Postmodernism, Traditional Cultural Forms, and African American Narratives

Postmodernism, Traditional Cultural Forms, and African American Narratives

W. Lawrence Hogue

SUNY
PRESS

Published by State University of New York Press, Albany

Printed in the United States of America

For information, contact State University of New York Press, Albany, NY, www.sunypress.edu.

Production by Diane Ganeles
Marketing by Michael Campochiaro

Library of Congress Cataloging-in-Publication Data

Hogue, W. Lawrence
Postmodernism, traditional cultural forms, and African American narratives / W. Lawrence Hogue.
pages cm
Includes bibliographical references.
Summary: "Examines how six writers reconfigure African American subjectivity in ways that recall postmodernist theory"—Provided by publisher.

ISBN 978-1-4384-4835-0 (hardcover: alk. paper)—
ISBN 978-1-4384-4834-3 (pbk.: alk. paper)

1. American literature—African American authors—History and criticism. 2. Subjectivity in literature. 3. African Americans—Intellectual life. 4. Postmodernism (Literature)—United States. I. Title.

PS153.N5H63 2013
810.9'9286'08996073—dc23

2012045528

10 9 8 7 6 5 4 3 2 1

Contents

Acknowledgments

The completion of this manuscript was facilitated by a Faculty Development Leave, Office of the Dean, College of Liberal Arts and Social Sciences (Spring 2011), and by summer stipends from the University of Houston, which allowed me to work uninterrupted. I benefited enormously from conversations with a number of colleagues and friends. I thank my colleague Hazel Pierre—an astute and very capable Caribbeanist and postcolonial theorist—who reminded me of the importance of history: if you do postcolonial theory, you must first study the anticolonials. If you want to examine the emergence of African American studies in the 1960s, you also need to study the precursors to the 1960s. I want to thank my colleague Patricia Yongue, who is always prepared and ready to pull up a chair and discuss any intellectual and/or political issue on my mind. I thank former students Sabrina Hassumani and Gregg Carleton who do not make a single demand on me but whose friendship commands me to continually grow intellectually. I also thank my dear friend Dr. Bill Taylor, who always lends me his ear for discussions about jazz and psychology. He pointed me in the appropriate psychological direction in my discussion of the jazz great Thelonious Monk, who lived with a form of schizophrenia. We also had conversations about drugs and music as they pertain to the bebop great Charlie Parker.

Although some of the chapters are drawn from existing publications, they were all reworked for publication here. The Toni Morrison and Clarence Major chapters are drawn from "Postmodernism, Traditional Cultural Forms, and the African American Narrative," *Novel: A Forum on Fiction* 35.2–3 (Spring–Summer 2002). The Wideman chapter is a revised version of "Radical Democracy, African American (Male) Subjectivity and John Edgar Wideman's *Philadelphia Fire*" that first appeared in *MELUS* 33.3 (Fall 2008): 45–69. *MELUS* is published by the Society for the Study of the Multi-Ethnic Literature of the United States.

Finally, I want to thank Dr. Michael Rinella, Senior Acquisitions Editor at SUNY Press, who recognized the importance of this manuscript and saw it through to publication.

— 1 —

Postmodernism, Traditional Cultural Forms, and African American Subjectivity

In the West, a notion we must divide because the European West is not the American West, people of African descent have always already been defined as Other. They are represented in an unequal, restrictive white-black binary opposition that defines whites as normative and superior and represents blacks as primitive, as deviant, as devalued Other, and/or more recently as the same.[1] The African American, to use the words of Madhu Dubey, is represented as "the negative term against which modern norms of body, identity, reason, or culture are defined and propped up" ("Contemporary African American Fiction" 158). He exists, to use the words of British psychoanalyst Christopher Bollas, "to contain unwanted destructiveness in the oppressor who insists at the same time that the [African American] be like a fecal entity that is so odious that it cannot be recognized, except if and when it is out of sight, and finally eliminated" (Said, *Freud* 6). As the less powerful negative term of the binary, the African American is "socialized in such a way that [he] cannot trust [his] own 'consciousness'" (Sylvia Wynter qtd. in Thomas, "Proud-Flesh Inter/Views" 2), which in many ways is the same as the normative consciousness. This means that since the middle-class puritan white norm—which is a space of difference that I am representing singularly—defines him negatively, he can also define himself in negative terms. Historically, how has the African American dealt with this predicament? How does he psychologically and socially liberate himself from this binary? Does or can he offer a different kind of subjectivity?[2]

There have always been African American social and political movements, individuals, scholars, black studies, and cultural forms that have resisted and/or countered this negative representation of the African American. These resisting entities seek to maintain sanity for African Americans through the insistence that the African American self exists even as the normative American society seeks to deny or eliminate it. Therefore, despite the fact that some African American movements, individuals, and scholars seek freedom by defining the African American as being the same as the middle-class puritan American norm and thereby reproduce the binary, I am interested in a different notion of (African American) freedom and subjectivity, one that is different from but equal to the middle-class American norm, one that knows the Other. Therefore, I am not just concerned with the African American flipping the white-black binary opposition and being defined/constructed as better than or the same as the middle-class puritan American norm, as a fixed and ontological subject in the modern sense. Flipping the binary means that the modern African American subject participates in violence similar to the mainstream hierarchy. This modern binary-constructed African American subjectivity does not or cannot know or empathize with the Other.

In her discussion of postmodernism in *A Poetics of Postmodernism,* Linda Hutcheon argues that the self-Other binary opposition belongs to what she calls a modern moment and that perhaps it has outlived its effectiveness. "The modernist concept of a single and alienated otherness is challenged by the postmodern questioning of binaries that conceal hierarchies (self/other)" (61). Binary oppositions, which are at the foundation of Western metaphysics in terms of how we define meaning, are inherently violent in their reduction or devaluation of their lower halves. The logic of binary oppositions is the logic of domination and subordination. Instead of binary oppositions, Hutcheon suggests that it is more useful to think of difference and the chaining movement of signifiers (originating in Ferdinand de Saussure's insights and developed further by Jacques Derrida) that describes not only the movement of meaning constitution within language but also self-constitution. "Difference suggests multiplicity, heterogeneity, plurality, rather than binary opposition and exclusion" (61). With difference, we can define situations, events, and subjectivities not in terms of binary logic and violent hierarchies but instead in terms of differences, without hierarchies.

In focusing on a different kind of (African American) subject, one that escapes the violence and repression of rational, linear, Eurocentric Enlightenment reason, I am most concerned with how African American individuals, scholars, and cultural forms define American/African American history (social real) and African American subjectivity or self-constitution in certain postmodern terms, as a new set of terms. I am concerned with a subjectivity or an *I* that has many selves, that is not an individual with definite limits that separate him or her from the Other, not a form of knowledge, but instead is a chaining movement of signifiers, a network of contextual, partial, contradictory, and shifting identifications. It is a subjectivity that is multiple because the individual is traversed by alterity and in so being is the very place of difference(s). It is a subjectivity, to quote Felix Guattari in *Soft Subversions,* that "establishes itself . . . in a complex relation to the other, mother, father, family, caste [race and ethnic] relation, class struggles, in short all levels of social interaction" (269), thereby having relations to people outside of itself.

I am concerned with an African American subjectivity whose existence is presented in the form of the mystery, which encompasses everything in life that is still unknown to us, or in the form of the open that is always out of reach. It is a subjectivity that is incomplete, that is processes, that is always becoming. Finally, and more important, in a multicultural cosmopolitan America,[3] I am concerned with a subjectivity that presupposes a certain heteronomy, that is, a certain acceptance of the law of the Other, of difference. It recognizes the exteriority of the Other, cohabitating and coexisting with subjects of different worth without hierarchy. Eschewing hierarchy, it presupposes neither servitude nor subjugation of the Other but instead presupposes a *knowing* of or an empathy with the Other.

But first, I want to discuss African American subjectivity within the context of the white-black binary opposition. Within the logic of this binary, the normative middle-class puritan American consciousness that the African American buys into is the same regime of power/knowledge (consciousness) that defines him or her as deviant. "The same educational process which inspires and stimulates the oppressor with the thought that he is everything and has accomplished everything worth while," writes Carter G. Woodson in *The Mis-Education of the Negro,* "depresses and crushes at the same time the spark of genius in the Negro by making him feel that his race does not amount to much and never will measure up to the standards of other peoples" (5–6). In addition, this white-black binary opposition exists within what Sylvia Wynter calls "the logic of a formulation of a [Western Christian middle-class] general order of existence; and this [order] is elaborated by intellectuals, whether theologians or shamans or ourselves" (qtd. in Thomas, "ProudFlesh Inter/Views" 19). To maintain its hegemony, this unbalanced white-black binary as a discourse needs secondary institutions to reproduce normative America, to reinforce what Michel Foucault in *The Archaeology of Knowledge* calls the "enunciation" that it wants to make about the African American (64–65).

Within the middle-class puritan American norm, the identity of the African American as a socially recognized deviant individual is only possible within the practices of this discourse, this power/knowledge network. E. Franklin Frazier writes in "The Failure of the Negro Intellectual" that "Under the slavery regime and for nearly a century since emancipation everything in American society has stamped the Negro as subhuman, as a member of an inferior race that had not achieved even the first steps in civilization" (64). From the American colonialists and legal slavery in the seventeenth century to the racial ideologies of the eighteenth century to Jim Crow laws and the eugenics, genetics, and hereditary arguments of the nineteenth and early twentieth centuries, the normative American regime of power/

knowledge, which was reinforced by the law, the courts, the educational institutions, the medical profession, the political system, the canon of American literature, and social and cultural practices and institutions, generated this particular representation of the African American. "Most of the history books and courses in American institutions of higher learning," writes Edward L. Cox, "either failed to mention blacks or did so in a most unfavorable light" (460). Historically, the African American has been defined as negative.

As the negative terms of the white-black hierarchy, the African American's body—the African American's identity, subjectivity, and history—was/is enmeshed in the West's construction of the African American as "deviant," as devalued Other, as victim, which is a space of isolation, of doom. The African American exists in an internal colonized space. But this "deviant" representation of African Americans contains "within [it] the frozen essence that condemns them to servitude and punishment," which America "sees as [its] present fate." This representation also "point[s] prophetically towards a whole series of implied developments that [its current and] later history disclose[] . . . , despite the radical severity" of the representation (Said, *Freud* 26). American and African American scholars and writers keep returning to this particular reduced representation of the African American, which gives it "its antinomian force, the intensity and power wrapped inside its [images], which demand an equal and opposite response" (26). And in the grip of this dehumanizing, racist representation, the individuals, social and political movements, and scholars revisit and push beyond it, "as history itself transforms even the most unyielding stasis into process and a search for greater clarity, relief, resolution or denial" (26). The return allows them to produce their own bodies of knowledge, to point prophetically toward a series of developments that challenge this reduced representation of the African American.

In the first implied development that history later discloses, as Albert Memmi argues in *The Colonizer and the Colonized,* those who have been colonized seek freedom by rejecting self and race because they have been negatively defined by the colonizer and by embracing and assimilating the colonizer's values. "By this step, which actually presupposes admiration for the colonizer, one can infer approval of colonization," or of the logic of the white-black binary (121). According to Memmi, the "crushing of the colonized is included among the colonizer's values"; as such, "[r]ejection of self and love of another are common to all candidates for assimilation" or, rather, common to all who want to buy into normalcy (121). Because they have access to social mobility, middle-class African Americans "strive to assimilate the virtues of the [mainstream] bourgeoisie in the assumption that by doing so they can lift themselves into a higher social sphere" (Wright, "Blueprint" 316). In having access to and in performing certain white values, they think they can socially and culturally pass for white.

Because they have been stigmatized, negatively marked, "denied opportunities for development" and advancement because they are black, middle-class or aspiring middle-class African Americans, the vocal group within African American communities, feel that this stigma is something they do not deserve, that their actions and behaviors are, in fact, exemplary. To gain respect, to erase the barrier of stigma, middle-class African Americans feel that they must "not only 'normify' their own conduct but also . . . clean up [purify] the conduct of others [African Americans] in the group" (Goffman 108). To "achieve acceptance in American life," argues E. Franklin Frazier, middle-class African Americans must "slough off everything that is reminiscent of its Negro origin and its Negro folk background" ("Failure" 56). They must deny, subordinate, or attenuate their historical and cultural differences, their otherness: the blues and working-class and subaltern African American cultures, the legacies of slavery, the historical struggles that define them, the experiences of internal colonialism, legal segregation, and second-class citizenship.

Equally as important, this means that to achieve the semblance of acceptance by mainstream society, middle-class African Americans must define subaltern and working-class blacks not as different, complex human beings who have agency but instead as a (pathological) problem to be solved, or to be made the same. Here, middle-class African

Americans are reproducing within black communities the same violent self-Other hierarchy that they contest in normative America. Finally, to achieve their goal of becoming the same as the middle-class puritan white norm, many middle-class or aspiring middle-class African Americans, who are terrified of falling into the negation of non–middle classness, devised a supporting discourse, the racial uplift narrative, with secondary social, political, educational, and literary organizations and apparatuses to seek sameness/equality.

Still operating within binary logic, the objective and success of these uplift institutions and practices are the transformation of the African American from his subaltern, "deviant" status to the values and definitions of the middle-class puritan white norm. The uplift canonical literature, writes Richard Wright in "Blueprint for Negro Writing," "became the voice of the educated Negro pleading with white America for justice" (316). But this uplift narrative or unequal, restrictive binary system psychologically entraps middle-class and aspiring middle-class African Americans. They become immobilized, erasing and/or suppressing aspects of themselves or their complex existence. A binary opposition, argues Gilles Deleuze in *Difference and Repetition,* "teaches us nothing about the nature of that which is thought to be opposed" (205). When the "difference" of African Americans is read as opposition, African Americans are "deprived of [their] peculiar thickness in which [their] positivity is affirmed" (205). They take the form of an empty opposition.

For those African Americans who are successful in becoming the same culturally and socially as the middle-class puritan white norm—in acquiring middle-class American education, values, manners, taste, jobs, and definitions, in passing—what emerges is an African American experience that is, to use the words of Hélène Cixous, "inside without being inside" (*White Ink* 170). They escape traditional black communities, black folk cultures, the historical experience of black struggles, and black modern traditions, becoming "more exposed to the contempt and discrimination of the white world" (Frazier, "Failure" 56). But middle-class blacks are not able to enter into that which they "had been admitted," living in "the exclusion," without it becoming a home (Cixous, *White Ink* 170). As the Other who wants to be the same as the middle-class white norm, middle-class African Americans reach a blockage, for they are the Other "in a hierarchically organized relationship in which the same is what rules, names, defines, and assigns 'its' other" (Cixous and Clément, *Newly Born Woman* 71). Therefore, they experience themselves in self-alienating terms. Because they are so defensive about the middle-class white norm, the tension, the power, the spirit, the desire, and the complexity of middle-class African Americans' lives, manifested in their differences, their otherness, are still latent, still colonized, still frozen and untapped. The higher up the social ladder you go, argues Gilles Deleuze in *Negotiations*, "the less scope there is for the expression of desire" (19). Therefore, middle-class blacks become spiritually, emotionally, and/or intellectually deprived, obstructed, and muzzled.

Because these middle-class or aspiring middle-class African Americans share many of the same values, definitions, and assumptions as the middle-class puritan white norm and because these particular middle-class African Americans share the same truth and knowledge (or consciousness) as the white norm—despite the fact that this truth and knowledge define their otherness as deviant or that this middle-class white norm has historically, until recently, "justified slavery, peonage, segregation, and lynching" (Woodson 5)—the middle-class white norm rewards them with jobs, educational and political opportunities, and a certain social capital. The middle-class white norm anoints them to represent the race, viewing them as "exceptional" blacks and thereby condemning all other African Americans. America needs the "exceptional" black, argues Sylvia Wynter, "to prove that all the Blacks in prison are right to be there" (qtd. in Thomas, "ProudFlesh Inter/Views" 14), that blacks who are different deserve to be unsuccessful. These assimilating African Americans deal, survive, and participate in America not on their own terms but instead on America's terms.

But as middle-class and aspiring middle-class African Americans are seeking freedom by becoming the same as the mainstream white norm, subaltern and other African Americans who do not have or want access to the abstract structures of civil society, who do not want to pass, who are "cut off from the lines of mobility," who exist "outside . . . the vectors of upward, downward, sideward, [and] backward mobility" (Spivak, "Subaltern Talk" 288–89) resist, with many practicing difference, not with hierarchal opposition. These African Americans seek freedom, agency, and identity through social and political movements and in their own indigenous/traditional cultural, social, and religious practices such as the blues, jazz, spirituals, Voodoo, black folk culture, working-class culture, etc., which are unsymbolized, fluid spaces in the American order. They develop a rapport with their unconscious, which is not stereotyped by the middle-class American norm, unleashing their latent/colonized tension, energy, spirit, and power. They revive themselves; cover their vital forces; accept their hybridity, differences, intermixture, and creolization; and dare to be themselves. Their existence contradicts and therefore is a relief from America's unyielding desire to construct them as the same, as negative or as primitive Other.

Historically, as a second implied development that history later discloses about the violent representation of the African American as deviant, there have always been American and African American intellectuals and activists—many of whom are tied to African American–based social and political movements—who resist the West's takeover of the world through its control of knowledge and information, who demand an opposite response, and who return to and deconstruct the West's devalued construction of the African American. Maria Stewart, Frederick Douglass, William Lord Garrison, Harriet Tubman, Sojourner Truth, the Salem Massachusetts Female Antislavery Society, and the slave abolitionist movement of the nineteenth century resisted slavery, gender oppression, and the representation of the African American as nonhuman. The first two decades of the twentieth century witnessed the Marcus Garvey movement that resisted the middle-class American norm and offered an Afrocentric perspective on the world. These decades also witnessed the emergence of civil and human rights organizations such as A. Philip Randolph and the Leadership Conference on Civil Rights (LCCR), C. L. R. James and Paul Robeson and the Black Communist Left, Roy Wilkins and the NAACP, Dorothy Heights and the Congress of Negro Women, Mary Church Terrell and Ida B. Wells and the National Association of Colored Women (NACW), Claudia Jones and Louise Thompson and the National Negro Congress (NNC) and the Southern Negro Youth Congress (SNYC), Nannie Burroughs and the National Association of Wage Earners, Martin Luther King Jr. and the Southern Christian Leadership Conference (SCLC), and Whitney Young and the National Urban League, all of which fought successfully to overturn or pass laws to support African American social equality. The legal arm of these civil rights organizations, particularly the NAACP's Legal Defense Fund, used the courts to challenge Jim Crow and segregation laws that barred African Americans from participation in normative/mainstream institutions and practices such as education at white colleges and universities, equality in the workplace and in housing, and access to electoral politics.

In the 1960s, Ella Baker and Bob Moses and the Student Nonviolent Coordinating Committee (SNCC), the Black Power movement (with such leaders as H. Rap Brown, Elaine Brown, Kathleen Cleaver, Stokley Carmichael, Bobby Seale, Huey P. Newton, and others), the Cultural Nationalist movement (with such leaders as Ron Karenga, Sonia Sanchez, Amiri Baraka, Haki Madhubuti, Toni Cade Bambara, and others), the Black Muslims (including early Malcolm X), and the National Black Feminist Organization (NBFO) again resisted the West's control of knowledge and Enlightenment reason and equated black progress and humanity with nation building, Afrocentric education, and women's liberation. Their existence confronts and gives greater clarity to America's denial of black humanity and agency.

These organizations, movements, and individuals achieved enormous feats and had a transformative effect on American society. Certainly we must give credit and praise to them for bravery and courage in challenging hegemonic

American racial, political, economic, and educational structures and apparatuses that excluded women and people of color. But we must also recognize and acknowledge that these organizations and movements, particularly the more prominent male-centered ones, reproduced the same or versions of the same violent hierarchies, subordinations, and repressions within black communities as in mainstream American society. In many instances, these were corporatist movements and organizations with leaders and rigid rules and regulations. They tended to impose their norms and standards from the top down, according to a model of absolute authority. In addition, flipping the binary, they established a hierarchal self-Other relationship with other African Americans and/or non–African Americans. For example, as we rightfully sing the praise of these civil rights organizations and movements for successfully advocating the vote and first-class citizenship for African Americans, we must also examine how in structurally reproducing mainstream American and Enlightenment patriarchal, heterosexual, middle-class, Christian practices and values, they also subordinated and repressed women, homosexuals, non-Christians, and non–middle-class taste and values. Here we are talking about how the male-centered leadership of the NAACP, the National Urban League, the Black Power movement, Black Cultural Nationalists, the SCLC, the Black Communist Left, and Black Muslims denied equality to women in their movements and organizations. African American women were denied access to leadership roles and positions in many of these organizations. The Christian and capitalist leaning of the NAACP and the National Urban League caused them to promote Christianity and capitalism and to exclude Islam, socialism, and Voodoo.

The patriarchal, heterosexual, Christian biases of many of these organizations cause them, on the one hand, to demand respectability and social acceptance for middle-class, heterosexual, Christian African Americans and, on the other hand, to deny or ignore the social acceptance of subaltern African Americans such as jazz and blues practitioners, working-class urban dwellers, and the urban and rural illiterate outsider. Bayard Ruskin, one of the architects of the 1963 March on Washington, and James Baldwin, the novelist and civil rights spokesman, were denied prominent places on the march's platform because they were or were suspected of being homosexuals. Subaltern and working-class blacks who did not advocate the Protestant work ethic were viewed not as complex individuals with their own cultures and distinct subjectivities but instead as (pathological) problems to be solved.

The middle-class, racial uplift, Christian narrative that, on the one hand, validates and provides cultural capital to the canonical texts of W. E. B. Du Bois, James Weldon Johnson, Langston Hughes, Booker T. Washington, Ralph Ellison, etc., also, on the other hand, subordinates or ignores blues- and jazz-influenced texts such as Langston Hughes's *Not Without Laughter,* Arna Bontemps's *God Sends Sunday,* Rudulph Fisher's *The Walls of Jericho,* and Gayl Jones's *Corregidora.* This racial uplift narrative also excludes Voodoo texts such as Fisher's *The Conjure Man Dies,* Don Belton's *Almost Midnight,* Ishmael Reed's *Mumbo Jumbo,* Mary Monroe's *The Upper Room,* and Gloria Naylor's *Mama Day.* This epistemic violence—the same kind of epistemic violence practiced when whites exclude or subordinate blacks and others socially and politically—is quite evident in the practices of many of these male-centered civil and human rights organizations and movements. Therefore, although these organizations and movements were instrumental in the transformation of American society and the economic, social, and political predicament of the African American, they also practice the logic of domination and subordination. They do not offer the kind of politics necessary for a postmodern, multicultural, cosmopolitan American society, which would require an alliance politics that eschews single-group identity politics or movement. These organizations and movements also would have to equally engage multiple political identities and movements and a conflicting set of social, economic, religious, sexual, gender, and racial/ethnic positions.

Also, as a third implied development in the historic representation of the African American as deviant, as primitive Other, there is a long tradition in African American scholarship that studies and examines the life, history, and experience of the African American, returning to, exposing/opposing, and pushing beyond this representation of the African American. This tradition creates counterhegemonic bodies of knowledge that challenge America's historiography, its claims of universalism, and its definition of civilization, and defines the African American with history, agency, and a distinct subjectivity. The tradition begins with George Washington Williams's *History of the Negro Race* (1882), William T. Alexander's *History of the Colored Race in America* (1887), Harold M. Taver's *The Negro in the History of the United States* (1905), Benjamin Brawley's *A Short History of the American Negro* (1913), and Willis D. Weatherford's *The Negro from Africa to America* (1924) and includes among others Anna Julia Cooper (*A Voice From the South*), W. E. B. Du Bois (*What the Negro Wants*), feminist Pan-Africanists Amy Jacques Garvey and Shirley Graham Du Bois, the sociologists E. Franklin Frazier and Charles S. Johnson, and historians Carter G. Woodson, John Hope Franklin, and Lerone Bennett.

Using current postmodern, poststructural, postcolonial, psychoanalytical, African American cultural, and feminist theories (and the issues of otherness, difference, heterogeneity, violent hierarchies, hybridity, etc.), I dust off and/or reopen and rethink the works of some of these past scholarly figures to liberate their potentialities from restrictive, partial, and indeed erroneous interpretations or to dramatize latencies in their work, making them relevant to today as forerunners of African American studies. Specifically, as intellectuals in the margins of the racially and socially hierarchically organized United States, Cooper, Du Bois, Frazier, Johnson, and Woodson were defined negatively by the mainstream society. They endured earth-shattering racial and gender experiences; were sensitive to and tormented by the injustice, the violence, and the real and symbolic murders; attended America's and Europe's best graduate universities; and traveled between two cultures. These experiences informed their historical and sociological research. I will focus on these five scholars for several reasons: because they offer alternative bodies of knowledge, perspectives, and representations of African Americans; because their works reconfigure the American symbolic order to include the African American and other excluded groups into the national political, social, philosophical, and literary rituals and narratives and to signify a new way to create an "American" subjectivity; because in their scholarship they think in terms of difference rather than in binary oppositions; and, finally, because they show traces of plural, multiple, and polyphonic African American subjectivities and/or genders that empathize with or know and acknowledge the Other.

The postmodern dynamics of contemporary American society, which advocates differences and nonhierarchies rather than binary oppositions, allow me, as someone from a different historical period and a different cultural background, to reread Anna Julia Cooper to instigate new thought, to illuminate the present. Without the kind of intellectual, institutional, and financial support received by her black male scholarly peers, Cooper—feminist, educator, scholar, activist, theorist, cosmopolitan, historian, and visionary—theorizes and remaps an American society where there are strong ethnic, racial, and gender differences without hierarchy. Through her writings (particularly *A Voice From the South,* a collection of essays and speeches written between 1886 and 1892), the black women's club movement, and community organizations, she rejects a patriarchal American social norm and education that control/devalue the black and the Indian and deny/subordinate the subjectivity of women, particularly black women. She defines her current (1880s) patriarchal capitalist norm as "when internecine war, originated through [the Euro-American] man's love of gain and his determination to subordinate national interests and black men's rights alike to considerations of personal profit and loss, was drenching our country with its own best blood" (128–29). With power to create a social, economic, and gendered hierarchy, the Euro-American male (in the 1880s and 1890s) serves his interest, totally subordinating women, the working class, and people of color. Race and gender blindness might keep a culture alive but also keeps it unhealthy.

Indicting the United States for having divided human beings into hierarchies of races and genders that reduced and dehumanized the subordinates and echoing what I interpret as certain postmodern and poststructural feminist sentiments, the biracial and bicultural Cooper proposes an American symbolic order that equally includes America's racially and sexually diverse and conflicting voices.[4] In *A Voice From the South,* reverberating against Ralph Waldo Emerson's *The Hermetic Book of Nature,* which advocates antagonisms and therefore hierarchies among different social forces rather than oppositions and harmony, Cooper writes that *"equilibrium, not repression among conflicting forces is the condition of natural harmony, of permanent progress, and of universal freedom"* (160). The concept of the symbolic order was conceived in the 1950s by the French psychoanalyst Jacques Lacan, who was concerned with reconceptualizing Western society into a unified and coherent social system. He elaborates a system according to which everything in the human world is structured "in accordance with the symbols which have emerged" (*Seminars* 29). This system is comprised of social, cultural, and linguistic symbolic networks. The symbolic order, according to the Lacanian scholar Jane Gallop, is "the register of language, social exchange, and radical subjectivity" (59). As the defining context for the self, it determines the "order of the subject" (Lacan, *Ecrits* ix). Individuals are transformed into signs and operated within a system of symbolic exchange. The symbolic is comprised of signifiers "extended into a generalized definition: differential elements, in themselves without meaning, which acquire value only in their mutual relations, and forming a closed order" (ix).

In devising his symbolic order, Lacan is not saying that everything is reducible to the symbolic but instead is saying that once symbols have appeared, they will be ordered, or structured, in accordance with those symbols and the laws of the symbolic, including the unconscious and human subjectivity. Lacan conceived of the symbolic order as a totalizing concept in the sense that it marks the limits of the human universe. As signs, we are locked within what Lacan calls a circuit of discourse.

> It is the discourse of the circuit in which I am integrated. I am one of its links. It is the discourse of

> my father . . . in so far as my father made mistakes which I am condemned to reproduce. . . . I am condemned to reproduce them because I am obliged to pick up again the discourse he bequeathed to me, not simply because I am his son, but because one can't stop the chain of discourse, and it is precisely my duty to transmit it in its aberrant form to someone else. . . . [T]his discourse produces a small circuit in which an entire family, an entire coterie, an entire camp, an entire nation or half of the world will be caught. (*Seminars* 89–90)

We are born into this circuit of discourse, which marks us before our birth and after our death. To be fully human, Lacan concludes, we are subjected to this symbolic order.

Although spoken universally and totally, Lacan's circuit of discourse/symbolic order does not occupy all the space available in the social. Rather, it represents those social, literary, psychoanalytic, political, media, religious, and economic discourses (and mythologies) that have the power to have their symbols and signs appear and enunciate. From the above quote and due to Lacan's statement that the child/subject accepts the father's name, Lacan's symbolic order is inherently phallocentric and Eurocentric in its structure of concepts. It is structured according to the law of the Eurocentric father, repressing and excluding the representation of the feminine and the non-European Other, who are the unacknowledged unconscious of Western culture. Depriving women and the non-European of "the fulfillment of their desire, of the 'fullness' of pleasure," argues Luce Irigaray, "the [Eurocentric] father introduces them, or reintroduces them, to the exigencies of the symbolization of desire through language, that is, to the necessity that desire pass by way of demand" (*This Sex* 63). Women and non-Europeans, even when they are visible within the symbolic order, are perceived as the absence and negation of the Eurocentric masculine norm. They are excluded from complex representation.

Arguing that the first settlers in the United States were racially mixed or plural with multiple circuits of discourse, the theorist and cosmopolitan Cooper in *A Voice From the South,* positing poststructural latencies that she might not have been fully aware of, reconfigures what Lacan would later call the symbolic order to include "the variety and warfare of the elements of [American] civilization, . . . [a] stable equilibrium of opposition" (160, 164), thereby signifying irreducible differences and a new way to name American subjectivity. She wants the variety and the conflicting political, social, economic, philosophical, psychoanalytical, gender, sexual, and literary symbols and signs of women, African Americans, American Indians, along with the symbols and signs of Euro-American males, to be equally represented in the American symbolic order. "Hence no one is or can be supreme. All interests must be consulted, all claims conciliated where a hundred free forces are lustily clamoring for recognition and each wrestling mightily for the mastery, individual tyrannies must inevitably be chiseled down, individual prejudices either obliterated or concealed" (164). According to Cooper, the remapped American symbolic order becomes an alliance between all subjects who share with each other, advocating a politics of equal respect for all. "Cooper," writes Janice W. Fernheimer, "works at the level of first premises to redefine American culture entirely. Cooper thus not only makes space for African Americans [and American Indians] on their own terms, but also legitimates their centrality and necessity to the nation's well-being" (289). As Jean-Francois Lyotard would argue almost seventy years later in *The Postmodern Condition* (1979), Cooper, in 1892, echoing Francois Guizot's belief that difference benefits the nation,[5] is arguing for the abandonment of a centralized, rational (grand) narrative; for the abandonment of the whole edifice of patriarchal Euro-American humanism, which has proven incapable of going beyond its own limitations of vision; and for embracing a vision of the world (America) in which multiple incompatible discourses or language games (Wittgenstein) flourish alongside each other. As Michel Foucault, Gilles Deleuze, and Jacques Derrida were to do, Cooper proposes an unregulated freedom of pure difference. The heterogeneity of language games leads to a multiplicity of justice.

In *A Voice From the South* (1892), Cooper, echoing the current discussion about the violence involved in the self-Other binary opposition, critiques/deconstructs classic binary oppositions such as Western–non-Western, men-women, strong-weak, male-female, white-black, white-Indian, and upper class–lower class that are constructed by the Euro-American patriarchal order and permeate society's social, political, religious, and economical institutions and practices. These binaries are not separate and equal or what Jacques Derrida in *Positions* calls "the peaceful coexistence of a *vis-à-vis.*" Rather, they comprise a "violent hierarchy" where "one of the two terms governs the other . . . , or has the upper hand" (41), and the lower half is defined in a reduced way. This lower half has been denied distinct subjectivity and full representation in the symbolic.

Understanding the obstacles and potentials confronting women and the oppressed in the United States, Cooper rewrites the center, undermining hierarchies and repositioning the Other—Woman, the African American, and the American Indian. Through education, she wants Woman, who traditionally takes the lead in transmitting the rules and laws of heteropatriarchy, to take the lead in transforming the American symbolic order for all Americans equally. The source of this responsibility comes from the potentialities of Christianity and the feudal system, "not on the fruition we now enjoy, but springs rather from the possibilities and promise that are inherent in the system" (12). It is the responsibility of women, argues Cooper in *A Voice From the South,* to use their energies to undermine these binaries and to initiate reconfiguration, thereby tapping into the inherent promises and possibilities of Christianity, "broadening, humanizing, and civilizing her native land" (116) and bringing to women "the same code of morality, the same standard of purity, as men" (17). Cooper argues that Jesus Christ "throughout his life and in his death . . . has given to men a rule and guide for the estimation of woman as an equal" (18).

In addition, long before French and American feminists such as Mary Daly, Adrienne Rich, Luce Irigaray, Hélène Cixous, Catherine Clément, and others of the 1960s and 1970s sought the first trace of women's oppression in the West, Cooper, who was denied opportunities because she was a woman, in 1892 traces the violent man-woman hierarchy in the West to the "barbarian brawn and brutality" in fifth-century Europe, which permitted "no feminine modification" (53). European heteropatriarchy repressed its feminine, which could teach "it to be pitiful, to love mercy, to succor the weak and care for the lowly" (51). It did not value or nurture empathy for the Other. Cooper attacks the patriarchal American symbolic order's "one-sided masculine definition" of Woman, which argues that if women are given an education and equality, "there would be an end forever to their sewing on buttons and embroidering slippers" (49, 50–51).

Believing that societal transformation comes not from the collective, which is artificial and is too quickly constructed, but instead from the individual, by putting influence on subjective structures, the feminist Cooper in *A Voice From the South* redefines Woman as one of the "vital elements of its [society's] regeneration and progress" not because she is "better or stronger or wiser than man but from the nature of the case, because it is she who must first form the man by directing the earliest impulses of his character" (21). Therefore, the visionary Cooper believes that in socializing, raising, and teaching the young, it is Woman's responsibility to deconstruct society's hierarchal self-Other binary order, which is at the foundation of Western metaphysics:

> Woman should not, even by inference, or for the sake of argument, seem to disparage what is weak. For woman's cause is the cause of the weak; and when all the weak shall have received their due consideration, then woman will have her "rights," and the Indian will have his rights, and the Negro will have his rights, and all the strong will have learned at last to deal justly, to love mercy, and to walk humbly; and our land will have been taught the secret of universal courtesy. (117)

Although she wants Woman to take the lead, Cooper also wants man to empathize with the Other, to "be a father, a brother, a friend to every weak, struggling unshielded girl" (32). In a cosmopolitan sense, Cooper wants America/the world to replace the violent hierarchy with difference, without hierarchy, and she wants Woman to take the lead. In many instances, in having "[t]he philosophic mind see[] that its own 'rights' are the rights of humanity," Cooper is insinuating that through education the female self can angle toward or empathize with the Other, the poor and the oppressed, which is the mark of being alive.

Likewise, deconstructing the unbalanced white man–black man and black man–black woman binary oppositions, Cooper in *A Voice From the South* argues that the white man, who cannot put himself in the dark man's place, exists in a violent hierarchy with the black man, who provokes "ceaseless harangues . . . but [is] little understood and seldom consulted" (i). Even Christian white men do not recognize black men, do not invite them "to take part in their deliberations" (37). Therefore, Cooper wants to overturn this white man–black man binary, arguing for the black man to speak for and represent himself. Although he is the lower half of the white male–black male binary, the black male becomes the upper half of the black male–black woman binary. But the black male, argues Cooper, does not "represent the race" and "can never be regarded as identical with or representative of the whole" (30). He cannot "fully and adequately . . . reproduce the exact Voice of the Black Woman" (iii). Therefore, the black woman should equally speak for and represent herself.

In *A Voice From the South,* Cooper undermines other classic Western hierarchies. She unearths the white woman–black woman binary by arguing for the "radical amelioration of womankind, reverence for woman as woman regardless of rank, wealth, or culture," which comes from "the Gospel of Jesus Christ" (14). She advocates not oppositions but rather the acceptance of differences and mutual recognition among women. Rejecting the selection of successful upper-middle-class men to represent the race, Cooper dismantles the upper class–lower class binary, asking that the poor be considered as different but equal, visualizing an American society where all groups and individuals are equal and different. Cooper "interpreted the Gospel as a liberation theology," argues Hazel Carby in *Reconstructing Womanhood,* "a set of ideals which argued for equality not only for women but also for the poor, the weak, the starving, and the dispossessed" (98). For Cooper, liberation theology should make everyone equal and different—that is, different socially, culturally, racially, and religiously—but with cooperation and mutual recognition among different individuals and equal representation in the eyes of the law, the American symbolic order. In short, Cooper desires an American society where the recognition of people in their range of diversity is acceptable.

But to circumvent constructing another violent hierarchy, Cooper in *A Voice From the South* does not define sex and gender by binary logic, as biological or as essential. There are moments when Cooper reads as if she is advocating something essential about Woman. "Her voice may strike a false note, but her whole being is musical with the vibrations of human suffering. Her tongue may parrot over the cold conceits that some man has taught her, but her heart is aglow with sympathy and loving kindness, and she cannot be true to her real self without giving out these elements into the forces of the world" (55). But if we reexamine Cooper more closely and fully, gender identity, for Cooper, is an oppressive, socially contrived role; it is performance, and subjectivity/sexuality is not unitary. Later in that same speech/essay, "The Higher Education of Women," she says that "I do not ask you to admit that those benefactions and virtues [tenderness, nurturing, emotion, etc.] are the exclusive possession of women, or even that women are their chief and only advocates. It may be a man who formulates and makes them vocal. It may be . . . a man who weeps over the wrongs and struggles for the amelioration" (60). Cooper in *A Voice From the South* believes that there is no gender/sexuality or value that is strictly feminine or strictly masculine, "that there is a feminine as well as a masculine side to truth" (60), and that both men and women possess this truth. This truth is "related not as inferior and superior, not as better or worse, not as weaker and stronger, but as complements" (60). We can see "women who reason . . . with the coolness and precision of a man, and men as considerate of helplessness as a woman" (60–61). For Cooper, then, sex and gender are complex, mobile, fluid, and open, admitting the components of the other sex and the other gender. Thus, long before Hélène Cixous and Catherine Clément in *The Newly Born Woman,* Judith Butler in *Gender Trouble,* and others discussed gender and sex as repressive social constructions, Cooper in 1892 had already argued for a femininity of the masculine and a masculinity of the feminine. Here, Cooper liberates gender/sexuality from the prison of gender stereotype.

In addition, Cooper in *A Voice From the South* rerepresents the black woman, who embodies lower halves of the gender and race hierarchies and who is described as "open-eyed but hitherto voiceless" (2), as possessing a unique, complex, and contradictory subject position in the social. This includes the poor black woman, the "untalented plodder who continues to want more" (qtd. in Gabel 78). Cooper—who became sensitive to sexism and aware of male privilege early at St. Augustine's Normal School in Raleigh, North Carolina, where female students were excluded from Greek classes—understands gender oppression. Therefore, she gives the black woman, whose subjectivity is formed amid social, racial, economic, and patriarchal processes of exploitation, voice and agency. "The colored woman of today occupies, one may say, a unique position in this country. In a period of itself transitional and unsettled, her status seems one of the least ascertainable and definitive of all the forces that make for our civilization. She is confronted by both a woman question and a race problem, and is yet an unknown or an unacknowledged factor in both" (134), with the black woman's unacknowledged position in the social giving her a unique angle/perspective. Because she knows and/or can empathize with the various "weak" or devalued subject positions in American society, Cooper believes that the black woman—whose experience teaches her heteronomy, an acceptance of the law of the Other—is in the best or most effective position to speak truth to power. If this black woman, whose "status seems one of the least ascertainable and definitive of all the forces," can speak and be heard, she might help the country "to a clearer vision and a truer pulse-beat in studying our Nation's Problems" (iii). As Patricia Hill Collins points out in *Black Feminist Thought,* Cooper views the black woman's struggle as "part of a wider struggle for human dignity, empowerment, and social justice" (41). Cooper wants to unleash the untapped power, spirit, and energy of the black woman, which is an unsymbolized representation of the black woman in the United States. Given her status within the social, when the black woman becomes different but equal, so will the rest of America.

Operating out of this critique of violent hierarchies, Cooper reacts against binary logic within American literature, particularly nineteenth-century white male writers such as William Dean Howells, Joel Chandler Harris, and George Washington Cable for their devaluation and erasure of African American subjectivity. In *A Voice From the South,* Cooper writes:

> Imported merely to be hewers of wood and drawers of water, no artist for many a generation thought them [blacks] worthy of sympathetic study of a model. No Shakespeare arose to distil from their unmatched personality and unparalleled situations the exalted poesy and crude grandeur of an immortal Caliban. Distinct in color, original in temperament, simple and unconventionalized in thought and action their spiritual development and impressionability under their novel environment would have furnished, it might seem, as interesting a study in psychology for the poetic pen. . . . Full of vitality and natural elasticity, the severest persecution and oppression could not kill them out or even sour their temper. (178)

Unlike the middle-class puritan American norm, which defines black life as deviant, as not "worthy of sympathetic study," Cooper paints a unique, complex, fluid portrait of African American subjectivity, its "unmatched personality" and its "spiritual development," which has been constructed under "the severest persecution and oppression."

She gives it agency and distinct subjectivity, asking why it is not as worthy of equal poetic portrayal as any other American.

For Cooper, African American subjectivity, or any subjectivity, is created not by some timeless, universal racial identity or by someone's racist mythology but instead by various, perpetual, conflicting forces of history.

> [N]o individual character receives its raw material newly created and independent of the rock from whence it was hewn. No life is bound up within the period of its conscious existence. No personality dates its origin from its birthday. The elements that are twisted into the cord did not begin their formation when first the tiny thread became visible in the great warp and filling of humanity. . . . The materials that go to make the man, the probabilities of his character and activities, the conditions and circumstances of his growth, and his quantum of resistance and mastery are the resultant of forces which have been accumulating and gathering momentum for generations. (234, 235)

And within their socially and historically constructed subjectivity, African Americans have desires or hungerings that are multiple.

> There are other hungerings in man besides the eternal all-subduing hungering of his despotic stomach. There is the hunger of the eye for beauty, the hunger of the ear for concords, the hungering of the mind for development and growth, of the soul for communion and love, for a higher, richer, fuller living—a more abundant life! And every man owes it to himself *to let nothing in him starve* for lack of the proper food. (257)

Hungerings or desires should be fulfilled. Finally, for Cooper, a balanced, peaceful subjectivity is one where "the individual [has] found the secret of true harmony in the determination to live and let live" (149). Here, Cooper constructs a complex African American subjectivity that is the product of social forces, that has multiple desires, that is open and mobile, and that belies deviancy.

For Cooper, the African American, stripped of all the labels and stereotypes inscribed on his or her body, is simply just like other complex human beings. "My 'people' are just like other people—indeed, too like for their own good. They hate, they love, they attract and repel, they climb or they grovel, struggle or drift, aspire or despair, endure in hope or curse in vexation, exactly like all the rest of unregenerate humanity" (112). She argues against assimilation, against the African American becoming the same as the middle-class puritan white norm, for assimilation denies the self. "Imitation is the worst of suicides; it cuts the nerve of originality and condemns to mediocrity" (175). After asking for "social equality" under the law but not "forced association" (110) (association is an individual election), Cooper asks for difference but equality, that is, for the acceptance of their racial differences but for the equal treatment and coexistence of blacks, Indians, and whites within the same social order. "What the dark man wants then is merely to live his own life, in his own world, with his own chosen companions, in whatever of comfort, luxury, or emoluments his talent or his money can in an impartial market secure" (112). The dark man wants to be himself, even if it means being at times culturally and socially different. But he also wants integration, equal access to, representation of, and protection of the law. If he wants "first-class accommodations on a railway train" (111) or wants to go to the opera or attend an expensive restaurant not in his community, he should not be denied these opportunities. If he has money, he should not "be forced into inconvenient or unsanitary sections of cities to buy a home and rear his family" (112). The acceptance of diversity as the norm, of difference without hierarchy, leads to a multiplicity of justice.

Unlike the mainstream middle-class white norm, which defines the African American as deviant, Cooper offers a representation of the African American that is complex, heterogeneous, and human, a representation that dismantles the white-black binary opposition, that angles toward the Other. In taking the 1892 Cooper for the as-yet unlived, still-shaping history that her vision partially, tentatively, foresees and provokes, I give you Cooper as a forerunner to and in the present.

Likewise, W. E. B. Du Bois also challenges the violent representation of the African American as deviant. The Lacanian and Deleuzian psychoanalytical dynamics of contemporary American society, with emphasis on decentered, multiple, or fluid subjectivities, allow me to reconsider and to rerepresent the works of Du Bois, particularly his now-famous concept of double consciousness, which is usually interpreted as warring conflicts to be resolved, making it speak to the present. The concept of double consciousness is also found in Emerson's 1852 essay "Fate," where it is put forth as "One key, one solution to the mysteries of human condition, one solution to the old knots of fate, freedom, and foreknowledge" (qtd. in Bremen 81). As Du Bois was to do, Emerson conjoins "individual consciousness with racial identity and national formations" (Bremen 81). This makes for a different kind of subjectivity.

Although Du Bois, historian, social critic, political theorist, novelist, and poet, was one of the founders of the Niagara Movement, later named the National Association for the Advancement of Colored People (NAACP), he was also, like Anna Julia Cooper, one of the early African American scholars who returns to and critiques/opposes Western knowledge for its devalued/otherized representation of the African American. Du Bois too offers a complex and open portrait of African American history and subjectivity. In books such as *The Philadelphia Negro* (1899), *The Suppression of the Slave Trade in America* (1896), *The Souls of Black Folk* (1903), *Black Reconstruction* (1935), *The Encyclopedia of the Negro* (1931–46), and *The World and Africa* (1946) and in his capacity as editor of *The Crisis* and director of the Atlanta University Studies Series, Du Bois—who, despite his PhD from Harvard and further graduate studies at the University of Berlin in Germany, was denied tenured professorships at America's white colleges and universities—provides the social, historical, political, artistic, and economical truth of the African American on his own terms. Providing the African American with history, agency, and distinct subjectivity and also reproducing some black stereotypes, Du Bois in *The Philadelphia Negro* examines the urban black in Philadelphia as a particular social phenomenon. *Black Reconstruction* was written in response to the racist put-down of African Americans by Claude Bowers in *The Tragic Era,* published in 1929.

In *The Souls of Black Folk,* Du Bois, who grew up as one of a small number of blacks in the mostly white town of Great Barrington, Massachusetts, and who with his concept of the talented tenth bought into class hierarchies, examines the strivings, longings, and yearnings of the African American within the unique cultural, musical, social, and economic milieu in the South. Against a country that denies it, Du Bois, offering an opposite response, shows the complexity of black life and humanity. But in a cursory way, he is best known for his statement of double consciousness—the contradictory dilemma of the African American being both American and black.

> [T]he Negro is a sort of seventh son, born with a veil, and gifted with second-sight in this American world—a world which yields him no true self-consciousness, but only lets him see himself through the revelation of the other world. It is a peculiar sensation, this double-consciousness, this sense of always looking at one's self through the eyes of others, of measuring one's soul by the tape of a world that looks on in amused contempt and pity. One ever feels his two-ness—an American, a Negro; two souls, two thoughts, two unreconciled strivings; two warring ideals in one dark body, whose dogged strength alone keeps it from being torn asunder. (9)[6]

And as Sylvia Wynter makes clear, Du Bois is fully aware that in America the African American is socialized to be antiblack, to hate his black/Negro self. The American symbolic order provides the African American with "no true self-consciousness." Instead, the middle-class puritan

American norm teaches the African American to reject/deny race and self and to embrace this white norm. As a consequence, it is difficult for the African American to be aware of oneself racially and subjectively outside of the way he or she has been socialized and negatively marked by the white norm. Most African Americans, as Farah Jasmine Griffin argues, can "see themselves only through the eyes of white Americans, to measure their intelligence, beauty, and sense of self-worth by standards set by others" (xvi). The African American in the United States, argues Michelle M. Wright in *Becoming Black,* is the "Other-from within" (69). Thus, because of the way he or she is represented in the American symbolic order/the normative consciousness, the African American can experience oneself as a foreign Other.

But Du Bois, who was bicultural—that is, he knows both American and African American cultures—refuses to be antiblack, to hate his black self, to define the African American as having "no true self-consciousness." In *The Souls of Black Folk,* he also refuses to choose either total assimilation or total separation, as the binary logic of the American symbolic order demands. Like Cooper and echoing the contemporary debate on the problem of otherness, Du Bois reconfigures the American symbolic order to include differences, the African American Other—black folk culture, the blues, the spirituals, and the experience and legacy of slavery and racial oppression. Viewing double consciousness as a "gift" of "second-sense" and rejecting the binary logic of subordination and domination, Du Bois, who at times was marginal to both subaltern African America and middle-class white and black America and echoing Emerson's "new principle" in "Fate" that hopes to conserve the Black race from extinction (Bremen 82), constructs African American subjectivity to be not either American or black but to be *both* American and black, "two unreconciled strivings," "two warring ideals," accepting the tension and the contradiction between the two *equal* terms. "The genius of *The Souls of Black Folk,*" writes historian David Levering Lewis, "is that it affirms" double consciousness as "a permanent tension. . . . [T]he destiny of the race could be conceived as leading . . . to [a] proud, enduring hyphenation"

(281). With the concept of double consciousness, Du Bois offers a fluid African American subjectivity.

As a subject with multiple, shifting identifications, the Du Boisian African American travels between the two or three cultures, thinking his or her differences from other Americans and accepting his or her equality to them, with the conflict and tension keeping the African American healthy, stimulated, progressive, and alive. The African American, argues Paul Gilroy in *Black Atlantic,* is "both inside and outside the veiled world of black America" (127). Double consciousness, writes Michelle Wright in *Becoming Black,* allows the African American to operate "both within and without the discourse of the white subject and the black Other" (69). Thus, the African American's double consciousness has an alien and critical perspective, one that can alter its focus as it moves between the two, seeing the gaps in both categories. Being hyphenated allows the Du Boisian African American to recognize his hybrid relations to the black and the American, "to form a conception of the other as the closest of all possible neighbors" (Cherif xvii). This means that in the experience of instability and hybridity, the Du Boisian African American comes to know, embrace, and empathize with and to be critical of both spaces. In short, the African American learns to empathize with and to know the Other. Du Bois "intended the divided self to be a phenomenon that was spiritually and socially evolving—one that would define itself through struggle and attain 'self-conscious manhood' through 'strife'" (Lewis, *W. E. B. Du Bois* 282). Like Cooper, with double consciousness, Du Bois is signifying a different kind of African American subjectivity.

Du Bois's acceptance of African American subjectivity that is plural, that is both American and black, means resisting the middle-class puritan American norm and defining black and the tumultuous history that it represents not as black Other but instead as something positive, as something that is different from the norm but equal to it in value. In *The Souls of Black Folk,* Du Bois writes that

> this longing . . . [is] to merge his double self into a better and truer self. In this merging he wishes

> neither of the older selves to be lost. He would not Africanize America, for America has too much to teach the world and Africa. He would not bleach his Negro soul in a flood of white Americanism, for he knows that Negro blood has a message for the world. He simply wishes to make it possible for a man to be *both a Negro and an American,* without being cursed and spit upon by his fellows, without having the doors of Opportunity closed roughly in his face. (9, my emphasis)

For Du Bois, the experience of being black in America "has a [valuable] message for the world." In pairing African American spirituals with European verses as epigraphs for each essay in *The Souls of Black Folk,* he symbolizes this African American subjectivity that is *both* American and black. "He twinned them in this manner," writes David Levering Lewis, "in order to advance the then-unprecedented notion of the creative parity and complementarity of white folk and black folk alike" (278).

It was Du Bois's decision to accept/embrace and study black life, history, and culture in the United States, which was unsymbolized in the American symbolic order, rather than to reject it that "redefined the terms of a three-hundred-year interaction between black and white people and influenced the cultural and political psychology of peoples of African descent throughout the western hemisphere" (Lewis, *W. E. B. Du Bois* 277). Like Cooper, this decision makes Du Bois a forerunner to black studies, to a body of knowledge that contests the mainstream American regime of power/knowledge that defines the African American as deviant, as inferior. Du Bois advocates the tolerance of difference, the acceptance of two sensibilities. Here, he acknowledges that African American subjectivity has more than one self, that it is complicated, mobile, plural, and open, implying that it is not the product of somebody's or some movement's rigid, identity politics. Du Bois's use of the term "American Negro," writes Michelle M. Wright, "suggests that even as the Black strives to be both Negro and American, he already *is*" (71). In being *both* American and black, the African American unearths the white-black binary opposition, challenges the American symbolic order, and angles toward the Other, toward differences.

In addition, sociologist E. Franklin Frazier also pushes beyond the reduced representation of the African American in the United States. The dynamics of contemporary sociology allow me to reread and to dramatize latencies in the work of Frazier that suddenly illuminate the present. Frazier, an admirer, critic, and friend of Du Bois and a product of the Chicago School of Sociology,[7] creates a body of scholarly and popular sociological works that revisit, contest, and prophetically push beyond the American middle-class norm's construction of the African American as deviant, as a simplistic reduction. In books such as *The Negro Family in Chicago* (1932), *The Negro Family in the United States* (1939), *Black Bourgeoisie* (1957), and *Race and Culture Contacts in the Modern World* (1965), Frazier challenges conventional social-problems texts that define the African American as devalued Other, explores the political economy of racism in a global context, and analyzes class differences within black communities. His *Black Bourgeoisie* interrogates and indicts an apolitical, materialistic black middle class, asking it to reexamine its assimilationist desire to reject its black cultural and historical past and to move into the white American norm and to reassess its responsibility to the black community.

But amid almost universal celebration of the decision of *Brown v. Board of Education,* which struck down legal racial segregation in public education, Frazier, who witnessed deep-seated racial discrimination in the United States, did not believe that racial integration could adequately address "the nation's entrenched socioeconomic inequalities" (Gaines 512). Although Frazier welcomed "the integration of the Negro into the economic and social organization of American life," he voices misgivings about assimilation, hoping that African Americans would retain their historical and cultural identity, "the traditional culture of the Negro peoples" (Frazier, "Failure" 53, 55).

And like Cooper and Du Bois, Frazier recasts the American symbolic order to include *all* Americans, even the African American. In his final essay, "The Failure of the Negro

Intellectual," published in 1962, Frazier theorizes studying "the problems of Negro life in America in a manner which would place the fate of the Negro in the broad framework of man's experience in this world. . . . [I]f the Negro is ever assimilated into American society his heritage should become a part of the American heritage, and it should be recognized as the contributions of the Negro as one recognizes the contributions of the English, Irish, Germans and other people" ("Failure" 60, 66). Like Cooper, Frazier wants the American symbolic order to include, in a nonhierarchical way, its diverse voices and heritages. In addition, Frazier's anticolonial worldview signals "the transformation of US society as it is remade in the image of the multiracial, multicultural global majority" (Gaines 526). In his reconfiguration of the American symbolic order, Frazier proposes the inclusion of the hyphenated African American and/or the African American as a transnational U.S. citizen in solidarity with African peoples, making the African American a cosmopolitan individual. In his final essay, Frazier clearly has a notion of African American subjectivity that is fluid and becoming.

But even in his earlier study of the black family, despite the fact that many intellectuals have accused him of pathologizing the black family, Frazier views black subjectivity or any subjectivity not as essential, or as a "person," but instead as fluid, social, and becoming, as the production of a way of existing. Reacting/refuting "the crudities of contemporary sociologists and anthropologists who insisted on finding in the disorganization of the Negro family something primitive," writes Nathan Glazer in the "Foreword" to *The Negro Family in the United States,* Frazier in the text insists "that the social characteristics of the Negro family were shaped by social condition, not by race or African survivals" (vii–viii). Whether it is the rural South or the urban North, Frazier argues that "whatever standards existed, whatever behavior we found, could be understood only in terms of the social conditions that had shaped them" (viii). Families and social forces construct African American subjectivity. If the American society wants to change the behavior of the African American, it simply has to change the social and economic conditions. For Frazier, there is nothing innate or essential about the culture of poverty or black behavior.

Therefore, if changing social and economic conditions shape African American culture and life, then African American subjectivity is open and mobile. It is never fixed but instead is continuously shaped by various forces, which act upon it. It is an expression of a relationship to time, space, and values. Stripped of his African cultural heritage by the institution of slavery, argues Frazier in *The Negro Family,* the African American

> acquired a new personality on American soil. At first his impulses knew no restraint except that imposed by the physical force of those that had enslaved him. But soon even the strongest of these impulses, sexual hunger, was modified and controlled by feelings of tenderness and sympathy toward those who shared his bondage and enabled him to escape from loneliness and isolation. Moreover, bondage could not crush out individual talent, and the division of labor on the plantation promoted mental differentiation and became the basis of differences in status. (32)

The African American psychological and social formation that continued in the United States was facilitated by the African American's assimilation into the household of the white master:

> There he took over more or less the ideas and attitudes and morals and manners of his masters. His marriage and family relations reflected the different stages and aspects of this process. Where the assimilation of western mores went farthest and the development of personality was highest, the organization of family life approached most closely the pattern of western civilization. (32)

But as Anthony Pratt argues, Frazier's position that racism and economic exploitation had "disorganized" the black family "did not constitute a negation of [black] culture" (5). As I have previously discussed, Frazier's last published article bears this out. In all the situations in which blacks found themselves, they had to adapt to the conditions, and life was complex, with much longing and yearning. This signifies a plural subjectivity that can speak to today.

Charles Johnson, a southerner who had very strong feelings and views about racial segregation, was a traditionally trained sociologist but also an overturner and a remapper of accepted or settled cultural, literary, and sociological geographies and genealogies, particularly when it came to the representation of the African American. He lends himself especially to a rereading in a different context and also opposes the reduced representation of the African American. Johnson was a distinguished American sociologist, the first black president of Fisk University, and a key figure of the Harlem Renaissance. Through his editorship of the Urban League's magazine, *Opportunity,* he gives expression to the cultural side of black life, doubling back to and challenging the myth of black inferiority. He believes that an "[a]rtistic work that equaled the quality of any other race would surely undermine white arguments of innate black inferiority" (Pearson 124). One of the leading patrons of the Harlem Renaissance, Johnson influenced the careers of such writers and artists as Langston Hughes, Zora Neale Hurston, Aaron Douglas, and Arna Bontemps.

Johnson also theorizes and remaps the American symbolic order to include America's diverse voices, traditions, and heritages. Although he wants blacks to achieve social equality, he, like Cooper, Du Bois, and Frazier, did not want them to assimilate, to become "a black Anglo-Saxon" (Gilpin 237–38), implying a desire for difference in the American symbolic order. Johnson wants to alter "the racial habits of functioning institutions through such tools as research and education, negotiation and persuasion, confidence and achievement" (Pearson 127), viewing black artists as playing a significant role in this reconfiguration and reeducation. In the *Nation,* Johnson writes that "The Negro writers . . . are now much less self-conscious, less interested in proving that they are just like white people, and, in their excursions into the fields of letters and art, seem to care less about what white people think, or are likely to think about the race" (qtd. in Gilpin 240). Seeing great value in black people as a cultural group, Johnson was encouraged by the Harlem Renaissance writers who discovered "the unique aesthetic values of African art, of beauty in things dark, . . . of harkening for the whispers of greatness from a remote African past" (qtd. in Gilpin 241).

Like Du Bois, Johnson, who was also bicultural, thinks of the African American as having a double consciousness, as being *both* American and black. Therefore, like Du Bois, because Johnson saw great value in African and African American life and culture, he rejects the mainstream American desire to represent the African American in negative terms, refusing to be antiblack. He also rejects the African American's own construction of himself as a pathological victim. In *Shadow of the Plantation* (1934), Johnson focuses on nonmainstream, nonnormative black folk culture, and as the editor of *Opportunity,* "he urged blacks to exploit the black experience to build the body of literature about black people that was necessary for liberation from the isolated world of segregation" (Gilpin 238). Johnson describes black artists' utilization of folk materials as "a new emancipation" (qtd. in Pearson 126), as creating a space outside the norm to define the African American. Within a remapped American symbolic order, Johnson wants the acceptance of racial difference and equality for all Americans.

In addition, Johnson, who worked in coalition with liberal white groups in the South, was one of the first sociologists to emphasize the psychological impact that racial discrimination and segregation had on African Americans. Through the research center in race relations at Fisk University, Johnson and his colleagues produced several important reports documenting the many manifestations of African American economic disadvantages in the South. Their reports on black communities in Tennessee are an important documentary source of rural and African American life in the mid-twentieth century. Johnson's books, *The Negro in American Civilization* (1930), *Shadow of the Plantation* (1934), and *Growing Up in the Black Belt* (1941), give history, agency, and distinct subjectivity to southern, subaltern African Americans, moving to combat the psychological behavior adjustments that African Americans "made to survive and function in American society" (Pearson 125).

In *Growing Up in the Black Belt,* Johnson does a sociological study of African American youths in Bolivar and Coahoma Counties in Mississippi, Macon County in Alabama, and Greene County in Georgia. Seemingly using a Freudian psychoanalytical framework, which focuses on the family and the environment, Johnson does ten personality profiles of youths in various settings, examining their attitudes toward family, community, religion, race, the South, and vocation and examining how being black affected the personality development of black youths living in the rural South (Stroman 163). Johnson learns that

> [t]heir personalities are profoundly influenced in a more realistic way by their familiar round of work and play, by the character and composition of their immediate families and their cliques, and by the level of education, the skills, and the social habits of their parents and all others who influenced them. . . . Inevitably their personalities and careers are influenced by the fears, hopes, and expectations bred by their status; by their isolation from the stimulating currents of a growing world; by the deep margins of poverty and the prestige and glamour of those who have escaped it; by the moral, aesthetic, and religious standards to which they are exposed; by the complex etiquette of race; and by the all pervading psychological and social implications of the traditions of race and class. (38)

As with Frazier, Johnson believes that these personalities or subjectivities are becoming and interactive.

Within this social milieu, the subjectivity of the African American is constructed among those processes of racial socialization and exploitation. African American youths develop complex subjectivities as they are forced to take various subject positions and to negotiate the various racial, economic, social, and religious forces and practices. We can discern their daily lives and their longings, their joys and sorrows. In short, the consciousness of African American youths is determined by historical and social situations. Thus, Johnson shows how African American youths are not simply passive victims but instead are social agents whose libido is not as effectively controlled by Freudianism and the closed, capitalistic family system. For them, desire is an element in the social field, an active participant in social life. Although they "occupy a subordinate position," they also struggle against rather than accept the status quo (Johnson 327), challenging and/or questioning Jim Crow laws. Economic changes in industry and urbanization undermine traditional patterns of race relations and cause changes in attitudes toward religion, family, sex, and whites. With education, these youths "enter skilled and white-collar occupations supposedly reserved for whites," and "whites . . . enter 'Negro' occupations" (326). Economically, there is a certain intermingling and interacting. This complex human portrait of African American youths certainly counters their image as devalued Other, as deviant.

Finally, the historian Carter G. Woodson also returns to and opposes America's representation of the African American as devalued Other. The dynamics of Foucauldian historiography, which defines history as a series of dispersions, ruptures, and discontinuities, allow me to dust off and reconsider Woodson, the "Father of Black History," bringing him in contact with theoretical, political, and epistemological formations undreamed of by him and making him speak to the contemporary moment. Working against a mainstream American middle-class and at times an educated norm that believed that blacks had no history and culture besides slavery, Woodson—whose childhood, youth, and adult life were poisoned by American racism—through his books, his Association for the Study of African American (Negro) Life and History, the *Journal of Negro History* (editor), Negro History Week (now celebrated in February as Black History Month), and the publication of the monthly *Negro History Bulletin,* offers an opposite response. He produces a body of knowledge about African American life, history, and culture that challenges a number of generally accepted myths about black inferiority. In *The Education of the Negro Prior to 1861* (1915), *A Century of Negro Migration* (1918), *The History of the Negro Church* (1921), the pioneering *The Negro in Our History* (1922), *Negro Makes History* (1928), *The Rural Negro* (1930), *The Mis-Education of the Negro* (1933), and others, Woodson revisits and contests the representation of the African American as being absent of history, consciousness, agency, and distinct subjectivity. Like Du Bois, Woodson, who was also educated at Harvard and earned a PhD in history but who was still considered as devalued Other by normative American society because he was black, rejects the binary logic that the African American should reject self and race and embrace mainstream values and definitions. Instead, like Cooper, Woodson theorizes and remaps an America that accepts and tolerates differences and cultural diversity, heralding the contributions of African Americans and black traditions.

In *The Mis-Education of the Negro* (1933), which includes the philosophical basis of his activities over the years, Woodson argues for an education that challenges the normative order of consciousness, or the American symbolic order, that does not define the African American as deviant. Woodson was aware that blacks are socialized in such a way that they cannot trust their own consciousness because it is very difficult to contradict the norm. He writes that

> the Negro's mind has been brought under the control of his oppressor. . . . When you control a man's thinking you do not have to worry about his actions. You do not have to tell him not to stand here or go yonder. He will find his 'proper place' and will stay in it. You do not need to send him to the back door. He will go without being told. In fact, if there is no back door, he will cut one for his special benefit. His education makes it necessary. (5)

Arguing that the education system within the hegemonic order of consciousness reinforces white supremacy and black inferiority, Woodson writes that "The thought of the inferiority of the Negro is drilled into him in almost ever class he enters and in almost every book he studies" (7).

But Woodson challenges this education system, the American symbolic order, by arguing for a multicultural, cosmopolitan American norm and education. First, in *The Mis-Education of the Negro,* and echoing what I interpret as the postmodern notion of difference without hierarchy, he reconstitutes the American symbolic order so that "the history [and subjectivities] of [all] races and nations, which have been purposely ignored," are nonhierarchally included and studied (107). Viewing the African American as an integral part of America's order of consciousness/symbolic order, he wants the African American socialized and educated in "the sense of being developed from what he is, and the public must be so enlightened as to think of the [African American]" not as a devalued Other or as a subject that is the embodiment of a political ideology but instead as a complex, fluid human being who has human virtues and human frailties. Furthermore, the remapped symbolic order has mutual understanding and respect among all its groups and individuals. All Americans must *know* the Other. No one can be "thoroughly educated [in America] until he learns as much about the Negro as he knows about other people" (95). This does not mean learning less about George Washington; instead, it means learning *also* about "the three thousand Negro soldiers of the American Revolution who helped to make this 'Father of our Country' possible" (108).

Second, within the order, Woodson redefines the African American as an active agent in the development and creolization of the West. Rather than focusing almost exclusively on "European colonists prior to their coming to America, their settlement on these shores, and their development here toward independence," American and African American historians should be "equally generous with the Negroes in treating their status in Africa prior to enslavement, their first transplantation to the West Indies, the Latinization of certain Negroes in contradistinction to the development of others under the influence of the Teuton"

(96). The African American is an integral part of the development of America/the West.

Third, arguing against the West's binary logic that reduces the African American to the negative half of the white-black binary opposition, to the subjugation of slavery, Woodson in *The Mis-Education of the Negro* incorporates African philosophy, alongside Greek philosophy, into America's national order of culture and consciousness, especially since Africans have "their own ideas about the nature of the universe, time, and space, about appearance and reality, and about freedom and necessity. The effort of the Negro to interpret man's relation to the universe shows just as much intelligence as we find in the philosophy of the Greeks. There were many Africans who were just as wise as Socrates" (96). Therefore, Woodson symbolizes the unsymbolized relationship between blacks and Americans, including a linguistic, social, cultural, theoretical, mythical, and/or religious representation of that relationship in the American symbolic order. With these remappings, the African American becomes not the same as the middle-class white norm but instead becomes its racial difference and its subjective equal.

Rather than learning about others and imitating them, Woodson in *The Mis-Education of the Negro* rerepresents African Americans to "function efficiently in society, . . . know themselves and the generation which they are to serve," and learn to think critically (97). More important, in his reconstituted American symbolic order, Woodson has the African American discovering oneself and understanding his or her own self-consciousness, own complex humanity. The philosophic penetration into the soul of the African American will find "a solace for the modern world" (99). Within African American life exists possibilities of a great drama for the person of color. The Middle Passage, according to Woodson, is one of the greatest dramas in history. The literature and art of the United States should capture this human drama. The study of African American folk songs shows incredible insights into African American humanity (98). In short, the genius of black music in the United States is inspired by incidents of the struggles of racial, economic, and social oppression. In Woodson's reconstituted symbolic order, the outstanding contributions that African Americans have made musically are included in America's diverse national symbolic culture.

Anna Julia Cooper, W. E. B. Du Bois, E. Franklin Frazier, Charles S. Johnson, and particularly Carter G. Woodson, with his *The Mis-Education of the Negro,* in their commitment to and focus on the life, history, and subjectivity of the African American and wanting nothing less than a radical transformation of American education and society, were precursors to black studies on black and white college and university campuses in the 1960s. The rise of black studies was spearheaded by black students—who were a part of or inspired by the civil rights movement, the Black Power movement, the assassinations of Malcolm X and Martin Luther King Jr.—at Cornell University, San Francisco State (College) University, Columbia University, Howard University, Morgan State University, Harvard University, Princeton University, Wesleyan University, Rutgers University, UC Santa Barbara, and others and demanded a remaking of American education and the inclusion of their realities—their history, culture, literature, and art—into the university curriculum. What they encountered on these campuses was a Eurocentric college curriculum where Europe and the United States were the center, the makers of history, while non-Europeans, non-Westerners, and women were the periphery. According to historian Nathan Huggins in *Afro-American Studies: A Report to the Ford Foundation,* what these students really encountered "was the parochial character of the humanities as taught," seeing the humanities as exclusive rather than universal. They saw "humanists as arrogant white men in self-congratulatory identification with a grand European culture" (13). These students challenged and contested this curriculum not only because they saw university education acting in complicity with the racism of the general American society but also because they recognized how this constructed European education and culture had excluded them or had defined them as deviant, or as devalued Other—as someone who is different and therefore less.

In the spirit of Cooper, Du Bois, Frazier, Johnson, Woodson, and others, what these students demanded was an education that spoke to the repressed margins and was relevant to their own lived experiences, included the history and culture and literature of African Americans in the United States, and acknowledged the contributions of Africans and African Americans in the United States and the world. In "Black Studies in the Midwest," literary critic Nellie McKay writes that "The common reference point is the validity of the African Diaspora experience—the creation of an active consciousness that a rich culture springs from Africa, which her children, scattered across the face of the globe, share and celebrate for its uniqueness, power, and strength" (26). These students wanted to hear African and African American voices that had been repressed by the ruling discourse of white (male) supremacy.

Therefore, between 1968 and 1975, in responding to the demands of African American students and communities, American colleges and universities established more than five hundred programs and departments in African American studies; added to their traditional curricula courses on African American life, history, sociology, and literature; and made efforts to include African Americans on their faculty and administrative staffs. Colleges and universities widened the curriculum, the range of intellectual inquiry, and the range of discussion to include the African American and successfully struggled to establish black studies as a "respected academic discipline" (Patton 1). The inclusion of black studies, argued Harold Cruse at one of the first conferences on black studies at Yale University in 1968, was to "facilitate equalization of the black man in American society" (22). Showing his skepticism at an emerging black cultural nationalism or the construction of black history "by emphasizing the oppressive aspects of this experience," Martin Kilson, who was also at this conference at Yale, argues "that the black experience is truly nothing more than a variant of the human experience" (15). Because he did not think that the "bloody and dehumanizing record of [the white-black] relationship" was "neither unique nor a startling event" (15), Kilson did not think that the relationship should become the focus of black studies.

The aim of these precursors and the main aim of black studies programs and departments, along with American Indian, Asian American, Latino/a American, and women's studies programs and departments, were to produce new bodies of knowledge, remap the American educational system and the American symbolic order, challenge Eurocentric intellectual control of knowledge, contest African Americans' investment in the middle-class American norm or in the order of consciousness, and advocate for an African American who has agency, history, and a distinct subjectivity. Black studies programs were to enable an exit from an American/Western system of knowledge that defined the African American as deviant. Writing in "The Case of Black Studies," Gerald A. McWhorter argues that "the traditional body of knowledge" offered in Ivy League American colleges and universities defines "the black community in pathological terms" (59). As Cooper, Du Bois, Johnson, Frazier, and Woodson had done, the purpose of black studies was to return to, challenge, and reconfigure this pathological representation.

But at some point very early on, if not in some cases from the beginning, many of these programs and departments were hijacked by careerists, ideologues, cultural nationalists, and Afrocentric scholars who reneged not only on the black students' wishes and demands but also on the scholarly foundations established by Cooper, Du Bois, Johnson, Franklin, and Woodson. While students' demands might have begun as requests for programs, departments, and activities relevant to African Americans, with no implication of being exclusionary, these programs and activities, argues Nathan Huggins, almost always evolved into de facto black dormitories, cultural centers, and programs. The demand for black turf generally resulted in separatism and ethnocentrism. Students and faculty in many of the first African American studies programs and departments in the late 1960s were, in fact, explicit in their demand for racially separate programs and facilities (Huggins 32). The assumption was that the United States consisted of two separate nations, two separate cultures—one black and one white—and despite the four hundred years of coexistence in the same society, there was no interpenetration or hybridization culturally and socially, thereby turning a deaf ear on Du Bois's double consciousness. In rejecting everything white and western, many of these programs and students assumed and advocated what Paul Gilroy in *Black Atlantic* calls "ethnic absolutism" (30), or a social and intellectual space that existed outside the West. They assumed that the construction of their identities also existed outside the West.

In the twenty-first century, some of these programs and departments, which existed mostly on soft money, have either been closed or have merged with ethnic studies programs and departments at such places as UC Berkeley, Stanford University, and Iowa State University.[8] The majority of these programs and departments, which are still standing, are chaired and directed by Afrocentric or neonationalist scholars.[9] Entering into a binary opposition with the dominant white society, this cultural nationalist approach to black studies focused on what is indigenous to black life to generate positive public images of the African American, or black studies takes a romantic return to a mythical Africa, hoping to retrieve a precolonial African past and totally ignoring Africa's complex human and colonial past. Although most of these programs and departments are approximately forty years old, they are defined and "practiced in many ways, which vary from institution to institution" (McKay, "Black Studies" 26). But despite this assessment by McKay, if we scrutinize closely many of these programs today, we can still surmise that the reaction and the objectives, expectations, and demands that brought them into existence still inform their construction today. But with the increase in doctoral programs in African American studies in the last decade, along with innovative African American scholars in traditional American disciplines, some diversity is coming to African American studies.

But today, a close scrutiny of many of these programs and departments shows the use of Afrocentric or neonationalist perspectives in representing African American life.[10] Although Afrocentrism emerged as a full discourse in the 1980s with Molefi Kete Asante and others, Black Nationalism, in one stage or another and as a term to describe a body of social thought, attitudes, and actions, has always been a part of the body politics of African American life. In its simplest form, it is the "expressions of ethnocentrism and racial solidarity. . . . It generally has no ideological or programmatic implications beyond the desire that black people organize themselves on the basis of their common color and oppressed condition to move in some way to alleviate their situation. The concept of racial solidarity is essential to all forms of black nationalism" (Bracey, Meier, and Rudwick xxvi). Understanding that the dominant white society denies African Americans their complex humanity, Black Nationalism, argues James Turner, believes that African Americans "must become transmuted into a conscious and cohesive group. The rationale is that a group giving a unitary response can more effectively and honorably confront the constraining dominant group. . . . Loyalty to group cultural attributes and commitment to collective goals provide the adhesive for the group" (235–36). Many African American studies programs are organized in accordance with this basic tenet of Black Nationalism. With Black Nationalism, African Americans can reverse/flip/interrogate the white-black binary, rediscovering and making those things—black skin, values, tradition, cultural attributes, and subjectivity—that had been suppressed by mainstream white society into things that are positive and good. I am not sure whether this Black Nationalist approach attempts a transformation of the American society.

Black Cultural Nationalism, which has much in common with Afrocentrism, is more ideological and has programmatic implications, especially when it comes to African American studies, culture, life, and art. Black Cultural Nationalism contends that black people in the United States or throughout the world have a culture, style of life, and cosmology and have an approach to the problems of existence as well as aesthetic values distinct from that of white Americans in particular and white Europeans or Westerners in general (Bracey et al. xxvi–xxvii). In "Black

Cultural Nationalism," Maulana Ron Karenga argues for an essential African-based culture and a revolutionary black art that support and reflect the black revolution, that do not get "bog[ged] . . . down in the meaningless madness of the Western world" (31), totally ignoring the fact that the African American is produced by and therefore belongs to the Western world. And if art produced by African Americans is not functional, collective (no individuality), and committed (to revolution), it is not relevant. For Karenga the blues are invalid, "for they teach resignation, in a word acceptance of reality" (36). Today, the blues "are not functional because they do not commit us to the struggle of today and tomorrow, but keep us in the past" (36).

Like Black Cultural Nationalism, Afrocentrism is rigidly ideological and has programmatic implications, especially for African American studies programs and departments and for African American life. Reinforced by the publication of *Afrocentricity* in 1980 by Molefi Kete Asante, chair during 1984–96 of the Department of African American Studies at Temple University, where he created the first PhD program in African American studies and still serves as a professor, and by Maulana Karenga's *Introduction to Black Studies* in 1982, many of these Afrocentric-based programs and departments work from the assumption that African Americans belong to an essentialist, diasporic African global unity, which determines their behavior, ethics, art, and rule of life and should be imposed on all people of African descent in the world. I am not arguing that nationalist and Afrocentric scholars are not aware of social, cultural, and ideological differences within Africa and African America. I am arguing that these scholars establish hierarchies and represent Africa and African America singularly and ideally, with all kinds of exclusions.

Afrocentrism, which is quite effective in critiquing racism, argues that African Americans belong to a permanent, timeless, isolated, separate, autonomous, and homogeneous culture in the United States—a culture that exists outside Western history and rationality, that harkens back to classical African civilizations and cultures, to a mythical Pan-African past, and therefore is oblivious not only to classical

European colonialism and the West's influences and interpenetrations but also to Africa's rich influence on the West. In *Afrocentricity,* Asante writes that "It is our history, our mythology, our creative motif, and our ethos exemplifying our collective will" (6). In response to Henry Louis Gates and Harvard University's Department of African American Studies, Asante, in a letter to the editor, further clarifying his Afrocentric view and mission for black studies, writes that

> Temple University's department is Afrocentric because we believe that African-American studies is not merely an aggregation of courses about African people, but the Afrocentric study of African people and phenomena. If you study African people from any other vantage point you are engaging in some other discipline, not African American studies. To view Africans as subjects and agents within the context of history is Afrocentric. ("Black Studies" A1)

In *Introduction to Black Studies,* Karenga writes that "This [black studies] enterprise is self-consciously Afrocentric. . . . An Afro-centric approach is essentially intellectual inquiry and production centered on and in the image and interest of African peoples" (xxiv). Any deviation by African Americans from this essentialized cultural base is perceived as betrayal or an aberration.

The underlying assumption of this ideologically racially constructed Afrocentric culture is the belief that African America is to be represented with exclusions, tacitly arguing that African America is not polluted by capitalism, heteropatriarchy, classism, the ravages of slavery, and modernity. In *Small Acts,* Paul Gilroy resounds this same note when he rhetorically answers the question, in a dialogue with bell hooks, of why Afrocentric scholars cannot talk about popular culture:

> I notice it most of all in the complete silence in that whole body of work about popular culture. There's nothing being said about popular culture there. . . . [T]o talk about popular culture, one has to confront

> the whole "contamination" of supposedly pure African forms. Africa provided the critical substance for that process of mutation and adaptation we call creolization. The serious study of black popular culture affirms that intermixture in some way. If you want to repudiate that process of adaptation and growth and are trying in its place to reconstruct some notion of a purified African culture, you have to stay clear of the vernacular. Investigating the black Atlantic diaspora means that you have to reckon with the creolization process as a founding moment, a point in time when new relations, cultures and conflicts were brought into being. (209)

To maintain its sense of purity and high culture, Afrocentrism, like Black Cultural Nationalism, also has to steer clear of the great African American musical forms such as the spirituals and the blues because they are products of hybridization whereby African forms and instruments intermix with Western forms and instruments. But the reality of the situation is that African America, whether we are referring to the rural margins or the urban pockets, belongs, as Du Bois argues, to Africa and to the West, to the modernization process, and to capitalism. It is a product of the "mutation and adaptation we call creolization," the product of cultural and social hybridization.

Of course, this narrow Afrocentric representation of African American life does not go uncontested by contemporary African American scholars, critics, and writers such as Manning Marable, Robert L. Harris Jr., Cornel West, Hazel Carby, Adolph Reed, James Boggs, Amiri Baraka, bell hooks, Michael Eric Dyson, and many others in organizing African American life differently and more complexly, who unearth and challenge this Afrocentric representation of black life. They argue that Afrocentricity fails to engage adequately with the complexity, hybridity, and heterogeneity of African American life, being quite rigid and rational, in the Western sense. For example, responding to the establishment of Temple's Afrocentric PhD program, Robert L. Harris Jr. states that while he respects "Temple's doctoral program, he disagrees with the way Temple defines black studies as a discipline rather than as an interdisciplinary venture. The experiences of African people are too vast . . . to fit under one discipline" (Magner A13). In an interview with Paul Gilroy in *Small Acts,* bell hooks states that "We've been talking a lot about ways that some of the more prominent strands of Afro-centrism in the United States really mirror certain white Western philosophical ways of thinking about the self. I was thinking in response to the comment you just made about how much there's an insistence in Afro-centric thinking on the importance of high culture. . . . Afro-centrism reproduces certain white bourgeois assumptions" (209–10), religiously peddling such Victorian values as the patriarchy; cultural and moral purity; chaste, compulsory heterosexuality; female subordination; and high art. According to hooks, Afrocentrism reproduces within these programs and departments versions of the same violent hierarchies and exclusions as in mainstream American university departments. It imposes its norms and standards with absolute authority, subordinating and repressing differences. There is all this African American culture and life, such as subaltern and working class black cultures, the blues, and Voodoo, in which Afrocentrics and cultural nationalists cannot engage except negatively. Pointing out the limitations of Afrocentrism and echoing hooks, Cornel West, in *Beyond Eurocentrism and Multiculturalism,* writes that "Some of the problems I have with certain Afro-centric thinkers is, I think they are too preoccupied with Europe" (28). Defining Afrocentrism as a fad, Leon Forrest argues that Afrocentrism is "another easy way out of a complex identity. Black people in this country are a new kind of people, a different people whose consciousness was forged on this continent" (qtd. in James 58). Finally, Stanley Crouch defines Afrocentrism as "another 'simple-minded hustle'" (qtd. in Boynton 96).

In short, a rigid Afrocentric approach to African American life, history, and culture prevents several things from happening. First, it recovers African cultural forms already established or, at least, infiltrated by the culture of empire, rerepresenting them as untroubled and authentic. As a consequence, it never engages Africa's complex, troubled past or present: its wars and conquest between indigenous nations, its colonial and postcolonial experiences, its globalized urban experience, its realities of capitalism and consumerism, and its subsequent hybridization and multiculturalism. Second, a rigid Afrocentric approach represses the polyvalent nature of African American life, especially the mysteries. It ignores the larger political, social, and economic movements and forces and African Americans' connections to them. Third, a rigid Afrocentric approach talks "about [a] black experience without a class [and gender] analysis that is coordinated to the analysis of contemporary racism" (Gilroy, *Small Acts* 218). Black women's existence and history are marginalized or completely ignored, and there is no discussion of class within black communities. "Nationalism," writes Edward Said in *Culture and Imperialism,* "can become a panacea for *not* dealing with economic disparities [and] social injustice" (217) within groups and nations. Because African Americans are products of the West, they have internalized and therefore reproduce much of the classism, sexism, homophobia, and patriarchal attitudes of the West.

Fourth and last, a rigid Afrocentric approach ignores, excludes, and represses subjectivities, differences, and modern and postmodern experiences in African American life. Unlike Cooper, Frazier, and Woodson, this Afrocentric approach does not position itself within the hegemonic space in order to be oppositional, to rewrite the center. It positions itself separately in the margins. Therefore, structurally, it never challenges the American symbolic order, adding black courses to the curriculum, but never challenges or transforms the center, the core Euro-American university educational curriculum.

But, more important, a rigid Afrocentric/neonationalist approach to black studies and black life, in defining Africa and African America singularly and ideally, eschews the complex, fluid portrait of the African American put forth by Anna Julia Cooper and E. Franklin Frazier, ignoring Du Bois's (and Charles Johnson's) double consciousness, whereby the African American is *both* black and American.

The Afrocentric approach fails to examine the African American in the context of the larger American and global societies, as Frazier and Woodson do. Finally, it represses or simply ignores Cooper's and Woodson's theorizing and remapping of the American symbolic order to include the African American as an integral component, to acknowledge the intimate blend between the black, the American Indian, the Asian American, the Latino/a American, and the European American and to know how they fertilized each other. The danger of essentialism is that in thinking about their own group, Afrocentrics ignore what is most interesting about being alive: being angled toward the Other. Rather, they think that it is more interesting to be victims.

Afrocentrism has been able to dominate the majority of these programs and departments until recently because the flagship Afrocentric department at Temple University has produced the majority of the PhDs in African American studies. Established in 1987 under the leadership of Dr. Molefi Kete Asante, Temple University's Department of African American Studies, according to Stephanie Y. Evans's research published in 2006, has produced 135 of the 153 PhDs in African American Studies (2). With Temple's department being the first and only PhD-granting institution in African American studies for many years, it produced the PhDs who would chair and direct many of the various programs and departments throughout the country. Discussing the creation of Temple's African American studies PhD program and the graduation of its first PhD, Asante states that "We are producing the next crop of scholars who will leave here and pursue Afrocentricity, not just at Temple, but across the country" (Magner A13). Writing in the introduction to the 2001 edition of *The African American Studies Reader,* whose first edition is heavily Afrocentric but whose expanded and revised second edition includes sections on women's studies, on black gays and lesbians, and on public policy, and echoing Asante, editor Nathaniel Norment Jr. states that "it could be argued that during the last two decades in African American Studies, no other conceptual framework or theoretical construct has contributed more to the discussion and debate of the academy than the theory of Afro-centricity as presented by Molefi K. Asante" (xxxix). From the beginning, many of the African American studies programs and departments have been hijacked by rigid Afrocentric and black cultural nationalist thought.

But more recently, and to a lesser degree earlier, other African American studies programs and departments have diverse faculty and diverse approaches to African American studies, thereby challenging the absolutism of the Afrocentric approach and making it one of many approaches to African American life and history. The movement away from the domineering, narrow Afrocentric approach to African American life, history, and culture is further assisted by the development of other African American studies PhD-granting departments at the University of Massachusetts at Amherst (1996), the University of California at Berkeley (1997), Harvard University (2001), Michigan State University (2002), Northwestern University (2005), Indiana University (2008), the University of Pennsylvania (2009), the University of Texas at Austin (2010), and others, which deal polyvalently with African American life and history. For example, the doctoral program at UC Berkeley focuses on comparative ethnic studies, examining black life in a larger global context. Through a Ford Foundation initiative, Berkeley's department strengthened its "emphasis on diasporic, interdisciplinary research" (O'Meally and Smith 126). Berkeley's ethnic studies PhD, which includes Asian Americans, Chicano/Latinos, and American Indians, along with African Americans, situates "these core groups within national and transnational contexts, and . . . understand[s] how racial and ethnic formation articulate with other axes of stratification such as class, gender, and sexuality."[11] It becomes interdisciplinary and multicultural.

Also, the interdisciplinary doctoral programs at the University of Massachusetts at Amherst (UMass), which is named for W. E. B. Du Bois, and at Michigan State are quite diverse. UMass's department "seeks to reproduce both the scholarship and the social commitment of Du Bois in a new generation of scholars who will carry into the twenty-first century the work that Du Bois accomplished in the nineteenth and twentieth centuries." With a multiracial faculty with diverse approaches to African American studies, UMass signals something different for African American studies. Michigan State's innovative PhD program in comparative black history is transnational and involves several continents (O'Meally and Smith 146).

The doctoral program at Yale, which draws heavily from nationally and internationally renowned scholars such as Hazel Carby, Elizabeth Alexander, David Blight, Jonathan Holloway, Christopher Miller, Naomi Pabst, Glenda Gilmore, and Matthew Frye Jacobson and from traditional disciplines, is quite eclectic, diverse, and theoretical in its approach to African American history, life, and literature, maintaining and building on an excellent undergraduate program established in 1969 by Charles Davis, Michael Cooke, Sidney Mintz, Roy Bryce La Porte, John Blessingame, and others. The African American studies PhD program at Yale is in conjunction with other departments, such as American Studies, Anthropology, English, Film Studies, History, etc., echoing and continuing the work of earlier African American scholars such as Cooper, Du Bois, and Woodson.

Finally, realizing that the contemporary world is increasingly interdependent and subject to diverse representations and questions, the African American studies PhD program at Northwestern University examines the "multicultural, multi-ethnic, multi-faith and gendered dimensions of national spaces and histories [that] are accelerating to prominence under the influence of economic and cultural forms of globalization."[12] Unlike Afrocentric-based doctoral programs and departments, these more recent doctoral programs and departments engage the law of the Other. They are interdisciplinary and transnational and are beginning to challenge traditional disciplines to address silences on black issues. In addition, many are changing their names to "Africana" and "Africana diaspora" studies and "broadening their courses from a focus on black Americans to black people in Africa, Europe, and the Caribbean" (Wilson A9).

More encouragingly, though, many contemporary scholars and intellectuals who write about black studies issues but are not affiliated with African American studies programs and departments continue to grow and mature as they deal with women issues, sexual identity issues, popular culture, globalization, feminism, sexuality, subjectivity, subaltern and working-class black cultures, jazz, blues, environmental racism, and difference rather than binary oppositions. "At the field's inception," writes editors Bobo, Hudley, and Michel of *The Black Studies Reader,* most of whose contributors are not housed in black studies programs and departments, "scholars defined it as an intellectual necessity linked with political imperatives: students activism, collaboration among diverse Black communities, and scholarship in support of changes in the larger society" (3). Today, with more "theoretical and methodological sophistication," black scholars are meeting the challenge of a global society and the African American existence within it. "The melding of cultures and research paradigms within black studies," write Bobo et al., "has demonstrated a commitment to issues of social, educational, and economic disparities, defining curricula vitally engaged with present-day societal issues. . . . Interdisciplinary and multidivisional, these approaches create original and innovative bodies of knowledge. . . . Black Studies engages issues about historical and contemporary forms of resistance and resilience in response to local and global crises" (4). *The Black Studies Reader* is divided into three parts: Theorizing Black Studies, Conceptualizing Culture and Ideology, and Sexuality, Education, Religion.

At the same time that many black studies programs and departments are still locked in Afrocentrism, other black studies programs and departments and black scholars in traditional departments (and in American studies and women's studies programs and departments) are using postmodernism, poststructuralism, feminist theory, queer theory, postcolonial theory, media studies, cultural studies, and African American cultural studies to reconfigure black studies in a very contemporary way, echoing Cooper, Du Bois, Frazier, Johnson, and Woodson; dealing contemporaneously with black issues; and bringing plurality, full complexity, and humanity to African American subjectivity. These more current programs and scholars interrogate Eurocentrism and the construction of the African American as devalued other, black essentialism, and rigid identity politics, opening up the field to what Dwight McBride calls a "broad analysis of black people" (Bobo et al. 10).

Finally, as a fourth implied development that history later discloses about the African American and in addition to African American scholars such as Cooper, Du Bois, Frazier, Johnson, and Woodson, along with a host of contemporary American and African American scholars of black studies, certain traditional African and African American cultural forms such as the blues, jazz, spirituals, Voodoo, African American folk culture, and others—which are spaces that still retain a wildness, that have not been completely mapped and taken over and trademarked by the normative American culture—can be reinterpreted to speak to contemporary dynamics or issues in African American life. Contesting the construction of the African American as "deviant," as devalued Other, or as the same in the West, they, as Charles Johnson and Carter G. Woodson suggest, allow African Americans to define their body, identity, subjectivity, reason, history, and culture not as the negative term of the white norm but as complex entities and histories with their own potency, agency, history, wildness, and distinct subjectivity. Despite the fact that they are discourses with certain hierarchies and exclusions, these cultural forms can be represented as unleashing the tension and the power and as fearlessly, courageously, and thoroughgoingly dealing with the complexity of black life, the black spirit, outside of limited and essential categories. "No true artist," writes Anna Julia Cooper, "can allow himself to be narrowed and provincialized by deliberately shutting out any class of facts or subjects through prejudice against externals" (116). These cultural forms also allow African Americans to redefine themselves outside the logic, reason, and values of the Enlightenment, which are the underpinnings of the white middle-class puritan norm. Finally, these traditional cultural forms possess intrinsic features and characteristics such as heterogeneity, open-endedness, chance, indeterminacy, play, hybridity, multiplicity, fluidity over rigidity, and the flow of desires that we currently associate with poststructuralism and postmodernism.

The blues idiom as an expressive musical form and as a way of life has been a part of African American life since the time of slavery, representing a definition of life that is different from that of mainstream middle-class Christian American life. "The blues was conceived," writes LeRoi Jones (also known as Amiri Baraka) in *Blues People,* "by freedmen and ex-slaves—if not as a result of a personal or intellectual experience, at least as an emotional confirmation of, and reaction to, the way in which most Negroes were still forced to exist in the United States" (142). The blues is the "material history" and the "psychological source" of an American people "who were not allowed to be American" (Baraka, *Digging* 13, 19). As a feeling, a sense-knowledge, the blues invites African Americans to embrace the reality and truth of black life, and in most instances that life is not patterned after the Enlightenment definition of life that emerged in Europe in the sixteenth century. In not being rational and linear, it does not always move toward a resolution. Rather, it accepts the spectrum of human life, including contradictions, differences, and the nonrational. It embraces flux, the flow of desires.

Philosophically, the blues is secular but also serves a theological purpose. It is closely related to the so-called slave secular music that is nonreligious, occasionally antireligious, and is often called "devil songs" by Christians. Blues people/subaltern African Americans—the field slave, the migrant, the convict, the roustabout, the working class and lower working class, and the urban or rural illiterate outsider—are escaping but not completely leaving Christianity, Enlightenment reason, middle-class respectability, features that comprise the American norm. "As the poetic voice of a people distinctively victimized by the whole gamut of the repressive forces of bourgeois/Christian civilization (economic exploitation, political disenfranchisement, racism, etc.)," argues Paul Garon in *Blues and the Poetic Spirit,* "the blues long ago found itself in the service of human emancipation by virtue of the particular manner in which it deals with such repression" (2). The blues has a different cosmology than the American norm.

Listening to great blues singers such as Mamie Smith, Ma Rainey, Robert Johnson, Bessie Smith, Blind Lemon Johnson, Son House, Big Bill Boonzy, Howlin' Wolf, Charles Patton, Leadbelly, Muddy Waters, Big Mama Thornton, and others, you find the major catastrophes (both personal and national), the triumphs, and the miseries that are shared by all yet remain private to one. The music of these blues singers reflects the family disputes and the upheavals, dislocation, and alienation caused by racial oppression, poverty, and migration as well as the violence and bitterness, the tears and the happiness. The blues allows all of these reflections "without falling into self pity and recriminations" (Gioia 12). In the blues, argues Paul Oliver in *The Meaning of the Blues,* an unsettled, unwanted people during periods of social unrest and dislocation find "the security, the unity and the strength that [they] so desperately desire[]" (32). The blues resists, limits, and modifies middle-class puritan American culture, affirming blues people's essential worth, even as the normative culture defines them as "deviant." Telling us about individuals who refuse to accept society's negative representation of them, the blues "offer[s] a catharsis, an idealization of the individual's plight," states Gioia, "and, in some strange way, an uplifting sense of mastery over the melancholy circumstances recounted in the context of the blues song" (12). The blues comprises a paradigm that engages contradictions, indeterminacy, and play, that embraces flux and the flow of life and desires, thinking differences rather than binary oppositions.

Many music historians trace the beginnings of jazz to New Orleans and the slave dances, with their clusters of individuals moving in a circular pattern, that took place in the early nineteenth century in the open area known as Congo Square—today known as Armstrong Square. Although the slave dances, also known as the ring shout, had their origin in West Africa, they intermingled and intermixed in New Orleans with European, Caribbean, and American elements, particularly the work song, truly becoming a great hybrid modern American music. "The ability of African performance arts to transform the European tradition of composition while assimilating some of its elements is perhaps the most striking and powerful evolutionary force in the history of modern music" (Gioia 8). Thus, the original spirit of jazz is to bring together and hybridize African, European, and American music, incorporating improvisation and group interplay and communicating on the spot. It keeps changing and evolving. In this sense, jazz is a uniquely American creation.

But jazz begins with the blues, the simultaneity of good and bad, the tradition of love and trouble. It was used to "cast off the blues and be happy, carefree, even in the midst of sordidness and sorrow" (Rogers 104). The earliest jazz makers were the itinerant piano players who would wander up and down the Mississippi from saloon to saloon, from dive to dive:

> Seated at the piano with a carefree air that a king might envy, their box-back coats flowing over the stool, their Stetsons pulled well over their eyes, and cigars at an angle of forty-five degrees, they would "whip the ivories" to marvelous chords and hidden racy, joyous meanings, evoking the intense delight of their hearers who would smother them at the close with huzzas and whiskey. Often wholly illiterate, these humble troubadours knowing nothing of written music or composition, but with minds like cameras, would listen to the rude improvisations of the dock laborers and the railroad gangs and reproduce them, reflecting perfectly the sentiments and the longings of these humble folk. (Rogers 106)

These early jazz makers (and their successors) produced a new way to inhabit and define the world.

Improvisation, one of the most salient features of jazz, dates to the rhythmic vitality or polyrhythms of African music. With every object of day-to-day life a source of rhythm in African life, play and the multiplicity of rhythms manifested itself in the music, which was transported to the United States by enslaved Africans. In the contemporary American jazz musical context, improvisation, which involves chance, is the signification or transformation of an original melody. It can be, according to Paul F. Berliner, the "most radical transformations of the melody, . . . from progressively subtler alterations, falling within the realm of variation, embellishment, and interpretation" (221). More important, jazz improvisation is when a blues song is transformed and new ideas are created. Jazz, writes Amiri Baraka, is a "blue[s] song, transformed by instrumental adaptation of rhythm and the harmelodic expansiveness of improvisation as acknowledged reorganization of the line the beat the melody the harmonic relationships" (*Digging* 295). Through transformation, jazz liberates.

Jazz embodies and generates the free flow of life, which explains its popularity in Paris, London, San Francisco, New York, New Orleans, Montreal, Sidney, and Tokyo. The spirit of jazz can almost express itself everywhere, for it is available for anyone who is oppressed and repressed by rigid rationalism, nationalism, and the narrow linear model. "The true spirit of jazz," writes J. A. Rogers in "Jazz at Home," "is joyous revolt from convention, custom, authority, boredom, even sorrow—from everything that would confine the soul of man and hinder its riding free on the air. . . . It is a release of all the suppressed emotions at once, a blowing off of the lid, as it were. It is hilarity expressing itself through pandemonium; musical fireworks" (104, 105). In this sense, jazz has features and characteristics similar to postmodernism, including the free flow of desire, indeterminacy, heterogeneity, becoming, open-endedness, chance, plurality, etc. Like the blues, jazz thinks differences rather than binary oppositions.

The racial uplift narrative, the social and political movements and organizations, the scholarship of Cooper, Frazier, Du Bois, Johnson, Woodson, and others, along with African American cultural forms such as the blues, jazz, Voodoo, the African American trickster figure, and others, as implied developments that Western history discloses, push beyond "the frozen essence that condemns" the African American "to servitude and punishment," beyond the West's construction of the African American as deviant. Through opposition, refutation, contestation, and the search for clarity and relief, these social movements, scholars and cultural forms transform the most unyielding stasis in the West, the notion that the African American is inferior, that he is deviant.

But more important, the scholarship and the cultural forms redefine the consciousness and the subjectivity of the African American, not only as a subjectivity that is fixed and ontological but also as one that is multiple, that is a movement of self-constitution within language, one that accepts the reason of the Other. They allow for a subjectivity that recognizes other subjects as different and yet alike, as others who are capable of sharing mental experiences. The scholarship and cultural forms allow for the emergence of an entirely new order of consciousness, a reconstituted, heterogeneous American symbolic order, which means a profound rewriting and reproduction of knowledge (Wynter qtd. in Thomas, "ProudFlesh Inter/Views" 11) and also means a regime of truth whereby the African American does not function as negation. Rather, the African American belongs to an American symbolic order where he enjoys the social power of being routinely connected psychologically to a whole spectrum of normative institutions and practices.

In *Postmodernism, Traditional Cultural Forms, and African American Narratives,* I offer a close reading of six African American texts that use marginal or peripheral cultural forms and paradigms as alternatives to European-centered and rigid African American–centered modernities to inform and reconceive their constructions.[13] I use deconstruction, postcolonial theory, Carl G. Jung, French psychoanalytical theory, feminist theories, Gilles Deleuze's theory of difference, and Enrique Dussel's concept of modernity to remake or to reposition the African American subject from a black Other to an American subject. Then, I show how these contemporary African American texts use American, African, and African American cultural traditions and belief systems, some of which had been denigrated by Western reason, not as romantic retreats to the past but instead as ways to redescribe, expand, and complicate the representation of the African American in a contemporary setting.

These traditions and belief systems include jazz, the blues, the African American trickster figure, Yoruba gods, African American folk culture, radical democracy, and virtuality, which operate within sets of rules that are different from the middle-class puritan American norm.

The social and cultural milieu for these writers and texts began in the upheaval of the 1960s but came to fruition in the 1980s and 1990s as African American writers, intellectuals, activists, and scholars achieved some psychological freedom from the daunting American historical narrative, which defined them and their history and culture negatively. Finding their voices, they dusted off and reclaimed their African and African American cultural traditions and belief systems, particularly those that are open and fluid. With an affirmative knowledge of the historical and cultural past, outside the lens of Eurocentrism and Enlightenment reason, and with the assistance of poststructuralist theory (either directly or indirectly), post-1970s feminist thoughts, modern linguistics, and/or African American cultural studies, these writers and texts disrupt Western binaries and challenge rigid mainstream African American categories and paradigms, such as the racial uplift narrative, identity politics, and racial essentialism, as they strive for a more complex, varied, and humane portrait of the African American. They also reverberate against mainstream American cultural and literary productions, especially those that reproduce a reduced representation of the African American.

First, I choose three texts each by African American male and female writers, which forced me to exclude other blues- and jazz-influenced texts. But I wanted to examine whether women writers have the same relationship as men writers to the Other and to the world. Second, I am particularly interested in contemporary African American texts that redefine the African American in terms of postmodernity, in terms of jazz and the blues, in terms of a plural subjectivity, with all of the above texts having one or several of these in common. In addition, these six texts present African American subjects who are able to accept the law of the Other, to empathize with and/or become the Other. These are African American subjects who, according to Toni Cade

Bambara, in telling the truth "plug into other kinds of intelligences," who use African American cultural forms "to invent, in addition to new forms, new modes and new idioms" (Salaam 58). In short, unlike some of the political and social movements discussed earlier and like the scholarship of Cooper, Du Bois, Johnson, Frazier and Woodson, these texts create models of subjectivity that speak to a multicultural, cosmopolitan, postmodern American society.

Third and last, I organize these six texts as they progressively leave but do not completely escape Enlightenment reason, heteropatriarchy, logocentrism, middle-class respectability, identity politics, black essentialism, and the realistic novel, beginning with John Edgar Wideman's *Philadelphia Fire* and Percival Everett's *Erasure,* which easily deconstruct the novel form (a subsystem of Enlightenment reason) and logocentrism, undermine black essentialism and identity politics, and reconfigure African American male subjectivity but become entrapped in heteropatriarchy and Eurocentric notions of masculinity and sexuality. Toni Morrison's *Jazz* in many ways escapes the traditional novel form and heteropatriarchy but reproduces some of the normative features of modernism, such as Western notions of gender and sexuality. The last three novels—Bonnie Greer's *Hanging by Her Teeth,* Clarence Major's *Reflex and Bone Structure,* and Xam Cartiér's *Muse-Echo Blues*—are much more open and fluid and experimental, as they play with the traditional novel form; challenge black essentialism, identity politics, and middle-class respectability; and undermine Eurocentric notions of reason, subjectivity, and heteropatriarchy.

Although *Postmodernism, Traditional Cultural Forms, and African American Narratives* begins with contemporary African American texts and marginal cultural forms and paradigms, its objective is to impose something that is African American difference on the equality of the American norm, reconfiguring and creating models for a genuine multiracial, multicultural, and cosmopolitan American society. This book makes a "conscious effort to enter the discourse" of mainstream America, "to mix with it, transform it, [and] to make it acknowledge marginalized or suppressed . . . histories," cultures, and subjectivities (Said, *Culture* 216). This book thus reconfigures the American symbolic order where differences, including a rearticulated African American subjectivity and history, are included and participate, making the African American a part of the performance of the general American culture.

Although the texts covered in *Postmodernism, Traditional Cultural Forms, and African American Narratives* increasingly undermine Enlightenment reason, challenge heteropatriarchy, interrogate rigid identity politics and racial essentialism, and advocate a different way to be human in the West, some of them still have what Sylvia Wynter calls "reflex valuations that [they] continually carry" (qtd. in Thomas, "ProudFlesh Inter/Views" 4). In their instinctive reactions to normative values and the subsequent construction of them as deviant, they cannot avoid the fact that they are produced/created in a world in which everything black has been negatively marked. Because everything black is defined by normative American society as being negatively marked, there is a reactive response.

— 2 —

Multiple Representations of Philadelphia and John Edgar Wideman's *Philadelphia Fire*

According to Jacques Derrida, meaning in the West is defined in terms of binary oppositions, "a violent hierarchy" whereby "one of the two terms governs the other" (*Positions* 41). Within the white-black binary opposition in the West, the African American is defined as devalued Other. One of the aims of many experimental/postmodern African American writers such as Ishmael Reed, Toni Morrison, Clarence Major, Bonnie Greer, Percival Everett, Samuel R. Delany, and Xam Cartiér has been to deconstruct in fiction this binary opposition, unleashing, liberating, and repositioning African American subjectivities. To escape but not leave Western logocentrism, of which the novel is a subsystem, these and other writers, as Charles Johnson earlier suggested, have returned to certain African and African American cultural forms such as the blues, jazz, Yoruba gods, the African collective unconscious, and Voodoo not to retreat from but instead to expand and/or reconfigure modernity/postmodernity and to challenge Enlightenment reason, particularly as it defines the African American, and the Eurocentric horizon of the novel. *Philadelphia Fire* (1990) belongs to John Edgar Wideman's postmodern literary phase, which also includes *Reuben* and *Brothers and Keepers.*[1] Of the three, *Philadelphia Fire* is most effective in challenging the traditional novel form, undermining the white-black binary opposition, rerepresenting African

American male subjectivity, highlighting the crisis in representation, and challenging the violent representation of the African American as deviant.

Philadelphia Fire uses a peripheral, cultural paradigm or technique to challenge the conventions of the novel. In this chapter, I examine how *Philadelphia Fire* contests the traditional modern novel as it aims to redescribe African American male subjectivity. I also explore how *Philadelphia Fire* undermines the Western quest narrative by giving heteroglossic perspectives on the MOVE (also known as the MOVE Organization) bombing. Finally, I examine how *Philadelphia Fire* shows its heteroglossic limits in its treatment of women in not having a femininity in its writing, that is, a writing that incorporates the self's relation to the Other.

In its desire to challenge the traditional novel, *Philadelphia Fire* plays with instrumental reason and other Enlightenment ideas. In an interview with James Coleman, Wideman discusses his conscious, overt efforts to violate the conventions of the modern/realistic novel, which attempts to impose a single, unitary language on heterogeneity, and to unleash differences. Wideman states that "I don't think that you can write a very meaningful book about a culture that's in flux, a culture that is changing all the time, and a culture [that] is infused with minority points of view . . . and [still] use the conventions and traditions of narrative fiction" (159).

Also, using a peripheral cultural paradigm, the concept of radical democracy—a diversity of perspectives and points of view that parallel, intersect, and contradict each other, without the desire for hierarchy, totality, or mastery—that he borrows from Africa, Wideman's *Philadelphia Fire* contests Eurocentric hegemony and gives a different perspective on the African American, one that does not construct him as experientially monolithic. In an interview with Lisa Baker, Wideman states that

> For African American people I am in the business of inventing reality—that stands on its own feet, that gives a different perspective on history, on crime, on art, on love. I'm very actively deconstructing the

> given formulas and definitions of African American culture and life, and trying to put in their place those that seem more reasonable, more real, more lively, more potentially positive. (264–65)

Engaging a democratic search for the flux, or multiple meanings, *Philadelphia Fire* gives the reader a radically democratic text where African Americans from different socioeconomic, educational, and cultural levels represent the same event/social reality, the bombing of the MOVE row house in Philadelphia. With each African American, *Philadelphia Fire* shows how each station in life, along with its own individuality, affects his or her construction/perception of the event/reality.

Although *Philadelphia Fire* is sensitive to the immense plurality of experiences among African Americans, the book does not disassociate difference from economic and social inequality. It gives us radical democracy at the narrative and ideological levels, but it remains Eurocentric and hegemonic in terms of subjectivity except for the masculine, where, theoretically, it affirms difference but obscures this difference by positing representations of the selfsame.[2] In *Philadelphia Fire,* the masculine narratorial *I* of Cudjoe and John Wideman the character is never deconstructed, mostly because its femininity has been "subsequently displaced, transformed by culture" (Cixous, *White Ink* 60). In addition to maintaining a masculine self-Other binary opposition, *Philadelphia Fire* fails to engage the reason of the Other,[3] particularly Euro-American women who participate in heterosexual coupling and love interests or who are the recipient of the male gaze. This masculine *I* thereby erases feminine differences.

Philadelphia Fire uses several textual strategies to push the boundaries of the traditional narrative, opening it up to other forms of speech. Wideman admits that he takes chances with the narrative:

> I like to take chances, and one chance that I have been taking lately, . . . is a chance with the texture of the narrative—letters, hymns, poems, song lyrics,

> thoughts, speech, time present, time past, future time, philosophical discourse, scatting, etc. . . . a kind of collage . . . [something] that you find in traditional African art. In masks or dance, you have that eclectic combination. (Coleman 159)

First, *Philadelphia Fire* consciously operationalizes what Bakhtin calls "heteroglossia, . . . the diversity of social speech types . . . and a diversity of individual voices" (262). Dispersed dialogically throughout *Philadelphia Fire* are multivoiced, multistyled, and often multilanguaged discourses and forms such as quotes, letters, conversations, interior monologues, multiplicity of social voices, plays, and the rewriting of Shakespeare. There are letters to John Wideman, isolated quotes from Shakespeare's *The Tempest,* Kunene's *Ancient Bonds,* and Bachelard's *The Psychoanalysis of Fire* intersecting and reinforcing, without a direct causal link, *Philadelphia Fire*'s main narrative, Cudjoe's search for the meaning of what happened in Philadelphia on Monday, March 13, 1985. The presence of these diverse literary forms in the text challenges the reader's expectations of a unitary language, disrupts the linear flow of the text, opens up *Philadelphia Fire* to a kind of collage of multiple meanings, and shows the inability of language to provide absolute truth. In *Philadelphia Fire,* argues Susan Pearsall, Wideman "assembles meta-fictional passages within a mostly nonlinear, open-ended narrative" (18). In pushing the boundaries and reconfiguring elements of the traditional narrative, *Philadelphia Fire* displaces Western Hegelian epistemology, which requires certainty, order, hierarchy, linearity, and coherence. *Philadelphia Fire* transforms the hierarchal center by redistributing the voice of the text to the many.

Second, to signify the flux in American culture, *Philadelphia Fire* disrupts chronological time, mingles persons, and collapses the past and present tenses. Chapterless, the book is divided into three unequal parts. In part 1, which comprises the first half of the novel, everything is filtered through Cudjoe's consciousness/memory, which is presented in the third person and contributes to the nonlinear associative flow of the text. John Wideman the character tells part 2 of *Philadelphia Fire* in the first person, but he tells it in a stream-of-consciousness, fragmented mold. Part 3 concerns the homeless plight of J. B., with the first half being told by an omniscient narrator and the second half being told by a MOVE snitch, Richard Corey, telling, in the first person, his story of betrayal. These stories and narratives flow in and out of the text without any clear markers, thereby collapsing the past and present tenses.

A third strategy that *Philadelphia Fire* uses to create openness and multiplicity in the text is to foreground the writing process as limited. As Wideman states:

> I try to invite the reader into the process of writing, into the mysteries, into the intricacies of how things are made and so, therefore, I foreground the self-consciousness of the act of writing. And try to get the reader to experience that, so that the reader is participating in the creation of the fiction. In fact, I demand that. (Coleman 159)

When Cudjoe gives the policeman's description of the boy escaping "with no clothes on screaming" (9), he reminds the reader that "he was not there and has no right to add details" (9). In using the tape recorder to capture the former MOVE member Margaret Jones's version of what happened in Philadelphia on Monday, March 13, 1985, Cudjoe stops, rewinds, and fast-forwards. This move and observation, along with poignant questions, allow him to get the information he wants and also to expose the selective process in his construction of Margaret Jones's story. In *Philadelphia Fire,* there is also an indication that she tells Cudjoe things that are not on the tape, showing the reader its "process of writing." In addition, *Philadelphia Fire* quotes other writers such as L. Zasetsky on the writing process.

> So, before I could go on and write my story, I had to jot down various words for the names of objects, things, phenomena, ideas. I'd write these down whenever they came to me. Then I'd take the words,

> sentences, and ideas I'd collected in this way and begin to write my story in a notebook, regrouping the words and sentences, comparing them with others I'd seen in books. (107)

In using these strategies, *Philadelphia Fire* is communicating to the reader that it is aware that it is being written, with all of the attendant problems of language and meaning.

Fourth and last, to expose/unfasten the authority of the author, Wideman inserts himself into the narrative, breaking through the traditional pose of removal taken by the author of fiction and thereby problematizing the authority of the author. Asked about this insertion of the self into his fiction, Wideman says:

> I write out of who I am, and my identity and my writing identity, my life as transposed into the art that I practice, are becoming more and more of a piece. I don't make distinctions. . . . I don't think of myself as writer only when I'm sitting down in the morning at my desk in my study. . . . I use my imagination. . . . And more and more the subjects of the fiction are this strange interpenetration of the imagined life and the actual life and the inextricability of the two. (Rowell 97)

As with many postmodern writers, Wideman is aware that the subject has many selves, that the John Wideman that appears as a character in the text is not the same John Wideman whose name is on the cover of the text. But the two John Widemans belong to the same subject. In becoming a character in his own novel, argues Susan Pearsall, Wideman "undercuts his authorial position of moral and critical superiority by erasing the potential differences between himself and his characters" (21). The John Wideman in the text becomes a self of John Wideman the author.

Ostensibly, *Philadelphia Fire* is about the modern quest for meaning. It concerns Cudjoe, another self of John Wideman, who has been in exile on the Greek island of Mykonos for the last ten years. When his marriage to Carolina (his white wife) falls apart, his relationship with his sons breaks up, his book is "orphaned," and his life reaches an impasse, Cudjoe leaves the United States. As the only black on the island, he lives the life of a lonely expatriate, writes a lot of "bullshit poems and unfinished essays," and does a lot of "drinking and hiding and running" (87). He has failed as a writer, a father, and a black man. On the island, writes Mary Paniccia Carden, Cudjoe "awaits a dissolution of his old self that will allow for a new self to emerge" (480). He wants to transform himself.

But Cudjoe is drawn back to the United States and Philadelphia, his hometown, when he reads about the bombing of the MOVE house, a "[s]tory of a fire and a lost boy" (7). He feels that the fire and the house are a part of the "terrible jaws of something shaking the life out of us" (22). Connecting with it, he wants to tell that story. When the city government of Philadelphia orders the bombing of the row house owned by MOVE members, the boy, Simba Muntu, is the only survivor. Friends of Margaret, who are nurturing him back to life, take him in. But one day, according to Margaret, his buddies teach him how to ride a bike, and he rides into oblivion (33).

The clash between MOVE and the city of Philadelphia is much more complex than Wideman's representation,[4] with everything about MOVE giving contested readings. The conflict is what Robin Wagner-Pacifici in *Discourse and Destruction* calls "a strange hybrid, a charged space at the intersection of race, modernity, class, nature, urban life, and culture" (x). In calling on other sources/representations, I want to offer a strategic representation of MOVE to problematize or make contingent Wideman's representation. MOVE was a radical, activist, counterculture organization that arose in Philadelphia in the 1970s, with John Africa as the founder and leader. Some have described MOVE's philosophy as "urban, back to nature, and primitivist" (Assefa 10). MOVE stood against everything that was "unnatural" and "man-made," defining its purpose as "stopping man's system from imposing on life," stopping "industry from poisoning the air, the water, the soil" (Assefa 11). Its mission was to put "an end to enslavement of life—people, animals, any form of life" (11). Because it believed that the city was at the heart of the problem, MOVE thought its organization should be based in an urban environment.

MOVE's lifestyle reflected its opposition to middle-class life and modern technology. According to Anderson and Hevenor, members adopted Africa as a last name, signifying that they were members of the same family (5). Growing their hair into dreadlocks, they live communally as an extended family where marriage and family are strongly encouraged among members and sexual relations outside of marriage are prohibited. Members avoid using machinery or electricity, processed food, heat in houses, or soap, and their diets are primarily uncooked fruits, vegetables, and nuts. MOVE members wash cars, walk dogs, and chop firewood for money (Bowser 72).

MOVE's oppositional lifestyle brought it into conflict with its neighbors. People complained directly to MOVE and to city officials and the police about garbage and fecal odor, rat infestation, and health and housing code violations. Because MOVE members took in homeless dogs, neighbors were concerned about the health hazard from the many unvaccinated dogs (Anderson and Hevenor 9). Also, MOVE's practices of not allowing babies to wear diapers and of dressing them minimally and not sending their children to school, even in winter, raised neighbors' concerns about child neglect.

Rhetoric intensified between MOVE and its neighbors, and the neighborhood conflict escalated. The neighbors who actively protested against MOVE complained that MOVE retaliated by threatening and harassing them, by picketing their houses and using bullhorns to shout obscene language at them (Anderson and Hevenor 14). By the mid-1970s, MOVE members began appearing at public functions, demonstrating against the Philadelphia Zoo for caging animals. MOVE members disrupted rallies, conferences, Board of Education meetings, and neighborhood block parties throughout West Philadelphia. Clearly MOVE was on a collision course with the city of Philadelphia.

The first clash between MOVE and the police came in 1976 in which several police officers and MOVE members suffered injuries, with charges being filed against three MOVE members. Other members complained that during this incident a baby was killed. In 1978, several MOVE members were jailed for shooting a police officer (Weiss 13). Finally, on Monday, March 13, 1985, after evacuating the neighborhood surrounding the MOVE house, the police commissioner, Gregor Sambor, ordered MOVE members to leave their house, and they refused. The fire started when a police helicopter unconscionably dropped a satchel of explosives into the roof of the house where it was suspected that MOVE had a storehouse of arms (Bowser 21). The fact that the fire chief let the fire burn for almost an hour before turning on "quirts" to curtail it resulted in the burning down of the MOVE house and in the deaths of eleven people, including five children (Wagner-Pacifici ix). The fire also burned fifty-three other neighborhood houses and left more than two hundred people homeless. A woman, Ramona Johnson Africa, and a child, a boy of thirteen known then as Birdie Africa, escaped the fire (Anderson and Hevenor xiv). The dropping of the explosives and the delay in putting out the fire created much of the outrage reported in the media. Nobody believed that the MOVE conflict was handled well. The situation was further exacerbated because the incident happened on the watch of Philadelphia's first black mayor, Wilson Goode.

In its representation of the MOVE incident, *Philadelphia Fire* reconfigures and simplifies the issues by presenting it as a clear binary opposition between the government and the premodern, innocent MOVE. According to *Philadelphia Fire*'s redescription of MOVE, King and his people did not bother anyone, keeping to themselves and refusing to participate in mainstream social rituals. Their house was bombed when "they refused to obey a police order to leave their home" (97), with only the boy surviving. For *Philadelphia Fire,* MOVE struggled for cultural recognition in a city that is dominated by capitalist, Judeo-Christian, Enlightenment values. MOVE is marked out as the Other and, at the same time, is rendered invisible. The government of Philadelphia is not willing to tolerate its difference.

More specifically, *Philadelphia Fire*'s rerepresentation of the bombing of the MOVE row house and the search for Simba Muntu function as catalysts to raise larger social, linguistic, racial, economic, and political issues. How does one survive the urban landscape? Who can survive the fire of Philadelphia? What has happened to race in the United States after the 1960s? What has happened to the American Dream? Can we tolerate difference? How do we mete out justice? Who will save the children and make the family whole again? How do our individual needs and invested interests affect how we respond to/represent the happenings in society? How does one become a successful father? In an interview with Steve Beeber, Wideman assesses:

> I think what happened in Philadelphia in 1985 with the MOVE business was really a watershed event that is directly connected to what's happening at this moment in larger American cities. The denial of race as a problem is a factor. . . . [We have] a country that's determined to demand of its citizen a bland conformity. . . . In *Philadelphia Fire,* I tried to show how seeds were planted, a lesson of fear taught, a warning rammed down the country's throat. (152)

Philadelphia Fire redescribes what happened in Philadelphia on Monday, March 13, 1985, especially since the redescription indicates that the events of that day have been erased, as a way of examining the condition of possibility for survival in the urban landscape, for preventing—echoing James Baldwin—"more fire next time" (198). It "yearns to make sense of Philadelphia, to render the city legible with dispassionate precision" (Lee 235), with the yearning becoming the issue to be resolved in the text.

As in the traditional detective story, which is used and abused here, Cudjoe's search for the meaning of the bombing and the boy mocks the detective story, taking on social, metaphysical, and spiritual dimensions. "Maybe this is a detective story, Cudjoe says to himself" (46). Knowing the crimes, he wants to find the criminals, to know the truth. "What caused it. Who was responsible. What it means" (19). As a detective, Cudjoe's search becomes a typical Western, Hegelian male quest for absolute knowledge, the father, and/or the law. "He would like to be named for something his father or grandfather had done well. . . . A name to stamp him, guide him" (3). For the son, discovering a relationship with the father corresponds to discovering the path of his incarnation as a man. The father becomes a focus for all the promises and status symbols that his son learns to expect will be his. Through identification with the father, Cudjoe hopes to acquire a masculine identity, a conscience, a sense of place within and his obligations to preexisting social (and gendered) systems, at the exclusion or reduction of the feminine.

In a modern sense, actually, Cudjoe's search is also about becoming spiritually whole:

> [T]he child who is brother, son, a lost limb haunting him since he read about the fire in a magazine. He must find the child *to be whole again.* Cudjoe can't account for the force drawing him to the story nor why he indulges a fantasy of identification with the boy who escaped the massacre. He knows he must find him. He knows the ache of absence, the phantom presence of pain that tricks him into reaching down again and again to stroke the emptiness. He's stopped asking why. His identification with the boy persists. . . . Like the Second Coming. (7–8, my emphasis)

Finding the boy, Cudjoe assumes, will make him whole, will save him, or will let him find himself, overturning his failure as a man, a father. "In returning to Philadelphia to find Simba," Jeffrey Prager argues, "he undertakes the arduous effort of confronting himself and striving for a single, unified self" (9). The search for and finding the boy implies resolution.

Equally as important, as a way of mastering Philadelphia and the self, Cudjoe wants to ascertain an answer as to why the City of Brotherly Love has not fulfilled its potential of being an egalitarian city. Sitting on the steps of the art museum after a basketball game, Cudjoe looks out over the city of Philadelphia, seeking answers. Observing the plan that William Penn, Pennsylvania's most celebrated governor and the founder of Philadelphia, envisaged for the city, Cudjoe thinks:

> This is how the city was meant to be viewed. Broad avenues bright spokes of a wheel radiating from a glowing center. . . . Scale and pattern fixed forever. Clarity, balance, a perfect understanding between the parts. . . . I belong to you, the city says. This is what I was meant to be. You can grasp the pattern. Make sense of me. Connect the dots. I was constructed for you. . . . All you have to do is speak and you reveal me, complete me. (44)

Discerning the layout of the city, Cudjoe is struck by the sanity and order of the streets and the architecture. Ironically, in the Penn epigraph at the beginning of *Philadelphia Fire,* Philadelphia was "never [to] be burnt, and always [to] be wholsome." Cudjoe realizes that Penn's "egalitarian ideals have never been honored. The city has never been morally vitalized" (Varsav 433). Instead Penn's plan has been betrayed, for in 1684, 150 Africans were brought to Philadelphia and sold as slaves, in 1850 there were race riots in the city, and in 1986 Philadelphia is on fire. Racism and racial oppression have always existed in the city. Cudjoe concludes that "no one has used the city yet. No one has pushed a button to start the heart pumping" (*Philadelphia Fire* 45). His aim is to find the button, to start the heart pumping.

As a result of the betrayal, there is urban renewal and the subsequent dislocation of the poor, the homeless, and the African American. Racial oppression, capital movement, and land-use decisions produce and reproduce injustices and inequality, where the rich live next to the homeless. Thus, Philadelphia becomes a city where the "rich [are] richer, [the] poor poorer" (79). Private developers purchase slum property and transform it into sites of luxury residences. Also, poverty, drugs, a decline in mainstream moral and civic values, urban decay, and corruption engulf the city. And since the 1960s, there has been a change in the power dynamics of the city: there is a black mayor and a substantial black middle class who enjoy "some of [the] good life" (76). But do they transform this city? Start its heart pumping? Stop the fire this time? Or do they reaffirm the status quo?

In *Philadelphia Fire,* Cudjoe asks questions, seeks answers, and offers a response to the fire, the bombing, and the city of Philadelphia. But other African Americans from different socioeconomic, educational, or cultural levels also struggle to make sense out of the bombing and the city, tacitly showing the limitations of Cudjoe's truth. In *Philadelphia Fire,* there is a plurality of discursive voices constructing interpretations and reactions to the bombing and the happenings in Philadelphia. All differences are worthy of recognition, and all are "specific points of view on the world, forms for conceptualizing the world in words, specific world views" (Bakhtin 292). In this polyphony of voices, each voice constructs its own irreducible discursive identity. Each conveys its own system of modeling subjectivity, its own logic, and each becomes a performance. Multiple voices, argues Tracie Church Guzzio, not only "transgress realistic time and reject linear history," fracturing "the narrative line, opening spaces for other voices to be heard," but also show the incompleteness and fallibility of language to provide the truth (179).

The different voices or the eclectic combinations in *Philadelphia Fire* do not exclude each other; rather, they intersect, contradict, interrelate, and parallel each other in many different ways. Some are isolated. Others are set against each other dialogically, where "everything means, is understood, as part of a greater whole" (Bakhtin 426). There is no center, and there is no hierarchy. However, there is the sense of an inclusive, egalitarian, participatory radical democracy in telling the story of the MOVE bombing and the changes happening in Philadelphia. In an interview, Wideman discusses these different points of view, this plurality of discursive American and African American voices. For Wideman, real democracy "decenteralizes the truth—it fragments the truth. It puts truth in the light of multiplicity, of voices as a kind of construct that you can't arrive at unless you do have a mosaic of voices" (TuSmith 198). In *Philadelphia Fire,* Wideman aims for that real democracy, that truth, as a way to reimagine and/or transform the representation of the African American and subsequently America:

> I try very consciously in the book to get different points of view. To find a character who is interesting who lived at the bottom of society—somebody who actually was a street person and had lived out of garbage cans, etc. I wanted young people, old people. I wanted people who were up near the top who were involved in city politics and rode around in limousines and traveled internationally. I wanted a college person, a college teacher to be represented and, in that sense, it's a potpourri of personality types and social types. . . . Each character was . . . chosen because he or she has a role in the particular story I'm telling—the story of the fire. (Presson 107)

Philadelphia Fire wants the voices of the exilic, the extraterritorial, and the unhoused as well as normative American voices, but it wants them as differences and equals.

But *Philadelphia Fire* does not celebrate difference or multiplicity uncritically, interrogating its relations to economic and social inequality. Within the various African American socioeconomic, educational, cultural, and political voices, *Philadelphia Fire* shows that there exist what Nancy Fraser in *Justice Interruptus* calls "class divisions or other deep-seated structural injustices" (185). The various African American characters struggle for voice/recognition in a world of oppression and material inequality in regard to income and property ownership, cultural disrespect, and access to paid work, education, and leisure time but also in regard to exposure to environmental toxicity. Here, oppression, to use the words of Iris Marion Young, "designates the advantages and injustices some people suffer . . . because of the everyday practices of a well-intentional liberal society" (41), pervading everyone's life.

In *Philadelphia Fire,* Margaret Jones, who is actually for a while a member of the MOVE organization, provides a second representation of truth of/discursive voice on the bombing of the MOVE headquarters and Simba. As a friend of his mother, Margaret is the only person who knew Simba personally. She is educated, having her "little piece of [a] degree" (12). But her education does not empower her economically or socially. She has been marginalized economically by the political-economic structure of Philadelphia, confining her to poorly paid work. Margaret is "tired and hassled" (12) because of her job, with bitterness running down to her feet, the same as her mother who was not educated. Margaret's precarious economic situation impacts her life and her perspective. She speaks for herself, and how she represents herself is informed by her needs and her social predicament, as a single mother with two children who are constantly in danger of getting into "[d]eep trouble. Bad, bad trouble" (12).

When Margaret first encountered Reverend King during her walks home from work, she noticed the smell "stinking up the whole neighborhood" (12). But although she is repulsed by the smell and the surroundings, she is seduced by King's message, especially since she has a need for recognition, a need to have her thoughts and feelings articulated and validated, and he speaks to her needs. "Got to [my] Christian mind. Got to my tired feet. Who I been all the days of my life" (14). Margaret likes Reverend King's ideas, giving in to his message because he offers her hope and faith in a better future. "Things spozed to get better, ain't they? Somewhere down the line, it ought to get better or what's the point scuffling like we do?" (14), she asks rhetorically. Giving up her children, Margaret rejects modern urban society and embraces, for a while, MOVE's retreat to premodern times and values. But she comes to understand that King is not egalitarian. Members of MOVE "let him [King] order us around like we was slaves" (11). King is as much a heteropatriarch as Philadelphia's founding father.

But even after she is rescued by her sister and leaves MOVE, Margaret is still at an impasse, seeing no way out of the rut of urban life, which she thinks has deteriorated because of drugs and prostitution. And although she has problems with King personally, Margaret does not believe that the mayor or the cops had the right to murder MOVE members.

> I still can't believe it. Eleven people murdered. Babies, women, didn't make no nevermind to the cops. Eleven human beings dead for what? . . . Why did they have to kill my brothers and sisters? Burn them up like you burn garbage? What King and them be doing that give anybody the right to kill them? (17)

Margaret's representation of the bombing of the MOVE row house is different from Cudjoe's, with his being cerebral and distant and hers being emotional and immediate. To understand what it means, he needs to write a book about the fire. Margaret does not "need a book. Anybody wants to know what it means, bring them through here. Tell them these bombed streets used to be full of people's homes. Tell them babies' bones mixed up in this ash they smell" (19). The difference in representations is personal and socioeconomical.

Next, in this polyphony of voices that makes up the text, Cudjoe interviews a diverse array of guys with whom he plays a game of basketball. Usually voices never heard, these men are empowered by the text, giving their perspective on the bombing and the racial situation in Philadelphia. They identify the social and economic forces that confront them daily. Many of them are unemployed or have precarious job situations, making them feel powerless. They too have been marginalized economically by the political-economic structure of Philadelphia, denied access to income-generating labor, and disrespected culturally. When they do find work it is as "menial labor," a category that Iris Marion Young identifies as one where blacks are exploited economically (51). They live in drug-infested crime-ridden communities and are subject to random police harassment and imprisonment.

Although some of these guys do not want to disparage the mayor because he is black, others think that he is a puppet of the white power structure downtown. "Mayor don't run the city, city runs him" (41). They think the happenings in Philadelphia are a conspiracy, that the mayor was put there by whites to control blacks, despite the fact that he was elected with ninety-eight percent of the black vote. The mayor can burn down the houses of blacks, some argue, but the white power structure will not "let him burn down white people's houses" (41). More importantly, they do not know the whereabouts of the boy, Simba, but only hope that he is far away from Philadelphia.

As the urban subaltern and despite the myriad mechanisms of hierarchy and subordination, these basketball players are full of knowledge, languages, skills, and creative capacities. As the most creative agents in Philadelphia, they use the game of basketball, which provides them with a sense of community, to survive urban decay:

> Pulling the game out was the best moment. Many high fives and a good, deep-down sense of pushing to the limit and bringing something back. After the winning basket they gathered under the hoop still shuddering from Sky's humongous dunk. Their eyes meet, their fists met for a second in the core of a circle, then just as quickly broke apart, each going his own way. (39)

Basketball allows them to forget their surroundings and their personal hardships:

> Pushing past the point of breaking but you don't break. . . . Doing your thing and nothing can touch you. . . . You forget everything you know and play. The wall you can't move, that stops you and makes you cry when you beat your head against it, is suddenly full of holes. (30–31)

With basketball providing them with rejuvenation and purpose, these ballplayers escape the reality of the fire and the harsh urban environment through conspiracy theory, basketball, storytelling, wine, and reefer. Although they live in its midst, they do not know what is happening to the city. They are simply victims of it. "[B]ut no one understanding the problem. Just this queasiness, this uneasiness. This tilt and slow falling" (43). Their truth is different from Margaret's and Cudjoe's. Whereas Margaret cannot answer the question of why the mayor bombed the MOVE row house and Cudjoe does not ask the question, some of the basketball players attribute it to a conspiracy and call it racism.

With Timbo, his 1960s buddy and the "cultural attaché to the Mayor" (72), Cudjoe gets a point of view on the bombing and the events in Philadelphia from the top. Timbo speaks for himself and his class interest, which has its own logic. He is the system's and the 1960s' success story. Born poor on a farm near New Orleans, he came to Philadelphia and was active in the Black Power movement of the 1960s. Today, he has moved downtown. "Timbo rolling along in his big car courtesy of the City, pocketful of money, the mayor's boy, the city cocking up her big legs for him" (86). He has class, if class means expensive tastes, wining and dining Cudjoe at an expensive restaurant at the mayor's expense. But Timbo is somewhat powerless because he does not belong to the monied class of Philadelphia.

Timbo believes that through the city's redevelopment program, Philadelphia will get rid of its "eyesores" and will become a "little version of Athens. . . . Museum's the Acropolis up on the hill. Cross by way of bridges and tunnels to the brain-power and computer power of the universities. Modern urban living in the midst of certified culture. . . . It's gonna work, too" (78). Timbo also admits that there are "sections of this great metropolis where nobody don't love nobody. Too ugly. Too mean" (79), that dope is king in the city, and that blacks are struggling to survive. But he still believes that the mayor is sincere in making the city a "better place to live and you can see progress, real progress" (79). As a part of the political and social elite in Philadelphia, Timbo speaks from his class interest.

Timbo's reasoning for the mayor's decision to bomb MOVE conveys his own system of modeling subjectivity. Timbo is a politician who believes in capitalist progress, and MOVE is counterproductive to this progress.

> They were embarrassing, man. Embarrassing. Trying to turn back the clock. Didn't want no kind of city, no kind of government. Wanted to live like people live in the woods. . . . A Garden of Eden up in West Philly. Mayor breaking his butt to haul the city into the twenty-first century and them fools on Osage want their block to the jungle. How the mayor spozed to stand up and talk to white folks when he can't control his own people? . . . Sooner or later those nuts had to go. Mayor got tired of them mocking everything he was promising. Talk about a thorn in his side. King and them were a natural thorn halfway up his behind. A whole brier patch growing up in the mayor's chest. Sooner or later, one way or another, them and their dreadlocks had to go. (81)

Having internalized the values of mainstream capitalistic American society, both Timbo and the mayor define the MOVE people as primitive people who remind them of their repressed, untamed self. MOVE, argues Stacey L. Barry, "calls into question the lifestyle and values of the majority" (163). Because the otherness, the difference of the MOVE people, threatens Timbo and the mayor, they move to violently destroy the MOVE people. Timbo and the mayor, like the dominant American society, refuse to tolerate difference.

Timbo belongs to that sector of American society that wants to erase the memory of the bombing. When Cudjoe tells Timbo that he needs to find the boy to finish his novel about the fire, Timbo tells him to forget the fire and to write his 1960s novel. "Forget the fire. Play with fire you know what happens. You'll get burnt like the rest of us" (88). As Timbo tells it, argues Susan Pearsall, "the victims of the fire were sacrificed to a higher goal, urban renewal" (27). This higher goal does not start the city's heart pumping, perpetuating business as usual.

Timbo's version of what happened on Monday, March 13, 1985, furthers the diverse, radically democratic, contradictory representation of the bombing. Timbo's truth is not Cudjoe's, and Timbo's response to the bombing is quite different from Margaret Jones's. Whereas Margaret and Cudjoe think the bombing of the MOVE row house is a tragedy and the ballplayers think it is a conspiracy, Timbo thinks it was necessary for progress in Philadelphia. And whereas Margaret as well as Cudjoe, who refers to the bombing as a holocaust, think the economic changes in Philadelphia are happening for the worse, Timbo thinks they are happening for the better.

In part 2 of *Philadelphia Fire,* John Wideman and his wife Judy enter the text, with John Wideman narrating Part II, which is told in a nonchronological, associative, fragmented manner where current ideas remind him of other ideas. Dispersed in Wideman's narrative are paragraphs on John Fanning Watson's writing about Philadelphia in 1850 and on Giacometti and sculptures, quotes and scenes from Shakespeare's *The Tempest,* a letter from Ramona Africa, a paragraph on Jackie Robinson breaking into professional baseball, and the story of Wideman's son in prison. Finally, halfway through this part, Cudjoe and Wideman take turns with the narrative. The fragmentation forces the reader to make sense out of its pieces.

By introducing the name "John Wideman" into the text, *Philadelphia Fire* creates another fictional self of John Wideman within the narrative. Queried by Rebekah Presson about the first-person speaker named John Wideman in *Philadelphia Fire,* Wideman says that "All the voices are fictional; they're voices that are made up to create certain effects within the novel, within the drama" (108). John Wideman the character is simply another role player telling the story of the fire. In the series of polyphonic voices reacting to and representing the bombing of the Osage row house, from Wideman, the writer and university professor, we get another view.

Wideman and Cudjoe share several things in common: basketball, writing, assimilation, white wives, and escape and return to the community. Both have lived on Osage Avenue in West Philadelphia. Wideman is "a middle-aged, middlingly successful writer, teacher, father, husband and all the rest" (*Philadelphia Fire* 106). He, like Cudjoe, has lost connection to his juvenile son, whom he knows "next to nothing about." Because they cannot communicate, they never "move beyond the ritual of greeting" (99). Wideman is watching as his "son gradually deteriorates" (16) in prison from psychological neglect. Also, like Cudjoe, Wideman is caught up in a search that is about the father, the son, and the law—the male economy. "Say the word father. Now say son. Now think of the space between father and son, as they are words, as they are indications of time and the possibility of salvation, redemption, and continuity. Think of these two words in natural order and sequence" (103). Within the masculine order, which is naturalized here, the father is suppose to initiate the son to reproduce continuity. But both John Wideman and Cudjoe are failures at being fathers.

Yet Cudjoe is not Wideman in that Cudjoe is not a published author and is not a university professor. But in having Cudjoe and John Wideman the character perform John Wideman the author, *Philadelphia Fire* achieves this sense of indeterminate authorship. You have the "interpenetration of the imagined life and the actual life and the inextricability of the two" (Rowell 97). In giving us the selves of Cudjoe and John Wideman, *Philadelphia Fire* creates a sense of fluidity in subjectivity, but it is a subjectivity that ultimately falls back on the masculine self-Other binary opposition, a subjectivity that subordinates the feminine.

Wideman the character hears about the bombing of MOVE's row house while in bed with his wife channel surfing the television one night in Laramie, Wyoming. His first question is, why is Philadelphia burning? Wideman is paralyzed by the burning city, thinking,

> Row houses in flames. Rooflines silhouetted against a dark sky. Something's burning. We watch. Wonder whose turn it is now. Whole city blocks engulfed. It must be happening in another country. A war. A bombing raid. We're watching a Third World shantytown where there's no water, no machines to extinguish a fire. Flames, true to metaphor, do leap and lick. . . . We are impatient for the voice-over to tell us what to think. (100)

Later in Amherst, Massachusetts, searching for the origin of the March 13, 1985, event, Wideman asks whether Jackie Robinson being denied access to a hotel in Philadelphia because he is black is another trace of racism in Philadelphia. When Wideman writes a review of a book about the fire, a former colleague who had read the review contacts him. In the conversation, the two discuss the denial of race, the reemergence of racism in the city, and the country's demand of its citizens for a "bland conformity" (Beeber 152). They discuss the denials of tenure for blacks, the dismantling of the School of Social Work that produced "graduates equipped intellectually, technically and emotionally to deal with the everyday runaway chaos of an ailing urban landscape" (*Philadelphia Fire* 111). Wideman, like Cudjoe who wants "to do something about the silence" (19), realizes that the "official silence" (114) around the bombing of the MOVE row house and the reemergence of racism become inseparable from his inability to write his son's story, to take responsibility for Philadelphia. "Will I ever try to write my son's story? Not dealing with it may be causing the forgetfulness I'm experiencing" (115). Wideman becomes a metaphor for America.

The friend, who was not "rehired" because the university has cut its community-based social work program, continues to speak out against racism and injustice. Despite the loss of a wife, he is leading a study group, and the "object of their inquiry and research [is] the fire on Osage Avenue" (111). Both Wideman and his friend use academic/intellectual discourses to respond to the bombing and racism. Wideman's friend invites him to attend a seminar and a memorial service for the dead victims of Osage Avenue.

Although Wideman and his friend think that the colleague's social work research is vital and necessary, at least from their point of view, and both want to write to make the "official silence" speak, Margaret Jones does not. And, again, we discern how an individual's socioeconomic level and/or intellectual interest impact how each responds to and interprets his or her surroundings. Earlier in the novel when the questing Cudjoe tells Margaret that he wants to find the boy so he can get his story and write a book, Margaret, accusing him of narcissism, responds:

> You mean you'll do your thing and forget Simmie. Write your book and gone. Just like the social workers and those busybodies from the University. They been studying us for years. Reports on top of reports. A whole basement full of files in the building where I work. We're famous. (20)

As Robert A. Morace points out, Timbo makes much the same point, only more cynically. In the City of Brotherly Love, the new golden rule is the bottom line: "you want yours and I want mine," which translates personal salvation into economic terms (98). Margaret points out the limitations of Wideman's and his social work friend's intellectual discourse.

Finally, part 3 gives the reader another socioeconomic voice, further equally redistributing the voice/perspective of the text from the center to the many. Part 3 concerns J. B (James Brown), who comes from the Philadelphia streets, surviving the harsh urban landscape of Philadelphia, a city on fire. As a "funky derelict emerging from an almost invisible wedge between two buildings" (*Philadelphia Fire* 180), J. B.'s existence at the bottom of society offers another perspective on the reality of the fire and the city of Philadelphia. J. B., whose mother cared for him but is now dead, is a powerless homeless man who has been marginalized economically by the political-economic structure of Philadelphia, denied an adequate material standard of living. He "inhabits many places, no place" (184), being "dispersed and ignored" by the city (182). J. B. is oppressed by the injustice of material deprivation caused by marginalization, and he is exposed to environmental toxicity. For J. B., everything is on fire. Penn's planned Garden of Eden, his "greene County Towne," have turned into hell, an "inferno" (Richard 606). "Loud pops of automatic weapons fire scything down naked bodies lined up against walls and fences. . . . Walls are tumbling, burning-hot walls on tender babies" (*Philadelphia Fire* 156, 157). J. B.'s fear is that the fire will destroy him.

J. B. becomes a gang member, and he and his tribe of gypsies rob the local store and roam the downtown area, sexually harassing women and robbing people. They also roam the streets looking for their next meal, coming to appreciate the wrapping of the food that they find in the garbage.

> Full of boxes and packets that seal flavor in. Almost like buying your own meal. Surprise. Surprise. You open a discarded orange-and-yellow–striped box and anything could be inside. Hunks of snow-white bun, lettuce, pickles, cheese, tomato, special sauce in finger-licking good puddles. Plastic envelopes with seals unbroken. . . . You're grateful for boxes which keep the treats safe inside the Dumpster's rotten maul. You feel blessed because someone packages each morsel, each ingredient in its own individual container. (176)

As they move around the city, they hear sirens from the police and constantly fear that they might be jailed. They are juxtaposed with the excessive waste of the city, with J. B. dying at the hand of the cops.

In the second half of part 3, the reader hears another voice: a white liberal Philadelphian, the MOVE snitch Richard Corey, who tells his story. Initially Corey is updating the "Book of Life" to make it relevant to the lives of poor inner-city black youths. Then he shifts his loyalties from his comrades in MOVE to the mayor, whom he calls a friend. "I squealed on my former soul mates, my comrades huddled in the arms of the Tree of Life. Squealed to the pigs" (167). He also plants evidence, "strand[ing his] good brown brothers out on a limb, high and dry" (167). In fact, Corey is partly responsible for the fire that destroys the row houses, as he now lives in the suburb away from the city. Like Timbo, Corey profits from the fire.

Finally, the ending of *Philadelphia Fire* has no resolution, further showing the hopelessness of the situation in Philadelphia. The memorial service, the culminating moment for the dead victims of Osage Avenue, does happen, but the square, a place where a riot took place against African Americans on July 4, 1850, is nearly empty. Haunted by the violence and racism of the past, of that 1850 riot, Cudjoe says, "Never Again. Never Again." He is ready to confront the past that has always been the "footsteps behind him" (199). But what could be the outcome of Cudjoe confronting the past? Although John Wideman and his colleague have promised to attend the service, they do not show. Margaret Jones and the basketball players are not present, and Richard Corey is absent. Timbo and the mayor are not present, and the city continues to refuse to take responsibility for the fire. "Why wasn't the entire city mourning? Where were the mayor and his official delegation from City Hall? The governor? The president? A dog hit by a bus would draw a bigger crowd" (195). Cudjoe does attend the service, and there is no crowd "confirming his reason for arriving" (191). The purpose of the program states:

> *Through observance, atonement, education, and cultural expression we aim to confront and move beyond the horrors of that terrible day, to contribute to healing the wounds of our city and its inhabitants, and to aid in the development of humane and peaceful methods of resolving our community's problems.* (191)

Although Cudjoe is ready to take responsibility, no one with power is there to solve the problems, to contribute to the healing of the city. When Cudjoe attempts to recruit a crowd for the memorial service, "[n]obody pays any attention" (193). In this anniversary of the bombing of the MOVE row house at 6221 Osage Avenue, "two black men, chest bare, dreadlocks to their shoulders, drum their way into the ceremony" (196). There is a MOVE minister who speaks, but there is no resolution to the text or to the social decay in Philadelphia. There is no remedy for economic injustice and cultural imperialism in Philadelphia (there is no remedy for economic redistribution offered) except in the text, which recognizes and positively valorizes a plurality of discursive voices. Wideman obviously hopes that this recognition of diversity will counter the country's "demand of its citizens a bland conformity" and reinforce tolerance of difference, hoping that *Philadelphia Fire* will counter the "denial of race as a problem" (Beeber 152). He also thinks that "if we look at certain events long enough and hard enough through the lens of fiction, maybe we can learn more of what we need to know" (Rowell 100). But will the recognition of diversity or the focused lens of fiction change social situations?

In addition, echoing James Baldwin, Wideman writes *Philadelphia Fire* as a warning about "more fire next time" (198). If something is not done about the violence and racism in Philadelphia and America, they, as in the 1960s, could go down in flames in the 1980s. "The urgency of Wideman's writing," argues Tracie Church Guzzio, "reminds us that if the past cannot be re-imagined, if new maps cannot be drawn, if new stories cannot be told, the children and the future are in peril" (188). In writing a novel that undermines the traditional, linear novel and that repositions African American male subjectivities, Wideman hopes to give Philadelphia and America those reimagined stories, that new map, that will transform them, that will let them know what they need to know. "Pretend we can imagine events into existence or out of existence. Pretend we have the power to live our lives as we choose. Imagine our fictions imagining us" (*Philadelphia Fire* 97–98). It is through writing and the imagination that Wideman tells a different story, that he deconstructs "the given formulas and definitions of African American culture and life" and reconceptualizes that culture and life as being "more reasonable, more real, more lively, and more potentially positive" (Baker 264–65). He wants to change the world by writing a different story, one of differences.

Despite the fact that each of the individuals is seeking answers or is simply trying to find a way to survive, *Philadelphia Fire* is left without a totalized resolution or logocentric closure. Artistically, Wideman never subordinates what Bakhtin calls the "heterogeneous stylistic unities" to a "higher stylistic unity of the work as a whole" (262). The ends are not tied up. First, William Penn's plan of a new egalitarian world order never materializes. Second, the black mayor and his administration of the 1960s are unable to bring possibilities to all the citizens of Philadelphia. Under the black mayor's leadership, Philadelphia "continues to code space by race and class" (Carden 486). Third, the back-to-nature alternative (the "Book of Life") offered by Reverend King and the MOVE people, early Margaret Jones, and Richard Corey fails to materialize in the urban center. As Madhu Dubey argues in *Signs and Cities,* "MOVE 'did it wrong' because, although based in the city, it sought to reinstate an organic ideal of community that is not only impossible to maintain in modern times but is also suspect even as a hypothetical construct" (75). The later Margaret Jones is at an impasse. The traitor Richard Corey finds that the seeds (children) of hope, the "Book of Life," that were meant to nurture have "degenerated into terrible weeds that are poisoning urban life" (81–82), causing him to commit suicide. J. B., who finds himself lost in the city, takes the "Book of Life" from Corey's briefcase. But J. B., according to Dubey, soon abandons "the effort to decipher the tiny and barely legible script and nods off to sleep" (82). Although the basketball game allows the players to temporarily escape the racism, the drugs, and the corruption of the city, they are still being destroyed by the decay of the city. Finally, even the option of poor urban black youths deconstructing and reconfiguring Shakespeare's Caliban to be their great-great "grandfather," to start the city's heart pumping again (131), to transform their lives, offers potential but is never actualized, leaving the children to become lost to the city. They have been "lost in time. . . . This new crop. Long live the kids. Come up like grass. And get trampled on. And new grass next spring" (*Philadelphia Fire* 117). Seemingly, each generation is born in the city and is then destroyed by the city.

Fourth, Cudjoe never finds the boy, reaching an impasse. As an almost religious, modern character, Cudjoe has a need for wholeness, salvation. He has a sense that if he could get and tell the story of the fire and the boy, he will have the answer to the riddle, will have mastered knowledge, or will have the answer to himself. If he can get the boy's story, he will have a successful narrative for surviving the fire of Philadelphia. As Cudjoe tells Timbo, in the novel that he is writing about the fire "the boy who survived is the key" (88). He will know how to be a man/father who takes responsibility for his sons and family, and he will know how to return to the community. But Cudjoe's narcissism stands in the way of his genuine desire for wholeness and peace of mind.

Cudjoe also has the assumption that a found Simba will also teach other kids how to survive the urban landscape of Philadelphia. "And . . . because a kid managed to survive. Survived bullets and flames and flood and bombs. . . . He's a symbol of kid power. He's a hero, magic, they say. Went through hell to show the others they can do it. Do anything" (91). All around Cudjoe, kids in America, particularly black kids, are not surviving. Families are broken, and children are lost. In addition to worrying about his own kids, Cudjoe "wonders what happened to the kids he taught" (117) before going into exile. There are the gang kids in Philadelphia who spray-paint messages/signs all over the city. But are the signs "[v]andalism or tribal art or handwriting on the wall" (88)? Cudjoe thinks there is a natural order, and "[a] child lost cancels the natural order, the circle is broken" (119). But in the end, Cudjoe does not find Simba and therefore has no model of survival for the kids of Philadelphia or himself. Asked what would happen if Cudjoe did find the boy, Wideman in an interview states:

> He would have found some aspect of himself. He would have found what he was looking for. That's what most of us find when we set out on some kind of quest, chase some sort of grail. We're projecting a loss or a need or an emptiness in ourselves. . . . I think Cudjoe would have found what he was looking for and then the real fireworks would have started. (Presson 109)

Finding the boy, Cudjoe would have found what psychoanalyst Jacques Lacan calls a "substitution" or replacement for the emptiness, the "lack," the perennial desire to return to the imaginary stage where the subject feels whole or is at one with the m/other (*Ecrits* 164). But it can never happen.

Unable to find the boy and write the book, unable to devise a narrative to survive the city, unable to successfully reconnect with the black community in Philadelphia, Cudjoe retreats to the past. He begins to look for "places" from his childhood and the 1960s that gave him a sense of home, safety, and wholeness. There were the neighborhoods, the swimming pool, markets, and the bars, but they have all been destroyed by urban renewal.

> You remember people, Timbo. I have places, almost like stage sets, in my mind. I've been trying to find them since I've been back but they're gone. Buildings, streets, trees. Stores I used to shop, bars where we partied. The Carousel. I can picture it perfectly. But there's no Carousel anymore. (*Philadelphia Fire* 85)

For Cudjoe, salvation lies in a past that no longer exists.

But if Cudjoe was successful in finding the boy/himself, he would shut down the play, the game, something that *Philadelphia Fire* defines as a possible solution for Philadelphia and America. "Multiple consciousness and energy, the fluid situation of freedom that multiple consciousness creates, that's what I mean by play" (Rowell 98), writes Wideman. This means that Cudjoe's modernist desire for wholeness, truth, and resolution in the present, along with that of other characters, is undermined by the structure of the text. (His nostalgia for the past is critiqued.) He cannot pin down, colonize, or master the subject of the text. Therefore, in not allowing Cudjoe to find the boy, in not allowing King and MOVE's narrative to take hold in contemporary Philadelphia society, *Philadelphia Fire* critiques modernist desire to survey it all and master meaning, showing the limitations of their various modernist narratives. This is also true for John Wideman the character. The fact that he cannot write his son's story, that he unsuccessfully seeks the origin to racism in Philadelphia, and that he cannot give a definitive read of the bombing of the MOVE row house means that he too has limitations and therefore cannot master knowledge/meaning. In *Philadelphia Fire* (and in Philadelphia), the modern metanarrative of human liberation and progress toward total meaning or logocentric truth has lost its force. We are left not with a successful distanced, epistemic subject who surveys it all and plans comprehensively but instead with many small narratives legitimating all sorts of practices or points of view.

More importantly, in reimagining the past, *Philadelphia Fire* offers a new postmodern way to comprehend knowledge, to understand freedom. Using diverse/different points of view, *Philadelphia Fire* plays with representation whereby each point of view/representation has its own validity and limitation. *Philadelphia Fire* gives us different individuals who are empowered to create meaning. Each speaks for himself or herself rather than for others. Each identifies the impersonal, physical, and mental forces that confront the individual, not knowing what oneself is trying to do until he or she begins to fight. "Being itself," argues Gilles Deleuze, "is in this sense political" (*Negotiations* 88). Each has the freedom to decide how the bombing and Philadelphia are represented, and each tells us how the harsh environment of the urban area impacts his or her life. Each perspective is presented as constructed, and each is told from its own economic, cultural, intellectual, or political interest. Matters of truth and its security of self become accepted simply as parts of what Michel Foucault, in "Truth and Power," calls the game of truth and falsity. "Truth is a thing of this world: it is produced only by virtue of multiple forms of constraint. And it induces regular effects of power" (131). *Philadelphia Fire* replaces the epistemic subject with a plurality of subjects. We know the world through diverse stories. Wideman is saying that if we want to change America and the African American, we need to tell a different story about both.

In short, *Philadelphia Fire* signifies the contradictory, heteroglot, multilanguaged world of the times of John Wideman and the United States. The book unmasks the illusion of unity in representation and in everyday reality in Philadelphia. Wideman, in *Philadelphia Fire,* thinks this diverse, heterogeneous approach is more effective in representing the tension, conflict, and contradiction that are a part of reality. In "The Architectonics of Fiction," Wideman states that "perhaps there are ways in fiction to achieve the dialectic, the tension, the conversation, the warfare of competing versions of reality English contains" (43, 45). *Philadelphia Fire* shifts the focus of the novel from consciousness to language, from the order of representations to that of speech-acts, and from denotation to performance. At the narrative level, it privileges the plural and multifarious character of contemporary black Philadelphia, rendering it unstable and perpetually in flux. It is ferreting out postmodern alternative, cognitive, and normative options.

For *Philadelphia Fire,* this is the ultimate democracy, and it is also quite postmodern. With these diverse, paralleling, intersecting, isolating, and contradictory voices/narratives, this "rainbow of [American and African American] faces, and types, and kinds" (Presson 108), *Philadelphia Fire* wants a sense of mutual relationship between the "multiple forms" of truth, the competing versions of reality, to emerge. It participates in nontotalizable multiplicities, freeing differences and refusing totalities. It presents a series of positions and a heterogeneous polyphony of voices in an indefinite, open-ended, and indeterminate frontier. This radical democracy challenges a single, unitary language that defines America and/or African America as homogeneous, undermining notions of racial essentialism, identity politics, and the racial uplift narrative. It also contests the notion of the African American as deviant, or as devalued Other. There can be no radical democracy "without renouncing the discourse of the universal and its implicit assumption of a privileged point of access to 'the truth'" (Laclau and Mouffe 192). In privileging difference and dissensus, *Philadelphia Fire* exposes the limitation of modern rationality and critiques it as an instrument of terror.

Philadelphia Fire creates dialogically a defer/differ chain of signifiers of the black male in the narratorial *I.* Cudjoe, John Wideman, and Caliban become different selves of the same subject/character. As a refigured scene from Caliban in *The Tempest* completes its interruption of Cudjoe's narrative, the text asks, "Why this Cudjoe, then? This airy other floating into the shape of my story. Why am I him when I tell certain parts? Why am I hiding from myself? Is he mirror or black hole?" (122). The three narrate this scene with shifts in voice and place without markers or indications. Cudjoe is Caliban and Wideman and not Caliban and John Wideman, all occupying the place of "omniscient narrator and limited character" (Pearsall 22). Cudjoe's "drama of consciousness," argues Leslie W. Lewis, also involves Wideman's "drama of consciousness" (154). Cudjoe's and Wideman's quest for identity is reflected in Cudjoe's "reinterpreted Calibanic quest for identity. The aching loneliness, the question of origins, of generations, and the desire for language in order to communicate [are] all characteristics of Caliban on his island prior to the moment of contact." Caliban's quest becomes part of Wideman's own "existential meditation" (155). The three belong to the same male subjectivity.

For *Philadelphia Fire,* African American male subjectivity is a nexus of meaning whereby "the subjects of the fiction are this strange interpenetration of the imagined life and the actual life" rather than an unchanging entity. This nexus challenges the devalued construction of African American subjectivity within Enlightenment reason's white-black binary but also creates another opposition in the black male–Other binary. This chain of black male signifiers always comes back to a story of phallocentrism.

Although the sovereign narrative *I* in *Philadelphia Fire* comes to accept a chain of signifiers of black masculinity within the quest narrative as a way of exalting the universality of reason and of signifying the flux within American culture, its perception of the quest narrative and of itself as narrator is never deconstructed. Although it desires both self-transformation and a confirmation of the self, it never changes. *Philadelphia Fire*'s *I* never renounces the demands of a self that wants to exert power over the Other. Its *I* is never thrown into crisis where it becomes powerless through its exposure to the irreducible Other, which is already a part of the *I,* where its "femininity is not forbidden" (Cixous, *Coming* 57), thereby opening itself up to the experience of the Other. This sovereign, masculine *I,* to use Cixous's words, "doesn't fantasize [its] sexuality around a faucet" (57). Instead, it refuses to take the risk of losing the I/self, to immerse the I/self fully, willingly, probably irrevocably and without return, into the unknown. It operates within a binary logic that regenerates the masculine order, subsequently displacing its femininity and homosexuality. Its desire to dominate and to protect its centered, privileged masculine position causes blind spots, which prevent it from understanding/acknowledging that it is murdering/erasing the feminine and homosexual Other. In addition, *Philadelphia Fire* shows how patriarchal assumptions pervade even the most destabilizing narratives. It is not fully aware of how structures of gender and sexual domination are embedded in psychic and social practices, which constitute phallocentric loss. The bellicosity of the patriarchal system is so vast and so extreme that even those such as Cudjoe, Wideman, and Caliban who benefit most are put to work maintaining it, and this takes a tremendous toll on the masculine subject's well-being.

In *Philadelphia Fire,* European and Euro-American women as Other are filtered through the masculine *I,* leaving the reader with a highly subjective version of events. European and Euro-American women inhabit the margins, serving to articulate and reinforce the patriarchal, compulsory heterosexual, masculine order. They are the only sexual or heterosexually coupled women in the text—the black Margaret Jones, who has subjectivity, is not constructed as an object of male gaze, yet she is a resisting Other to the dominant masculine narrative[5]—and they are constructed as the underrepresented Other in the various male quest narratives. As the Other, they are not invested with agency, voice, their own distinct subjectivity, or their feminine Other. Many are simply the objects of male gaze.

For example, in Cudjoe's failed attempt to have his students stage a reimagined version of *The Tempest,* from Caliban's point of view, his goal is to replace Shakespeare's colonial and dehumanizing representation of Caliban with one that shows him with agency and equality. Cudjoe's job is to "demonstrate conclusively that Mr. Caliban's behind is clean and unencumbered, good as anybody else's" (*Philadelphia Fire* 131). In addition, Cudjoe recognizes the political parallels between Miranda and Caliban: both are properties of Prospero. Miranda is as oppressed by the patriarchy as Caliban is by colonialism. "She's trying her best to be her own person. She wants to share. But she can't. She's a prisoner, too. Hostage of what her father has taught her. A language which Xeroxes image after image of her father, his goodness, his rightness, his deed to the island. . . . Her womb perpetuates his property" (141). Yet when Cudjoe reconfigures Caliban's part, giving him agency and distinct subjectivity, he rerepresents Miranda not as a subject but instead as property, as a sexual object, as body parts. Caliban achieves masculine selfhood by raping Miranda to spite Prospero. "But is Caliban the snake on this island paradise or is the serpent wound round old Prospero's wand? Or is it Caliban's magic twanger, his Mr. William Wigglestaff he waggled at Miss Miranda and said: C'mere, fine bitch. Make this talk" (140). Caliban's motivation for raping, objectifying, and devaluing Miranda, who can perpetuate her father's property, is to use her to attack Prospero's empire. Yet he never thinks to liberate her from the patriarchy.

Likewise, within Cudjoe's own detective/quest narrative, European and Euro-American women are reduced to sexual objects. Before he leaves Mykonos for Philadelphia, Cudjoe will "spend part of his day with her on the beach. . . . She will teach him the Greek for her *body part*" (6, my emphasis), never mentioning her name, only her body parts. Upon his return to Philadelphia, Cudjoe daydreams of leaving the bar with Teresa, the bartender, and making love to her in "the moment when she's weak and exhausted" (25), which can be read as misogynistic. As he walks through Clark Park to meet Margaret Jones, he sees a woman who could be Teresa. The woman reminds him of naked bodies he had encountered daily on the island of Mykonos. Later he peeps through the window and gazes at the woman's naked body. For Cudjoe, she becomes all Euro-American women.

> Dark hair, slim, compact, but generously rounded in butt and breast. Like the woman in the park. Like the woman he'd married. Perfectly formed and proportioned the way only small women can be. When his neighbor walked naked through the rooms of her apartment, he could almost hear Caroline's bare feet thumping. (54)

There are other moments of male gazing and misogyny in these quest narratives. In some remembered scenes with his estranged Euro-American wife, Caroline, Cudjoe reduces her to body parts. "When he sat reading with Caroline in the quiet of an evening, . . . why did she always close her robe or shut her knees if she noticed his eyes straying from his book, peering between her naked legs?" (56). He also objectifies Cassandra, the eighteen-year-old daughter of his friends Rachel and Sam:

> Below him in the moonlight a white body hugs itself, twisting slowly, tentatively into spray from an outdoor shower sheltered in this nook of the house. Cassandra must have been swimming in the ocean and now she's warming herself, rinsing salt and sand from her body before she goes to bed. (63)

In his violation of Cassandra, Cudjoe thinks not of her but of her father. He "hears himself trying to explain to his dead friend why he's spying on his daughter" (63–64). The conversation is between the two men about the daughter, Cassandra, who has no say in the matter. Again, for Cudjoe, European and Euro-American women do not possess individuality or distinct subjectivity. They are objectified bodies to be gazed upon, existing as objects of male desire. They have no voice or agency, and they belong almost exclusively to the male economy.

Even in John Wideman's narrative in part 2, his Euro-American wife, Judy, does not have any agency or distinct subjectivity. "She screams without uttering a sound" (100). He refers to her as the "woman beside me" in bed (100), thinking of her in terms of "breast" (101). Although she is in the bed with John Wideman when he learns of the Philadelphia fire, the reader never gets her reaction or hears her voice. He says, "How do I know what she's thinking" (101). And although John Wideman is totally preoccupied with his son psychologically deteriorating in prison, one would think that Judy, the son's mother, is not affected by her son's predicament. The reader never hears her voice on the issue; her thoughts are unrepresented.

In a final instance of male gazing, John Wideman the character describes watching a friend's little girl's genitals in a very graphic way, sexualizing the child. "A little girl. Shy. Yet her body knows for sure it's on its way to being a young woman and she's ready and anxious to share that knowledge. . . . She cracks the surface and smiles, enjoying what she is, enjoying being watched, secure, teetering on an edge. . . . [She] does a handstand with her head submerged, her spraddled legs kicking in the air, her sex displayed seamed and taut as a fist" (123). Afterward, Wideman reflects on the moment of seeing the little girl, Becky, as a female/woman although she was just a child.

In the various male-dominated quest narratives throughout the text, European and Euro-American women are abandoned and are represented as silent wives or sexual objects. Nowhere do we get their desires, fantasies, agency, subjectivity, and so on. Euro-American woman is the Other or the mirror for man. In the male quest narratives in *Philadelphia Fire,* "there is no place for the other, for an equal other, for a whole and living woman" (Cixous and Clément, *Newly Born Woman* 79), white or black. *Philadelphia Fire* reproduces a gender system that generates relations of domination and objectification. The objectification and misogyny in *Philadelphia Fire* prompt the questions: Why do Cudjoe and Wideman desire only Euro-American and European women? Why do they hate these women? Is such hatred of European and Euro-American women an intentional narrative move injected by Wideman to deepen the scope of *Philadelphia Fire*? Or is it simply there because Wideman himself is a misogynist? Disappointingly, there is nothing in the text to suggest the former. There are no clear consequences for Cudjoe's and Wideman's objectification and misogyny, which exist in the text untroubled. Like Caliban in Cudjoe's reconfigured *The Tempest,* are Cudjoe and Wideman using European and Euro-American women to defile the white man's empire, to undermine his rule? Is the black woman ignored, or is she of no use to Cudjoe and Wideman because she has no value in defiling the white man's empire?

Philadelphia Fire understands clearly how the white-black binary system in the West has devalued the representation of the African American, particularly the African American male. The book critiques this binary system and the modern novel, using the African concept of radical democracy or eclectic combination to challenge the conventions of the novel and, as Anna Julia Cooper, W. E. B. Du Bois, E. Franklin Frazier, and Carter G. Woodson have done, to redescribe African America as diverse and the African American male as having his own logic, agency, and distinct subjectivity, thereby challenging the mainstream American society's representation of the African American as deviant. *Philadelphia Fire* gives us a different way to look at truth, freedom, and reality and produces a fluid, indeterminate, and open postmodern text. But in not giving us a fluid subjectivity outside the black masculine and in constructing all European and Euro-American women and female children as sexual objects, *Philadelphia Fire* leaves but does not escape Western logocentrism and heteropatriarchy. *Philadelphia Fire* successfully reimagines the African American male but does not completely reimagine America or the past.

— 3 —

The Trickster Figure, The African American Virtual Subject, and Percival Everett's *Erasure*

In *The Invention of the Americas,* the Argentinian philosopher Enrique Dussel identifies two basic paradigms of modernity—the Eurocentric and the planetary. The Eurocentric paradigm believes in reason, progress, hierarchy, sameness, and center, conceptualizing the phenomenon of modernity (and later postmodernity) as exclusively European, with Europe and the West as the center and with the rest of the world as the periphery (138). The planetary paradigm formulates the phenomenon of modernity (and later postmodernity) as the culture of the center of the first world-system, through the incorporation of the periphery (137). Within the Eurocentric paradigm of modernity, the African American is underrepresented. Historically, at least since the European Renaissance, he has been defined as the negative half of the Western self-Other binary opposition, where he is constructed as inferior, as a victim, or as deviant. He is locked in a rigidly defined racial category, which is defined as essential to one's DNA or biological makeup. But within planetary modernity, the African American is a subject with agency and distinct subjectivity who accepts the law of the Other. Race is a mere fact of life, being one component of one's identity. Percival Everett's *Erasure* struggles between these two paradigms of modernity. In this chapter, first, I will examine how Everett's *Erasure* challenges the novel form, opening up the literary space for a different notion of reality and of the subject. Second, I will explore the condition of possibility for an African American to socially and culturally pass. Third, I will examine Everett's strategies in *Erasure* to escape racial labeling. Fourth and last, I will discuss how Everett in *Erasure* uses the African American trickster–folk hero Stagolee (also known as Stagger Lee) to construct a plural African American male subjectivity that escapes categorization/labeling and pushes beyond the reduced representation of the African American in the United States.

In *Erasure,* published in 2001 and the only novel in his vast oeuvre that deals directly with race, Everett,[1] working within the assumptions of the Eurocentric paradigm, unhinges and complicates this negative, reductive construction of the African American, particularly the African American male. To achieve his goal, Everett, like Wideman in *Philadelphia Fire,* plays with Eurocentric modernity's notions of Enlightenment reason, closure, totalization, and linearity as a way of opening up the novel form and of reconceptualizing the African American outside the norms of reason. Then, Everett flips the binary and gives us an African American who defies the negative stereotype by being the same as the American upper-middle-class educated elite norm: an African American who graduates summa cum laude from Harvard, has doctors in his family, is a Western renaissance man, and writes experimental novels that have nothing to do with the African American experience. This upper-middle-class elite representation belongs to the Eurocentric paradigm of modernity. But by the end of *Erasure,* Everett undermines this upper-middle-class elite representation, using the African American folk hero Stagolee to signify a representation of the African American male that escapes language and categories.

But in his effort to redescribe the African American male, Everett in *Erasure,* like Wideman in *Philadelphia Fire,* creates differences within African American male subjectivity, otherizing and reducing the feminine and the homosexual. Like *Philadelphia Fire, Erasure* does not have a femininity in its writing, that is, a writing that incorporates the self's relation to the Other. In *Erasure,* the masculine narratorial *I* is never deconstructed. In addition to maintaining a self-Other binary opposition, the *I* fails to engage the reason of the Other, women and gays, thereby erasing their differences. In this sense, *Erasure* expresses planetary desires but ultimately fails to become a planetary postmodern text.

In *Erasure,* Everett begins with but unfastens instrumental reason, undermining the conventions of the traditional novel. He is not concerned with chronological and developmental narrative system building or in naturalizing a set of idealizing literary and social presuppositions. Rather, like Wideman in *Philadelphia Fire,* Everett in *Erasure* wants to liberate the African American novel from a normalized and predictable literature and from a publishing industry that supports it. He also wants to reframe the representation of the African American outside of certain otherized but acceptable stereotypes that continually *erase* complex, varied, and diverse African American subjectivities and experiences. In the "Foreword" to *Making Callaloo: 25 Years of Black Literature,* Everett defines what he thinks is the predicament of African American literature:

> Standing at the mercy of the publishing industry . . . , African-American writers were, and in some ways still are, stuck trying to supply fictions that are palatable to American culture's tastes and expectations and that do not upset the way America wants to see black people and itself. The black reading public has never been a sizeable market, and no doubt it wouldn't matter if it were, African-Americans falling as much victim to the culture as anyone else, learning the same ways, reading the same, predictable ways, and wanting to read the same, predictable literature. The market for the novels of social protest, from [Richard] Wright in the 1940s to John A. Williams in the 1970s, was mostly white, middle class, and young. Black novels were . . . novel: a people's statement about black life, about being black in a racist, oppressive society. It all fit neatly into the rehearsed rhetoric of the 1960s and 1970s. New York publishing houses were trying to find the next, blacker work. (xvi)[2]

To disrupt the African American social protest/traditional novel's expected conventions and its rules of totalization, which are subsystems of Enlightenment reason, and not create a new set of conventions and rules, Everett in *Erasure* gives us a text that asserts itself as a plurality. Through the heterogeneous and open-ended forms, rather than through the content, Everett tells the reader that *Erasure* cannot master meaning, cannot capture in language its subject. But in trying, it tells a good story. *Erasure* is Everett's novel and Monk's journal, which create "ambiguity about to whom this narrative actually belongs" (Eaton 223). As Monk, the main protagonist in the text, writes his saga in his journal to be read by others after his death, he includes a vast network of texts, conversations, influences, images, and ideas that informed the writing of his story. Dispersed throughout Monk's narrative are other texts and discourses: other ideas for stories, foreign words and phrases, which are not translated, and conversations between Hitler and Eckhart about Jews contaminating German culture, which are really notes for a novel inspired by Monk's witnessing the fascist antiabortionists outside his sister's clinic. Interspersed throughout the central narrative are also short italicized conversations between prominent Western male writers and intellectuals such as James Joyce, Jacques Derrida, Ludwig Wittgenstein, Oscar Wilde, Theodore Roethke, Richard Wright, and Robert Rauschenberg that concern issues pertinent to the text such as erasure, representation, play, and the process of writing. They assist in authoring the text. Also, within the text there are letters, plays, flashbacks, dreams, television interviews, an interview to be on a television show, a curriculum vitae, and a diary. Finally, halfway through *Erasure,* Monk presents a novel-within-a novel, renaming himself and creating a mirror and a challenge to *Erasure.*

These diverse forms, narratives, discourses, foreign words and phrases, and a novel-within-a novel that intersperse *Erasure*'s main narrative break the flow of the narrative (and the idea of a totalized narrative and a unified subject) and further undermine the traditional notions of linearity, causality, and progress. Through disruptions, transgressions, and explosions of the traditional realistic narrative, *Erasure* exposes the way narratives are constructed, using the deconstruction of narrative to raise metaphysical and linguistic questions and to show that the novel is a linguistic invention. These various forms, languages, and spaces create mystery, difference, and openness in the text by not allowing the text to create the illusion of wholeness and mastery.

In repeatedly renaming its subjectivity, *Erasure* presents the subjectivity of the main protagonist, Thelonious "Monk" Ellison, as one that is multiple, pointing to the great jazz musician Thelonious Monk and the novelist Ralph Ellison, with Ellison also being called "Monk" throughout the novel. Monk also moves relatively freely and simultaneously through several narratives, which are told in different persons and voices, without establishing an obvious causal relation between them or without building a narrative consensus. There is the central narrative of Monk and his family, which is told in the first person and through flashbacks. There are also the stories of fishing and woodwork, told in the third person, that are woven throughout the novel. Unlike writing, which allows him to search for metaphysical truths, the woodworking grounds him, signifying a pre-Saussurian referent or foundation outside the play of language whereby the word is actually equivalent to or reflects the object. "[T]he wood, the feel of it, the smell of it, the weight of it. It was so much more real than words. The wood was so simple . . . a table was a table was a table" (139). His pursuit of the trout is also a pursuit of metaphysical truth. "A trout is very much like truth; it does what it wants, what it has to" (199).

In addition to plural subjectivity, *Erasure* makes references to the process of writing/producing the novel. "In my writing my instinct was to defy form, but I very much sought in defying it to affirm it, an irony that was difficult enough to articulate, much less defend" (139), says Monk, the narrator. "*Story ideas. A woman gives birth to an egg*" (19). "*Story idea—a man marries a woman whose name is the same as that of his first wife*" (30). By including notes for other stories within *Erasure,* Monk makes the reader aware of the process of storytelling or of the fictiveness of fiction.

To further attack simplified reason and to open up the novel to nonrational experiences and other forms of speech, *Erasure* presents the real and the imagined without resorting to a priori context-independent standards, which can adjudicate hierarchal differences between them. While in Washington, D. C., Monk "imagined [his] sister treating a patient, a little girl with a name [his] sister despised, looking into her ears, joking with her, asking her if purple was her favorite color because that was the color of her throat" (47). As he watches his sister deal with the ordeal of taking care of their mother's worsening Alzheimer's disease, he imagines her smoking "an entire pack of imaginary cigarettes" (10). Discussing taking care of his mother with his brother Bill at her dining room table, Monk imagines a return trip to Los Angeles. "In my imagination, I told Mother I'd be back, took a leave from my teaching, put things in storage, packed bags, flew east on an L1011 seated next to a woman my mother's age" (51). In another and final instance, he imagines his character in his created novel "giving a reading at the East St. Louis Public Library" (234). In giving us both the real and the imagined equally, *Erasure* extends reality and makes human possibilities deeper and richer, signifying a mental world where Western logocentric structures do not dominate and allowing chance, probability, coincidence, and the imagination to be a normative part of his textual real.

Like *Philadelphia Fire, Erasure* also undermines the authority of authorship, which usually takes on qualities of godliness, by giving the author multiple selves. The distinction among author, narrator, and character—that is, among Everett, Monk, Stagg Leigh, and Thelonious—becomes increasingly blurred. Thelonious Monk has the same social and educational attributes as Percival Everett; both like fishing, woodworking, and painting; and both are experimental/postmodern writers who teach at universities in southern California. Both are told constantly that their books are too experimental and not "black enough." Finally, Everett and Monk wrote both the paper Monk delivers at the conference and the novel-within-a novel, *My Pafology.*[3] Everett and Monk, according to Everett in an interview, have "real similarities . . . in the way" they approach "the making of art in this culture" (McDaniel). "Monk's experience is very much my own," states Everett, "though he of course is not me at all" (McDaniel), with Monk becoming a self of Everett. Here, *Erasure* creates a fictional self within the narrative, thereby problematizing the authority of the author.

Finally, in the paper "F/V: a novel excerpt," which Monk delivers at the Nouveau Roman Society in Washington, D.C., he creates a framework or model for not imposing narrative or structure on texts, arguing for a plurality of meaning in texts. Barthes's enterprise in *S/Z* is to move the reader toward a "writerly" reading process, one in which the reader is "no longer a consumer, but a producer of the text. . . . [T]he writerly text is *ourselves writing,* before the infinite play of the world . . is traversed, intersected, stopped, plasticized by some singular system . . . , which reduces the plurality of entrances, the opening of networks, the infinity of languages" (4, 5, emphasis in original). Richard Howard in his "Preface" to *S/Z* describes Barthes's writerly criticism as "literature" that "makes upon us strenuous demands, exactions" (xi). These demands are manifested in a reader's ability to construct meaning in the text as multiple, pointing in many directions, beyond the denotation and connotation of words. Barthes writes that "In this ideal text, the networks are many and interact, without any one of them being able to surpass the rest; this text is a galaxy of signifiers, not a structure of signifieds; it has no beginning; it is reversible; we gain access to it by several entrances, none of which can be authoritatively declared to be the main one" (5). In the interview with Anthony Stewart, Everett acknowledges his debt to Barthes and multiple meanings. "I do expect a reader to study. If you want to get through *the layers of meaning,* it requires some work . . . that's the kind of literature I'm interested in and that's what I make" (320, my emphasis). In *Erasure,* Everett is concerned with plurality of meaning.

In his paper, Monk ruminates on the impossibility of mastering knowledge/meaning, of shutting down the play of differences, the galaxy of signifiers, placing writing and meaning *under erasure.* Writing as representation is inadequate but necessary. Satirizing Barthes's method of analyzing Balzac's *Sarraine* in *S/Z,* Monk presents his views on the possibility of storytelling, exposing the arbitrary nature of the story's title by showing how it can have not one but many different meanings. *"So, is the title the name of a work or the name of a mere shadow of a work?"* (*Erasure* 14). He demonstrates how the word "bean" has multiple meanings. "The bean of course implies the seed which it both is and contains" (15). In attempting to use a word to establish a particular intended meaning, the text shows how the meaning of that word "need[s] not and does not confine itself to that intention" (44). Words have infinite meanings.

Then Monk, in his paper, discusses how the slash between unequal binary oppositions combines and divides equally, creating multiple contradictory meanings. *"The '/' itself becomes a signifier and in each reference to the title it will be a sliding, conflicting element which behaves similarly to its function between S and Z"* (14). In a Derridean sense, Monk, in his paper, destabilizes the *I* and puts it back into play, pointing out how it also belongs to a chain of signifiers and therefore has many different meanings. *"Is the 'I' the Roman numeral one or is it the English pronoun* I" (*Erasure* 15)? In this instance, he shows the notions of individuals existing contrary to or with a narrative that is ephemeral in nature.

Next, in his paper Monk discusses how commercial publishing houses attempt to master fiction by controlling its definition, forcing differences into sameness, "plasticized by some singular system." Publishing houses perpetuate the idea of extracting *"from each tale its model, then out of these models we shall make a great narrative structure, which we shall reapply . . . to any one narrative"* (*Erasure* 17). With this model, all fiction must follow recognizable formulas, including the creation of an identifiable plot. When a writer deviates from this narrative structure, the publishers ask *"You call this a story?"* and thus force the writer to conform. Monk wants to *"come to dismantling of the endeavor as the endeavor of the text at hand, Sarrasine, not being chosen as a model at all, but accepted as one treated in a way which in turn is a model for the treatment of other texts, as is this text"* (17). In this short paper there is fervor, a commitment to language that keeps you reading. *"A reiteration of the obvious is never wasted on the oblivious"* (17), Monk concludes. Finally, even the fight that ensues between Monk and Davis Gimbel, who feels condescended to, after the paper's delivery also enters this crisis in representation.

Barthes in *S/Z* uses five notorious codes to reveal the meaning of Balzac's *Sarrasine.* In "F/V: Placing the Experimental Novel," which was published "as a piece of fiction . . . [or] as parody of its subject text," *S/Z,* before it appeared in *Erasure,* Everett recursively breaks down Barthes's first three sentences to demonstrate the inadequacy of this kind of literary analysis. "F/V" is a parody of Barthes's method of analysis, with Monk denouncing literary criticism in which "the method is subsumed by the analysis" (21). The problem with Barthes's method is that "the initial desire to analyze a particular text is rather quickly replaced by a fascination with the analysis itself as text" (21). Barthes's analysis reduces *Sarrasine* to a jumble of codes in the name of mastering knowledge of it, and it is the analysis of those codes—those signifiers—that become important in the process. "The direction of this *novel* . . . is back to the conventional [realistic] novel" ("F/V" 21). In "F/V," Everett/Monk endorses Barthes's project of writerly reading and making multiple meanings, even as he satirizes Barthes's method.

But to escape Barthes's inadequate and flawed method and the return to realism, Everett/Monk proposes to "affirm the novel's existence as novel while taking on as *stuff* the critical theory which has pretended to uncover the novel's so-called tricks. . . . The *new* new novel will rely less on ego . . . and more on the stuff of its own fictive reality" ("F/V" 21). Gimbel, who fancies himself as a kind of Hemingway, and his "entourage" of "young, aspiring writers" are provoked because they think Monk is accusing them, along with Barthes, of "defensive posturing. The posturing to which [he] refer[s] is painfully evident and representative in nearly every bit of criticism written by practitioners of *innovative* or *experimental* novels" (20, emphasis in original). But Monk thinks that Gimbel's reaction is "inappropriate and extreme" because he has not understood his paper. Monk's main criticism of Gimbel and the other postmodernists is their "disturbed, certifiable, and agitated postmodern state" (*Erasure* 36). Rather than being alive and open, they are "defunct practitioners of defunct art" (37), relying more on ego than on the text's "own fictive reality" ("F/V" 21). After the commotion that his paper provokes, Monk "saw people . . . bolting for the outside, where they would offer their versions of *the fight*" (*Erasure* 18). The paper serves as a metaphor for the inability of language/the novel to pin down meaning, to master its subject, and for the privileging of play and multiplicity.

In writing a self-conscious text that relies on the "stuff of its own reality," that normalizes play and multiplicity, Everett is producing a fiction that "upset[s] the way America [as well as New York publishing houses] wants to see black people and itself." He is writing a fiction that does not reduce black life to a people's statement, to a "set of stereotypical fictional tropes: the ghetto, the deep South, the angry pimp, the street hustler, or the triumphant victim" (O'Hagan, "Colour Bind"). He is writing a fiction that contests and problematizes the primitive picture that America has drawn of the African American and that shows complex individual African Americans living, surviving, and making sense out of a modern/postmodern American society. In the "Foreword" to *Making Callaloo,* Everett states that the African American experience is "an experience that is as varied as any other American experience but which has been funneled into a tiny vessel of clichés and set pieces" (xvi). Everett wants to unhinge African American life from this "tiny vessel of clichés and set pieces" and to show its variety and multiplicity.

Therefore, Everett in *Erasure* uses satire and deconstruction to present a different representation of the African American. Everett's characters in *Erasure,* particularly the main character, are black, but race is not their total identity; race is a construct designed by society. In *Erasure,*

Monk constructs an upper-middle-class family narrative that is typical and predictable, thereby creating a conventional middle-class narrative to supersede the conventional ghetto narrative. But Monk's upper-middle-class narrative is constructed under enormous repression, especially as it deals with race. As the novel opens, Monk is "isolated through a combination of circumstances and preferences from all the communities of which he might seem on first examination to be a part: his family, colleagues, industry, race, and class" (Powell 79). He also has a number of expected problems: His family is being erased, his mother is disintegrating into the abyss of Alzheimer's disease, and he feels estranged from the rest of his family, especially his physician sister, Lisa, whom he has not seen in three years. She has "very little use for [him]" (3). He is also estranged from his homosexual physician brother, Bill, whom he has not seen in four years. Having his family or having his racial past erased forces Monk to search for meaning and identity.

Monk does not fit into any of the categories of the existing social norm, refusing to be racially marked. Yet he is preoccupied, almost obsessively, with being racially constructed by the social. At the beginning of the text, Thelonious "Monk" Ellison informs the reader that he has "dark brown skin, curly hair, a broad nose" and that "some of [his] ancestors were slaves" (1). He cannot escape race. But he does not want race and racism to define him, to erase or reduce his diverse individuality/subjectivity to a singular system or category. He does not think that race is a valid category into which an individual can be slotted and therefore quantified. As Barthes does with *Sarrasine,* Monk does not believe that race can be reduced to a set of signifieds. Like mainstream white males, Monk, to escape racial marking, defines himself as a "galaxy of signifiers," constructing himself as a modern Western renaissance man, an American individual, with many interests, searching for his own truth, expressing himself freely. "What is most interesting to me about Monk is not his color," states Everett in an interview, "but his selfless examination of himself. He does not want to be constrained or reduced by society's demands or expectations. He's alert to that all the time" (O'Hagan, "Colour Bind"). Monk seeks an individuality that does not trap him in the socially enforced constraints of race, which assumes collective or stereotypical identity.

Unlike the stereotype, Monk is the product of a heterogeneous upper-middle-class America. In his self-description, he delights in undermining racial assumptions about himself. He grows up in Northwest Washington, an upper-middle-class section of Washington, D.C., with a physician father in the home and with a servant. The family owns a summer home or bungalow on the beach in Highland Beach, Maryland, near Annapolis. Since age twelve, Monk has aspired to be a serious writer, wanting "to write books like *Crime and Punishment*" (143). Unlike most African Americans, he was not raised a Christian, and when he was young he "despised religion." As an adult, he views the "trappings [of religion] with vague amusement and almost always finding the practitioners somewhat dull of spirit and thought" (50). He tells the reader he attended Harvard, graduating summa cum laude, and his eclectic taste in music and books allows him to listen to Mahler, Charlie Parker, Ry Cooder, and Aretha Franklin and to read the fiction of James Joyce, Zora Neale Hurston, and Jean Toomer. But he is careful to distance himself from traditional markers of African Americans, informing the reader that he cannot dance or play basketball and that he did not grow up in the inner city or the rural South.

Also, Monk has grown up an Ellison, and the family has had an enormous impact on him. But as a teenager, he begins to emerge as an individual and to have issues of identity, wanting to be the strong individual who stands out against his family and society. During this time, without a clear sense of self, he begins to perform identity, "want[ing] badly to fit in" with his peers. Wanting to "talk the talk," he "watche[s] [his black] friends, who didn't sound so different from [him], step into scenes and change completely" (166). But he is not successful, becoming the "awkward one" (167). As a young adult, Monk has "interpersonal failures" (152), having difficulties relating to and being intimate with other people, particularly women.

During his years in college, Monk is still searching for his place and continues to perform identities, becoming a member of the Black Panther Party because he needs to prove that he "[i]s *black* enough" (2). In his current social life, as a professional he is performing the identity of a renaissance man, an American individual, and race does not matter. He is also passing in "terms of his class background, cultural affiliations, modes of behavior" (Moynihan 106). He is performing some of the privileges of whiteness. He hardly ever thinks about race, and when he does think about it, it is because he feels guilty for not thinking about it. "[He doesn't] believe in race" (2).

Absent of race, Monk represents himself as a racially *unmarked,* multiple individual, as being "a son, a brother, a fisherman, an art lover, a woodworker . . . and a writer of fiction" (*Erasure* 1). He drives a pickup truck, and he can be "flighty . . . , live in a swirl of abstracts, removed from the *real world*" (3). Monk is a student of French poststructuralist theory, writing noncommercial novels retelling "Euripides and [writing] parodies of French poststructuralists" ("The French hold his work in high regard") (*Erasure* 2). Monk has many desires and many interests.

But society is not simply content allowing him to be an individual and a writer, to completely pass, to speak as the Other who is the same and is heard. Whatever his position in the social, Monk is separated from whites by a symbolic coefficient that negatively affects everything that he is and is the source of a systematic set of homologous differences. Unlike mainstream white males whose representation of themselves (as white) remain racially *unmarked* because of the pervasive nature of white privilege and domination, Monk's representation of himself as a racially *unmarked* individual is not reinforced by the social. Against his wishes, he is constantly racially *marked.* In an interview with Anthony Stewart, Everett discusses this inability of the African American to escape racial marking. "Even though, I, with every anthropologist in the world since the beginning of the twentieth century, dismissed race as a category, it is a bogus yet *real* category that's perpetuated by culture. By everyone in the culture" (315). Therefore, the daily effects of living with dark skin and of being reminded of what it is to live in a racially conscious society are an inescapable part of Monk's identity. Because Monk is marked as black, white policemen stop him, and "[s]ociety tells [him he] is black" (*Erasure* 1). Other black and white people who are defined racially by society, which they essentialize, mark him as being black. "Some people in the society in which I live, described as being black, tell me I am not *black* enough. Some people whom the society calls white tell me the same thing" (2). Society constructs nonwhite individuals racially, making race an integral marker of identity.

But Monk rejects the labeling, wanting to pass, to be a racially unmarked American. He becomes what Hélène Cixous calls "inside without being inside," not being "able to enter into that . . . which [he] had been admitted" (*White Ink* 170). He will always live in the exclusion. And even when he rethinks himself, he has "reflex valuations that [he] continually carr[ies]" with him (Sylvia Wynter qtd. in Thomas, "ProudFlesh Inter/Views" 4). Monk compensates for his exclusion by arguing for differences within that exclusion, which he hopes will become a home. For Monk, there are *many* black experiences, and his is as valid as any other, including the ghetto one. The problem is that the simplistic, reduced, primal ghetto version of black life, promoted by mainstream American society, keeps erasing his complex, complicated, modern life.

Also, in addition to his subjectivity being reduced to a set of knowable signifieds, Monk's art is constantly being reduced. His nonblack fiction books are placed in the African American section of bookstores. His novel, *The Persians,* as a reworking of Aeschylus's *The Persians,* is dismissed, causing one white reviewer to say that "One is lost to understand what [it] . . . has to do with the African American experience" (*Erasure* 2), assuming that Monk could and should only write about the black experience. At a party in New York City, a literary agent approaches Monk to tell him that he needs to settle down and "write the true, gritty real stories of black life" (2). Despite his protestation, Monk's literary expressions are colonized by racial markings. He is unable to speak and be heard.

Therefore, in addition to a rigid racial marking of him and his work, Monk is angry and disgusted with the way book publishers cater to the black politburo, the unspoken sentiment that anything from a black writer must automatically deal with being black, or the problematic of race. He despises those black authors who cater to white liberal sentiments, for turning blackness into a commodity, albeit a seamy and reprehensible one. He hates the mainstream publishing industry because it promotes for profit a narrow, otherized, victimized, authentic representation of black life: "the real people, the earthy, gutsy people . . . *the true story of what it is like to be black in America . . . the pain of those people*" (217, 235). The fallacy in this general assumption about African Americans is in thinking that any one book—or person or image—can signify meaning for an entire race.

This kind of generalized, authentic representation of the African American has grave consequences. To define African American life only as "true, gritty real stories" is to erase other African American representations/drawings. It is to assume that African American life is completely Other; that it is primal; that it exists outside the norms of Western language, history, and rationality; that it has not been touched by modernity/postmodernity. To write "the true, gritty real stories of black life" is to write black life as being in the myth of a precivilized state: unself-conscious, spontaneous, and peaceful. More important, to be "black enough" is to approximate this primal construction or stereotype, to suggest that race can be quantified in such a way as to circumscribe it. Although an authentic representation of African American life/subjectivity "purports to give access" to that subjectivity in an unmediated way, it is, to use the words of Sanchez-Arce, "as constructed as that which is other" or normative (141).

Why does the white West in the late twentieth century and the early twenty-first century still have a need for the primitive black? Why does the white West insist on defining the African American outside the norms of Western history and rationality? Interestingly, in *Erasure* the New York publishing houses, awarding agencies, and television shows have the same desire for the primitive black Other as Humes, Hegel, and Kant of the eighteenth and nineteenth centuries.[4] Why? "The real secret of the primitive can be—has been, will be—whatever Euro-Americans want it to be," writes Marianna Torgovnick in *Gone Primitive.* "It tells us what we want it to tell us" (9). In most instances, Euro-Americans want the primitive to tell them that they are defined as normative, superior, and advanced, that the white norm is produced around the positioning of the black/African American as devalued Other. In defending their literary/social space from black intrusion, from *recognized* intermingling, the white publishing houses and awarding agencies, to use the words of Pierre Bourdieu in *Masculine Domination,* are "trying to protect their most deep-rooted idea of themselves as" whites, especially in the case of categories such as highbrow literature that generate much to their image of whiteness (96). Although Monk is clearly different from normative black stereotypes, whites and blacks expect him to obey the logic of the traditional model of the division between whites and blacks. In their expectations, both blacks and whites avoid the problem of Monk's representation.

But the world/life that has allowed Monk the luxury of socially and culturally passing, of being a free-thinking health-conscious (he does not eat meat) single individual, to be a lover of woodworking, fishing, and intellectual humor, is more immediately threatened with erasure by family happenings. Until his sister's murder, he has lived in his "own little bubble" (*Erasure* 28), where he has never thought of things such as his mother's welfare, financial responsibility, and growing old. But now he must deal overtly with the happenings in his family. Seven years earlier his father committed suicide; Monk must begin to understand that suicide. His sister, Lisa, is shot to death at an abortion clinic, and he must now not only deal with her murder but also take responsibility for his mother's Alzheimer's disease. His brother, Bill, married and a father, comes out of the gay closet, forcing Monk to deal with his homosexuality. Monk realizes that he has become the "captain of a sinking ship" (159). He must grow up and become a responsible adult.

After the murder of his sister, Monk, in many ways and in an American sense, is forced to grow up. This much he admits. "Mother needed caring for and I didn't believe that Bill was up to it. Lorraine was nearly as old as Mother and would perhaps require the same care. . . . My skin crawled, my head ached, my neck itched, all as I watched my life as I knew it change before my eyes" (51). As his mother's Alzheimer's disease worsens, Monk moves outside his ego, putting his life on hold and making difficult but intelligent decisions about his mother. In short, he takes on "familial duties" (48).

In a kind of existential way, Monk's life is like the lives of most middle-class American families. It has to do with a Freudian, rational bourgeois family life that causes all kinds of repression in its members and that creates problems, such as jealousy, sibling rivalry, and distant parents. And as with any other family, it has to do with losing your father, burying your murdered sister, negotiating a relationship with your distant brother, and taking care of your ailing mother. His life has to do with the search for knowledge of the self, the father. It is an "obsession with the autonomy of reason that manifests itself in a conception" of Monk as an "isolated and essentially self-sufficient" being (Code 268), but experientially, he thinks, it has very little to do with race.

In examining and reflecting on his family and his own isolation and alienation, Monk is forced to reassess and to revise the narrative of the family's past. In retrospect, he becomes fully aware that his father was not perfect; that he made mistakes; that he probably loved his mistress, Fiona, more than he loved his wife; and that his life was as complicated as Monk's is today. In reading his father's correspondence from the gray box, Monk hears "a voice of [his] father's that he had not heard directly in life, a tender voice, an open voice. [He] couldn't imagine the man who had run off to New York to have an affair. . . . Knowledge of the affair gave [him], oddly, more compassion for [his] father, more interest in him" (150). Although Monk thought his father was a kind man, living with him, he realizes later, "was like living on the crate of Vesuvius" (154). Monk also ponders how his mother must have felt/reacted when she read the letters of the affair, considering "his mother's discovery that all those years of somehow feeling she was not quite enough were in a few minutes made valid" (152). In reexamining the legacy of his father and mother, Monk surmises that they were "not outwardly affectionate"; he "thought they were decidedly distant, cool to one another" (152). This attitude, he thinks, "would seriously impair [his] attempts at relationships later" (152). Now he knows that his parents affected who he is.

In addition, in coming to grips with his family, Monk revisits his past relationship with Lisa and Bill. In a poignant scene that he reremembers from his childhood, he acknowledges that being his father's favorite puts distance between him and his siblings. The scene occurs during the Christmas break of Monk's freshman year at Harvard. When he tells his father, who thinks he has a "special mind" (9), that he has read Joyce in a class, Monk and his father get into a long discussion about Joyce's word play in *Wake.* Since the two had begun to read and discuss serious literature, the father "had forced the rest of the family to endure [their] discussions at the [dinner] table" (184). Despite the fact that Bill is in his second year of medical school and Lisa is finishing up her final year at Vassar before going off to medical school, Ben Ellison puts them down. At the end of the discussion on Joyce, "[he] looked at me for a long time. He then looked at his other two children and put his fork down. 'I hope before you go to bed this evening, you kiss your brother.' Then he stood and left the room" (185). Later, after Monk attempts to apologize, Bill calls him a "geek," and Lisa, who gives him an almost "sympathetic look, shrugged and stepped into her room. The closing of her door was just ever so slightly louder than a normal closing of a door and so she too managed to slap [him] about some" (186). Reremembering and reexamining this childhood incident, Monk understands "how bad Lisa and Bill must have felt" (186), wondering if at ten years of age he "had unknowingly and accidently shaded [his] father's perception of [his] older brother" (145).

But in the midst of sorting out and taking responsibility for his family, frustrated by his book sales, unable to get a decent-paying visiting teaching position at American

University, in need of money to help take care of his mother whose sums have dwindled, Monk is angered, again, by the high profile and success of Juanita Jenkins's *We's Lives in Da Ghetto,* which is *"the ghetto . . . painted in all its exotic wonder"* (40). Monk is angry because Jenkins not only claims to represent the black race but also profits off of a life in which she has almost no contact. She admits that "[w]hen [she] was twelve [she] went to visit some relatives in Harlem for a couple of days and that's what the novel come from" (53). Her novel has become a national best seller, with paperback and movie rights bringing in millions of dollars. This time, he decides to react.

In the heat of inspiration, energy, and anger, Monk writes a fierce parody on the kind of exploitation ghetto wannabe literature (and television) represented by *We's Lives in Da Ghetto,* Richard Wright's *Native Son, The Amos 'n Andy Show,* Alice Walker's *The Color Purple,* and Sapphire's *Push.* It is the type of novel that he, because he is marked as "black," is *expected* to write—the dystrophic novel of violence, poverty, and abuse that he calls *My Pafology,* which he later retitles *Fuck.* It is written under the pseudonym of Stagg Leigh because Monk does not want to put his name on it. Loaded with imitation, humor, and satire, *My Pafology* tells the story of nineteen-year-old Van Go Jenkins, a tough, streetwise narrator deep in the language and culture of subaltern, inner-city, hip-hop black life. He has four children by four different women, and he does not take care of any of them. He hangs out with his homeboys, Yellow and Tito; runs women who are always referred to as "bitches" and "hos"; steals; plays pool; and gets into fights. Constantly nagged by his mother to get a job, Van Go relents and shows up at the affluent black Daltons. In a parody of Richard Wright's *Native Son,* Van Go becomes the chauffeur for the Daltons. When the Dalton's daughter Penelope, who is a recent Stanford graduate, along with her boyfriend, Roger, asks him to drive them to his community, as Mary and Jan do with Wright's Bigger Thomas, he becomes angry but obeys. Interestingly, Stagg Leigh's black Daltons, who, like Monk, constitute a different black experience than Van Go, treat blacks in the same patronizing and ignorant way as Wright's white Daltons. Penelope and Roger, who have internalized the mainstream representation of black life, respond to Van Go and his life with contempt and condescension, finding it humorous that Van Go has four children. They too define Van Go's life as raw, honest, and savagery, outside the norms of Western history and rationality.

In *My Pafology,* the parody comes with its imitation/exaggeration of stereotypical situations in Wright's novel for comic effects. We get the uneducated violent black teenager who makes babies he cannot support. We also get the humorous misspelling of chapters, the language that shows the futility of life on one level and the lightness of that life situation on another. For example, describing stabbing his nagging mother, Van Go says:

> So, I stab Mama again. I stab her cause I scared. I stab Mama cause I love her. I stab Mama cause I hate her. . . . Then I walk out the kitchen and stand outside, leavin Mama crawlin round on the linolum tryin to hold her guts. I stands out on the sidewalk just drippin blood like a muthafucka. I look up at the sky and I try to see Jesus, but I cain't. Then I wonder which one of my fo' babies I'm gone go see. (65)

Later Penelope gets drunk, and Van Go, like Bigger Thomas, becomes terrified with getting her home, thinking that he will be caught. After Van Go puts his hands on her breast, because he is expected to do that, the blind woman enters the pool area calling Penelope, and Van Go panics. "A woman is standin by the pool. Shit, I thinks. I'm in here with this drunk bitch. They gone throw my ass in the jail for damn sho" (108). After he murders Penelope, Van Go is invited on the *Snookie Cane Show* because there is "a guest who wants to surprise [him] with something. Someone who has a crush on [him]" (109). Instead, on the show, he is confronted by one of his babies' mother because he has failed to pay child support. "You gave me the baby, Now where's the money" (113). Being a setup, cops arrive to arrest him for the rape of Penelope, and as with Bigger Thomas in Wright's novel, he runs, and the chase is on.

Monk writes *My Pafology* as "an expression of [his] being sick of" what is being published as African American literature (132), wanting to erase/undermine the urban ghetto, primal narrative and to redescribe complex black life. Constructed easily without play, *My Pafology* "inhabited no space artistically that [he] could find intelligible" (160); yet later, when he changes the title to *Fuck,* he says it is "in fact a work of art" (221). But when his agent, Yul, sends this literary indictment out to publishers, its intended parody is ignored or not received, and it is greeted not as a "caricature" but instead as an "authentic" new voice in African American literature. "What Monk is trying to achieve with this narrative," writes Toiya Kristen Finley, "is not in doubt—create the most offensive, vile, and perverse depiction of 'the black experience.'" Again normative society, both black and white, refuses to let him speak, to let Monk successfully involve himself in representation.

Just as mainstream critics, reviewers, talk show hosts, and movie producers like Jenkins's novel because it reinforces "the way America wants to see black people," Monk's *Fuck* receives similar endorsement, making him another middle-class black writing about authentic black inner-city life. (But *Erasure* is completely silent on subaltern or non–middle-class blacks writing about subaltern black life.) The Oprah-like talk show host, Kenya Dunston, thinks it is "a gripping and truly realistic tale" (*Erasure* 248). One judge from the Book Award Association describes it as "a true, raw, [and] gritty work" (254). Another judge thinks that in *Fuck* "the energy and savagery of the common black is so refreshing" (254). Reviewing *Fuck* for the *New York Times,* Wayne Waxen writes: "The life of Van Go Jenkins is one of sheer animal existence, one that we can all recognize. Our young protagonist has no father, is ghetto tough and resists education and *reason* like the plague" (260, my emphasis). The editor at Random House calls it "true to life . . .[that] it was magnificently raw and honest" (136), offering a $600,000 advance.

Just as in the case of Juanita Mae Jenkins, Monk is offered money, fame, and success because he has written a novel that is "palatable to American culture's tastes and expectations and that [does] not upset the way America wants to see black people" (xvi). The mainstream media endorse *Fuck* because it reinforces a representation of black people as being primal/primitive/exotic, as not having been touched by modernity. "Monk's financial success and recognition," argues Kimberly Eaton, "reveal that the public's desire for literature, which reinforces [racial] stereotypes, causes a lack of space for alternative narratives to exist" (228). But as demand builds for meetings with and appearances by Stagg Leigh, Monk is faced with a whole new set of problems.

Until Monk writes and sells *My Pafology,* there is a clear binary opposition operating within *Erasure* concerning art and the subjectivity of the African American male. On the one hand, there is Monk, the individual, and his middle-class, high Western notion of art, desperately trying to pass as a Western renaissance man. On the other hand, there is the African American Other, embodied in Juanita Mae Jenkins's *We's Lives in Da Ghetto,* Monk's *My Pafology,* and other perceived African American lowbrow literature that define the African American as victim, that define black life in terms of the inner city or the rural South. It is a literature that says that to be *truly* black, you need to be downtrodden. Monk's objective thus far has been to assert himself and to counter the erasure of *his* individual black life.

But in simply reacting to the stereotype of the African American as victim, as primitive Other, Monk finds himself

> sadly a stereotype of the radical, railing against something, calling it tradition perhaps, claiming to seek out new narrative territory, to knock at the boundaries of the very form that calls me and allows my artistic existence. . . . [M]aybe I have misunderstood my experiments all along, propping up, as if propping up is needed, the artistic traditions that I have pretended to challenge. (155–56)

His reaction/protest is a part of the binary system. To simply flip the binary and privilege his representation of life as the African American experience, Monk would remain entrapped in the violent system. As we learn in the conversation between Rauschenberg and de Kooning, erasure is not simply reversing the binary opposition or creating and destroying an object and getting a blank. Rather, in the "erased drawing" (228), you get something else. "Language never really effaces its own presence, but creates the illusion that it does in cases where meaning presumes a first priority" (44). Therefore, in writing *My Pafology* as parody, Monk does not successfully erase the stereotype of the primitive black Other; he simply reconfigures it, using another lens. More important, in encountering other texts and images of the primitive black on television, in the movies, and in literature, *Erasure*'s primitive black Other is continually rewritten and renamed. Monk continues to fail to assert himself as a passing Western renaissance man.

In selling *My Pafology,* Monk is torn between his need to have all that money and his disdain for the publishing industry and its representation of blacks. He ponders the idea of being a sellout, asking how he "should take [his] Stagg Leigh performance. I might in fact become a [Ralph Ellison's postmodern, trickster] Rhinehart, walking down the street and finding myself in store windows. I yam who I yam. I could throw on a fake beard and a wig and do the talk shows, *play the game, walk the walk, shoot the jive.* No, I couldn't" (162, my emphasis). But he does. When Monk tells his agent to "take the deal" (136), he implicates himself in the same kind of commodification of blackness as the middle-class Oberlin-educated Juanita Mae Jenkins. "This news of the money came and I breathed an ironic and bitter sigh of relief" (137). Monk's decision has much more play than that of Ms. Jenkins.

To rationalize taking the check and dealing with looking himself in the mirror, Monk redefines *My Pafology* "as a functional device, its appearance a thing to behold, but more a thing to mark, a warning perhaps, a gravestone certainly" (208–09). More important, though, Monk admits that his writing is not marked by race, that he does not write for social or political purposes, and he does not believe that art/literature frees people or reflects the social real.

> I didn't write as an act of testimony or social indignation . . . and I did not write out of a so-called family tradition of oral storytelling. I never tried to set anybody free, never tried to paint the next real and true picture of the life of *my* people, never had any people whose picture I knew well enough to paint. (212)

Yet despite the fact that he does not comply with any of the conventions of African American literature, including not writing novels about being black, Monk is still *marked* as a black writer. Therefore, he becomes the lawless trickster Stagolee figure who takes various subject positions and who plays the "game"; he wears "the mask of the person [he] was expected to be" (212), becoming Rine the runner, taking subjective positions, and performing roles, which is something he has done most of his life.

Stagg Leigh, or Stagolee, is the pen name for Lee Shelton, who was a carriage driver and a pimp and was convicted of murdering William "Billy" Lyon in St. Louis in 1895. The crime was immortalized in popular songs, ballads, African American folk culture, and African American literature.[5] Ultimately Stagolee is transformed from a street pimp into a legendary trickster folk hero. Becoming "one of the most significant figures in our [African American's] folk culture" (Brown x) and "a classic of the black verbal arts" (Holloway 162), Stagolee becomes the embodiment of the tough/bad black man—one who is duplicitous, streetwise, and potentially violent and who defies white authority. According to Cecil Brown in the "Preface" to *I, Stagolee,* the folk hero Stagolee has both savory and unsavory elements (x).

In reproducing and reconfiguring the folk hero Stagolee, Everett's Monk/Stagg Leigh in *Erasure* takes subject positions and performs different roles. He lives a life that is based on difference and becoming. When Monk speaks to Paula Baderman, the editor at Random House, on the phone, he performs the bad man folk hero Stagg Leigh. When Paula asks him how long it took him to write the novel, Monk responds, "It took me just a little over a week." Paula is surprised by his time frame and put off by his diction; it was not what she expected. But when Paula tells him that his novel "is just perfect for summer reading," Monk, changing his tone and attitude and performing Stagg Leigh, responds, "Yes, white people on the beach will get a big kick out of it" (156). This response "sent walking fingers up her spine" (156). Has the novel-within-a novel challenged the singularity not only of *Erasure* as a traditional realistic novel but also of Monk as a middle-class American individual who is a Western renaissance man?

Writing in *Of Grammatology,* Jacques Derrida argues that "[t]he meaning of the outside [the Other] was always present in the inside" (35). In having *Erasure* and *My Pafology* in the same text, Everett is not choosing either side of the binary but instead is choosing both, allowing him to both condemn and lionize the texts, to intermingle and intermix both representations of black life and black male subjectivity. It is a reality or subjectivity that is not governed by any fixed norm; rather, it is a self in flux (difference) and becoming. Everett locates and maintains a relation between the two representations of black life (or self and Other) in which both can exist, insisting on the plurality of selves. For example, Van Go's life in *My Pafology* is not absolutely Other to Monk's life in *Erasure.* Both Monk and Van Go are estranged from their families, both have black ancestors, both are Other in the United States, and both know black talk (Monk created Van Go). In addition, both Monk and Van Go have had run-ins with the law. Within the middle-class, individualistic, Western renaissance man Monk, the feared Van Go has to be cancelled (but not annihilated) because Van Go erases for Monk the presence of the selfsame.[6] As Margaret Russett makes clear, Van Go "ultimately occupies the same fictional space as his fictional creator" (364). Van Go is always already within Monk. In his anger at Juanita Mae Jenkins, Monk hears himself speaking like Van Go: "Why fo you be axin" (*Erasure* 62). Both Monk and Van Go have been produced by the United States, both have been touched by modernity, and both have been packaged for television and/or fiction. The reader must contend with and interrogate the multiple worlds.

Discussing trace, "the origin of origin," as a way of showing the heterogeneity of the transcendental signified,

Jacques Derrida in *Of Grammatology* borrows and rerepresents Heidegger's concept of *under erasure.* "[T]he value of the transcendental arche . . . must make its necessity felt before letting itself be erased. The concept of arche-trace must comply with both *that necessity and that erasure*" (61, my emphasis). *Erasure* is not simply reversing the binary opposition between the middle-class, individualistic, erudite Monk and the urban, raw, primitive, thug-like Van Go. It is putting both under erasure, preserving and undoing the two. Both are inadequate yet necessary to describe the more general play of differences common to both Monk and Van Go. The result is that this "original" category or transcendental signified, "African American subjectivity" is, at base, heterogeneous. But as with Cudjoe, Wideman the character, and Caliban in Wideman's *Philadelphia Fire,* can Monk accept Van Go as one of his selves? Can he accept that which he hates? Can he accept a virtual subjectivity?

In *Erasure,* after the publication of *Fuck,* Monk/Stagg Leigh sends double signals, displaying his decentered, multiple subjectivity. When Monk, dressed as Leigh in dark glasses, meets the movie producer, Wiley Morgenstein, for lunch and Morgenstein wants "more street . . . black," Monk, performing the African American trickster folk hero Stagg Leigh and, again, changing his tone and attitude, says, "They say I killed a man with the leather awl of a Swiss army knife" (218). When he puts on his "dark glasses," he is becoming everything he hates. "Not only are we divided, harboring within 'ourselves' alterities we can sometimes hardly bear," writes Julia Kristeva, "but this polyphony gives us pleasure" (*Revolt* 63–64). More specifically, Monk is allowing himself to be racially marked for success. Becoming ambivalent, he refuses to submit completely to the stereotype that the movie producer expects. At lunch, Monk orders "the carrot and ginger soup. That's served cold, isn't it?" (*Erasure* 218). When Monk is asked by his agent, Yul, what he is going to do about appearing on the *Kenya Dunston Show* and being exposed, Monk, shifting to a distant third person, replies, "You mean what is Stagg Leigh going to do" (236). When Monk arrives at the studio and is offered makeup, Stagg Leigh "says, his voice flat, black. 'No makeup'" (246).

Stagg Leigh becomes one of the selves of Monk, where Thelonious, Monk, and Stagg Leigh move in and out of the same fluid subjectivity. "Thelonious and Monk and Stagg Leigh made the trip to New York together, on the same flight and, sadly, in the same seat" (237). Monk is performing and empathizing with the masculine African American outlaw, trickster Other. "Stagg Leigh had slipped away from me in my concern about discovery. I closed my eyes and conjured him again" (247). In slipping into "an actual condition of dual personalities" (247), Monk deconstructs the modern logocentric notion of a unified subject and rerepresents the subject as decentered or as, according to Foucault in *The Order of Things,* "explod[ing] in different directions" (346), which involves a constantly shifting identity. "So, I had managed to take myself, the writer, reconfigure myself, then disintegrate myself, leaving two bodies of work, two bodies, no boundaries yet walls everywhere" (*Erasure* 257). Here, subjectivity is constructed as plural, multiple, and polyphonic but ultimately, like Cudjoe's subjectivity in *Philadelphia Fire,* falls back on the masculine self-Other binary opposition, especially when it comes to women and gays.

Just as there is a version of Stagg Leigh in Monk, there is also a version of Van Go in Monk. Like Monk, Van Go in *My Pafology* also appears on television. At the end of his appearance on the *Kenya Dunston Show,* Monk says "egads I'm on television" (265). With Van Go saying "Look at me. I on TV" (131) at the end of his appearance on television, Monk repeats his character's words. Is it a parody at this moment or the same voice? The "egads" signifies that Monk is not subsumed by Leigh; both exist. But the line harks back more fully to Van Go. All the selves are present. Monk is Stagg Leigh and Van Go but also not Stagg Leigh and Van Go, standing firmly yet standing nowhere. He acts as two or three rather than one, and he incorporates differences into the felt sameness of existence. *Erasure* shows both that subjectivity is multiple and that it cannot be controlled or constructed by any one individual.

This idea that Monk's masculine subjectivity is plural and multiple continues and culminates at the ceremony of the Book Award, with Monk fighting the nomination and the eventual winning of *My Pafology* "in order to maintain his artistic integrity" (Gysin 76). "I had to defeat myself to save my self, my own identity" (*Erasure* 259). He attends the ceremony knowing that "he would be exposed" (262). When Stagg Leigh is called to the stage, Monk stands up and begins to approach the front of the room. As he approaches the stage, a small boy, perhaps Monk as a boy, "h[olds] up a mirror so that [he] could see [his] face and it [is] the face of Stagg Leigh" (264). Stagg Leigh informs Monk that he is not "free of illusion" (264), but after the television camera looks at him, Monk looks at the "mirror, still held by the boy. He held it by his thigh and [he] could only *imagine* the image the glass held" (265, my emphasis). This is the moment of Monk's conscious acknowledgment of himself as a plural, virtual subjectivity, witnessing himself as a trickster figure with many selves, as a being in flux and becoming. The quote raises the question of what a decentered multiple-selved individual sees in the mirror. Can it be represented? The mirror shifts position, and his identity becomes a mystery, both to himself and to the reader. Here identity/subjectivity is indeterminate. This moment shows that Monk's Eurocentric high-art renaissance man's passing subjectivity proves inadequate in a world where he is contaminated and swallowed up by other images of the African American. Multiple copies and images of him create a virtual subjectivity.

Thelonious "Monk" Ellison exists in the space of the two or three. Did Stagg Leigh emerge because Monk annihilates his "own presence," thereby asserting "the individuality of Stagg Leigh"? Or was it *My Pafology* itself that had "given him [Stagg Leigh] life" (248)? Here Monk stands both in presence and in representation. Representations of Monk are not simply less real than what they represent. They, to use the words of Thomas McEvilley in *Art & Otherness,* "are not . . . just *re*-presences, but presences. They are parts of [Monk]" (106). In performing the role of the dutiful son in his mother's final days, in performing the trickster Stagg Leigh on the phone, in person, before the Friends of Books Society, and on television, in echoing his creation Van Go, and in performing Stagg Leigh at the Book Award committee, the character Monk is able to take subjective positions or to reinvent himself into selves, presences, as long as they are of the masculine selfsame.

With the constitution of Monk's decentered subjectivity, reason has failed to reduce differences to unity. The fact that Monk and Stagg Leigh are the same person means that Stagg Leigh was always already there waiting to surface, that the dis-privilege of blackness and the tumultuous racial history of African Americans, as manifested in Stagg Leigh and Van Go, in the United States were a part of Monk and his repressed past. In this instance the binary opposition is overturned, and in overturning the binary opposition, *Erasure* makes the black male experience neither the middle-class Monk nor the ghetto Van Go but instead the intermixing and intermingling, the mélange, between both halves of the binary opposition. In synthesizing and intermingling Monk, Stagg Leigh, and Van Go, *Erasure* creates a new plurally dimensional trickster masculine identity/subjectivity of Monk that is outside of and challenging to existing narratives/binaries. Here, in plugging into aspects of the African American trickster folk hero Stagolee, *Erasure* reconfigures a different African American male subjectivity, thereby, like Charles Johnson and W. E. B. Du Bois did in their sociological research, opposing and pushing beyond the reduced U.S. representation of the African American. Everett in *Erasure* rerepresents black subjectivity in such a way that readers, New York publishing houses, mainstream reviewers, and the media cannot take it as being a unified representation of black life. For *Erasure,* the black male self, like the text with its different planes of meaning and worlds, is a nexus of meaning, with the ultimate subjectivity that emerges from the liminal spaces being created between the juxtaposed selves. This virtual, plural subjectivity is really the racially unmarked African American subjectivity in *Erasure,* and it is the one that is unsymbolized and therefore not represented in the American symbolic order. Here, Everett in *Erasure* has produced an African American male subjectivity that upsets the "way America wants to see black people," that, because it is plural, escapes racial categorization.

At the ceremony of the Book Award, Monk acknowledges but does not celebrate this (trickster) multiplicity within himself or within the category "African American male." Although he is a part of it, he, as a modern subject who has not embraced all of his selves, unlike the text, is not fully aware of thinking of subjectivity and the social real in terms of difference and plurality. He is not fully accepting of the idea that he is a subject constituted as a consequence of all kinds of exclusions, that he is a subject in process.

Although Monk becomes a trickster, decentered character who can adapt to the postmodern world, his growth or becoming is reduced to a proliferation of the selfsame. Heteropatriarchy reduces all things to a singular, "phallic" meaning. There is no equal relation between the same and the different (Other). Although *Erasure* creates fluidity and difference and play at the narrative, male subjective, author, and content levels as a way of challenging the universality of instrumental reason, there is no constant relation between the same and the different subjectivity. A poststructural feminist reading of the margins of the text shows that it resorts to binary logic with a violent hierarchy when it comes to sex and gender—a binary logic that entraps it in some of the modern values and structures that it is trying so desperately to escape/deconstruct/expose. *Erasure* assumes that it has grasped/mastered what is gender and sex, losing the power of sex and gender differences. The text operates within a gender code that is never opened up, never questioned, creating blind spots and preventing it from understanding/acknowledging its own discourse fully and the discourses of the Other.

With gender in *Erasure,* there are no "layers of logical play" (195); there is no multiplicity. For example, the text does not challenge the heteropatriarchy of Monk's narratives, which operate according to binary logic of self and Other, with the Other being sex and gender. It does not renounce the demands of a masculine self that wants to exert power over the Other. Writing in *The Newly Born Woman,* Hélène Cixous states "that there is no *invention* possible . . . without there being in the inventing subject an abundance of the other, of variety" (84). Yet in Monk's invented male subjects, we get no gender or sexual Other, no variety. They assume that there are fixed, stable ways of knowing and understanding sex and gender. They do not have the awareness of what feminist psychoanalyst Jessica Benjamin calls an "inter-subjective experience of space" (131), which allows recognition from subject to subject and is outside the world of the phallic.

In addition, *Erasure* shows how heteropatriarchal assumptions pervade even the most destabilizing narratives, not being fully aware of how structures of gender and sexual domination are embedded in psychic and social practices, structures, and processes. Because *Erasure*'s notion of differences and fluidity does not construct all aspects of the text, including gender and sexuality, it retraces previous modes of social domination. For example, Monk's relationship with women is mostly gaze and objectification. In defining women and sex as disassociated objects, he speaks in a language that originates in the male economy, which prevents him from empathizing with the feminine Other.

In fact, outside of his mother, Monk does not connect in a human and intimate way with women. At his sister's clinic in Southeast Washington, he is uncomfortable in the company of women. "I felt awkward, out of place, like I had so much of my life, like I didn't belong" (21). His dealings with Linda Mallory are mostly sexual with very little intimacy, feeling uncomfortable with her, and obviously wanting to control her aggressive sexual nature. When they meet for drinks at her hotel in Washington and he decides not to go back to her room for sex, he says, "I finished my scotch and became painfully aware that I had nothing to say to Linda" (12).

His potentially intimate relationship with beach neighbor Marilyn ends ostensibly because she thinks Jenkins's "book was a good story. . . . Lightweight stuff, but it was fun" (188). Marilyn has all of the attributes to be a different kind of black woman. She has grown up outside Boston with her brother and physician parents, gone to Vassar and then to Columbia for law, and now works as a federal defender for the Sentencing Guidelines Group. Her life is also defined outside of existing stereotypes. Yet Monk puts

Marilyn down and ends his relationship with her because he thinks that she is the stereotypical dumb black woman who reads *We's Lives in Da Ghetto.* Although Monk later blames himself for his outburst against Marilyn, he still does not develop Marilyn into a complex and interesting character. He does not deconstruct the binary opposition of intelligent Monk and dumb Marilyn. His "constitution seemed to make [him] an unsuitable candidate for the most basic of friendships, new or old, and romantic involvement seemed nearly ridiculous to [him]" (221). Monk has problems connecting with women.

Furthermore, despite his "interpersonal failures," Monk still operates out of a ready-made heteropatriarchal identity, functioning as a compulsory heterosexual patriarch and repressing "the other sex as a component" and his homosexual dimension that would make him "much richer, more various, stronger, and . . . very fragile" (Cixous and Clément, *Newly Born Woman* 84). He is a prisoner of the dominant, masculine representation. He, to use Luce Irigaray's words, cannot be "faithful to the reciprocity in touching-being touched" (*to be two* 23). He searches for himself within or against a masculine order that includes his grandfather, father, and uncle. For Monk, his existence "[r]eally appears as an always already cultural reality, linked to the individual and collective history of the masculine subject" (Irigaray, *je, tu, nous* 35).

Despite Monk's teenage insecurities, as an adult he becomes rational and methodical—key features of the heteropatriarch. Even his detective work and his search for self and identity are conducted in the mode of the Western heteropatriarchal quest narrative. His hobbies are fishing and working with wood—traditional masculine endeavors. Walking his sister to her office amid antiabortion picketers, he feels guilty for not being the "protective brother" (29). Working to become financially able, Monk takes care of his mother, his half sister, and Lorraine. In taking care of his mother in her final days, he becomes the "dutiful son, the good man, the family rock" (236). And although he becomes Rine the runner and performs several masculine selves, none of them take the risk of the Other or challenge or undermine their heteropatriarchal images. They are multiple representations of the selfsame.

Monk, as with Van Go, to use Cixous's words, has been "trained . . . to aim for glorious phallic monosexuality" (*Newly Born Woman* 86). Therefore, he never risks immersing himself into the unknown or grows into a concept of manhood/masculinity that allows him to know the Other, to express a range of complex emotions, competing passions and desires, or to engage his tender, feminine self, his sexualities outside the phallus, or his spiritual self. He never becomes aware of his own body. "The male subject's relation to his body," argues Irigaray in *je, tu, nous,* "to what it has given him, to nature, are yet to be developed" (35). His body remains what Jonathan Rutherford calls an "instrument to [his] will" (26). Monk holds steadfastly to a heteropatriarchal masculine notion of manhood, never relinquishing the borders of masculine consciousness and never becoming completely processed, remaining a constructed modern individual who represses differences. In short, and more to the point, Monk does not make an intervention into the politics of heteropatriarchal domination, never throwing it into crisis. *Erasure* uncritically accepts the Eurocentric modern notion of the masculine, making compulsory heterosexual masculinity beyond question. This heteropatriarchal masculinity not only oppresses/dominates women but also makes men—who insist on the primacy of the phallus—victims. There are many aspects/dimensions of men's existence that they cannot explore or experience. "Men's loss in phallocentrism," writes Hélène Cixous in *The Newly Born Woman,* "is different from but as serious as women" (83). But unlike Eurocentric modern white males, Monk cannot assume that he is the privileged center and the end of history. The white supremacy narrative and his marginal, racially marked status remind him constantly that he is not mastering the world, that there are social forces that render him invisible and unrecognizable.

Likewise, Monk constructs the sister, Lisa, and the mother, Ruth, as essential categories. There is no indication that they posses what Kristeva calls "'I is an other' and even several others" (*Revolt* 63). They are the embodiment of the maternal function, which reproduces the heteropatriarchy, with their subjectivities confining them to the intention of their names. Lisa is a devoted daughter who is divorced; she becomes the space of the professional, nurturing woman doctor. The reader never gets a sense of Lisa occupying subjective positions or as a lover who desires. In addition, Monk's mother, Ruth, fills the space of the dutiful, long-suffering wife. Her existence is inseparable from the fact that she was Dr. Ellison's wife. Neither of their constructions has differences or otherness. In constructing them, Monk does not give them "any abundance of irony or play with language or ideas" (214), leaving unchanged a binary masculine-feminine code that gives him his sense and privilege. In *Erasure,* women fill "the space" rather than occupy it. They do not live the space of their categories; they become the categories. In situating Lisa and Ruth in the margins of Monk's quest narrative, *Erasure,* to use Luce Irigaray's words from *Speculum,* "enjoins women . . . from ever imagining, fancying, re-representing, symbolizing, etc . . . [their] own relationship to beginning . . . a definitive prohibition against establishing one's own economy of the desire for origin" (83). In constructing the Other—women—without differences and play, *Erasure* incorporates it/them into a Eurocentric unitary language of culture.

Also, *Erasure* does *not* play with sexuality, thereby repressing/erasing the chaining movement of signifiers that describes not only the movement of meaning-constitution within language but also self-constitution. *Erasure* allows the heterosexual/homosexual binary to remain unturned. In discussing his brother Bill's homosexuality and in discussing the French-speaking "gay" men in the restaurant, Monk, who accuses his father of not knowing that "sexual preference" exists (45) and for referring derogatorily to gays as queens, again uses binary logic, which connotes subordination and domination rather than differences. "[T]he establishment of homosexuality as a separate category," argues Jeffrey Weeks in the "Preface" to *Homosexual Desire,* "goes hand in hand with its repression" (36). For Monk, who needs a category, Bill and the Frenchmen must be either heterosexual or homosexual. Assuming that the Frenchmen are homosexuals, Monk stereotypically comes to their aid because he thinks they are weak and therefore need protection. We have Monk guarding his compulsory heterosexuality when he cringes (ashamed) when Bill's lover calls him "darling" or when he sees Bill "walking hand in hand with another man. . . . What I really felt was envy. . . . I wanted to hold a hand too, albeit a girl's hand, but a hand nonetheless" (*Erasure* 45, 182). Even the construction of his brother is not one of sexual fluidity or hybridity or as someone who has competing passions that make him attractive to men and women, which is how he has lived, but as someone who is gay but has lied to his wife "for fifteen years" (50).

Monk's heteronormative value constructs gays, to use the words of Nancy Fraser and Alex Honneth, as being "subject to sexually specific forms of *status subordination*" (18). This is an injustice of misrecognition. Monk's response to gays is completely absent of the play, satire, irony, fluidity, and intermingling that dominate his attitude toward art, narrative, authorship, and heterosexual male characterization. In *Erasure,* we have no fluidity in sexuality and no intermingling between categories such as heterosexual and homosexual, men and women, words that remain stable, pinned-down meaning. *Erasure* participates in the crushing of the feminine of masculinity by the masculine. In constructing the Frenchmen and his brother as the homosexual Other, Monk leaves unchanged the binary heterosexual-homosexual code that gives him sexual/gender privilege and centeredness.

Before Monk can empathize, intermingle, know, and intermix with the Other—women, gays, and so on—or accept traces of the Other in himself, before he can define himself completely as processes, he has to *know* and experience his own Other, his femininity and his homosexuality. He would have to use the foreignness within him, which is the most spectacular incarnation of his otherness, as the source of his ethical connection with others. He would have to accept the separateness and difference of others while also identifying with them. Equality in differences requires the sharing of some characteristics by all, a characteristic that serves as the warrant for the claim of equality. In being completely closed, or blinded, to the Other, including the Other within, Monk amputates a part of himself.

Erasure includes a novel-within-a novel to create a mirror and a challenge to itself, presenting the novel as a galaxy of signifiers and defining heteropatriarchal, African American male subjectivity as plural, thereby defying racial categorization. After putting both narratives under erasure, *Erasure* ends with the Latin phrase "*hypotheses non fingo,*" which means "I theorize about only what I observe/see." Sir Isaac Newton used this phrase to decline to speculate on the origins of gravity, satisfying himself with merely proving its existence and consequences. Monk tells us that *My Pafology* is a constructed text. With this phrase, Everett/Monk tells us that *Erasure* is also constructed, reminding the reader of the Twain quote "*I could never tell a lie that anybody would doubt, nor a truth that anybody would believe*" at the beginning of *Erasure,* which leaves the text subjective, relative, and open. Yet *Erasure* feels incomplete because it never returns to or mentions the present journal moment in which it begins. At the end, it does not read like a text that is completed and left after the author's death.

Everett's *Erasure* points to an elsewhere, to a form of the novel and to a plural, heteropatriarchal, trickster, African American male subjectivity that exists outside the repressive and reductive norms of Western reason, allowing other metaphysical, social, subjective, and psychological dimensions to exist. But *Erasure* also demonstrates how Eurocentric postmoderns may criticize modern reason as a reason of terror but still practice the sacrificial violence of the myth of Eurocentric modernity by failing to engage *the reason of the Other.* Here, in using the word "Other," I am referring to women and gays. In leaving the male-Other hierarchy in place and in erasing differences in the Other, *Erasure* reproduces gender and sexual systems that generate relations of domination. Despite its attempt to unfasten traditional power dynamics, *Erasure* produces a narrow/limited conception of postmodernism, one whose truth claim is circumscribed by an unmarked African American male desire and, finally, one that accepts uncritically Eurocentric modern (male) notions of the masculine and of the Other.

— 4 —

Using Jazz Music and Aesthetics to Redescribe the African American in Toni Morrison's *Jazz*

Because they belong to a different epistemological system, certain African American cultural forms such as the blues and jazz challenge Enlightenment reason and the Eurocentric horizon of the novel. In offering definitions of life that are different from a middle-class, Eurocentric, Christian life, these cultural forms expose its limits and boundaries. Toni Morrison's *Jazz,* her only novel to do so overtly, uses these cultural forms to escape but not leave the Eurocentric paradigm of modernity, including the modern Western novel, which is a subsystem of Enlightenment reason. In this chapter, first, I will examine how *Jazz* takes a peripheral jazz music–jazz aesthetics paradigm, which has been defined as negative Other by mainstream American society, particularly in the 1920s, and reconfigures it to improvise on the conventions of the novel and, like Anna Julia Cooper in *A Voice From the South* and W. E. B. Du Bois in *The Souls of Black Folk,* to rerepresent an African American who is not deviant or devalued Other but instead has her own logic, agency, and distinct subjectivity, which can empathize with and accept the law of the Other. Second, I will show how Morrison in *Jazz* improvises on the form of the novel and on subjectivity but fails to improvise on gender and sexuality.

Toni Morrison's *Jazz,* published in 1992, assumes and plays with both of Enrique Dussel's modern paradigms—the Eurocentric and the planetary. Like Everett's *Erasure, Jazz* undermines instrumental reason—the reduction of the social world to "thing-like" equivalences—and other Enlightenment ideas as a way of redescribing the African American. But unlike some postmodern texts that do not offer a valid economic, political, or cultural alternative, *Jazz* offers southern black folk culture and a jazz/blues[1] urban lifestyle. The two function as alternatives to and/or as refuges from the dominant, capitalist, modern, middle-class, Christian American lifestyle, which is unbalanced and restrictive. But like some Eurocentric postmodern texts, *Jazz* offers southern black folk culture as being merely different in the postmodern sense, which does not include differences. *Jazz* also offers a jazz/blues urban lifestyle, which includes differences, for those individuals who are able to critique and/or work through the difficulties brought on by modern urban living, with jazz becoming the sign of planetary modernity. As a consequence, *Jazz,* on the one hand, is "only partially effective" in its postmodern critique of modernity, insofar as it remains "locked within the binary structure of the Eurocentric paradigm of modernity" that it seeks to contest (Dubey, "Contemporary African American Fiction" 159). This aspect of its postmodernism is Eurocentric. On the other hand, *Jazz* is quite effective in using a jazz/blues urban lifestyle to offer planetary postmodernity as a way of contesting Eurocentric modernity and of offering differences. *Jazz,* we can say, in playing off the Eurocentric and the planetary critiques of modernity, is simply blowing a jazz/blues tune that serves as a critique and an alternative to Eurocentric modernity.

Set in Harlem in the mid-1920s, *Jazz* deals not with the expected middle-class writers, artists, and musicians of the Harlem Renaissance but instead with the plight of the large numbers of poor and working-class African Americans in Harlem who migrated from the South. "I wanted to show how ordinary people lived and viewed that period [the 1920s] in history," says Morrison in an interview (Micucci 275). Approximately two million African Americans moved North during the Great Migrations (Lilienfeld 55). More specifically, the text is about the ordinary people of Harlem as represented by the blues lives of Joe and Violet Trace, transplanted Virginians who have lived in Harlem for almost twenty years. When the novel opens, both are in their fifties, and Joe has had a three-month affair with Dorcas, an eighteen-year-old girl who lives with one of his clients, as he tries to deal with a troubled loveless marriage and an absent mother. But Dorcas loses interest in him and ends the secret affair. Out of jealousy, Joe follows her to a party, where he shoots her as she dances with a younger man. Dorcas dies because she refuses to go to the hospital (*Jazz* 209). Violet, who cries the blues for her childlessness and bemoans the failure of her marriage, goes to Dorcas's funeral and tries to disfigure the face of her corpse. The summary of this blues story is mostly told on the first page, with the rest of *Jazz* retelling, revising, expanding, and ultimately transcending this blues story.

The historical backdrop for this unhappy triangle among Joe, Violet, and Dorcas is the Jazz Age, an age defined by African American culture, music, and literature, and the backdrop for the novel encompasses much of American and African American history. *Jazz* reaches from post–World War I Harlem back to the South and Reconstruction, recounting migration, sharecropping, town burnings in the South, economic hardships, and hopes. Discussing the migration of blacks from the rural South to urban centers in an exchange with Cornel West, Morrison states that "There was an enormous political shift in the lives of many, many black people post-Reconstruction, post–World War I. . . . Whole towns were wiped clean of black people, running from want, running anywhere mostly to cities" (Morrison and West 19). They end up in northern urban centers such as New York City.

Within *Jazz*'s historical backdrop, there is the structural apartheid-type racism in the South in the nineteenth century and Jim Crow laws. There are the segregated poor, middle, and upper-middle-class blacks in Baltimore, and in East St. Louis there are race riots. There is the migration of blacks from the rural South to cities, which, according to Dubey in *Signs and Cities*, "spawned fears of economic competition and social conflict" (132). The southern migrants brought with them the blues, Voodoo, and other African American musical and cultural forms, and these forms intermix and intermingle with existing American urban cultural and social forms. In the 1920s, black music adapts to and permeates the city. "Morrison clearly regards the music that reverberates throughout the novel," writes Andrew Scheiber, "as distinctly urban music, music that is the product of radical social change and cultural instability—in short a product of modernity, which in some ways differentiates it from the rural and vernacular blues taproot" (486). In the city, blacks face oppression due to economic exploitation, marginalization, cultural imperialism, and systematic violence, causing many of them to not survive and others to forget their relations to nature, the past, and a larger cosmos. There is the heady tempo and daring temper of black life in Harlem, along with disgruntled veterans returning from World War I, where they served in all-colored units, looking for their payday.

Told in a spiraling/circular/linear jazz/blues, collective, improvising ensemble where the presentation of narrative situations, events, and characters is one of improvisation, differences, and multiplicity, with Joe and Violet taking turns with the multifaceted narrator and improvising solos about their past in Virginia, *Jazz* is, according to Morrison, a "performance in which the musicians [narrator and characters] are on stage. And they know what they are doing, they rehearse (sometimes getting it wrong), but the performance is open to change" (Carabi 41). With each version or retelling of an event or situation, the narrator or a character adds additional information, thereby revising and expanding the event.

Although the issues of indeterminacies, fictive history, lack of closure, multiple subjectivity, and self-conscious narrative in *Jazz* are akin to the postmodern fiction that develops out of the critique of Dussel's Eurocentric paradigm of modernity, these same features also situate *Jazz* within the tradition of African American jazz music. Morrison uses African American music as her metaphor in creating and structuring her text. In an interview with Cornel West, Morrison states that she wants *Jazz,* in its construction of black life in Harlem, to "represent the anarchy, the originality, the improvisation, the practice, the anger, [and] the daring of the music. . . . But the point of the novel is not to re-render it [jazz]; it's to take from it its compositional qualities, its ferocity, its seduction, its temptation and the fact that it was so enormously complex" (Morrison and West 18–19). Also further discussing jazz as a model for writing in an interview with Nellie McKay, Morrison states:

> Classical music satisfies and closes. Black music does not do that. Jazz always keep you on edge. . . . There may be a long chord, but no final chord. And it agitates you. . . . There is something underneath [it] that is incomplete. There is always something else that you want from music. I want my books to be like that—because I want that feeling of something held in reserve and the sense that there is more. (155)

Discussing the spontaneity of Duke Ellington's jazz orchestra, Clark Terry says that Duke makes "the end of a song sound like it's going somewhere" (qtd. in Hentoff 146), avoiding the sense of closure or resolution. In the interview with Dana Micucci, Morrison speaks about jazz improvisation: "Jazz itself is one of the most vital artistic forms in the world. It symbolizes an incredible kind of improvisation, a freedom in which a great deal of risk is involved" (275). Time in jazz and blues works outside and inside the prescribed meters, existing all over the map. As light is both a particle and a wave, meter in jazz is circular and spiral; it is also linear at times. It is multiple, functioning within the parameters of the music as well as acts against it, a kind of war machine.

Morrison's *Jazz* uses jazz music and jazz aesthetics to improvise on the conventions of the traditional/realistic novel form and on the blues story of Violet, Joe, and Dorcas. The narrator alters particular features of the novel as she explores their maneuverability with features of jazz. The chapters are numberless and without titles. As in a musical score, writes Eusebio L. Rodrigues, *Jazz* "has been cut into unnumbered unequal sections, ten of them, divided by blank pages. . . . Each section is further cut into a number of unequal subsections" (246). Language is made to "syncopate, the printed words loosen up and begin to move, the syntax turns liquid and flows" (Rodrigues 247). Black vernacular blends harmoniously with standard English. *Jazz,* to use Morrison's words, "remove[s] the print-quality language to put back the oral quality, where intonation, volume, and gesture are all there" (Tate 126).

The style of *Jazz* reflects the sounds and rhythms of jazz, and the structure mirrors the patterns and configurations of jazz composition, with improvisation being central. On one level, to create a contradictory, multiple narrative voice that combines first-person limited narrator and third-person omniscient narrator is jazz because this combination "symbolizes an incredible kind of improvisation" (Micucci 275) and entails a freedom that involves a tremendous literary risk. As with bebop, the combination is "open in its defiance of conventions" (Gioia 277). On another level, we can say that *Jazz* draws upon jazz music as its "structuring principle." The novel is told as if it were playing a jazz composition. "A disembodied narrator slips easily and guilelessly from third-person all-knowingness to first-person lyricism, without ever relaxing its grip upon our imagination" (Gates 53–54).

In the jazz/blues ensemble, *Jazz* is also told by a contradictory, multifaceted, narrative voice that smashes/unmasks the rules, conventions, and expectations of the traditional novel. "So, when I was thinking of who was going to tell this story," Morrison states in an interview with Angels Carabi, "the idea of 'who owns jazz,' . . . came up. . . . I decided that the voice would be one of assumed knowledge, the voice that says 'I know everything.' This is a kind of dominant ownership: without sex, gender, or age" (41). The contradictory, multiple narrative voice in *Jazz* is "indeterminate: it is neither male nor female; neither young nor old; neither rich nor poor" (Gates 54), constantly shifting person, gender, sex, and narrative point of view. The voice is, to use Derrida's marker for the indication of overturning violent hierarchies, "both/and" (*Positions* 41).

Improvising on the narrative voice as it is "constantly adding, revising, inventing, shifting back and forth among various characters" (Grandt 304), *Jazz* gives us this contradictory, multiple narrative voice that is part limited narrator (character) and part third-person omniscient narrator, with both, as in a jazz performance, taking turns and telling the story. This narrative strategy reflects the egalitarian nature of jazz. First, there is the confiding, gossipy tone of the subjective and personified first person (character): "I know that woman. She used to live with a flock of birds on Lenox Avenue. Know her husband, too" (*Jazz* 3). This first-person narrative voice becomes personified, speaking personally and intimately about the city, and sympathizes with Dorcas's life as being unbearable. "And when I think about it, I know just how she felt," says the narrator (63).

Although it watches everyone and everything trying to figure them out, this first-person narrator (character), as in a jazz rehearsal, sometimes fails or gets it wrong. He/she does not know "whether she [Violet] sent the boyfriend away or whether he quit[s] her" (5). It speculates that the boyfriend may have come to feel that Violet's "gifts were poor measured against his sympathy for the brokenhearted man in the next room" (5). At the end of *Jazz,* the limited narrative voice incorrectly interprets Violet, Felice, and Joe as "a mirror image of Dorcas, Joe and Violet" (221). Also at the end of *Jazz,* this first-person limited narrative voice returns and, further undermining its authority and veracity, states: "I thought I knew them and wasn't worried that they didn't really know about me. Now it's clear why they contradicted me at every turn: they knew me all along. . . . They knew how little I could be counted on; how poorly, how shabbily my know-it-all self covered helplessness" (220). Finally, when the voice goes on to confess that it is lonely and longs above all for love, it says of Joe and Violet: "I envy them their public love. I myself have only known it in secret, shared it in secret and longed, aw longed to show it—to be able to say out loud what they have no need to say at all" (229). This first-person limited narrative voice (character) shows that it is human, fallible, and unreliable, challenging its and our desire for mastery of knowledge.

Second, improvising on the narrative voice, there is a capacious, all-knowing, objectively instructing voice of the third-person omniscient anonymous speaker: "The wave of black people running from want and violence crested in the

1870s; the '80s; the '90s but was a steady stream in 1906 when Joe and Violet joined it. Like the others, they were country people, but how soon country people forget" (33). Describing African American patterns of migration to the city, this third-person omniscient narrative voice states: "Some were slow about it and traveled from Georgia to Illinois, to the City, back to Georgia, out to San Diego and finally, shaking their heads, surrendered themselves to the City" (32). Later, discussing the rioters, this third-person omniscient narrator states: "Some said the rioters were disgruntled veterans who had fought in all-colored units, were refused the services of the YMCA, over there and over here, and came home to white violence more intense than when they enlisted" (57). In contrast to the subjective, personified first-person narrator, this third-person omniscient narrator is distant, objective, and omnipotent.

Caroline Rody argues that Morrison in *Jazz* plays with the convention of the omniscient speaker (621) by making it plural. In most (modern) literature, the omniscient narrator is a *naturalized* convention. It is all-knowing and all presence. But I argue that in *Jazz,* Morrison gives us a contradictory, multifaceted narrative voice that behaves like a jazz musician, taking turns and playing all of its parts, with the omniscient narrator being one of the parts. This multiple narrative voice and its various parts riff on the various situations and events in the text. Because its limited narrative voice (character) shows vulnerability and limitations, at the end the contradictory, multifaceted narrative voice is left without having mastered the characters, without a definitive conclusion. Thus, *Jazz* remains open-ended.

Finally, in the jazz ensemble, Violet's and Joe's rerememberances (solos) of the past emerge as improvised jazz solos, further contributing to the egalitarian nature of the jazz ensemble. Walking through the streets of the city, looking for Dorcas/Wild, and taking turns with the narrator, Joe tells the blues story of being born without a mother and being raised by Victory Williams's family. Then he tells of meeting Violet, of them getting married and living in Rome, and of their eventual move to the city. Likewise, going solo and taking turns with the narrator, Violet's early years in

Virginia are reremembered, including her suicide mother, Rose Dear; Vera Louise and Golden Gray; the visits by her grandmother, True Belle, from Baltimore; and her unsuccessful desire to have children.

Thus, it is the contradictory, multifaceted narrative voice, riffing from first-person limited to omniscient narrator that improvises on the situations, events, and characters, along with the reconstruction of the past through Violet's and Joe's memories, and constitutes the ensemble that narrates *Jazz*. All forms of presenting and narrating information in *Jazz* are subjective and relative. It is the pluralizing, problematizing, and humanizing of the contradictory, multifaceted narrative voice that have caused some critics to represent *Jazz* as postmodern.

Other critics identify other features in *Jazz* that deconstruct instrumental reason and other Enlightenment ideas and therefore allow them to represent the text as a critique of the Eurocentric paradigm of modernity, as postmodern. In "Traces of Derrida in Toni Morrison's *Jazz*," Philip Page argues that Morrison's published work is "infused with postmodern themes." For example, *Sula* is structured around the interplay between supposed "binary oppositions (such as Bottom/valley, white/black, male/female), and *Beloved* examines the necessary dangers of both memory and its repression" (55). But Page seizes on Derrida's concepts of trace and differance to speak postmodernly about subjectivities/characters in *Jazz*. Throughout Morrison's fiction, and particularly *Jazz*, subjectivities are caught in a flux of becoming. In their quests for viable identities, characters are compelled to negotiate solely within the white-black polarity. As a result, the exploration of roles and identities is both narrowed and skewed because the one pervasive and unyielding polarity of white-black displaces other possible sites of identification.

Morrison's characters have trouble, argues Page, developing a fulfilled self for lack of adequate relationships with parents, spouse, family, neighborhood, community, and/or society (55). For example, because Joe was deprived of his parents and therefore had to rely solely on himself, he exaggerates "the importance of self, to the exclusion of anything else" (55), changing identity seven times (as he searched for substitutes to make him whole) and creating a subjectivity of many selves. As in a jazz solo where each take is different, Joe constantly reinvents himself. The first time is when he goes to school and "had to have two names" but only had one. Naming himself, he tells "the teacher Joseph Trace" (*Jazz* 124). The second change occurs when he was taught to hunt and "was picked out and trained to be a man" (125). Without a father, Joe has to live independently and to be able to feed himself. A third change in identity happens for Joe when Vienna "burned to the ground" and he "met Violet" (126). They get married, set up housekeeping at Harlon Ricks's place, and start a life. Joe changes identity for a fourth time when he takes Violet to "Rome . . . and boarded the Southern Sky for a northern one" (127), beginning a new life in New York City. The move from West Fifty-third to Harlem constitutes a fifth change, the one Joe thinks is his "permanent self" (127). But Joe changes again when, during the riots of 1917, a white man rescues him. Then, two years later, Joe changes for the seventh time when he "danced in the street" as the colored soldiers marched in the streets of the city (Lewis, "Function of Jazz" 275). In a kind of Lacanian sense, Joe lives in a world that requires him to shift identities to accommodate different situations and places. This shifting identification plays with the idea of character development in the realistic novel. It also points to the inability of language to successfully represent subjectivity.

Likewise, when Violet is represented in language, she has a subjectivity that unfolds in the multiple. She is Violet to her husband, but in her community of Harlem, she becomes "Violent" as the star of Dorcas's funeral. There is Violet who wakes up and sees another one of her selves doing something. "But she does not see herself doing these things" (*Jazz* 22). There is also that other Violet who "walked about the City in her skin; peeped out through her eyes and saw other things. . . . Where she . . . noticed a child's cold wrist jutting out of a too-short, hand-me-down coat, *that* Violet slammed past a white woman into the seat of a trolly four minutes later" (89). As with Joe, Violet in *Jazz* is constructed as a multiple subject, as a subject who takes different subjective positions. For Violet, the self is conceived as an achievement of linguistic positioning that is always contextualized in concrete relations with other persons. She is a shifting and always changing intersection of complex, contradictory, and unfinished processes. In her conversation with Felice, Violet echoes this fluid self. Felice says, "[S]he talked like that. But I understand what she meant. About having another you inside that isn't anything like you" (208). Violet is represented as a multiple subject.

Furthermore, as in a jazz performance, Dorcas is also constructed as having multiple components to her subjectivity, representing different subjects for different people. Alice constructs Dorcas as someone who has a free sexual nature. After learning of Dorcas's affair with her husband, Violet defines her as "ugly. Outside and in" (205). Felice, who was her best friend and who thought she was "cold," thinks that Dorcas loved to live dangerously. "Everything was like a picture show to her, and she was the one on the railroad track, or the one trapped in the sheik's tent when it caught on fire" (202). Joe, who was in love with her, constructs another Dorcas. When Felice tells him that Dorcas was cold and that she "never saw her shed a tear about anything," Joe responds, "I did. You know the hard part of her; I saw the soft" (212). In *Jazz,* African American subjectivities are represented in multiple ways, which can be interpreted as improvised jazz or as postmodern. Like the subjectivities of Anna Julia Cooper and Charles Johnson, these jazz/postmodern African American subjectivities are uncoded in the American symbolic order or the Eurocentric paradigm of modernity/postmodernity.

In addition, there are also those moments when *Jazz* makes the reader aware of language as a discursive process and of its inability to *really* capture the real. When Joe is trying to make sense of his estrangement from Violet, he realizes that he could have told his friends, including Victory, but "what ever [he] said to them would be something near, but not the way it really was" (123). Language cannot accurately reflect his feelings. Also, after Golden Gray has constructed his story about meeting Wild in the ditch en route to his father's house, the narrator comments: "I know he is a hypocrite; that he is shaping a story for himself to tell somebody, to tell his father" (154). As in a jazz performance, the multifaceted narrator in *Jazz* exposes the imprecise process by which language is used to construct narrative and meaning.

Also, other scenes are built in this improvisational jazz mode, which adds, revises, and retells the blues story of Joe, Violet, Dorcas, and the other characters. When she is composing the Violet/Violet split, the narrator does jazz riffs on "*that* Violet" (90–96), improvising through riffs on the crazy, out-of-control Violet. We get a second kind of linguistic improvisation when Alice gives three riffs on her waiting for Violet's first visit to her house in February, after Dorcas's funeral (75–80). Each riff/version is incomplete, which keeps it open and raises additional questions. There is a sense that there is more. The second version/riff provides additional information, but it too leaves the reader with this sense of incompleteness and of wanting more. In this sense, we can discern how the jazz/blues version/riff on a particular event is never complete, demonstrating how social identities are not coherent. It, like postmodernism, is open-ended and continually becoming.

Likewise, the narrator and Joe take turns blowing/telling their version/riff of how Joe meets Violet (68, 122). We have the narrator giving his version/riff of the early Joe in Vesper County from Violet's perspective (106), and later we get Joe's longer version/riff of meeting Violet in Vesper County (123–26), adding what the young Violet sees in his "high-yellow skin instead of black" (97). Joe becomes a substitute for the white-looking Golden Gray. We get a version/riff of Rose Dear's mother, True Belle, returning from Baltimore to Rome in Vesper County (99) and a revised longer version/riff of True Belle returning. But in this second version, we learn that True Belle is Violet's grandmother (138), allowing for the continual renewal of True Belle's returning. As in a jam session, two or more narrative soloists alternately improvise on the same event, hoping to best the others. These riffs show how history/the social real is not some objective, coherent narrative but instead is subject to interpretation, questioning the veracity of "knowledge" and "its origins" (Lilienfeld 44).

In another instance, Joe and Violet have two different riffs on the photograph of Dorcas on the mantelpiece, creating a call-and-response. When the lonely Joe tiptoes into the living room and looks at Dorcas's picture, "the face stares at him without hope or regret and it is the absence of accusation. . . . Her lips don't turn down in judgment. Her face is calm generous and sweet" (12). If it is the angry Violet who tiptoes into the living room and observes Dorcas's picture, "The girl's face looks greedy, haughty and very lazy. The cream-at-the-top-of-the milkpail face of someone who will never work for anything; someone who picks up things lying on other people's dressers and is not embarrassed when found out" (12). The construction and meaning of Dorcas's picture is subjective and relative. As if in three different solos for the same note/situation, Joe, Dorcas, the narrator, and Felice do their versions/riffs on the affair between Joe and Dorcas. Each version/riff provides a different angle or variation on the affair/murder. Finally, thinking differences rather than binary logic, the clubwomen's response to Joe has a blues/jazz vision: he was "ridiculous and delicious and terrible" (70–71). In all these instances, there is a riff/improvisation upon each event as a jazz musician riffs on a standard composition. Each time the riff is repeated, the reader receives additional information, causing him or her to revise the truth of the riff. Just as some jazz chords are longer than others, certain of *Jazz*'s versions are longer. In each riff, we get the notion that representation of an object or an event cannot be grasped in language but that representation and meaning are always in flux and becoming.

Finally, the jazz improvisational mode manifests itself in Golden Gray's search for his black father, Hunter, and his encounter with the body of Wild (144, 149), who is with child. We get several versions/riffs of Golden Gray's arrival at Hunter's cabin. First, we have an omniscient narrator in the third person giving us Golden Gray's version (151–52), telling of him finding the body of Wild en route to locate and kill his father. It gives a detailed description of the objects in the cabin, later focusing on Wild and the potential sexual attraction that Golden Gray might have for her. "[T]here is nothing to prevent Golden Gray from believing that an exposed woman will explode in his arms, or worse, that he will, in hers" (153). But it is incomplete. Then we get Patty's son, Honor's, first-person version of Golden Gray's arrival at the house (155). In this version/riff, the black boy (Honor), who is not mentioned in Golden Gray's version, encounters Golden Gray coming down the steps of the cabin drunk. "He thought this whiteman, this drunken gent, was looking for Mr. Henry" (156). The three different solos/riffs by Golden Gray, the narrator, and Honor are "countering, subverting, expanding, and ultimately" attempting to topple each other (Grandt 309).

Later, we get a third-person narrative voice giving us Honor's version of the event (168). This version presents an external view of Golden Gray's presence at the cabin. Noting that it rained all day, Honor "later . . . told his mother that the whole cabin was rainbowed" (168). Viewing Golden Gray exiting the house, Honor "looked at his wet yellow hair and creamy skin . . . [and] thought a ghost had taken over the place. Then he realized he was looking at a whiteman" (168). Each version/riff of Golden Gray's arrival at Hunter's cabin provides relevant but additional information. It also raises additional questions. As in jazz chords, the riffs are incomplete, holding something in reserve and creating not closure but instead "the sense that there is more." Repetition, argues Gilles Deleuze in *Difference and Repetition,* is not the recurrence of the same thing over and over again; to repeat something is to begin again, to renew, to question, and to refuse to remain the same (2, 21). Here, representation is multiple and remains open-ended.

Jazz, in using jazz aesthetics to signify change and difference in the various events, themes, narrations, situations, and characters, creates Derridean play. This improvisational jazz aesthetic construction of events, characters, and social situations not only plays with Enlightenment reason and the idea of narrative unity, unified character development, hierarchy, and closure but also signifies a life/social reality that is multiple, heterogeneous, and open to contradictions and differences. It constantly renews and questions the representation of life/social reality. *Jazz* creates a more fluid social reality that overturns hierarchies and plugs into/incorporates mystery, chance, probability, and other nonrational dimensions of human life.

Furthermore, this kind of blues/jazz ensemble/mode of representing events and social reality undermines Western linearity. In *Jazz*, events are presented in this circular, spiraling, nonchronological, and, at times, linear fashion, where aspects of/different angles on information is repeated. For example, the reader witnesses the presence of the effects of Dorcas's photograph long before Violet visits Alice and Alice gives it to her "to get her out of the house" (82). We get riffs and consequences of Dorcas's death before we get actual accounts of her murder, which is "repeated over and over again by the ensemble" of characters and the narrator (Lewis, "Function of Jazz" 278). The narrative of Joe looking three times for his mother, Wild, alternates and collides with the narrative of him searching for Dorcas. Morrison's *Jazz* uses a postmodern/jazz mode "to undermine teleological development, rationalist epistemology, authorial mastery, and other features associated with the realistic novel" (Dubey, "Contemporary African American Fiction" 159) as it constructs the lives of ordinary blacks in Harlem.

In the whirling and exciting Harlem of the 1920s, the characters are caught up in the paradox of the city, including the hopes and possibilities, on the one hand, and a racially oppressive urban, modern life, on the other, and *Jazz* plays this paradox like a good jazz/blues tune. These characters are also caught up in an array of social, economic, cultural, and religious forces, not only in black music—a music "that begged and challenged each and every day. 'Come,' it said. 'Come and do wrong'" (*Jazz* 67)—but also in the African American religion Voodoo. Some use (Voodoo) "signs (the weather, the number, their own dreams)" to read social situations (9), to make sense out of the world. For example, when Dorcas is murdered, "[a] host of thoughtful people looked at the signs . . . and believed it was the commencement of all sorts of destruction. That the scandal was a message sent to warn the good and rip up the faithless" (9). In addition, other characters in Harlem are also caught up in their desire for the American Dream, progress, and the Protestant work ethic, which is in total contrast to the jazz/blues life that surrounds them. Finally, some are caught up in an emerging mass, modern, consumer American culture that objectifies and exploits them. Movies and magazines provide Harlemites with images of clothing, dress, and hairstyling and of European subjectivity/identity. Just as in a jazz/blues song, *Jazz* gives us an array of the people, the feelings, and the experiences—from the sad to the angry to the jealousy to the happy—in Harlem. Jazz music is everywhere. The pages of *Jazz,* argues Geta LeSeur, "are alive with the sights, sounds, colors, shouts, [and] touch of the pulse of city life" (21), giving us the possibilities and the failures.

In capturing the southern migration and the survival of poor and working-class blacks from the rural South to the urban North, especially to New York City, *Jazz* gives us "people [who] think they can do what they want and get away with it" (8). They arrive in the city thinking it is "better than perfect" (107). They come on a whim and surrender themselves to the city. "They came for a visit and forgot to go back to tall cotton or short. Discharged with or without honor, fired with or without severance, dispossessed with or without notice, they hung around for a while and then could not imagine themselves anywhere else" (32).

Once in the city, they are overcome by freedom, fascination, risk, and danger. "What they start to love is the way a person is in the City" (33), with the city becoming what they want it to be. In short, the city unleashes all kinds of unacknowledged and nonrecognized desires, curiosities, and fascinations, changing who they are.

In Harlem in the 1920s, everything a person wanted was right there, except education and the law.

> The church, the store, the party, the women, the men, the postbox (but no high schools), the furniture store, street newspaper vendors, the bootleg houses (but no banks), the beauty parlors, the barbershops, the juke joints, the ice wagons, the rag collectors, the pool halls, the open food markets, the number runner, and every club, organization, group, order, union, society, brotherhood, sisterhood or association imaginable. (10)

Harlem is a place "where you [could] find danger or be it; where you can fight till you drop and smile at the knife when it misses and when it doesn't" (11). It is a place where, due to a fast-pace life and overexposure, people grow old quickly, where there is "no such thing as midlife" (11). Harlem is a place where a bluesman positions himself "in the middle of the block to play a six-string guitar" (119). Syncopated jazz music suits this urban lifestyle, the throbbing beat of modern Harlem.

Although the city in the 1920s is devastating and alienating for some and trying for others, many, in a blues kind of way, did find ways to survive, to hope for the best but to expect the worst, to empower themselves, and to find social spaces that gave them psychological and social refuge from objectification, economic exploitation, cultural imperialism, and commodification. First, generally, in learning to survive, the people in Harlem care and support each other, enjoying the numbers. Culturally they have a mutual understanding of each other. Crowded into apartment buildings and wooden houses, when the snow shuts down the city, people "knock on each other's doors to see if anything is needed or can be had. A piece of soap? A little kerosene? Some fat, chicken or pork, to brace the soup one more time" (10). The Salem Women's Club and the National Negro Business League offer financial assistance to those in need. The clubwomen use their organization to create a nurturing community in the heart of the city, being "[h]ard workers for themselves and [for] anyone who needed them" (70). In the spring in the city, "people notice one another in the road; notice the strangers with whom they share aisles and tables and the space where intimate garments are laundered" (117). In addition, they made adjustments; they improvised life. This diverse array of people in Harlem, living according to their own narratives, reminds the reader of blues, jazz, and postmodernism.

Second, in Harlem there are the good-time blues women who were never socialized into the repressive, Freudian, heteropatriarchal narrative or in the strictures of the American Dream and therefore live according to their desires, intellects, and instincts. They are open and are sensitive to differences. Being free and light, they wait "for the ease, the space that need not be filled with anything other than the drift of their own thoughts" (16). Being nonjudgmental, they are "women who wake in the afternoon, pour gin in their tea and don't care what she [Violet] has done" (13–14), being good to Violet "when nobody else" is (84). These wise, inventive, and creative women, who own themselves, belong to the city, but we do not get a full exposé on them; they exist in the margins of the text.

Third, various other city dwellers successfully struggle to survive, with variant degrees. There are the armed black women who empowered themselves by learning to fight back and protect themselves. They are "dangerous and the less money they had the deadlier the weapon they chose" (77). Alice Manfred, Dorcas's guardian, worked once for a Swedish tailor who had a scar from his earlobe to the corner of his mouth, inflicted by an armed black woman who "cut [him] to the teeth" (77). The few exceptions of African Americans who survived their old age had "[a] last courtship full of smiles and little presents," or they had "the dedicated care of an old friend who might not make it through without them" (11). Sometimes "they concentrated on making sure the person they had shared their long lives with had cheerful company and the necessary things for the night" (11). Finally, there are also the men who used music to insulate themselves, albeit temporarily, from the ugliness of the city. These men are

> playing out their maple-sugar hearts, tapping it from four-hundred-year-old trees and letting it run down the trunk, wasting it because they didn't have a bucket to hold it and didn't want one either. They just wanted to let it run that day, slow if it wished, or fast, but a free run down trees bursting to give it up. . . . That's the way the young men on brass sounded that day. Sure of themselves, sure they were holy, standing up there on the rooftops, facing each other at first. (197)

Although many blacks found ways to survive the city, many suffered psychologically, and many failed. As with the blues, the good comes with the bad. As the Traces and other blacks arrive in the city after World War I, they want the American Dream but encounter poverty, discrimination, psychological dislocation and displacement, and exploitation. There is segregated residential housing and structural discrimination in jobs. Some of the women in Harlem in the 1920s have a sense of displacement and anger, surviving but living unhealthy lives, including the "little hungry girls acting like women. Not content with boys their own age, no, they want somebody old enough to be their father" (14). To avoid confronting their anger, most of the women in Harlem were in constant motion.

> They are busy and thinking of ways to be busier because such a space of nothing pressing to do would knock them down. . . . They filled their mind and hands with soap and repair and dicey confrontations because what is waiting for them, in a suddenly idle moment, is the seep of rage. (16)

The rhythm of jazz is suited for the quick pace of the Machine Age.

There are also the unarmed black women in the city who found ways to escape or displace their fears, vulnerabilities, and frailties, including those "who found protection in the church and the judging, angry God whose wrath in their behalf was too terrible to bear contemplation" (77). Unarmed black women also include "the ones who thought they did not need folded blades, packets of lye, shards of glass taped to their hands. Those who bought houses and hoarded money as protection and the means to purchase it. Those attached to armed men" (78). Finally, some unarmed black women in the city become causalities, including those who are "silent or crazy or dead" (78) and those who are physically, sexually, and emotionally abused. The newspaper headlines read:

> Man kills wife. Eight accused of rape dismissed. Women and girl victims of. Woman commits suicide. White attackers indicted. Five women caught. Woman says man beat. In jealous rage men. (74)

As specific examples, Joe and Violet represent ordinary struggling individuals who had left the South because the landowner wanted "soft money" (81) and ultimately ran them off the land. They dance excitedly into the city, where they are able to make money. "Her hip bones rubbed his thigh as they stood in the aisle unable to stop smiling. They weren't even there yet and already the City was speaking to them. They were dancing" (32). In the city, Violet, the daughter of a suicide, Rose Dear, and the granddaughter of a slave, True Belle, does "day work," and Joe, the son of Wild, "clean[s] fish at night." Next he waits tables, with it taking a while before he could get "hotel work" (81–82). Later he begins to sell Cleopatra beauty products door-to-door, and Violet gets into hairdressing, becoming an unlicensed beautician. By 1925, according to Joe, they "had made it" (129), but they have paid a human price. The city makes Violet "tighten up" (81), and Joe "changed once too often. Made [him]self new one time too many" (129). They lose control of their lives.

The conformist pressure of the city, or what Andrew Scheiber calls "the stresses of radical social and historical dislocations" (489), and their own personal demons begin to undermine their sense of self and their marriage, and they change. "[T]he music itself, as disseminated through the City's dance clubs and the nascent recording industry," argues Scheiber, "proves a diverting pleasure that severs generational linkages painstakingly maintained and restored in the years during and after slavery" (477). Violet, who has the potential to be or is an armed black woman, begins to display "cracks" or "public craziness" (22). Before she came to the city, she had this yearning "to be 'White. Light'" (208). And even before Joe's affair, Violet sits down in the streets because she is tired. It is also rumored that she stole a baby, obviously suffering from "mother hunger" as she reremembers and is haunted by her last *miscarried* child (Lewis, "Function of Jazz" 274). In the city, she looks for her identity in magazines such as *Collier's*, which possesses images that tell her white is normative and superior. Likewise, in the city, Joe changes. He ceases to be the "Virginia Joe Trace who carrie[s] a light inside him, whose shoulders [are] razor sharp and who look[s] at [Violet] with two-color eyes and never s[ees] anybody else" (*Jazz* 96). He spends much of his time in the city psychologically searching for his mother Wild. Deprived of the southern ritual space, ceremony, and opportunities for *ekstasis,* which they maintained during their early years in the city, Joe and Violet lose their orientation and health. Although Violet longs for "rest" and a "carefree afternoon to decide suddenly to go to the pictures, or just to sit with the birdcage and listen to the children play in the snow" (16), she never gets them. The two fall prey to the malaise of modernity: mental illness, personality disorder, affairs, depression and anxiety, and self-destructive behavior, developing troubled blues lives. In addition, when rationality takes over, when the acquisition of material things destroys cultural values, when personal issues remain unresolved, and when mind triumphs over the subtle levels of existence, the soul suffers and perishes.

Because of the pressure of the city, Violet and Joe change, with the reader never being able to pinpoint the origin of the change. Violet begins "sleeping with a doll in her arms" (129). As a result, she neglects Joe. She begins to take

> better care of her parrot then she does of [Joe]. Rest of the time, she's cooking pork [he] can't eat, or pressing hair [he] can't stand the smell of. Maybe that's the way it goes with people been married long as [they] have. But the quiet. . . . She don't hardly talk anymore, and [Joe] ain't allowed near her. (49)

But in a kind of spiraling jazz-line way, the reader learns later that it was Joe's neglect of Violet that prompts her to sleep with her doll. He develops a masculine subject-object relationship with Violet, saying, "I treated Violet like a piece of furniture you favor although it needed something every day to keep it steady and upright" (123). Even later, we are told that Violet participates by allowing herself to be reshaped by Joe's masculine subjectivity. "[H]e tells me when he doesn't like it. I never wear glasses when he is with me and I changed my laugh for him to one he like[s] better" (190). Now the marriage is broken, and the two are not communicating.

> Twenty years after Joe and Violet train-danced on into the City, they were still a couple but barely speaking to each other, let alone laughing together or acting like the ground was a dance-hall floor. Convinced that he alone remembers those days, and wants them back, aware of what it looked like but not at all of what it felt like, he coupled himself elsewhere. (36)

As a consequence of these changes, actions, and awarenesses, they grow apart. To survive psychologically, the two seek out other avenues for comfort and satisfaction. Joe wants to "lighten [his] life a little with a good lady" (49), becoming hungry for the "one thing everybody loses—young loving" (120). Therefore, he has an affair with the eighteen-year-old Dorcas, who is to fill the empty space created by Wild's "chief unmothering" (167). To punish Joe, Violet gets a boyfriend and lets him visit her at home. She capitulates to the conformist pressure of urban life by repressing her emotional and psychic life, thereby losing her sense of self as she slowly cracks psychologically. She is haunted by thoughts that what happened to her suicide mother Rose Dear, who threw herself into a narrow place, and Rose Dear's husband might happen to her and Joe and of the stories her grandmother told her about Golden Gray. Hers is a "life . . . splintered like a cheap windowpane" (197). "I messed up my own life," Violet later tells Felice. "Before I came North I made sense and so did the world" (207). But in their pursuit of jobs, material possessions, and middle-class respectability and in the guilt for being childless and wanting to be white, Violet has allowed New York City to change her, and Joe, in his failed attempt to maintain young love, to find Wild, pursues and murders Dorcas. Both Joe and Violet develop cases of the blues. Both are potential casualties of the city. But Joe and Violet would eventually reconfigure their lives, move beyond their troubled blues lives, and use jazz to reinvent themselves.

This was not the situation with the middle-class Christian Alice Manfred, who is an example of one of those ordinary persons who becomes alienated in the city, failing to survive. She is marginalized by black and white societies. Alice, whose husband ran off, leaving her "starving for blood" (86), resists the city and the objectification of her body by white men who "leaned out of motor cars with folded dollar bills peeping from their palms. It was where salesmen touched her and only her as though she were part of the goods they had condescended to sell her" (54). She fears the "cold black faces, speechless and unblinking because what they meant to say" (54). Alice is also made uncomfortable and rendered invisible by white women—including those who did and did not speak English—in stores who say to other white women in her presence "Don't sit there, honey, you never know what they have" (54) and/or who called her by her first name.

To cope with her alienation, fear, vulnerabilities, objectification, and a strict upbringing from which she rebelled, Alice internalizes mainstream American values of emotional repression, the Protestant work ethic, and Christian morality, thereby living a restricted life, making her the same as the American norm. For this, thinking in binary logic, she believes that she is better than the good-time women, whom she defines as different and less. She also internalizes mainstream America's cultural imperialistic reaction to jazz—believing that jazz has a savage spirit, which she blames for the rioters being in the street. "She knew from sermons and editorials that it wasn't real music—just colored folks' stuff: harmful, certainly; embarrassing, of course; but not real, not serious" (59). In the reactionary newspaper articles on jazz in the 1920s by Walter Kingsley, John R. McMahon, William Morrison Patterson, and Anne Shaw Faulkner, jazz is defined as a threat to Western civilization. For most of its critics, jazz's wildness is associated with the African American. With its African roots associated with violence, jazz was accused of bringing out man's "lower nature in a number of ways ranging from crime to suicide to the break-up of the home" (Leonard 36). As one critic writes in the *New York Times*, "Jazz is a relic of barbarism. It tends to 'unseat reason' by setting sensuality free, along with its allegedly lascivious side effects" (Leonard 36). Convinced that jazz represented a threat to the social and moral order, mainstream America tried to "keep jazz in its place and to impede its dissemination" (Lemke 62). Jazz was defined by mainstream society as something negative.

In internalizing this negative representation of jazz, Alice alienates herself from the life of Harlem in the 1920s, repressing the freedom and possibilities advocated by black music and the life force on the streets of Harlem. She is afraid of this music that "made you do unwise disorderly things. Just hearing it was like violating the law" (*Jazz* 58). Alice resists the "songs that used to start in the head and fill the heart [that] had dropped on down, down to places below the sash and the buckled belts" (56). She is able to hear "a complicated anger in it; something hostile that disguised itself as flourish and roaring seduction" (59). Finally, she resists to the end the music and the life that made her hold her hand in her apron pocket "to keep from smashing it through the glass pane to snatch the world in her fist and squeeze the life out of it for doing what it did and did and did to her and everybody else she knew or knew about" (59). She snuffs out the music because it agitates that repressed part of her that wants to live. She tries to raise her niece, Dorcas, "to keep the heart ignorant of the hips and the head in charge of both" (60), but Dorcas rebels. After Dorcas's murder, Alice moves back to Springfield, Massachusetts.

Although some blacks fail and others are able to survive and get on with their lives in the city, many still have a sense of loss and nostalgia for the rural southern folk black culture, one where blacks are connected to the land, animals, and nature. Salvation, at least psychologically, for many urban blacks in *Jazz* is in Joe's and particularly Violet's subjective memories of an almost idealized rural South and its folk culture. Despite its "postmodern skepticism," *Jazz,* argues Kimberly Chabot Davis, "also retains an African American and modernist political commitment to the crucial importance of deep cultural memory, of keeping the past alive in order to construct a better future" (75). As with

Sula and *Song of Solomon, Jazz* notes the loss encumbered upon African Americans as they left the rural South and migrated to the urban North in search of the future, the American Dream, and Enlightenment progress, where they are affected more directly by industrial capitalism and mass modern American culture.

In the city, the southern migrants forget and therefore become disconnected from their past, from nature. The migrants to the city must forget the past, argues Dubey in *Signs and Cities,* "in order to participate in the exchange system of commodity consumption" (138). Although these African Americans survive, they forget a lot, which includes forgetting "what loving other people was like" (*Jazz* 33). The members of the Dumfrey family come to the city "trying to sound like they ain't from Cottown" (19). These urban blacks forget nature, "little pebbly creeks and apple trees" (34), and they forget "a sun that used to slide up like the yolk of a good country egg, thick and red-orange at the bottom of the sky" (34). Some of these urban blacks who migrated from the South forget their connection to the past, to nature.

Others have this nostalgia for the South and nature. Joe struggles a long time with his loss of the memory of the South. He "tries to remember the way it was when he and Violet were young" (29). In Vesper County, Virginia, Joe "loved the woods" (106). In his nostalgia for the past, he can recall dates, events, purchases, activity, and even scenes about Vesper County, but "he has a tough time trying to catch what it felt like" (29). Violet acknowledges later that the person she has lost in the city and wants to regain is the person produced in the South. Although the hardworking clubwomen at Alice's house had their own community in the city, they still used the rural South as their frame of reference. They liked Joe's voice because

> it had a pitch, a note they heard only when they visited stubborn old folks who would not budge from their front yards and overworked fields to come to the City. It reminded them of men who wore hats to plow and to eat supper in; who blew into saucers

> of coffee, and held knives in their fists when they ate. (71)

Jazz offers the memory of the reconstructed periphery in Wild, Hunter, and early Joe and Violet. They embodied what some urban blacks desired: southern black folk culture. As with the good-time women in Harlem and with Joe and Violet in the city at the end of the novel, these are social spaces where African Americans have refuge from objectification and commodification, where they can escape supposedly reduced representation by the dominant society. These are also social spaces that allow the African American subject to connect to the otherness of the world, possessing an openness toward the transcendent in self and others.

Wild is defined as being different, a creature of nature that is primal and chaotic. She is nameless and does not speak, representing herself with archaic sounds: grunts, howls, laughter, and earth songs—she sings "the music the world makes . . . some combination of running water and wind in high trees" (176). Like other animals, she is unhoused; she is sweaty and dirty, living in the wilderness. Initially in *Jazz,* Wild enters language and the symbolic order through Golden Gray, the racially mixed son of Vera Louise and the "black boy" (140), whom we later learn is Henry Lestory, or Hunter. She is represented in multiple ways. Using binary logic, Golden Gray is trying to construct himself as white, openly displaying his self-hatred. When he gets down from his wagon and finds Wild's body, Golden Gray constructs her as Other than reason, as savage. "[T]he awful looking thing lying there in wet weeds was everything he was not" (149). When he enters Hunter's cabin, he "thinks first of his clothes, and not the woman" (151). As Other, Wild's exposed body threatens him. Therefore, he wants to stuff it "into the ticking along with the bits of rag, stitched shut to hide her visible lumps and moving parts" (153). Golden Gray represents Wild as a "thing" that does not belong to the same human species as he, despite the fact that the narrator keeps apologizing for him.

Thirteen years later, Hunter rerepresents Wild in language and the symbolic order, saying that Wild lived "not way off in the woods or even down in the riverbed, but somewhere in that cane field" (166). She did not stay in the house, nurse her baby, or learn "how to dress and talk to folks" (167). Incapable of making even the connection of motherhood with her child, her ontological difference is terrible and at the same time quite natural. Because she is defined as being close to nature, she becomes animal, with the redwings staying close to her. Hunter represents Wild as

> a simple-minded woman too silly to beg for a living. Too brain-blasted to do what the meanest sow managed: nurse what she birthed. . . . [She] orphaned her baby rather than nurse him or coddle him or stay in the house with him. . . . She was powerless, invisible, wastefully daft. (178, 179)

Andrea O'Reilly argues that Wild represents a primal, premodern, and primitive state, the "archetypal wild woman. . . . Her lexicon is specifically the primal, original 'language' of the body" (373). In not speaking and in not participating in the rituals of the social, Wild signifies Jacques Lacan's real, which is prior to the assumption of the symbolic. The "real is the impossible . . . that which is lacking in the symbolic order" (*Ecrits* x). If the signification of the real enters language and the symbolic order, is it still the real? Is Wild merely different in the postmodern sense? Does she *really* exist as a primal, original language outside the norms of Western history and rationality? Or is she an intermingling of the reasoned and the unreasoned?

The southern black rural culture is embodied in Henry Lestory, or Hunter, who is also defined in *Jazz* as being merely different, becoming one with the differential flows of life. He lives in a "cabin with a dirt floor" (151), which has two beds, one chair, a table, a fireplace, and a cookstove. In a precapitalist sense, Henry's cabin is a communal way station where "all country people were free to enter a lean-to . . . [to] take what they needed, leave what they could" (170). He is connected to the otherness of the world, which promotes psychic health. He, like Wild, is also constructed as being close to nature; he listens to "the music the world makes" (176). He is a tracker who reads trails. Hunter was the man "so expert in the woods he'd become a hunter's hunter" (168), communicating with other animals. Like Wild, Hunter relies on "redwings, those blue-black birds with the bolt of red on their wings" (176), as signals, surviving by hunting and fishing. This is the close-to-the-earth lifestyle that Joe has nostalgia for.

In assuming that Wild, Hunter, early Joe and Victory, and black folk culture are merely different in the postmodern sense, ensemble members Joe and Violet, in their riffs on the past, assume that southern black folk culture is not touched by modernity and capitalism. But this notion of modernity omits any reference to the peripheral weak capital that Wild, Hunter, early Joe, Victory, Violet, and rural southern black folk culture must use to compensate for the value (labor hours) they transfer to central capital. Within the national capitalist system, weak capital, argues Dussel in *The Invention of the Americas,* "increases excessively labor hours and augments absolute surplus value by heightening the intensity and rhythm of labor . . . and by disproportionately diminishing absolute and relative salaries. . . . All this occurs because peripheral capital must compensate for the value it transfers to central capital" (129). There is a dialectical relationship between rural and central capitalism.

For example, in the cotton crops of Palestine, Virginia, where people traveled twenty miles to pick cotton, "the pay was ten cents for young women, a quarter for men" (102). It was "nine dollars a bale" if you grew your own and "eleven dollars if you had a white friend to carry it up for pricing" (102–03). Rural southern blacks traveled all night in wagonloads, assembled at dawn, ate what was handed out, and shared the meadows and the stars with local people who saw no point that heightens "the intensity and rhythm of labor" (Dussel, *The Invention of the Americas* 129). Before she meets Joe and moves to the city, Violet works "the fields like everybody else" (30), earning $2.20 for three weeks of picking cotton. When Joe meets Violet, he is a "double-eyed nineteen-year-old who lived with an adopted family, worked gins and lumber and can and cotton and corn, who butchered when needed, plowed, fished, sold skins and game" (106). These minimum subsistence salaries of Violet, Joe, and other southern blacks are forms of capitalism and are linked to metropolitan capitalism. Peripheral capital compensates for the value that it transfers to central capital. The young Joe and Violet *are* touched by modernity.

Others in rural Virginia are also touched by modernity/capitalism. The fact that Wild lives on the "back part of the woods on a whiteman's farm" (176) makes her a part of capital. The cane field that Wild hides in and that burns belongs to peripheral, rural capitalism. The "short work at a sawmill in Bear" and the "steady work" that Hunter and Victory find in Goshen after the fire in the cane field belong to peripheral, rural capitalism (175). In hunting and selling foxes and other animals for his livelihood, Hunter is participating peripherally in the capitalist enterprise. On his way to Palestine after not being able to find his mother, Joe "took every job offered or heard about. Cut trees, cane; plowed till he could hardly lift his arms; plucked chickens and cotton; hauled lumber, grain, quarry rocks and stock" (179). These jobs belong to peripheral, rural capitalism. As Dubey in *Signs and Cities* concludes, "The conditions of an exchange economy shape human . . . relations even in the rural south" (143). So what kind of elsewhere does southern folk culture represent in *Jazz*?

In constructing Wild, Hunter, and early Joe, Violet, and Victory as well as southern black folk culture through memory, which is selective and subjective, as primitive, or as premodern, Joe, Violet, and the narrator in their retelling of the southern past neglect the systematic linkage between the central capital of industrial metropolitan society of the 1920s and peripheral, rural capitalism. Industrial capitalism subsumes living labor by offering minimum subsistence salaries to competing marginalized individuals such as Wild, Hunter, early Joe, early Violet, and other black folk individuals who must sell their labor at subhuman prices.

In viewing the peripheral world of Wild, Hunter, and early Joe, Violet, and Victory as well as black folk culture as a "passive spectator of a thematic that does not touch" modernity, "because it is a 'barbarian,' a 'pre-modern,' or simply, still in need of being 'modernized'" (Dussel, "Beyond" 17), rather than as a constitutive moment of modernity, the reconstructed past history of Joe, Violet, and the narrator in this instance views the crises of modernity (and the subsequent postmodern critique) solely within the centralized, urban white European–North American moment. Rather than affirm the periphery, *Jazz*'s periphery/rural southern black culture, as it is reconstructed through Joe and Violet's memories, is romanticized/otherized. They do not construct it as belonging to a complex historical situation. Joe and Violet's memories recall some of the personal stuff from the past but not the social and historical stuff. "The bad stuff. The things-nobody-could-help-stuff. The way everybody was then and there. Forget that. History is over" (7). "Violet's perception," writes Darryl Dickson-Carr, "becomes problematic, given the rural South's lack of simplicity" (175). Her perception fails to ascend or constructs these peripheral characters in the absence of the social and racial dehumanization and the hardship. Unlike in New York City, in rural Virginia we get the effects rather than the presence/manifestation of these oppressive social, racial, and economic forces on black life. For example, in the South some white men exoticize (and rape) black women bodies just as they do in New York City. But Violet's reconstructed past is silent on this southern sexual phenomenon. Also in the South, whites openly discriminate against and objectify blacks. But Violet's memories exclude this aspect of southern history. In short, Joe and Violet's reconstructed narratives in *Jazz* subordinate the social, racial, and historical reasons why, to use Morrison's phrase, "[w]hole [southern] towns were wiped clean of black people" (19). Although their narratives do give some of the economic reasons, they subjectivize and revise history.

But Wild, Hunter, early Joe and Victory, black folk culture, and the periphery are not simply the premodern. They are the "*other face,* the alterity, essential to modernity" (Dussel, *Inventions* 26). They interact and intermix with the values and definitions of capitalist American society, easily breaking out of the prison house of unreason and having bouts of reason. They exist in a dialectical relationship with the center and are "victims of modernity's irrational action in contradiction to its own rational ideal" (137). Only a planetary postmodernity will affirm and give subjectivity to black folk culture and the reason of the Other.

In addition to Joe, Violet, and the narrator romanticizing/otherizing rural black folk culture, the ensemble in *Jazz* has other blind spots. Despite the fact that its contradictory, multifaceted narrative voice comes in different person, gender, and sex, none of *Jazz*'s characters are fluid in gender and sexuality. *Jazz* does not improvise on sex and gender. The characters are constructed with difference subjectively but also as belonging to essential gender and sexual categories. For these characters, *Jazz* assumes that it has grasped what is sex and gender, that there are fixed, stable ways of knowing and understanding sex and gender, and therefore the text is losing the very power of gender and sexual differences. As with situations, the narrator, and events in *Jazz,* there is no play or improvising on the gender and sexuality of these characters. In addition, although the ensemble in *Jazz* provides difference at the narrative and subjective levels, it does not construct white males with difference. Whether they are members of the Klu Klux Klan in the South or the passengers in the cars in New York City objectifying black women, they are constructed monolithically. Finally, the ensemble in *Jazz* is completely silent on questions, aspirations, and desires that ordinary poor and working-class people in Harlem might have about school, education, and the law.

On the one hand, *Jazz,* through the retold memories of Violet, Joe, and others, provides the retreat to a romanticized/otherized past as the possible solution to the longings and yearnings of those urban blacks who have failed to achieve the American Dream. On the other hand, *Jazz* provides a jazz/blues urban lifestyle as a different, and perhaps contradictory, option/solution for those African Americans, such as the good-time women and later Joe and Violet, who hope for the best but are prepared for the worst, who critique, work through, and adjust to the pain, confusion, and violence of modern urban living. Unlike Cudjoe in Wideman's *Philadelphia Fire* and Monk in Everett's *Erasure,* Joe and Violet transform their lives, creating new values and new desires. This jazz/blues lifestyle challenges mainstream middle-class Christian life in Harlem and New York City.

Violet's relationship with Alice and the many conversations in Alice's home allow her to work through the situation and to grow and mature. From Alice, Violet wants to learn why her husband desires Dorcas and if she has to "take" Joe's infidelity, and from Violet, whose visits cause "something" to "open up" for Alice (83), Alice wants conversations about youth and misbehavior. With Violet's visits, Alice also receives "clarity" about her own relationship with life and men (83). Despite the initial reluctance by Alice, the two, who are the same age and have had similar problems with the men in their lives leaving or going astray, end up becoming friends, offering mutual support, understanding, and companionship for each other. They learn to laugh together. "[T]he women had become so easy with each other talk wasn't always necessary" (112). It is, to use Luce Irigaray's words, "a real rapport between two concrete individuals" (*Conversations* 13), between two subjects.

Violet emerges from the conversations fully aware that she has "messed up [her] life," that in her desire to participate in the exchange system of commodity consumption she has forgotten her life and has let Joe and life change her. Until this moment, Violet has been living and existing in accordance with the demands of the social. She had ceased to *imagine,* to improvise, thereby allowing her female nature to be reduced to the masculine becoming. Now, like a jazz musician, she knows that it is her life to improvise: "What's the world for if you can't make it up the way you want it? . . . 'Don't you want it to be something more than what it is'? If you don't [change the world], it will change you and it'll be your fault cause you let it. I let it. And messed up my life. . . . Forgot it was mine" (208). If she is to regain her life, Violet will have to look for it. In this realization, she moves beyond what Curtis White calls the "middle mind," the idea that there is "no thought from any quarter that is a threat to business as usual" (vi), to a state where she has the "capacity for critique and invention" (viii), reconnecting to the otherness of the world.

With Violet forcing him to face reality, Joe, as in a jazz tune, is also transformed in the text. After he murders Dorcas, he is thrown into solemnity and despair; he feels something. He learns by mourning his love for her for a long time. Dorcas was his "personal sweet—like candy" (*Jazz* 120), which is fine if you are young, a kid, but he is not young. Joe had been in the city for twenty years before he met Dorcas, but he has become emotionally arrested. He is "one of those men who stop somewhere around sixteen. Inside" (120). Although he has changed seven times, he has not lived and matured, for none of these changes prepare him for Dorcas. He shoots her because he was "[s]cared," not knowing "how to love anybody" (213). Unlike the old men, he has never known how to be "new and stay the same every day" (135). Because he has never messed with another woman and because he selects the young Dorcas to love, Joe thinks he is free, "free to do something wild" (120). But he is not free; this is the way the city spins him. He has to suffer, to experience heartbreak and loneliness—and know that the world does not come to an end—before he can understand and transcend his troubled life/the blues, before he can become a mature person. The experience with Dorcas makes Joe a more mature person. Now he and Violet are "working on it [their marriage]. Faster now, since [Felice] stopped by and told [them] what [she] did" (212).

Joe and Violet Trace are able to pick up the pieces of their lives after the murder, the affairs, and the pain and suffering and after they have reconnected with their memories of the South—Violet in her drugstore ruminations about the past and Joe as he wanders the streets of the city "on an icy day in January" (180), looking for Dorcas/Wild and reremembering his fragmented past. "Golden Gray, along with Henry Lestory, Rose Dear, and True Belle," writes Natalie Stillman-Webb, "haunts their [Joe's and Violet's] attempts to integrate their rural Southern past into their present lives and identities in Harlem" (337), reestablishing a viable community.

After they have worked through their feelings and emotions and have had a final conversation with the young Felice, Dorcas's friend who brings them food and music, the two begin to mend their lives. It is not a welding together of two into one. Communicating with each other again, they develop a "non-hierarchical" relationship that is "respectful of the needs and desires of each person" (Irigaray, *Conversations* 4). Staying at home, they figure "things out, telling each other those little personal stories they like to hear again and again" (223). Joe rediscovers the Other, Violet, as a subject beyond his universe of objects, and Violet perceives Joe as an Other, with a body but also with a world and an interiority that are specific to him. In addition, she comes to grips with that part of her that has internalized the grandmother's stories of Golden Gray (skin color and beauty) and reconnects to her own female nature. Violet, write Perry and Maddox, has "found a viable identity and has reconstructed her marriage" (65), or as Dubey says, Violet has "killed her object self and affirmed the 'me' that remains" (*Signs and Cities* 140). Both Violet and Joe maintain their civil identities and their individual desires while also maintaining an ever-changing relationship. As in a jam session, Joe and Violet play off each other. She continues to cook pork that he dislikes but tolerates. At the drugstore, she has her "vanilla malt" and he has his "cherry smash" (*Jazz* 223). She gives a dark, tragic riff ("People are mean"), and he comes back with a light, comic riff ("No. Comic is what they are") (*Jazz* 214). They both laugh. Joe and Violet, after she has exorcised "the racist discourses implicit in the stories of Golden Gray and vowed to be her own black self" again (Lai 600), are now able to listen and dance to this urban music. Felice states that

> Somebody in the house across the alley put a record on and the music floated in to us through the open window. Mr. Trace moved his head to the rhythm and his wife snapped her fingers in time. She did a little step in front of him and he smiled. By and by they were dancing. (*Jazz* 214)

In this scene, argues Nick Pici, *Jazz* "illustrates jazz music's marked powers of restoration" (26). Jazz music finds expression in the body of Joe and Violet, allowing them to move beyond or transcend the social and their troubled lives. It allows them to cast off the blues and to get back in touch with bodily sensations, or a sensual self, that exists outside of language and commercial culture. "Jazz allows the musician to instantly communicate exactly how he or she experiences life as it is felt," writes Wynton Marsalis in *Moving to Higher Ground,* "and the instant honesty of that revelation shocks listeners into sharing and experiencing that feeling, too" (8). Violet and Joe are using their "musculatures to *represent* music, modeling the most important features" of jazz patterns "by means of physical movements" (Jourdain 325). Unlike Alice and Dorcas, and as they were able to do upon taking their first train ride to the city, Violet and Joe, in dance, can give themselves to the openness and fluidity of the music with abandon.

Joe and Violet can live a jazz/blues urban life that is unrecognizable by public norms. By resisting the American Dream, the American-taught self-hatred, and Enlightenment reason, they explore the texture of life and consciousness in a new free-floating way, living more according to intellect, feeling, and desire. They develop freer personality types that challenge the sacrificial character structure needed to sustain modernity and capitalism. Joe does not want to be a white patriarch. "Joe copies neither the successful white man's visual appearance," writes Erika Spohrer, "nor his patriarchal claim to breadwinning status in the home" (83). Instead, Joe develops a new self, one that is not whole, as some critics contend, but instead is fluid and becoming. They are "[c]aught midway between was and must be. . . . [T]hey are the sound of snapping fingers under the sycamores lining the streets" (*Jazz* 226). Joe and Violet develop autonomy, dignity, and freedom from the demand of money. Joe finds work at "Paydirt, a speakeasy night job that lets him . . . run around with Violet in afternoon daylight" (222), working not for profit but for necessity. This shift in attitude toward work tacitly critiques capitalism, the Protestant work ethic, and their subsequent repression, commodification, and objectification. The two will do enough to survive and maintain their values of love, freedom, and happiness.

Violet and Joe live more in harmony with their bodies, busying themselves according to how they think and feel and developing a different kind of community in Harlem, with jazz music serving as a vehicle to join people together. They eat breakfast and then break routine and take "short naps whenever the body insists. . . . The rest of the day goes however they want it to," such as "fussing with the bird Violet bought" (223). Since Joe has to be at work at midnight, they cherish after-supper time, developing a friendship with Felice. If they did not play bid whist with Gistan and Stuck, or "promise to keep an eye out for somebody's children, or let Malvonne in to gossip," they play poker "just the two of them until it was time to go to bed" (224). With other members of their community, Joe and Violet improvise life, making it up as they go along.

Through jazz, Joe and Violet arrive at a symbolic life that includes reason within itself but also transcends reason in a movement toward mystery and unknowable reality. In the end, they enjoy an intersubjectivity not mired in the ethical and moral dilemma of Enlightenment middle-class interpersonal relations. They are extended across objects and worlds, connected to an otherness that they may not even know: "They are so under the covers because they don't have to look at themselves anymore; there is no stud's eye, no chippie glance to undo them. They are inward toward the other, bound and joined by carnival dolls and the steamers that sailed from ports they never saw" (228). They belong to a new day.

As a consequence of this symbolic life, Joe and Violet invent their own schedule, living arrangements, and environment, but most of all they play it by ear—the desired outcome being a feeling of being alive, human, and dangerous. They give themselves to the music and adapt to the ever-changing pace of Harlem. "Violet decided, and Joe agreed, nothing was left to love or need but music" (224). Like jazz music, their lives are always in a state of becoming. For Joe and Violet as well as Dorcas, as in postmodernism, subjectivity and life are composites, mixtures, processes rather than products. They are plural, fluid, multiple, open, and heterogeneous.

As a consequence of their growth and self-transformation, Joe and Violet will continue to have epistemic changes in their subjectivities. They are ones who are not on the order of strict rationalism. Here, I am referring to what Gayatri Spivak calls subject-formation that produces "the reflexive basis for self-conscious social agency" (Chakravorty 116). They find an urban symbolic life, one that will also accommodate the nonrational (nature), that welcomes the mystery and surprise back into their life, unleashing the tension, the power, the desire, and the spirit from within. They develop their own reason for existence and create oppositional values and a different way to think and be, escaping but not completely leaving modern Eurocentric values such as rationalism, progress, capitalism, the Protestant work ethic, moral and metaphysical idealism, and open up new horizons.

Becoming more open, mobile, curious, and spontaneous and responding to possible differences, they reestablish an attitude of reverence toward the whole of life, a sense of the sacred in the everyday, an openness toward the transcendent in self and others. They adjust to Harlem's complex call, integrating the jazz lifestyle into modern American life, welcoming jazz's vitality and improvisation, and living each day in a fresh, spontaneous way. They continue to become.

Providing two viable options/solutions—the urban and the rural—in its critique of modernity could be a paradox for *Jazz*. But if we interpret this paradox within jazz aesthetics, it could simply be *Jazz*, again, behaving like a jazz musician. The paradox—the idea of having incompatible/contradictory responses to the text's alienation and fragmentation—symbolizes improvisation, risk, multiplicity, and the defiance of conventions and expectations that are at the heart of a bebop/blues solo. This jazz/blues life signifies planetary postmodernity. In addition, the viable options are two of several places, as I have discussed earlier, where the African American can leave but not completely escape materialism, commodification, racism, and white supremacy and can be in touch with her or his desire and nature, the world. In *Jazz,* as Carter G. Woodson advocated in his discussion of black music in *The Mis-Education of the Negro,* Morrison takes a jazz aesthetic style, which has been defined as dangerous, barbaric, and operating below the belt, and then reconfigures it and allows Joe and Violet to transform themselves, to transcend their troubled blues lives, to presuppose a certain heteronomy, which does not presuppose servitude or subordination, and to live beyond the dictates of the strictures of Enlightenment reason.

Like Carter G. Woodson in *The Mis-Education of the Negro,* Toni Morrison in *Jazz* understands clearly how the reason (and subsequent stereotypes) of the Eurocentric paradigm of modernity has devalued the representation of African American life and existence. Critiquing this paradigm and the modern novel, Morrison in *Jazz,* like Woodson in *The Mis-Education of the Negro,* uses jazz aesthetics to challenge the conventions of the novel and to redescribe the African American where he or she has her own logic, agency, and distinct subjectivity. Morrison in *Jazz* envisions an African American life that is no longer bound by the rules of Enlightenment reason, producing a fluid, indeterminate, and open postmodern/jazz text. In using jazz as an alternative paradigm to the Eurocentric paradigm of modernity and in giving us multiple subjectivity, Morrison in *Jazz* counters the violence of the modern myth, which denies the subjectivity of the Other, and offers a reason of the Other.

— 5 —

Revolting to Sustain Psychic Life

Bonnie Greer's *Hanging by Her Teeth* and the Encounter with the Other

In the Eurocentric West, the black woman has been called many names, almost all of them negative: Sapphire, Auntie, Jezebel, Mammy, Aunt Jemima, Brown Sugar, and girl, among others. With her body so inscribed with other people's fears, fantasies, desires, and foreboding, how can she possibly know her name or speak? How can the marginalized and the body of the black woman have voice and representation when the only language available to her is the language of white supremacy and heteropatriarchy? How can the black woman involve herself in representation? Bonnie Greer, a playwright, critic, and political commentator who is based in London, is the author of two novels, *Hanging by Her Teeth* and *Entropy.* But it is Greer's blues novel *Hanging by Her Teeth* that seriously explores the condition of possibility for the black woman to achieve subjectivity, agency, history, and a questioning psychic life outside the racial, sexual, and patriarchal institutions and practices of the West. It is *Hanging by Her Teeth* that creates a female subjectivity that can go to the Other. Just as Charles Johnsons' *Shadow of the Plantation* focuses on nonnormative black folk culture, Greer's *Hanging by Her Teeth* explores how a black woman uses the blues and other African and African American cultural forms to revolt, to speak differently and equally, to redefine herself, to go elsewhere, and to escape the stereotypes of and the prescribed social positions for black women. According to the French feminist psychoanalyst Julia Kristeva in *The Sense and Non-Sense of Revolt,*

revolt serves to renew and sustain the life of the psyche. "[H]appiness exists only at the price of revolt. None of us has pleasure without confronting an obstacle, prohibition, authority, or law that allows us to realize ourselves as autonomous and free" (7). *Hanging by Her Teeth* demonstrates how writing has the audacity of permanent freedom, has the power of creation and transformation, allowing Greer to involve the black woman in her own rerepresentation.

Published in London in 1994, *Hanging by Her Teeth,* unlike other blues texts by African American women writers such as Gayl Jones's *Corregidora,* Kristin Hunter's *God Bless the Child,* Toni Morrison's *Sula,* and Jane Phillips's *Mojo Hand,* opposes Eurocentric and Afrocentric modernity's notions of Enlightenment reason, closure, progress, totalization, linearity, and heteropatriarchy. It also undermines any notion of black essentialism and plays with the conventions and expectations of the novel as a way of opening up the literary terrain, engaging the Other, revealing a myriad of potentials and possibilities, and reconceptualizing African American women's subjectivity. Unlike Wideman's *Philadelphia Fire* and Everett's *Erasure, Hanging by Her Teeth* has a femininity in its writing, what Hélène Cixous in *White Ink* calls a "style of behavior which is in relation to a libidinal economy, . . . the expenditure of the self, the relation to the other" (22). *Hanging by Her Teeth* is a writing that accepts the law of the Other.

Utilizing/plugging into peripheral/marginalized/repressed musical, cultural, mythical, and historical forms, knowledge, and discourses such as the blues, the black Virgin, nonrational African American folk wisdom/knowledge, Elegba (Esu) of the Yoruba pantheon, Voodoo, and Edgar Degas's paintings, particularly *Lala Au Cirque Fernando, Paris,* as oppositions, *Hanging by Her Teeth* challenges and unfastens traditional power dynamics by incorporating different and alternative bodies of knowledge and paradigms, reterritorializing language and opening itself up to the Other. These repressed or stigmatized bodies of knowledge challenge/disrupt the center/norm. *Hanging by Her Teeth* exhumes and remakes a repressed black woman ancestry or lineage that gives her agency, history, and distinct subjectivity, allowing her to think pluralistically. The novel offers an "alternative to the alienated other, the individual subject of late capitalism" that has been the subject of collective, modern narratives (Hutcheon 63).

The novel opens as Lorraine Williams, its heroine, an overweight, midforties African American who was born and raised in Chicago but currently lives as an expatriate in London, is serving as "the chaperone" to a group of black schoolgirls from London on a trip to Athens, Greece. On their first night there, Lorraine is drinking ouzo—a popular Greek anise-flavored liqueur that when drunk slowly for hours puts one "into another dimension" (3), into a profoundly calm state of mind where all is beautiful and life is fine. As she drinks ouzo, which causes her to hear, think, and remember too much, she reflects on her life. While lying in her bed staring up at the shadow on the ceiling and while walking through the streets of Athens, she encounters repressed processes and begins to think anxiously "about the past" (3), a past that is given to us in fragments and pieces. Lorraine wants to articulate in language who she is, to see her face, and the rummage through the past is to provide the opportunity. But she cannot. She will have to use the Other to catch a glimpse of her face or to know the self. For Lorraine, anxious thinking becomes a revelation, an exploration, an opening, a place of freedom. *Hanging by Her Teeth* ends with Lorraine again walking through the "winding streets" of Athens, anxiously rethinking her decision to "stop moving around" (3), to get married, and to stay put and "settle" down when she returns to London.

But between its beginning and closing, *Hanging by Her Teeth* gives us the already-made blues woman Lorraine as she looks back on her past "like a parade" (3), giving us the arduous journey she has traveled to become a blues woman, learning to think and live independently, sensually, and pluralistically; uncoercively rearranging her desires for her own future; and telling us how it made her who she is. As she lays in her hotel bed or walks down the streets of Athens, a little drunk on ouzo, occasionally looking in the mirror trying to catch a glimpse of her face, with her antennas up for the sound of the blues, which speaks to her inner feelings, woes, and desires, fully aware of her female blues ancestors and African and African American folk wisdom, and completely open and honest about her sexual needs, realities, and desires, Lorraine floats "in the sea of [her] own past" (5). She wants to capture the self in language. And as the reader contingently pieces together memories and images from her past, along with created myths about the past, the reader understands her actions in the present. At age fifteen, Lorraine learns from Paris, the most beautiful woman in the world who works in the "Rib Shack" in Chicago, that alcohol is "the true holy water, a thousand times more redemptive than what was in church" (76) but that you should never overdo it. Alcohol brings clarity and understanding and connects her to everyone and everything (especially when blues music is playing), causing the trees to sparkle and also causing a delight with all creation. "It was like the elevation of the golden monstrance at high Mass" (76). Drinking and listening to the blues, Lorraine, like her father, can hear "the music in the voices of the people around" her (77). As an African American expatriate in London, Lorraine, like her great-aunt Muriel, is suspended between the two worlds, between motion and stasis, between the same and the different (Other), where she lives, hanging by her teeth. Lorraine, to use the words of Julia Kristeva in *Strangers to Ourselves,* knows that she is not "unitary and glorious," for she has already discovered and accepted her "incoherences and abysses," in short her "'strangeness'" (2) from within.

Lorraine's past emerges randomly, selectively (there are gaps between the dates of the letters), in reverse, in fragmented and multiple discursive forms in several ways: through an anonymous letter to "To Whom It May Concern," which she writes to herself; through letters to her father, written and presented nonchronologically and in reversed order with a twenty-year-old gap because her mother told her he was dead; through letters from her father in Europe, which we never read and she does not read until after her mother's death; through notes and diary entries; through a magic cinema, which tells her everything she wants to know about her mother and father; through college files; and through fantasy sequences and a third-person omniscient narrative. The veracity of each form is weighed equally, with all possessing meaning. The various forms, genres, and versions make *Hanging by Her Teeth* a constantly shifting narrative that questions the structure and shows the limitation of many types of forms. The multiple forms indicate *Hanging by Her Teeth*'s unsuccessful struggle to master or pin down meaning, to represent truth/the self absolutely. Yet in these different forms/spaces and levels, Lorraine's unstoppable, naked life exists, the misreading and mishearing happen, setting the reader on the track of the mysteries of language and forcing us to take up a variety of reading positions.

These dispersed and fragmented forms undermine the traditional modern novel, which is a totalized, rationalized subsystem of the Enlightenment world-system. To give us a freer and more open literary form, *Hanging by Her Teeth* gives us a circular rather than a linear novel, ending where it begins, with a fragmented, dispersed interior. Also, in playing with the conventions of the novel, *Hanging by Her Teeth* disorientates, delights, and challenges the reader, forcing the reader to accept another way of moving through the text and revealing the full spectrum of potential and possibility within it.

The endless play of differences in *Hanging by Her Teeth* also displaces the notion of the center. These dispersed and fragmentary forms, which shift from the first person to the second person to the third person, in pointing to their fictiveness, disrupt the rules of totalization, move backward and forward, abandon cause and effect, and undermine the whole idea of linearity and centrality, whose structure negates certain kinds of experience, opening up the text to other kinds of intelligences or forms of speech. They create spaces between and within themselves for the Other—the repressed and new sexual, social, spiritual, and psychological dimensions, along with mystery, coincidence, and other nonrational elements—to emerge and to exist. These self-conscious forms intersect, interrelate, parallel, contradict, revise, and/or expand each other as they incorporate these other excluded or non-Western forms of speech, with the combination and intermingling, allowing new experiences, imaginings, and human dimensions to emerge. They also allow for the existence of a more fluid, multiple subjectivity in Lorraine, which thinks pluralistically.

These diverse self-conscious narratives, letters, forms, and discourses produce instability, which is radical and creative, showing that meaning/representation of events and situations is multiple and problematizing the whole idea of historical or personal representation. A crucial moment in the text is of Lorraine, at age fifteen, standing on the corner and getting into a white man's car. As in a jazz/blues mode, the scene is presented several times, and each time its meaning is different depending on the perspective. When Lorraine represents the incident in her November 25, 1968, letter to her father, she constructs it according to Cat-eye's observation, which insinuates that the act is sexual. Speaking to Elvira, Lorraine's mother, in Lorraine's presence, Cat-eye says, "That's why she got into that white man's car that day when she was hardly fifteen years old. I saw. I see everything" (35). When Lorraine rearticulates this same scene in the section called "the Other," she explains it in the context of her desire to escape her narrow life, wanting to know the Other, to know herself. It takes on a different meaning: She is standing on the corner "because there people [are] moving. They [are] going somewhere" (70), and she wants to go with them. In her letter of October 13, 1967, to her father, Lorraine provides another version of why she gets in the white man's car. "I just got in. I didn't think about the fact that he was a white man, or that somebody could've seen me, or that I could have been dead. I just did it" (40). Still, again, in her July 22, 1964, letter to her father, Lorraine's expanded version of what happened includes meeting Claude, who is lost, at the Rib Shack. She gets in his car to show him to a particular address. In this version she tells us, for the first time, that Claude, the white man, took her to a blues club. The repetition and "variations" in pitch and tone in the bridgeless retellings of the scene remind one of a blues song, with "the second line echoing the first, and I-IV-V chord progressions moving back and forth" (Davis, *History of the Blues* 29–30).

Also, in the various representations of the death of the blues singer Magic Al, there is multiple meanings/

representations, again problematizing the whole idea of complete representation. In the letter of July 22, 1964, to her father, Lorraine mentions Magic Al getting up to sing and falling over and dying. When he hits the floor, he knocks out his gold tooth, which she picks up and puts in her pocket. But a third-person narrative about "the day magic al died" gives a different version of his death, telling us that before watching Magic Al sing, Lorraine visits his room and has sex with him (87). Subsequently her felt sexual power within her body kills him, with his gold tooth being her homage. We discern the risky ways in which the real is produced.

Finally, another crucial scene in *Hanging by Her Teeth* also has multiple meanings, pointing to the difficulties of pinning down meaning. We get two different versions of the shattered mirror. In the note "Chicago 1956" written by Lorraine, we are told that Lorraine crosses the street to meet her father, who has been standing outside her school continuously for two weeks. He gives Lorraine a "mirror with tiny sea shells encircling it" (25). When she holds it to her face, it slips from her grasp and shatters at her father's feet, causing him to react by stepping away and picking up the shards and the frame. Then he puts them in his pocket, pulling his "hat down deeper over his eyes" (25). In shading his eyes, he shades hers as well. The repeat of the scene in Lorraine's film has Lorraine clumsily dropping the mirror, which shatters into a million pieces. The father, Oswald Williams, reacts by getting in his car and driving away out of her life. By giving us two or three versions of the same situations, *Hanging by Her Teeth,* like a blues tune, unmasks the illusion that meaning can be mastered through interpretation and language, forcing the reader to accept the idea that truth/meaning is provisional and contingent. More important, *Hanging by Her Teeth* structurally undermines the traditional novel by organizing multidimensionally and thinking pluralistically.

To assist in further opening up the narrative and Lorraine's subjectivity to otherness and differences, *Hanging by Her Teeth* exhumes from the periphery/margin certain cultural forms or creates imaginary worlds. Because these forms assume different logics and/or definitions of life, they show the limits and boundaries of Enlightenment reason, providing Lorraine with other models, possibilities, and alternatives as she ferrets out a decentered, fluid, female subjectivity, escaping but not leaving heteropatriarchy, racism, black essentialism, and sexism. For example, the section called "the magic cinema," which is "a place where it would be possible to see events that happened before our time, events that for better or worse irrevocably shaped us" (52), provides Lorraine with a female model to escape from the stifling rigidity of the patriarchy and middle-class respectability, to learn to think pluralistically. In this imaginary movie, Lorraine sees her mother examine the paintings of Edgar Degas, especially *Lala Au Cirque Fernando, Paris,* the black acrobat so strong that she could hang by her teeth. As Elvira asks what it would be like to hang above the world, Lorraine watches as Elvira "dream[s] she [is] Lala. Not only the seen, but because of her elevations, the seer. The power of the seer. The power of Degas. The power of a painter" (59). As a seer, Elvira can see all of life.

Lorraine hears another version of Miss Lala from her Auntie Muriel. Sitting in Auntie Muriel's lap as she tells Lorraine about the circus, Lorraine "could see all the people watching her [Auntie Muriel] as she hung by her teeth, twirling around and around, holding those burning torches in her hands. I [Lorraine] wanted to do that so much, be so high up that I could see everything, all at one time" (37). Here, the social real mingles with the imaginary to expand options in the textual real. In bringing different, incompatible definitions/models together, the text unleashes new imaginings and invents new possibilities of life. The movie and Auntie Muriel's story provide Lorraine with female ancestral contexts to reimagine and redescribe her life, teaching her how to escape being colonized by closed, reductive, and repressive systems.

In another example, in the movie, the Yoruba Elegba (Esu), the god of the crossroads, sometimes known as the Devil who delights in playing pranks on the unwary, grants Oswald Williams's father a telepathic vision: "the sight of his granddaughter walking through a leafy green park. She was grownup and carrying the pieces of a shattered mirror in her hand, her feet barefoot and bleeding, her eyes clouded over as if she were blind" (54). As the Devil and the blues itself, Elgeba is a part of the world's cosmology, being as much a part of life as God. The Devil Paris also does good: she warns Lorraine against drinking too much alcohol and is also quite protective of Lorraine. The movie provides Lorraine with another model for redefining the social real. Later as a college student, Lorraine, traveling on the train in Chicago to see the play *Hair,* uses the Yoruba Elegba to reimagine a black woman with the Bible into Yemoja the mother, queen of the goddesses, to reconceptualize the drunken man with his piercing eyes into Elegba, the trickster, the Guardian-at-the-Threshold, the Devil-at-the-Crossroads, the blues itself (101–02). In this reconfiguration and reconceptualization, she is able to redefine this man and woman outside the existing norm, which defines them negatively.

In this random, selective, and nonchronological recollection of her life, Lorraine points to a picture of herself when she is five years old. In it she is hanging over a branch of a large tree, with her parents kissing underneath. Everyone looks so happy. At this moment, she "knew exactly who [she is]" (29). When she is ten years old, her father gives her a shiny foil box with a mirror in it, which slips and shatters. Lorraine cannot see her own reflection in the mirror, with her identity being her father's daughter. Looking in the mirror, one can imagine a place "far away from the drudgery and boredom of life" (53), with the shattered mirror putting her on the search for the Lacanian imaginary stage, her father, and her life.

In the "Mirror Stage," the French psychoanalyst Jacques Lacan discusses what happens when the child looks into the mirror and sees a coherent face that she accepts as her identity. For Lacan, the mirror stage signals the child's entrance into language and the patriarchal symbolic order, where the father is the law (*Ecrits* 2–5). In dropping the mirror, Lorraine does a reversal/rejection of the Lacanian mirror stage, becoming fragmented and identity-less, as she searches for the unity and wholeness or the m(other) that characterizes Lacan's imaginary stage. Absent of an identity or image of self that is submitted to law, but feeling that she should have one, she spends much of her life searching for glimpses of her face/herself in mirrors in all kinds of situations. Ultimately, she thinks she is searching for her father, hoping that he "would return the face she could not see, return it to her in a blinding white light of recognition, of benediction" (*Hanging by Her Teeth* 133).

From the various discursive narratives and forms but especially from the invented movie "oswald and elvira: the movie," you can provisionally and contingently piece together the lives of Lorraine's parents. Her parents' marriage is one between the father, Oswald Williams, the nomadic bluesman, and Elvira Taylor, the "preacher woman," with Lorraine caught hanging between the two. The marriage embodies the classic encounter between the nomadic and the religious, movement and stasis. Initially Elvira is a blues woman, having the blues all around her. Watching the paintings of Degas, she becomes fascinated by *Lala Au Cinque Fernando, Paris,* and the power of the seer, dreaming of becoming a great painter. But her father, observing her interest in painting, insists that Elvira "spend more time with the Bible. She was destroying his reputation by her failure to attend service" (59). Elvira thinks that by getting married, she can escape the wrath of her father's stifling religion. Meeting Oswald in Chicago, she asks him to marry her, praying that he would "take her away to Paris where she could paint" (60). She loves the life that Oswald lives on Maxwell Street, the heart of the blues community in Chicago, and she knows all the blues singers. She comes to feel at home in the blues milieu, associating and befriending up-and-coming blues women singers such as Millie.

But Elvira takes bluesman Sonny Boy Williamson being stabbed to death with an ice pick as "a message to her. She had strayed too far. She had gone to the Devil, and away from God" (63). She vows that night to dedicate her life and her daughter's life to God, becoming religiously dogmatic. Therefore, exactly one day after Sonny Boy's funeral, Elvira destroys her blues records, pours her paint down the toilet, and becomes a church deacon, desiring to lead her people away from sin. She rejects everything worldly and secular in her life except the small box she kept hidden. The British royal family, not Africa, becomes her external symbol. Henceforth she would suspend her life, becoming a totally stabilized individual. Writing in *A Thousand Plateaus,* Deleuze and Guattari argue that religion, which is absolute, is a piece in the state apparatus. "The absolute of religion is essentially a horizon that encompasses, and, if the absolute itself appears at a particular place, it does so in order to establish a solid and stable center for the global" (382). In her "world of order and knowingness, and surrender" (*Hanging by Her Teeth* 7), Elvira allows no wander or search, establishing "a solid and stable center," shutting down the complex flow of desire, and causing herself to be enormously unhappy (*A Thousand Plateaus* 382). Since her life is taken and caged, it is *less* true, having lost what is life itself, "which is always in the process of seething, of emitting, of transmitting itself" (Cixous, *Hélène Cixous rootprints* 4). Elvira's failure to successfully revolt is connected to an underdeveloped subjectivity. When Elvira is most depressed or in despair, she buys whiskey she does not drink and sings the blues, which signifies her spiritual anxiety driving her religious dogma.

The father, on the other hand, is a nomad, a wandering bluesman who listens to all kinds of sound. "His uncle told him that if he listened well and listened hard, he could hear the voices of the river goddesses Yemanja, and Oshun" (*Hanging by Her Teeth* 52). For his entire life, he will not follow in the "illustrious footsteps of his father and his uncle, prophets renowned for their wisdom" (53). After the death of his mother, Oswald enters the army, where he discovers clarity and understanding in playing the blues. After the army, back in Chicago, he takes a job as a sleeping car porter, which keeps him on the move. In Chicago he also meets Elvira, who is "wide-eyed and beautiful. She had the blues all around her" (55). He is given second sight and has a telepathic vision of his own daughter, the child who would be born to them. After Elvira becomes a deacon and Lorraine is born, Oswald is away from home off and on for the next five years, disappearing permanently except for the blues records he leaves behind and the visit he makes to Lorraine's school when she is ten years old. Except for one phone call and several sightings, Oswald is not seen again until Lorraine tracks him to a park in London years later. He has been constantly on the move from one point to another. Since religion/the state repels the nomad, Lorraine and Oswald cannot get along. "It is a vital concern of every State," argue Deleuze and Guattari, "not only to vanquish nomadism but to . . . establish a zone of rights over an entire 'exterior,' over all of the flows" (*A Thousand Plateaus* 385). But Lorraine is left hanging between the two worlds of her parents.

A second crucial moment recalled in Lorraine's young life comes with her entrance into Catholic school. Elvira sends Lorraine to a convent school "so that she could get the best education you can. There's nothing else a poor Negro mother can do when she wants the best for her child" (*Hanging by Her Teeth* 20). Elvira wants Lorraine socialized "to blend in," to become the normative selfsame, even as she admits that she is "special" (20). But the restrictive Catholic school shuts down her desires, causing her to suffocate. I would like to use Gilles Deleuze and Felix Guattari's notion of "desiring machine" to discuss and contextualize the repression of Lorraine's desires. In *Anti-Oedipus,* Deleuze and Guattari argue that the body, or one's subjectivity, is not unified, rational, and expressive. Rather, it consists of desiring machines/nomads that are in a constant process of becoming and transformation:

> Desiring machines are binary machines, obeying a binary law or set of rules governing associations: one machine is always coupled with another. The productive synthesis, the production of production, is inherently connective in nature. . . . Desire constantly couples continuous flows and partial objects that are by nature fragmentary and fragmented. Desire causes the current to flow, itself flows in turn, and breaks the flow. (Deleuze and Guattari, *Anti-Oedipus* 5)

Desire is the constant production of affective and libidinal energy generated by the unconscious, which is mechanic and productive, in various types of syntheses. Modern forms of identity and stasis repress desire, which is decentered, fragmented, and dynamic in nature. Desire "operates in the domain of free syntheses where everything is possible," running in discontinuous fluxes and "break-flows," always making connections with objects and other desiring machines (54). Lorraine comes to live in the space in between repressive, stable social forms and identities and the desiring machine, the complex flow of desires. She learns, to use the words of Irigaray in *Conversations,* "to coexist in difference" (81).

Thus, when a nun catches Lorraine playing with her petticoat underneath her white Communion dress, she "slaps her hand, and pulls the scratchy slip down over her knees" (*Hanging by Her Teeth* 19). Putting her hand under her dress, argues Jeana DelRosso, Lorraine "ventures into the taboo territory of autoeroticism that the church forbids" (32), a site of Lorraine's repressed sexual desires. Enforcing the church's edict on women sexuality, the nun shuts down Lorraine's sexual desires. Feeling tight in the modern suits of the Catholic Church and of black middle-class respectability (she began to gain weight, so her mother made her wear a girdle; her body is deodorized; and her hair is straightened), Lorraine's desiring machines are smothered, and she feels the world closing in on her:

> Something was closing around her. She could see it in the few black girls who attended her school. It was the Mantle of Respectability . . . She, along with the others, was the product of a dream. They were expected to carry a race on their back, expected to honor their history, to be better than any black woman who had gone before. There was no questioning this. Only death or madness could liberate her from her destiny. (*Hanging by Her Teeth* 69)

If she remains a good soldier, life would be easy: all she has to do is play the expected role, be "a part of the Great Plan, look thirty at twenty, . . . marry respectably, then eventually take over her mother's Tabernacle. And she would surely disappear, not only to the world, but to herself" (69–70), erasing her individuality and suppressing her father's blues genes.

But Lorraine decides not to disappear and instead to revolt against these repressive, closed systems, against her "bourgeois nightmare of black suburbia" (11), forming her subjectivity. For Kristeva, "revolt is a very deep movement of discontent, anxiety and anguish" (*Revolt* 99), referring to a state of permanent questioning, of transformation, change, and endless probing of appearances and becoming the essential gesture in the constitution of individuality. The Catholic Church and this essentialized middle-class African American dream police Lorraine's and others' discontinuous fluxes and break-flows, pushing these flows and fluxes into the unconscious (secrets) and subordinating their subjectivities to the laws and strictures of the church and the dream. Lorraine is frustrated and anguished because she is about to lose her sense of self.

At fifteen years of age, Lorraine's primary instinct and desire are to revolt, but she does not "understand the thing in her that urged her to move on" (70), to rebel, that causes her to stand on the corner because people are moving. They are "going somewhere. Somewhere else" (70), and she wants to follow them, to let go of all sense of familiarity and to go to the foreign parts of the self. She wants to know the Other, for how could anyone "know themselves unless they knew The Other. And she want[s] to know herself" (70). One cannot know what one does not know, and an Other is required for exposure to such knowledge. For Hélène Cixous, the Other is *everything*. "The other in all his or her forms gives me *I*. It is on the occasion of the other that *I* catch sight of *me*; or that *I* catch *me* at: reacting, choosing, refusing, [and] accepting. It is the other who makes my portrait. Always" (Cixous, *Hélène Cixous rootprints* 13). Much of what Lorraine is supposed to be, or think, is provided for and kindled by the Other. In short, Lorraine's identity is founded on otherness and difference.

The idea of pursuing the Other becomes a catalyst for the transformation of the self, makes her become alive. In *What We Owe to Each Other,* Thomas M. Scanlon considers knowing the Other as "the idea of a reason as primitive" (76). It is not problematic: it is the original ethical constellation. This reason is what Emmanuel Levinas in *Totality and Infinity* calls "the first philosophy": you should not kill the Other (79). According to Levinas, the "Face" is how others make moral claims upon us. "To respond to the face, to understand its meaning," interprets Judith Butler of Levinas's notion of the face, "means to be awaken to what is precarious in another life or, rather, the precariousness of life itself" (134). The Other *facing* me makes me responsible for him or her. It is the subject's desire or ability to pertain to the Other, argues Peperzak in *To the Other,* that allows him to be defined as a "living being that is reasonable" (26). Connections with the Other enhance and clarify life. Lorraine wants to know the Other.

At almost fifteen, Lorraine's desire to know or to empathize with the Other is sparked when she moves to the suburb with her mother. In this secretive, quiet community, young white males explode through the community in souped-up cars, throwing rocks at their window. With her mother asking her to pray for them, Lorraine wonders if they prayed for her. Therefore, she decides to "spend her life crusading against these blond barbarians who thought themselves the center of everything" (*Hanging by Her Teeth* 67). But her focus on a particular white male worker causes her to think about "the existence of the unknown" (67), the Other, his difference helping her to learn more about herself. Lorraine begins empathizing with him by imagining his life as different but equal to hers,

> that he lived further south, in the working-class districts where the sons and daughters of Polish immigrants lived. She imagined his house, too, dark, small, and cluttered. Completely devoid of light, of books, of music. He ate lunch meat sandwiches with mayonnaise on white bread. . . . He had probably been brought up to hate her. Her people competed with his people for jobs, for housing, for respect. . . . Yet, in spite of all she knew, all history taught her must be true, yet—she held imaginary conversations.

> With him. . . . He taught her how to deal with the basic things. (68)

He teaches her to want to know or to empathize with the Other, to learn more about herself. Here, Lorraine deals with the Other as Other, meaning she does not define the young white worker in terms of herself but instead in terms of his own logic and distinct subjectivity. She respects and recognizes the young white worker, considering him as a unique individual. Empathizing with the Other requires her to move outside of her own ego, or to recognize the Other within herself, thereby experiencing something other than her individuated self. Getting to know the Other is also getting to know herself.

Lorraine's visit to the Rib Shack is her second transgression, her second risk with the Other, with difference. Personally, it is her first encounter with the Other. At the Rib Shack, "[e]verything and everyone who was considered not respectable came there," with her mother considering Paris, a good-time lady, to be a "Devil's woman" (75). These subaltern African Americans or blues people and everything they represent have been defined as devalued Other for Lorraine by legitimate, Christian, middle-class society. But rather than otherize/devalue these people, reduce them to nothing, or define them as negative Other, Lorraine identifies with and becomes one of them because they let her see herself. They speak to her inner desires and needs. "These people were herself. They were her father, too, and her mother. These people, who, in their way, had always loved her, had always been her eyes, her ears, her very self" (77). Later when she walks with Claude on Maxwell Street, Lorraine is "one with the blues people who crowded the pavement. . . . Nomads of the blues. These were her people" (89). Lorraine and the crowd come to know and recognize each other. These people as Other give Lorraine her *I*, making her portrait.

Lorriane is "entering humanity via other people—namely, the Other Self" (Cixous, *White Ink* 4). A transformation of perspective and an epistemic change in subjectivity is occurring. The exterior, the Other, lies at the heart of the interior such that, according to Jacques Derrida in *Of Grammatology,* "[t]he meaning of the outside was always present within the inside" (35). Otherness is what mediates identity/subjectivity, which means that she is always already outside herself and therefore is decentered. Facing the people at the Rib Shack and on Maxwell Street, Lorraine becomes responsible for them and they for her. These people become others to her *I* itself. She comes to understand, perhaps for the first time in her life, what is precarious in another life. The Other plays within being.

From Claude, Lorraine begins to learn about the blues, a place "where ordinary black women found voice" (Collins 107). He is the "someone driving past" who gives her a "lift into the unknown, into the world beyond. To the Other" (*Hanging by Her Teeth* 71), provoking her anxieties and freeing her creativity, further expanding, transforming, and enriching her psychic life. The blues becomes an Other, something else for her to experience in understanding herself. Claude tells her that "[t]he blues was the only music in the world. Everything came from the blues" (79). For Lorraine, the blues is not about believing; rather, it is about recognizing certain values and being able to question them continuously. When she follows Claude to the club on Maxwell Street, she discovers the meaning of life. The blues is about the pain and pleasure of life, about having "no hope, only reality" (85). It teaches her that there is an "inherent joke in everything. . . . Life, mysterious, unpredictable. Life was not what someone else told you . . . It had to be experienced. On your own terms, in your own way" (76, 80–81). Immediately, Lorraine is learning freedom and how to live not according to an external metanarrative or fixed norm but instead according to her own needs and desires. The blues becomes a tool that allows her to resist the oppressive normative world.

In the car ride to the blues club, Claude also tells Lorraine about the black Virgin. "She is found . . . by serendipity. You must wander in order to find her. Not search. She is not on a deliberate route. My father called her '*La Retour.*' *La Retour* had no face. This was so she could reflect back the inner truth of those who gazed upon her" (84). After telling her about the black Virgin, Claude hopes/wishes that she may find *La Retour* someday, "so that She could reflect her truth to you" (84). The anxiety provoked by Claude plays itself out for Lorraine on a spiritual level. Gorging herself with the blues becomes a prerequisite for living and seeing the world, for being on the road, for dealing with the Other. Therefore, on this eventful day, she has sex with the blues-man Magic Al, the embodiment of the Other, who "look[s] evil, also very beautiful. And very definitely The Unknown" (85). He recognizes her desire to know the Other. As he sexually penetrates her, robbing her of her virginity and naïveté, Lorraine "could see New York . . . the Tree Of The Knowledge Of Good And Evil" (87), two main blues principles. In the midst of the sexual encounter, she "felt her own power" (87), discovering her own unique feminine sexual energy/power, submitting to a man and also making him vulnerable. For Lorraine, the encounter is more than sexual; it is spiritual and mystical, awaking within her the power of her own body. Because the blues brings the spiritual into the secular, she is empowered by the sexual encounter. Now, she is free to do whatever she wants. After being introduced to the power of the blues at age fifteen, along with the powerful sexual encounter with Magic Al, Lorraine understands the human cost of living a middle-class Christian life. "She knew she was not in fellowship with her mother's congregation, nor with the nuns and their plans for her vocation, either" (88–89). For Lorraine, the search for a different subjectivity/her face is still in progress.

From Auntie Muriel, a blues woman who lives life her way, Lorraine learns not only about the blues but also about how to live a blues life, which means learning a different/alternative model of subjectivity and a different order of cognition. According to Auntie Muriel, "the blues were the most important music of all for black people. It was the basis of everything, of all music sung in America." For her, "the blues was not only music, *it was a way of being in the world.* The blues was about living inside and outside at the same time. It was about being on the open road. It was about seeing things as they really are" (38–39, my emphasis). Auntie Muriel is the person who tells Lorraine that it was black women blues singers such as Bessie Smith, Ma Rainey, Victoria Spivay, Ida Cox, Trixie Smith, Clary Smith, and Sippie Wallace who made the blues "big, wide open" (38). "The great classic blues singers," writes LeRoi Jones in *Blues People,* "were women" (91). Blues singers such as Ma Rainey and Bessie Smith brought polish and professionalism to the "blues that it had never had before" (89). They also were the first blues singer to record. Angela Davis concurs but also takes a feminist approach to these women blues singers. Writing in *Blues Legacies and Black Feminism,* Davis concludes:

> The songs recorded by Gertrude Rainey and Bessie Smith offer us a privileged glimpse of the prevailing perception of love and sexuality in post-slavery black communities in the United States. Both women were role models for untold thousands of their sisters to whom they delivered messages that defied the male dominance. . . . The blues women openly challenged the gender politics implicit in traditional cultural representations of marriage and heterosexual love relationships. . . . They forged and memorialized images of tough, resilient, and independent women who were afraid neither of their own vulnerability nor of defending their right to be respected as autonomous human beings. (41)

The anxiety provoked by Auntie Muriel plays itself out for Lorraine at a cultural level. In opening up the narrative and providing Lorraine with the blues and knowledge of the black Virgin, the text is giving Lorraine the necessary information to transform the self, to devise an oppositional subjectivity that challenges the repressive one given to her by her mother and normative society. In *Black Feminist Thought,* Patricia Hill Collins argues that the blues becomes "a site of the expression of black women's self definitions" (106). The blues idiom or lifestyle serves as an alternate path for Lorraine.

Hanging by Her Teeth also possesses other forms of speech that challenge Enlightenment reason and contribute to the text's cosmology and to Lorraine's postmodern/blues subjectivity. Throughout her life, Lorraine is provided nonrational information and folk wisdom from members of the community and the ancestors who assist her in her journey to selfhood, to a nonnormative subjectivity, to thinking pluralistically. Writing to her father on July 22, 1964, she tells of her trip to the fairgrounds with her mother when a gypsy woman tells Lorraine that she is "going on a long journey," that "the journey would last a long time," that "she was filled with the spirits of [her] ancestors," and that "the spirits with [her are] wandering spirits" (48). On her first visit to the Rib Shack, Cat-eye tells her that "You'll find your daddy, Lorraine, you'll find him on the road through a stranger" (78). In the summer of 1969 when Lorraine is twenty-one years old and in college, her boyfriend Winston, after they have been fighting all weekend in Michigan and she considers suicide (94), drops her off in downtown Chicago. She encounters an old woman, a Goddess, on a bridge who tells her, long before she will search for her father in New York and the cities of Europe, "You goin far. Far away. Far. Don't throw yourself off this bridge. Not yet. You got too far to go. Your daddy's still around" (95). In another instance of Lorraine being provided with folk wisdom, on the train with her boyfriend Bernard to see the play *Hair* in downtown Chicago, the Yoruba Elegba, the Devil-at-the-Crossroads, shows "up to remind her that she had a journey to take. That she was just passing through" (102). While Lorraine is in Athens, she thinks of Mr. Kaminski, who owned the deli on the corner of her block in New York City and who is a wanderer who listens to the blues, because he "had told her once that she would have to go far to find what she was looking for" (5). When she visits Winston and his African girlfriend in Paris, the woman, who was small and wise, says in Twi "Go to London . . . your daddy is there" (161). In all of these instances, the nonrational, non-Enlightenment, intuitive knowledge is presented as being a part of Lorraine's body politics, her plural-dimensional mind-set, regenerating and reinforcing her blues life. This storehouse of wisdom and folklore, established by the elders and the ancestors and distilled from the African and

African American historical experience, provides Lorraine with guidance. The storehouse, along with the blues music that she listens to throughout the text, generates, resignifies, and reaffirms her journey to a blues life.

After she turns fifteen, when she learns to empathize with the Other and is introduced to the blues and other cultural forms such as the black Virgin and Miss Lala by Claude and Auntie Muriel, Lorraine revolts, which is central to the formation of the self and subjectivity and achieves a certain psychic liberation, a form of liberty. She possesses a different subjectivity or consciousness, one that battles against the hegemonic Western Judeo-Christian regime of truth, one that thinks pluralistically, one where alterity and difference go through her, one that makes room for and values the Other as Other, one that has the reflexive basis for self-conscious social agency. With this different consciousness, Lorraine becomes the seer, moving beyond a limited point of view of good and evil to an expanded point of view that sees all values as effects of the flow of life. This means moving beyond morality to ethics, where she creates and selects those powers that expand life as a whole, beyond her limited perspectives. In this sense, as a seer she is what Hélène Cixous calls a nonpatriarchal woman, "never settling down, . . . going everywhere to the other" (*Newly Born Woman* 87). In being introduced to the blues and other cultural forms, Lorraine completes an epistemic change in subjectivity.

This different consciousness, this change in subjectivity, allows her to connect with and to hear the blues all around her, particularly black women blues singers who speak to her inner needs and whose music brings a certain clarity to her life. As Lorraine and Artesia approach the club, a man in a Lincoln Continental pulls up alongside them, converses, and leaves, "blasting the blues in its wake" (*Hanging by Her Teeth* 16). In college when Lorraine goes to a bar off campus with her boyfriend Bernard, she hears "[o]n the jukebox Dinah Washington, 'Queen of the Blues,' . . . singing 'Blue Gardenia'" (105). Drinking Jack Daniels with Marion, the civil rights recruiter, at a club in Chicago, Lorraine feels the blues music everywhere, coming "not from the jukebox, but from the afternoon itself, to issue forth from the streets, from the very earth low and sweet. The earth where there was peace" (106). Later they go to a club on a street to hear the blues queen KoKo Taylor. When Lorraine visits Bernard's apartment in Amsterdam, he plays Bessie Smith's "Back Water Blues," and when Lorraine goes to Dr. Turner to get an abortion, she hears Dinah Washington playing on the radio in the reception area. Finally, at Maria's flat in Amsterdam, they talk about Bessie Smith, "Empress of the Blues." Singing and explaining something about the philosophical basis of their lives and the listeners' lives, these women blues singers provide Lorraine with clarity, understanding, and the healing that she needs. They reinforce and resignify her blues vision of life. These black women artists, argues Patricia Hill Collins in *Black Feminist Thought,* offer an alternate narrative and definition of what it means to be black and a woman at the same time. Their lyrics "challenge the externally defined controlling images used to justify Black women's objectification as the Other" (106). In addition, "[t]he blues is a vaccine," writes Wynton Marsalis in *Moving to Higher Ground,* "it's the controlled dose of something bad that prepares someone to deal with the approaching uncontrollable bad" (48). The blues allows Lorraine to live in and deal with the world, in all of its dimensions and absurdities.

In drinking and listening to the blues, to mostly blues women singers who are "defiant and wild" and who stay "on the move" (*Hanging by Her Teeth* 55), Lorraine connects/empathizes with others, with everything and everybody, not necessarily always agreeing with them. She comfortably befriends the transsexual Voodoo practitioner Artesia, going to clubs with him and watching his shows. "He treat[s] her like a lady at all times" (15). Lorraine nonjudgmentally accepts Morris, the once "chief alter boy at her school" (17), but is now a hustler in the Greyhound Bus Station. Even now, his face is still "full of that angelic essence which caused the nuns to call him a 'chocolate angel' behind his back" (18). When she returns to care for her mother in her final two years, Lorraine pities and loves members of the Tabernacle. Although they "would wander around like lost sheep until another shepherd came along to direct them to the Promised Land, . . . [t]here [i]s something touching about them, in the twilight of their lives, cast out into the darkness of uncertainty" (126). These people as Other give Lorraine her *I*, making her portrait.

As for the blues, the music is satisfying anticipations. Lorraine brings what Robert Jourdain calls "a flood of anticipations" and "patterns and deep connections" to her listening of the blues (318). When those anticipations are satisfied, she gets pleasure. She becomes a seer who hangs above the world and can see everything, who could move inside and outside of systems and identities. Her blues mentality drives her to abandon traditional religion, career, and home, to go where she is truly happy, moving from place to place, free and unburdened.

Thus, with the blues, the Elegba of the Yoruba pantheon, and the folk wisdom and support, Lorraine is free to think pluralistically, to move to uncoerced desires, to have a liberating and emancipating dimension, to have the sensation of finding herself prey to a multiplicity of languages. She has "wandering spirits" (*Hanging by Her Teeth* 48), and she wanders when the spirit moves her. Like blues people, she is a nomad. In *A Thousand Plateaus,* Deleuze and Guattari take the model of premodern nomadic tribes that roamed de-territorialized spaces while resisting the efforts of state powers to subdue them and apply it to postmodern subjects who resist modern structures and identities. For Deleuze and Guattari, nomadic movement is a metaphor to describe the way intensities circulate on the body-without-organs and a normative goal for the postmodern subject who should "keep moving, even in place, never stop moving" (159). With nomads providing new models for existence and struggle, the nomadic self breaks from all molar segments and cautiously disorganizes itself. Nomadic life is an experiment in creativity and becoming and is antitraditional and anticonformist in character. The postmodern nomad attempts to free oneself of all roots, bonds, and identities and thereby resists the state and all normalizing powers.

Lorraine Williams is a postmodern nomad, eschewing African American racial essentialism; breaking with a repressive, representational identity politics; and producing the fragmented, libidinal body. She roams freely across modern categories, institutions, and identities, moving from point to point "only as a consequence and as a factual necessity" (Deleuze and Guattari, *A Thousand Plateaus* 380) and combating totalizing modes of thought and social regulation and normalization. Distributing herself in an in-between space, she occupies, inhabits, and holds that space, possessing a close range vision. Despite the rigid social organizations and identity structures, her desiring subjectivity, at least since she was fifteen, moves "inside and outside at the same time," having a constant relation between the same and the different (Other). "The life of the nomad," argue Deleuze and Guattari, "is the intermezzo" (*A Thousand Plateaus* 380). The in-between space has taken on all the consistency and enjoys an "autonomy and a direction of its own" (380). In being inside and outside at the same time, or being what Linda Hutcheon in *A Poetics of Postmodernism* calls ex-centric, is to have a "different perspective" (67), one that is always altering its focus since it has no centering force. One is aware of simultaneous dimensions, of the gaps of all systems, contesting the authority of the center and challenging "models of unity and order" (57). As a seer, Lorraine hovers above static structures, coming to perform roles, to take various subjective positions, to share mental experience with others, as a way of escaping but not completely leaving rigid and rational racial, sexual, and metaphysical practices and institutions, as a way of undermining oppressive language centers. She accepts the good and the bad, God and the Devil. For her, the truth of life was living it, "day by day, moment by moment" (*Hanging by Her Teeth* 81). In this sense, Lorraine's subjectivity is always arriving or has arrived. There is never a point in time when her subjectivity can be said to finally emerge as a stable and complete entity. It is always in process.

Much of her role-playing, subjective positioning is the result of desire and pleasure. According to Jacques Lacan, to become a subject, one must take a position in relation to the desire of the Other (*Ecrits* 311). Because she has a desire "to get next to one of them" (*Hanging by Her Teeth*

10), Lorraine gets involved with the Black Panthers, giving breakfast to school children as part of the Panthers' breakfast program. Because she longs to be one of the girls he spent "an evening with after a hard day dodging power hoses and police batons" (10), she marches with Martin Luther King Jr. She becomes associated with the Black Muslims because buying *Muhammed Speaks* weekly allows her to watch Elijah Muhammed's elite shock troops. "That tiny bow-tie was the secret of their sex appeal" (11). Although she never took anything he said seriously, she likes Malcolm X's "mind. It [i]s searching, refining" (11). In her search for truth in the interrogation of these social structures, Lorraine experiences conflict, pleasure, and *jouissance* in her fragmentation.

Throughout the construction of her life, Lorraine's desiring machine or nomadic mind-set causes her to live in the in-between, challenging the authority and naturalization of what Michel Foucault in *The Archaeology of Knowledge* calls "these pre-existing forms of continuity" or already-made "syntheses" (25). She could not settle; she had to keep moving, becoming, and thinking pluralistically. Freedom lies in the in-between, the alternative space, which is polymorphous and undefined, in empathizing with the Other. When she is twenty-one and seriously in love with Winston, she has a desire to settle. "All she wanted was to be with her man. Time and circumstances were wearing her down. Making her toe the line. Act right" (*Hanging by Her Teeth* 92). But she becomes uncomfortable in this static, rigid role because she knows she belongs to a people who "[s]corned those people who conformed" (93). Between college and leaving for New York City, she works "forty different jobs so that she wouldn't have to tie herself down to anything" (112). These instinctual needs give her moments of pleasure. Later in New York City in 1984, Lorraine falls asleep during the discussion of the Black Women's Caucus separating from the Women's Group, not wanting to be just another sister. For Lorraine, the conflict is eternal because there is pleasure and freedom in conflict.

In college, clinging to the in-between space, Lorraine could not "accept things like everyone else did. There were too many questions with too few answers" (99). She moves into the Black House, "where 'authentic African' cuisine and not so authentic 'African' customs were observed" (98), and tries to settle down, to fit in. In the Black House, there were all kinds of black music but no blues, which was not welcomed because her housemates "were not interested in life as it really was" (99). The Black House has a rigid program that repressed differences. Again, "tired of being left out of the great mass of those who were convinced of the rightness of their lives" (99), she tries to settle. But, again, she realizes that she cannot just accept things like everyone else. Although the black girls had their own sororities and organizations, she "intended to join the other ones, too, because she had to experience everything" (93). Like her Auntie Muriel, Lorraine "lived her life her way. The only law she respected was the one that came from her" (39), that came from her desires, wants, and needs.

In short, beginning in college, Lorraine's subjectivity, to use Michel Foucault's term, "explode[s] in all directions" (*The Order of Things* 346), which is characterized as being in flux and becoming, a way to remain alive. She is a nomadic subject who forms multiple identities through various actions and interventions. This meant that she could not commit herself to one singular, static identity, thereby taking a stance against all forms of exclusion and abuse. She is always traveling, questioning, escaping repressive, rigid, and essentialized structures. She was a part of the Women's Collective, the Black Women's Collective, and the Black Lesbians' Collective, and she lives in the spaces within and between the three, coexisting in difference and in equal, journeying in intensities, recognizing the exteriority of others, and enjoying her own autonomy and a direction of her own. Unlike the other African American students, she could not be like the "middle class ones who have the world sewn up so they can afford to be 'afro-centric' for four years. Or the hippies, or the egg-heads. Sometimes [she is] all of them, but most of the time [she is] nothing" (*Hanging by Her Teeth* 30). She runs "from the Black Students' meeting to the Anti-Vietnam rally, and back again" (30–31), cohabitating and coexisting with subjects of different but equal worth, escaping the codes of both and understanding that political movements are not places of freedom. In reacting to and in refusing the taken or caged other, Lorraine catches a glimpse of her *I*. She is de-territorialized par excellence because "there is no re-terriorialization" (Deleuze and Guattari, *A Thousand Plateaus* 381). Frustrated, Lorraine wishes she could "get on a cross-country bus, throw away all [her] i.d.s and vanish" (31). As Marion the recruiter says to Lorraine after she tells him about her abortion, "I don't think a blues person . . . ever stays still. They just roam the world, looking for more blues. Somewhere in their heart they try to settle down. But it is no use. The blues come down on them" (*Hanging by Her Teeth* 108). Lorraine's subjectivity is not unified and fixed, the norm in Western thought. It is multiple, encompassing *and* deconstructing, both fragmentation and unification, both motion and stasis. She negotiates the contradictions without the promise of resolution. Her subjectivity transgresses the limits of our ordinary concept of subjectivity.

Lorraine's sexuality is also quite different, characterized as flow. It is expressed very much in the tradition of the great blues women/singers. "Blues women," writes Angela Davis, "rarely sang about mothers, fathers, and children, . . . [finding] the mainstream cult of motherhood irrelevant to the realities of their lives" (13). They also invoked their music and lived as independent women who were different from the domestic orthodoxy of mainstream society. Bessie Smith and Ma Rainey, writes Collins, "sang of sex and sexuality with a startling frankness for their times" (108), with many of these singers believing in and practicing bisexuality or fluid sexuality. Likewise, Lorraine's sexuality is not defined by love, motherhood, procreation, compulsory heterosexuality, and/or possession. Rather, it is shaped by desire, joy, and pleasure that flow in all directions, undermining social conventions and expectations. After she has sex with Professor McClaren and he tells her that he loves her and promises to leave his wife for her, Lorraine tells him to "buy [her] some bell-bottoms instead" (*Hanging by Her Teeth* 30). When she gets pregnant with Winston's child, she has an abortion. She is a woman with sin. All the reasons—God coming to condemn her or the notion that a black woman never kills a child—that should prevent her from having the abortion are irrelevant. She no longer goes to church, and she no longer believes. "The sacred place of religion," state Deleuze and Guattari, "is fundamentally a center that repels the obscure *nomos*" (*A Thousand Plateaus* 382).

Sexually, Lorraine's desiring machine moves in and out of sexual, gender, and racial categories, trying to create a different kind of sexuality. Defining the Other as "a component of the self," writes Cixous, is the "condition that we invent" (*Newly Born Woman* 84). Lorraine is fully aware of her sexual energy. In high school, she has lesbian encounters with her Polish basketball coach, who every Friday night takes her to the Illinois-Indiana border and "stretch[se] her across the back seat and suck her breasts" (8). Later in London, looking for her father, she rents an attic room from a witch, who had discovered the Goddess and women. The two make love, and the "lovemaking was soothing. It did not feel alien" (162). But problems arise when the witch became "possessive" (162), and Lorraine ends the relationship. In Venice, she gets a thrill out of thinking about making love to a stranger in the open air while the old women heard Mass. She has a one-night stand with a Chinese sax player. At the Hilton Hotel in August 1968 when teargas wafted up the elevator shaft, Lorraine and a campaign worker, with a naked pink backside, "were wrapped around one another" (12). Lorraine's sexual behavior/actions undermine sexual norms, pointing to a sexual elsewhere. Her sexuality is shifting and unstable, allowing her to sexually coexist in difference and equal. We can say that Lorraine, to use Derrida's terms, has a "multiplicity of sexually marked voices" or possesses a "mobile of non-identifiable sexual marks" (Derrida and McDonald 40). Lorraine's sexuality exists in a place where there is no law. In short, with her fluid sexuality, Lorraine, to use the words of Jeffrey Weeks in *Homosexual Desire,* is "rejecting Oedipus, rejecting the artificial entrapment of desire and rejecting sexuality focused on the Phallus" (39). She embodies a non–sex-based rearrangement of desires.

In Lorraine's healthy sexual and loving relationship with Winston, whom she has known since she was eleven, she becomes what Hélène Cixous calls bisexual:

> Bisexuality does not consist in being heterosexual and homosexual at the same time, that is, in leading a double life, acting now like a man, now like a woman, rather it consists in being with another, a woman with a man, in a state of dynamic exchange which is so intense, an oscillation of this exchange which is so rapid, in desires which are so strong, that the very process of crossing toward and through the other is made possible, and that something happens that allows woman to go as far as possible into the masculinity of the other, not into her own "masculinity." Of course it also has a reverse effect so that if she has a particularly strong streak of masculinity, it is reactivated. I see bisexuality being played out between two people; in no way do I confuse it with "androgyny." ("Rethinking Differences" 78)

Despite Winston's refusal to surrender to the vulnerable in college and to engage his "woman side," which is "never far from the surface" (*Hanging by Her Teeth* 91), and experience bisexuality, Lorraine, who is sexually empowered and constantly complains about black men's failure to be bisexual or sexually open, has the desire, imagination, and vulnerability to be bisexual, to move from the masculine to the feminine within another. "Winston knows me. That seems strange to say that a boy would know me. But I am him, and he is me. We know that. When I miss my face so much I can't take it anymore, I go to Winston and look deep in his eyes. When I look at his face, I feel that I am looking at mine" (46). Later when she encounters Winston in Paris, she recognizes that "something had finally broken through out of all the years of male reserve" (160). Now he can show his vulnerability, allowing his femininity of the masculine to break through. Now she can place him on his "back in the tall grass, undress him, [and] love him" (160), allowing the dynamic exchange of bisexuality to happen. "That beauty was still there, so mesmerizing, so immediate, that there were times when she thought him her twin, the very mirror of her being" (158). With Winston, Lorraine undermines gender and sex categories.

In continuing her journey in becoming a blues woman, Lorraine liberates herself from "secrets" (50), the repression, and lives fully. After her revolt and subsequent change in subjectivity and consciousness, her "insides are open" and she cannot "close them up anymore" (51). Not ever wanting to settle, she travels or is constantly in motion. Travel becomes the only freedom from the tyranny of stasis and the status quo, freedom from white supremacy, heteropatriarchy, black essentialism, compulsory heterosexuality, and rigid Enlightenment rationalism. She accepts no certainties, believing that "being wild was just about the most important thing a colored woman could be. We didn't invent the rules, so we don't have to go by them" (37). Freedom for her means moving constantly.

Although Lorraine is constantly moving, questioning, and transgressing, the motion, at least ostensibly, is in the direction of her father. Since her face was shattered in the mirror when she was ten, she has been looking for her father, who is also a free-spirited, wandering bluesman and has "itchy feet" (61). She thinks that the father will return her face, that he will put the "pieces back together again" (6), that he will "rescue her from this half-life of hanging by her teeth" (133). She believes he is "living [his] life" (50). Finding her father, she thinks, means getting the answer to her prayer, the solution to her problem. If she could look into his eyes, she would "see her miracle" (6) and the broken pieces would be put back together again. Therefore, from 1964 to 1969 and again in 1984, she writes her father letters because she thinks he knows her name (34). When she turns thirty years of age in 1978 after her mother's death, Lorraine physically pursues him in New York, Amsterdam, Paris, and London.

When Lorraine leaves the United States in 1986 for Europe, searching for her father, her miracle, she connects with black American expatriates, and they, being blues people, help her catch sight of herself. In Amsterdam there is Bernard, Joe Smith, and Shirley, who takes Lorraine to the Congo Museum, "the place where they have the dead statues" (147). Bernard, who collects black images, likes Amsterdam because he became a person there. In Amsterdam and Brussels, Lorraine connects with Maria, who is from the Moluccas, the island group off Indonesia. It is when Lorraine looks into the eyes of black Henrik—who has been adopted by a Dutch family, lives in a town with no black citizens, and is lonely for his own kind—that she sees a glimpse of her face, "A glimpse reflected in his eyes" (157). In reacting to, empathizing with, and accepting these other individuals, Lorraine begins to catch a glimpse of herself. In Paris wearing dark glasses because she has not seen in a long time, Lorraine's face—the "face in all its different ages, the face that had become distorted, lost in an attempt to live a life that had never been her own" (157)—begins to emerge. Encountering Winston in Paris allows her to use her new eyes.

Finally, in London, she tracks down her father in a park, but now it is too late. She does not need him because it is on the occasion of the Other that she catches sight of herself. She "had discovered her face all on her own. . . . She . . . had found what he had taken. . . . She could sit beside him forever, father or no father" (163). Earlier in Paris, in the Gare du Nord on her way to the English Channel, Lorraine has a vision of "all of those who had died, those who missed her, those she missed. So many gone, now crowded into this station, traveling with her on the journey south to cross the water" (161). Looking among this ancestral nomadic crowd, she sees "herself, her own face. The face she had when she set off from Chicago years ago and into life" (161). Here Lorraine accepts not a fixed image of herself that has been submitted to law but instead one that is in flux and becoming.

As Lorraine and her father sit on a park bench, there is "peace" and "quiet" around them, and when she moves to show him her face, she realizes that Oswald Williams is blind in a number of ways. "Blind to all she had gone through, blind to what she had been, blind to who she was now" (163). He is a prisoner of his blindness in the sight of others. Watching her father walk away, being "swallowed up in the people" (166), she acknowledges that she "had not been searching for him at all" (164), that he was not her miracle. Instead, she had found herself and her face in the blues, particularly historical and ancestral blues women, through life's lived experiences, and in Miss Lala.

In the opening and closing scenes of *Hanging by Her Teeth,* it is Lorraine, the nomadic blues woman, whom the reader encounters. She is living her blues life and is telling us about how it came to be. She is still in a state of questioning, transforming, and becoming. Although she tells us that she is committed, she has a moment when she wants to "jump in that sea and swim out as far as possible" (2). She teaches at Our Lady Queen of Peace High School in South London and has convinced herself, again, to stop moving and put down some roots and maybe marry the nice head teacher from Barbados. But she is still a seer who hovers above seeing all. She is still living in the fluid space between two worlds, the worlds of motion and stasis; she is still hanging by her teeth. "The blues is an art of ambiguity," writes Ralph Ellison in "Remembering Jimmy," "an assertion of the irrepressibly human over all circumstances" (48).

As a consequence of the blues awareness as well as her ability to empathize with the Other, Lorraine, on the trip to Athens, Greece, understands the well-meaning nuns and their mission: they miss "their colonial days in Africa and [have] decided to minister among the disadvantaged in Brixton." She recognizes "this type of white woman," but she refuses to be enlisted in their "fantasy." When the nuns see the school girls, they see "some kind of bush station with barefoot little girls with dust on their feet." When the seer Lorraine sees these schoolgirls, she sees "a posse of homegirls bent on total chaos" (1). She understands and deconstructs the quest for "cartoon" African "roots," exposing it as a romantic place where "everyone was royalty and the streets were paved with gold" (19). She understands the complex history of Africa and the role that the Catholic Church played in slavery. "Some ancient beach in Africa was where it had all begun with guns, and chains, crucifixes and mirrors" (84).

But Lorraine does not transform herself completely and permanently until she encounters the icon, the black Virgin, in a church on her second visit. In Athens, in the opening scene of *Hanging by Her Teeth,* Lorraine hears bells, but these are not the sound of the Catholic bells of her youth. "These are ponderous, heavy, dark bells. They sound like human beings talking" (5). She walks into the church and sees "an icon hidden amidst the incense smoke. It is a black Virgin. Her face is flat, her eyes large and still. The Holy is like her, too. The icon must have been waiting hundreds of years for her to arrive. . . . [B]lack Virgins are miraculous, much more powerful than white Virgins" (6). Having no face, the black Virgin represents a space of difference and becoming, allowing her to "reflect back the inner truth of those who gaze upon her" (84). Lorraine turns it from side to side, hoping to catch a glimpse of her reflection, but the miracle does not happen. For Lorraine, the black Virgin represents an image that counters the one perpetuated by the mainstream American Catholic Church: her face is not the white face of the traditionally depicted Blessed Virgin Mary, whose reconfigured European looks "belie her Jewish, Middle Eastern heritage" (DelRosso 34). Therefore, the black Virgin is affirming; it is empowering. Looking into the face of this Holy Child, Lorraine sees and connects with her spiritual female ancestors, the Sisters of the Tabernacle of Radiant Energy, who live in a world of silent corridors, praying in the darkness. Though she admires and desires their "world of order and knowingness, and surrender" (*Hanging by Her Teeth* 7), she rejects it and keeps moving. Their world contains no wander or searching, meaning that the miracle has not happened. However, she does accept the fact that "there is no peace, not even now, not even in the icon of this 'woman born without sin'" (7).

After she retrospectively reexamines her past and ultimately finds herself without the need of her father, Lorraine, in the closing scene of *Hanging by Her Teeth,* reassesses her decision to return to London, get married, find a house, and settle down. "[S]he is tired of moving" (165), she says. For a moment, she thinks of settling and becoming her mother. "She'll decorate it like her childhood home. Funny, she laughs to herself, how much you become like your mama when you get older" (164). But the ringing of the bells lures her back to the same church and the black Virgin. Peering into the ancient face of the black Virgin the second time, Lorraine sees another reflection: "Herself. Old. She is walking across a flat plain. Not in America. She is walking unattached, walking back to the place where she had come before. The lost home. Long ago" (165). This time, Lorraine receives a reflection of her inner truth. Despite her desire to settle, she is a blues person, and she cannot remain still. She has to live for the present moment. As one of the first (post)modern cultural forms in the West, the blues belongs to a culture of dislocation, interrogation, and revolt. At this moment, Lorraine is still self-interrogating and self-questioning. Hearing the blues again, which speaks to her inner blues needs and desires, she takes off her fiancé's engagement ring and places it, along with her identification, at the base of the icon, indicating a rejection of everything that is not apart of her inner truth. Again, she needs the Other to make her portrait. She rejects marriage because the reflection tells her that she is "unattached." She rejects her teaching job because she cannot imagine herself "standing at a school gate at fifty-six with a ten-year-old waving frantically at her" (164–65). She rejects the settling ("order" and "surrender") because it causes one to shrivel up and die inside. Because she knows too much, she rejects self-sacrificing aspects of Catholicism (virginity, innocence, freedom in certainty, and motherhood), knowing that she is not born without sin. These aspects stifle desire and prevent her from moving.

The back and forth between motion and stasis, between the same and the different (Other), exploring the multiplicity of languages, is a part of the nomadic model for existence and struggle, for remaining alive. One gives and opens the door to the other. "What is most interesting about being alive," argues Gayatri Spivak, is "being angled towards the other" (Chakravorty 64). This dual coupling is the (post) modern vision of psychic truth. Hanging between the two is the space where we are most alive, most mortal, where life happens, where desires flow, where we encounter the spectrum of life. It is the place of heightened pleasure and creativity, a place of difference and constant becoming, a place where infinite enrichment becomes apparent. Finally, it is a place of naked life and, according to Cixous, where "the world written nude is poetic" (Cixous, *Hélène Cixous rootprints* 3).

Leaving the church, Lorraine thinks about the people on the streets, the opening of shops and the ragga girls whom she has come to Athens to chaperone. She looks "back in the direction [toward the girls from where] she came. Then she turns, plants her feet firmly on the road, and walks away. In the opposite direction" (165). She refuses to capitulate to settling, realizing that questioning, change, and conflicts are the source of her human freedom and that revolt is about patience, return, distance, and continuously starting over. According to Auntie Muriel, to settle is "to shrivel up inside," to not be alive, to close down the world, to live a life that is *less* true. "The world closes down for most people, or they close it down. It's called settling in" (36). To settle into "sameness, equality, and identity," argues Irigaray in *Conversations,* prepares us not for peace but "for conflicts, because [in sameness and settling] people . . . remain in a quantitative viewpoint" (81). But human beings are not supposed to settle in; they are "made to roam. Nomads. Not sleep their lives away" (*Hanging by Her Teeth* 36). Therefore, Lorraine chooses permanently to doubt by remaining in motion, accepting life as it really is, and "living her life her way" (39), with the blues as a sound track and a blueprint for her journey. She chooses questioning desire through a continuous process of self-examination. No one can tie her down, and she can face herself because she accepts the fact "that human beings are essentially and unalterably alone" (82). The nomad has no history; she only has a geography.

In *Hanging by Her Teeth,* Greer challenges the very notion of Enlightenment goals and ambitions, or any definitions that are closed, re-creating new values, new desires, and a new image of subjectivity of what it is to be and think. While Western Enlightenment leans toward security and stability, Greer's heroine, Lorraine, a blues woman, signifies a new way to think about life, thereby contesting and resisting all the devalued stereotypes of black women mentioned at the beginning of this chapter. She finds that she is happiest while remaining in motion and living in the moment. Like her favorite painting, she feels most in touch with herself when she is "hanging by her teeth," between the same and the different (Other), accepting the fact that her identity is always already being disrupted by otherness and difference. In accepting this coexistence in differences, without hierarchy, Lorraine also accepts that no particular set of values is the sole and unique values, a position that paves the way toward peace and tolerance rather than conflict. For Lorraine, fate has not "confined her to the prison of her sex and race" (154). Lorraine connotes an unsymbolized representation of the black woman in the West. This creation by Greer raises plural thinking to a level of thought, to a somewhat ontological level. "[R]ecognizing the other and seeking to meet and coexist with respect for our difference(s)," writes Luce Irigaray in *Conversations,* "could be our guide for reaching another stage of our becoming humans" (82). Lorraine accepts becoming as the norm, which frees her from subject identity and from the illusion of transcendence—the illusion that there is a ground or law other than herself that simply needs to be obeyed or revealed.

Only when Lorraine stops looking for her father and others to tell her who she is does she find the freedom to define herself. In this instance, Greer creates a novel that challenges Enlightenment notions of linearity, unity, and coherence. Like Anna Julia Cooper in *A Voice From the South,* Greer in *Hanging by Her Teeth* uses African and African American cultural forms, as Charles Johnson urges, to create a space of liberation, to find a new mode, a new idiom, outside white supremacy, black essentialism, and heteropatriarchy. Like the sociologist Charles Johnson's *Growing Up in the Black Belt,* Greer's *Hanging by Her Teeth* also constructs a plural, African American, female subjectivity that emerges only through a continuous process of subjectification, which also challenges the Enlightenment's concept of subjectivity, particularly its stereotypes of the black woman. In short, like *A Voice From the South, Hanging by Her Teeth* launches a new (black female) subject, one that allows for the presence, rather than the devaluation or murder, of Others, thereby pointing prophetically toward a development that challenges the reduced representation of the black woman in the West. To know the Other is to know the self. In angling subjectively toward the Other, *Hanging by Her Teeth* eschews identitarianism. Finally, although *Hanging by Her Teeth* begins and ends with the blues, it is not restricted to the blues, especially as it plugs into other kinds of intelligences. It is open-ended, transforming rigid, rational categories at the narrative and subject levels and advocating commingling, intermixing, and difference.

— 6 —

Virtual-Actual Reality and Clarence Major's *Reflex and Bone Structure*

In the introduction to *Clarence Major and His Art,* Bernard Bell defines the value of Clarence Major's literary postmodernism as its ability to move "beyond traditional literary limits and cultural boundaries in experimenting with different, occasionally multiple, narrative voices" (1). Major's postmodernism, Bell continues, is derived from the "particular experiences of difference, marginality, and Otherness" (3). Like Donald Barthelme, Ronald Sukenick, Paul Auster, Steve Katz, Raymond Federman, Ishmael Reed, and other second-wave postmodern American writers who believe that the novel is a linguistic invention, that the novel does not reflect the social real, Major wants a writing that disseminates, that "works over the signifier, that listens to itself being written and that retraces its own steps" (Cixous, *White Ink* 12). He wants a "writing that re-describes" (12), creating an inexistent (virtual) space of its own. This kind of writing is self-reflexive; overturns binaries; liberates desires; engages differences/otherness; redefines the novel; moves beyond the limited point of view of good and evil, of morality; broadens lives; and ultimately reconfigures the subjectivity of the African American. In this chapter, first, I will examine how Major in *Reflex and Bone Structure* uses virtuality and the African American cultural form jazz and improvisation to challenge the traditional black novel and to reconceive reality and African American subjectivity outside existing stereotypes, which oppose a reduced representation of the African American. Second, I will examine how Major in *Reflex and Bone Structure* is aware of gender and sexual stereotyping. Yet ultimately, he fails to completely escape the masculine economy.

In *Reflex and Bone Structure,* Major defies "the linear and formal notions of realism traditionally practiced by Negro and Black American writers since William Wells Brown's novel, *Clotelle* (1857)" (Bolling and Major 29), minimizing representational effects in his fiction. He deconstructs traditional notions of the realistic novel—which are linear, progressive, utopian, and causal—perceiving and structuring reality (Weixlmann, "Clarence Major's Singing Voice[s]" 243). As Joseph Weixlmann states, *Reflex and Bone Structure* "eschews even the most fundamental tenets of realism" ("African American Deconstruction" 68), which is a direct challenge to Enlightenment reason. Instead, Major's *Reflex and Bone Structure* exists "as [an] object[] through which the reader can have an experience rather than an (ill-conceived) reflection on life" (Bolling and Major 29). In an interview with John O'Brien, Major states that "the novel . . . takes on its own reality and is really independent of anything outside itself. . . . You begin with words and you end with words. The content exists in our minds. I don't think that it has to be a reflection of anything. It is a reality that has been created inside a book. It's put together and exists finally in your mind" (130).

For Major, *Reflex and Bone Structure* is simulation/virtuality, realities represented in other forms, creating a new environment and reproducing appearances, images, and styles that are not grounded on anything other than their own becoming. These appearances and images are not "sustained by the depth of reality behind [them], but . . . [are] decontextualized appearance[s] which fully coincide[] with real being[s]" (Zizek 6). *Reflex and Bone Structure* does not reflect the social real but instead is an addition to it or is an artistic object in itself to be admired for what it is. *Reflex and Bone Structure,* argues Alide Cagidemetrio, "make[s] fiction reality itself" (4). The novel has its own presence in the world—extracting from the confused reality its own inner form and representing complex networks of ideas, images, and feeling—and refers to itself and to other texts.

For Major in *Reflex and Bone Structure,* like the Swiss linguist Ferdinand de Saussure, language is arbitrary, further undermining the reflectionist theory. In an interview with Larry McCaffery and Jerzy Kutnik, Major states that "a word is just a sign, a symbol, and as such it can never really represent the thing it names. Words are entirely different from things, separate from their referents" (81). Playing off the Saussurean notion that the relationship between the signifier and the signified, the word and the thing, is arbitrary, Major in *Reflex and Bone Structure* plays with the arbitrariness of the two. For example, in describing the word "Cora" (signifier) for the physical person Cora (signified), Major shows the limitation (and the arbitrariness) of the word: "The word Cora, she thinks, is the extent of her presence. This is a word" (*Reflex and Bone Structure* 73). He does the same thing for the word "table." Cora is sitting with her elbows on the kitchen table. "The table has a word that is used by people, like Cora, who wish to refer to it. That word is table" (73–74). The signifier and the signified are arbitrary, except as they are constituted in language. For Saussure and Major, language does not reflect the social real but instead signifies it.

Major then exposes this inability of the signifier to totally represent the signified when he discusses the concept of murder: "Cora does not pretend to know murder. Even Canada does not know murder. He is a man who spends time making up things. Writing words on paper has a powerful effect on his mind. If he writes murder, it means something terrible has happened" (83).

When the narrator/protagonist in *Reflex and Bone Structure* tries to recall the "trees and grass, clear sky and insects" from his trip to the country with Cora, he loses them when he tries "to bring them back, even for description. *The image tries to represent something it is not*" (108, my emphasis). He unsuccessfully tries "to bring the wholeness of this unquestionably human moment back. . . . But [it] get[s] away and never come[s] back" (108). Language, according to Jacques Derrida in *Dissemination,* involves delay, deferral of meaning, ambiguity, and some degree of the speaker's distance (168). In demonstrating the inability of the signifier to represent the signified completely, Major further exposes the inability of language to capture the real, showing again that fiction is a product of a signifying practice.

In addition, like Wideman in *Philadelphia Fire* and Everett in *Erasure,* Major in *Reflex and Bone Structure* exposes the writing process. Throughout *Reflex and Bone Structure,* the narrator makes references to the process of producing the novel. He states, "It's snowing outside. I'm in here making this novel. . . . The loneliness kills me" (51). Halfway through *Reflex and Bone Structure,* the narrator states, "I want this book to be anything it wants to be. A penal camp. A bad check. A criminal organization. A swindle. A prison. Devil's Island. I want the mystery of this book to be an absolute mystery. Let it forge its own way into the art of deep sea diving. . . . This book can be anything it has a mind to be" (61). This self-aware and self-conscious narrator and this exposure of the processes of writing fiction demonstrate that *Reflex and Bone Structure* is a construct, that it is necessarily bound to social reality only by its status as an artifact within that world and by virtue of it being an extension of an author whose imaginative acts brought it into existence. Every element of *Reflex and Bone Structure*'s composition—characters, theme, action, and event—argues Jerome Klinkowitz, "expresses the self-apparent nature of its making" ("Self-Apparent Word" 202).

Furthermore, *Reflex and Bone Structure* is in the "digressive tradition" rather than the sequential (linear) tradition (Bolling and Major 30), beginning not with an origin but instead where it already is: the narrator/character starts speaking, with no particular starting point, with no particular introduction. *Reflex and Bone Structure* starts out of its own necessity, ending not with a resolution or a conclusion but instead ending where it is: with the narrator still speaking. Also, it encompasses a multiple narrative, nonlinear voice. For example, the narrative of the explosion that kills Cora is juxtaposed with dispersed individual narratives about the lives of the other characters.

Further complicating language's ability to capture meaning completely or to tell the truth, in *Reflex and Bone*

Structure the narrative switches time, place, and physical ties, which disrupts linear plot development, signifying a new virtual way to configure time. An event will begin in the present and end in a previous century, where characters do not share the same context and time. For example, the narrator begins carrying the "wreckage off stage" in the present before the curtain closes, but the "first curtain takes place back in the seventeenth century" (102). In using the digressive way of constructing the textual real, Major collapses the past, present, and future, eliminating what Marshall McLuhan calls "time and space factors in human association" (9). Referring to his thinking about the future, the narrator states: "I want to blur the distinctions between it [the future] and the past" (*Reflex and Bone Structure* 49). Now that he knows that fiction does not reflect the real or tell the truth, Major uses it for other purposes: to imagine a different world, to create human potentials and possibilities, a fuller and richer human subject.

As a consequence, Major's *Reflex and Bone Structure* is a departure in form and content from the various established (modern) literary norms. It is a fiction where processes are more importance than conclusions, totalizations, and resolutions, where "imaginative space commands more attention than story line, plot, and character development" (Bolling and Major 30). Plugging into other kinds of intelligences or forms of speech, *Reflex and Bone Structure* juxtaposes elements of realism (the actual) with repackaged images from television, movies, dreams, the stage, and the imagination to expand reality, to create a virtual real—a world of copies and images, a world free of illusion of transcendence, free of the illusion that there is a law other than ourselves that simply needs to be obeyed. The real in *Reflex and Bone Structure* is the actual-virtual.

Published by Fiction Collective in 1975, *Reflex and Bone Structure,* like many second-wave postmodern American texts, is a parody of the surface closure of the detective story. It is, according to Major, a "mock detective story or a kind of murder mystery . . . a very strange murder mystery" (Bunge 36). The detective form has certain surface conventions and expectations. Historically, the classic detective stories and novels of Edgar Allan Poe, Arthur Conan Doyle, Willard Huntington Wright, and others and the hard-boiled detective fiction of Dashiell Hammett, James M. Cain, and Raymond Chandler complicate and problematize the detective search. In seminal stories such as "Murders in the Rue Morgue" and "The Mystery of Marie Roget," Poe presents a surface closure and intricate reasoning that he simultaneously mocks. Poe, according to Landrum, Browne, and Browne in *Dimensions of Detective Fiction,* provides "stories which oriented readers to a particular form of tension between the ordinary and the bizarre, between sentiment and reason, and between appearance and reality" (1). Poe's "Imp of the Perverse" makes clear the author's belief that the nonrational is a fundamental aspect of social and human reality. The hard-boiled detective genre is also marked by what Larry Landrum in *American Mystery and Detective Novels* calls "bizarre premises upon which it might be based" (8). In it, the detective discovers that the real case is not the case he thought he was working on or that the search is not about what it at first appeared. Unexpected corruption and perversity are revealed in the search, and some people's identities are not what they were initially presented as being.

Major's *Reflex and Bone Structure* is in this classic and hard-boiled detective fiction tradition, which provides "an apt referential code for self-reflective fictions" (Cagidemetrio 7). The *I* narrator/author/detective in *Reflex and Bone Structure* mocks the detective genre, showing that the real case is not a murder mystery but instead is life. The narrator also deconstructs the detective genre, showing an inability to solve the crime, reflect the real, or find the truth. Clues/details concerning the crime/murder of Cora and Dale pop up periodically, only to have the narrator inform us that he made them up. The police detectives who attempt to scientifically disclose the "truth" of Cora's and Dale's murders have flawed and inconclusive methods, with them not knowing how to operate "their gadgets." Therefore, they "hook them up to whatever they want to inspect. Even hook them up to people" (34). The narrator even suspects "the law enforcement officer of murdering Cora" (31). While we do learn on the text's final page that the narrator has, in one sense, caused the characters' murders—"They step into a house. It explodes. It is a device. I am responsible. I set the device." (145)—his device is a literary one. Thus, the search begins with who murdered Cora and her lover Dale but never solves the murders. Meaning is deferred, the crime is never solved, and truth is never found or told. Joseph Weixlmann observes of *Reflex and Bone Structure* that "[n]ot only do we never learn, in any meaningful sense," who commits the murder, but we also "get fragmentary and not infrequently conflicting accounts of the details of the murder" ("African American Deconstruction" 68).

Rather, the search is not about what it at first appeared. In exploding the surface conventions of the detective story, Major in *Reflex and Bone Structure* hijacks the detective story, critiques the search for absolute knowledge, points to the crises in representations, and exposes the ways that narrative realism is constructed, as being "socio-historically constructed, and so contingent" (Healy 5). In demonstrating the writer's confusion in the process of writing, or at least the writer's sense of exploration, in accounting for all complexities, Major in *Reflex and Bone Structure* humbles and makes the reader move, at least temporarily, more carefully but fully through life.

The structure of *Reflex and Bone Structure* not only mocks and deconstructs the detective story and echoes the works of other postmodern American writers, but its repetitive, improvisational nature/structure is also informed by jazz aesthetics. In an interview with Major, Jerome Klinkowitz characterizes the repetitive language in *Reflex and Bone Structure* in terms of jazz, and Major agrees: "Because you keep repeating sections . . . they're almost like [jazz] takes or cuts. . . . Sometimes . . . you go over the same scene a few different times, but each time the language is the slightest bit different" ("Clarence Major" 34). Improvising on the same scene or incident as in a jazz piece permeates *Reflex and Bone Structure.* For example, as Morrison in *Jazz* does with the Violet/Violet split, we get several riffs on or versions of the police at the bomb scene. The first presentation of the police at the scene of the explosion describes it straightforwardly. The policemen gather evidence at the crime scene, but they are also "very funny. . . . One had a Polaroid MP-3 camera for copy work. . . . Another one wore rubber gloves and picked his teeth with a toothpick. Still a third moved around the place with a scalpel scraping up the blood." There is no dialogue among the policemen. The scene ends with the narrator saying "But I didn't hang around" (*Reflex and Bone Structure* 2).

In a repeat of the scene, there are variations. The narrator indicates that the names of the policemen are unimportant, but they all continue to come around, and the "rumor is Canada and I [the narrator/author] are both very much under suspicion and closely watched" (31). After the narrator/protagonist informs the reader that "one night he kissed naked Cora in a musty hallway" (31), the bomb scene appears again, beginning with "They found some of her teeth near the window" (34). This particular repetition of the scene has some dialogue among the police. The police captain talks authoritatively to the crowd as he draws "a line around the bodies." When the narrator/author says to him, "I want to draw a line around her body, myself. I don't trust you people" (128), the policemen laugh. Each time the bomb scene appears in the text, it is redescribed anew as in an improvised jazz riff (Bradfield 121). Major uses jazz aesthetics to further explode the surface structure of the detective story, as a totalized, rationalized system, and to point to an elsewhere, to plurality and multiplicity in representation.

In addition, serving as guidance, relaxation, reinforcement, and comfort, jazz and blues in *Reflex and Bone Structure* play in the background, with real jazz musicians sometimes becoming characters within the text, creating an actual-virtual real, which is less stable and concrete. The record *The Jimi Hendrix Experience* plays on the turntable at one of their parties. The music "jumps through the room with the force of Goya dancers" (22). "Through the floor or from the hallway" (24), the narrator can hear Wilson Pickett's recorded "voice screaming from a turntable" (24). Pickett seems to animate the narrator. Needing to relax, Canada "sends for Red Garland to play piano. . . . Stan Getz follows

Red. . . . The tenor sax is an art of love. Canada closes his eyes. He's back in 1938 listening to Ella sing, 'A-tisket, A-tasket.'" Afterward, he feels "better" (52). As with Lorraine in Greer's *Hanging by Her Teeth,* the music has a therapeutic, transformative effect on Canada, enhancing the mood. Throwing a party to celebrate nothing, they invite Duke Ellington. For years, Cora has listened to Buck Clayton, Thelonious Monk, Bix Beiderbecke, Benny Carter, Hoagy Carmichael, and Chico Hamilton. "They drench her. She sleeps with the records, dances through the music" (61). For Cora, these musicians embody emotion and will. In another example, Cora and Canada catch Gerry Mulligan playing "Venus De Milo" in baritone sax. Then, we get the scene where Cora is in a lumber yard, and "[m]usicians are coming out of the woodwork. Clarinets piano vibes trumpets tenor sax trombone drums are speaking a language that rhymes" (57). Canada gets high and listens to jazz. "A stack of Armstrong Ella Prez Bird Billie on the turntable sets him straight for hours" (83), clarifying and enhancing his mind. With actual characters mingling with virtual jazz musicians, the actual-virtual impacts the dynamics of knowledge creation. In this actual-virtual reality, there is an absence of shared context and time for the characters and the musicians, making the representation less stable. But the music, again, serves therapeutic, transformative purposes. The jazz, in its openness, spontaneity, improvisation, and flexibility, facilitates these virtual characters's transgression of rigid rationalism and the linear model and permits the acceptance of the unknown, the Other, and a more expansive reality.

It is obvious that *Reflex and Bone Structure* does not have a clear linear plot. But from the desperate images and fragments, it is possible to piece together a provisional narrative: the narrator/author/protagonist belongs to a group of friends—Dale, Canada, and Cora—who live in the Village in New York. It is a virtual community, moving beyond the limited point of good and evil, of morality. Since the other three characters have relations with Cora, she could be considered the center of the text. All four main characters attend parties, where they are free with sex, drugs, and alcohol. Although historically women "have been victims of eroticism," Cora, the lone female in the group, is sexually free and ends up sleeping with and being romantically involved with the narrator, Dale, and Canada (Major, "Erotic Facts of Life" 264). "She needs variety" (*Reflex and Bone Structure* 39). Cora and Dale audition for plays and look for theatrical work. Dale also acts. At some point Cora and Dale are killed, but the reader does not know exactly how, why, when, or where. Was it the result of a bomb explosion? a car crash in southeastern Connecticut? an airplane crash en route to Russia with Canada as the pilot? a speeding taxi with the narrator as the driver? Suicide? or the result of four thugs, one of which is Cora herself? All are offered as possible reasons, creating multiplicity or layers of signifiers but no clear singular answer or resolution.

Because it is a text that neither begins nor ends, *Reflex and Bone Structure* is constantly shifting and unstable, nonlinear as well as noncyclical. Characters and their development are at the mercy of the narrator/author who is up front about his limitations, biases, and inadequacies. The narrator states that "everything that Cora [and the other characters] does happens first in my mind" (140). Therefore, at times the reader cannot nail down characters or plots, with the text defying meaning and embracing uncertainty and indeterminacy. The action in *Reflex and Bone Structure* is filtered through the consciousness of the *I* narrator/author/protagonist, taking place in dispersed geographical locations—Cuba, New York, Arizona, North Dakota, Maryland, southeastern Connecticut, a fishing village in a foreign country, the police station, on the stage—with an ongoing flow of segments of empirical scenes, television and movie images, dreams, and events radically different in kind, inhabited by beings of different ontological status, and governed by different physical laws. There is no distinguishable causal link between the various dispersed narratives and fragments and the geographical locations, and there is no clear connection between the desperate images. These virtual segments contribute to and further aggravate the plurality of the text's worlds.

The *I* narrator/author observes, creates, and participates in the action of the text. As the private eye, he provides the "logic to the text," he is the "organizer of time and space" (Cagidemetrio 9). Major represents the *I* narrator's consciousness as hybrid and open, encountering/plugging into various forms of otherness, or virtual realities, but not forcing them into an oppressive hierarchy. Within the narrator's consciousness, desire flows. Freed from the conventions of linear, sequential narrative and the belief in a unified subject or an objectively verifiable reality, the text is structured by the thoughts running through the consciousness of the *I* narrator/author as he draws on television, cinema, dreams, and the stage to create what Gilles Deleuze calls virtual reality and virtual characters. In *Difference and Repetition,* Deleuze defines virtuality as "[n]othing but the potentiality of an Idea, its determinable virtuality" (201). Virtuality is what is to become, what is not yet. For Deleuze, "The virtual is opposed not to the real but to the actual," being "fully real in so far as it is virtual" (208), or a re-presented form of reality. "When it is claimed that works of art are immersed in a virtuality," argues Deleuze, "what is being invoked is not some confused determination but the completely determined structure formed by its genetic differential elements, its 'virtual' or 'embryonic' elements. The elements, varieties of relations and singular points coexist in the work or the object" (209).

In *Reflex and Bone Structure,* television, dreams, the stage, movies, and the imagination are its coexisting "differential" or "virtual" elements, constructing realities and providing the potential for virtual reality and virtual characters in the text. "Cinema, television, and the press," writes Felix Guattari in *Soft Subversions,* "have become fundamental instruments of forming and imposing a dominant reality and dominant significations. Beyond being means of communication, of transmitting information, they are instruments of power. . . . [T]hey participate in the elaboration and transmission of subjective models" (146). With television and media technology, we can extend our subjectivity, argues Marshall McLuhan in *Understanding Media,* into "a global embrace, abolishing both time and space" on the planet (3). The virtual becomes an integral part of the actual.

Combining the actual and the virtual, Major in *Reflex and Bone Structure* gives us the fully real, the potential, making imagistic leaps, fracturing the identity of his characters and the world they live in, and moving existence/life from the human to the animal to the virtual. For Deleuze, life is desire, and desire is the expansion of life through virtual creation and transformation. Television, cinema, the stage, and dreams become active agents in the text, broadening lives and creating new environments and new knowledge. Characters who watch television move in and out of their actual space and into the virtual space of the television, blurring the line between the two, acquiring additional knowledge, and expanding or transforming their subjectivity, with the virtual space creating a less unitary subject. "Full of eggs and cheese, Cora takes a swim in a television commercial full of salad dressing. It's delicious, creamy, thick and sensuous" (*Reflex and Bone Structure* 64). After watching and becoming "completely submerged" in five Edward G. Robinson movies on television, Canada turns into "Edward G. Robinson. He's smoking a cigar and wearing a three-piece dark gray suit" (28). After a party, Cora and the narrator are in bed watching a movie. Suddenly they become a part of the movie: "It's 1938. *A Slight Case of Murder.* Edward G. Robinson and Jane Bryan" (3). Watching the movie transforms them and their reality. Later, watching the late-late show, the narrator/protagonist gets up and goes to the bathroom, and looking in the mirror upon returning to bed, he sees "Little Ceasar . . . and wink[s] at him in the mirror. He winks back" (3). Here, television meshes with rather than overrides ongoing empirical activities. Rita Haywood is "screaming in the room" (46), and Canada looks around and realizes that she is on television, showing how television casually interacts with the empirical world. Performing at the Concept West Village Theatre, "Dale's best strongest voice open[s] the performance" (17). The worlds of television and movies unceremoniously mingle with the ongoing empirical-world activities, creating a new environment. Television, movies, and the stage allow *Reflex and Bone Structure* to extend reality, to move beyond the actual, and to extend life to its fullest potential. *Reflex and Bone Structure* demonstrates the virtual power of becoming, which is empathy with the Other's movements and perceptions.

In *Reflex and Bone Structure,* Major's virtual characters escape from the kind of negation found in the logic of consciousness, "where everything appears to be stratified and definitively crystallized" (Guattari, *Soft Subversions* 198). Canada and the narrator travel about and through virtual power to "invent new identities" (*Reflex and Bone Structure* 35). Canada does a "transatlantic lindy hop from Europe to the states and land[s] in a courtroom in the South," where "he accidently gets sentenced to the penitentiary as one of the Scottsboro boys" (46). As a boy plays with the mirror, he becomes "a baby goat" (9). There is a time when "Canada thinks himself a sledgehammer" (36) and when plants "move about in deep silence and warm rocks . . . live with emotions of their own" (136). In becoming a goat or a sledgehammer, the boy and Canada do not become what they are; they do not behave like a goat or a sledgehammer. Rather, they feel for or empathize with the movements and perceptions and the becomings of the goat and the sledgehammer, using their virtual power to imagine seeing the world as if they were a goat or a sledgehammer. The process creates new knowledge and expands their subjectivity. Also, as Canada, Dale, the narrator, and Cora sit around playing cards "to the sounds of Scott Joplin's piano. Roman soldiers break in. They say Agatha Christie sent them. They drag Cora outside and nail her to a cross planted in the sidewalk" (123–24). Listening to Joplin's music changes their reality. In a final example, John Wayne rings Cora's doorbell and asks if she has seen a wandering prairie dog. Cora shows him a picture of Canada, and Wayne says, "Nope. That aint him" (86). Human beings can be animals and animals can be human beings. In these scenes, the space between the textual actual/real and the imagined real collapses. They intermingle and intermix, creating a different and more expansive subject and reality.

In addition, dreams and dreaming, which is not "all that different from living" (62), become a suitable parallel for fiction and expand reality in the text. Cora sees her death in a dream. The narrator/protagonist awakes Cora in the middle of a dream. "She [is] in the house, the one with the Gallic accent. She'd spent a lot of time in it, eating, fucking, dreaming and, of course, loving Canada, Dale, and me" (70). When the narrator/author is sick, Cora brings him his medicine and tells him her dreams (87). Unable to find a book that arouses her or to show that she is smart, Cora dreams the narrative where she returns home, goes "to sleep and dream[s] she [is] in the Kingdom of Navarre being raped by thousands of Spanish and French soldiers. It was no fun being sore and all, so she [wakes] up and [eats] a whole cream cheese pie and a gallon of pure ice cream" (95). Cora becomes erotically obsessed with food. In *Reflex and Bone Structure,* dreams are woven into the fabric of the actual, which joins with the virtual as the fully real and creates a different notion of reality, creating a more expansive notion of the psyche. Eschewing rational underpinnings, *Reflex and Bone Structure* mixes television, cinema, facts, fiction, dreams, and imagination to unleash desire, to create new knowledge, a new virtual reality, and new human potentials and possibilities.

These transformed/invented characters, events, and situations that bring different elements together, that combine the real with the fantastic, the actual and the virtual, the human with the object, signify a planetary mental world where rigid oppositions do not apply but instead are processes that Guattari call becomings—"virtualities of meaning and praxis that are extrinsic to the opposition reality/representation" (Guattari, *Soft Subversions* 198). Oppositions, which are violent and negative, are replaced by differences, which are nonhierarchal and equal. Major in *Reflex and Bone Structure* is inventing new potentials for and possibilities of life. Human forces come into play with infinitary forces, also producing different imaginative social spaces.

In disrupting language, traditional assumptions, and literary formal narration and in mixing television, facts, fiction, dreams, movies, the virtual, and imagination, Major unleashes fresh energy and imaginings, creating new spaces and allowing the reader "to *think* and to *imagine* certain possibilities or impossibilities" (Bolling and Major 31). In the world of *Reflex and Bone Structure,* Major is doing "everything [he] like[s]," making "up everything," and "extending reality, not retelling it" (*Reflex and Bone Structure* 49). In this virtual world, which refers "more insistently inwardly for its own validity" (Bolling and Major 28), there are enormous potentialities. It is possible for the narrator to be in bed watching the movie *The Bright Shawl* on the late show and be transformed to 1923, where he is "taking Mary Astor home in a yellow taxi. Dorothy Gish is jealous" (3). It is possible for Cora's cooked Thanksgiving turkey to begin to move (*Reflex and Bone Structure* 137), for Duke Ellington to attend the party. In the transformed and imaginative virtual spaces of *Reflex and Bone Structure,* it is possible for Canada to come home and find the "rubber plant is doing the dishes" (46). Extending reality into infinite possibilities and impossibilities rather than retelling it makes it possible for Cora to be gang-raped by fifty white cops, and

> while the last cop is opening his pants, a boy child slides out of Cora's vagina, grows up instantly. A big, strong young man. Suddenly, he starts beating the shit out of the fifty cops. With his bare fists he beats them into a pile of pulp. He releases his mother then vanishes. (124)

Television and movies give these characters the sense that they can transcend biological, cultural, and historical limitations and live disembodied, free-floating existences. In the age of media, when our subjectivity "is technologically extended to involve us in the whole of mankind and to incorporate the whole of mankind in us," writes McLuhan in *Understanding Media,* "we necessarily participate" (4). Mixing television, facts, fiction, movies, and imagination make possible all kinds of human and social possibilities.

In *Reflex and Bone Structure,* all time is present in the mind, and all narrative threads are held simultaneously in the *I* narrator's mind, displaying the absence of shared context and time. Cora is killed in the explosion on the first page. Yet throughout, *Reflex and Bone Structure* narrates

Cora's and Dale's lives in the present tense, with occasional mentioning of their deaths. In the next scene on the first page, Cora is at a party in New York with Dale and Canada. Cora is flirting, Dale is using the bathroom, and Canada is drinking too much. Two paragraphs later, we are told that "The scattered pieces of bodies were found" (1), referring to Cora's and Dale's deaths. Next, the narrator/author bakes a Middle Eastern dish of eggplant, cheese, and rice, and he and Cora eat it. Later, the two "make love on the table with the dishes beneath" them (1). In *Reflex and Bone Structure,* time is always present. In another example, one sentence says that "Cora goes to too many parties and she gets drunk easily." Four sentences later, the narrator says that "They found some of her teeth near the window" (34), again referring to her murder/death. In a scene after Canada breaks down because he cannot deal with Cora's sudden death, the text juxtaposes a scene where Cora is playing with her teddy bear inside of a boat (36). Finally, as the television anchorman announces Cora's and Dale's deaths, Cora is playing Mozart on a piano in a Greenwich Village restaurant with Canada and the narrator (81). Throughout the text, Cora and Dale are dead and alive simultaneously, making an interesting statement about beginnings (origins), linearity, time, finality, and closure and the inability of language (narrative realism) to represent social reality. More important, the simultaneous depiction of Cora's and Dale's lives and deaths demonstrates the possibilities of the imagination.

Major understands violent hierarchies, rigid rationalism, the limited linear model, the limited point of view of morality, and the repression and exclusion involved in Enlightenment reason and the traditional novel. He is desperately working to escape all of these closed systems, understanding that within the Eurocentric paradigm, or the white-black binary, the white is defined as normative and superior, while the African American is underrepresented. The African American is defined as inferior, as victim, as deviant, as the same, or as devalued Other. Major knows that the United States, to use Sylvia Wynter's term, "is itself based on the insistent negation of black identity, the obsessive hypervaluation of being white" (Scott 173). He also understands that African Americans contribute to their own particular negative representation. "How do you deal with the [negative] stereotyped view of yourself," asks Sylvia Wynter, "that you yourself have been socialized to accept" (Scott 131)? Albert Memmi in *The Colonizer and the Colonized* would argue that the first option for freedom/escape for the African American, as the lower half of the white-black binary, is to become the same as the white norm (121).

But Major understands the violence of this hierarchy, this freedom, which means the creation of another violent binary opposition whereby the assimilated black becomes the upper half of the binary. He wants to complicate/unhinge/deconstruct this negative, reductive stereotype by rethinking and redescribing the African American. In *Reflex and Bone Structure,* Major assaults the white-black binary (hierarchy) construction. In the interview with McCaffery and Kutnik, Major states:

> Despite all the different agendas throughout all the various periods, black writers were always working against a single dominant impulse in American culture: the use to which white America put blackness. Whiteness was about not being black. Thus, black people were invested with all the negative crap against which white America defined itself. Black writers worked always to humanize black people and to overthrow the burden of this symbolism. To be human meant to be whole—good and bad, complex, and so on. (73)

Major wants to free the African American from official markings, "the negative crap," and to redescribe the African American as complexly "human," as a complex person with human frailties as well as human virtues. In the "Introduction" to his anthology *Calling the Wind,* Major further delineates the limitations of the normative society's imposed, reduced representation of the African American:

> This white image, contrasted against the black Other, is in fact only a mythic American. The

> American presence is so varied and so complex that exchange and conflict between the black image and the white image tend absurdly to diminish the richness of a network of ethnic cultures that truly is the American human landscape. Most individuals in these groups feel some sense of doubleness, feel their otherness *and* their Americanness. One indication of an integral struggle can be seen in their tendency to hyphenate the names signaling the two different selves—African-American, Native-American, Asian-American, Mexican-American, and so on. (xviii)

Major's awareness of "the American human landscape," the varied and complex "American presence," causes him to want to redefine the African American as hybrid, as a product of the "doubleness," the intermingling between the African American and the American (echoing Du Bois's double consciousness), as a part of "the richness of a network of ethnic cultures." Representing the African American as hybrid overturns/challenges the white-black binary construction of the African American as deviant.

Thus, in *Reflex and Bone Structure,* Major virtually plays with modernity's notions of Enlightenment reason, closure, totalization, and linearity not only as a way of writing a postmodern fiction to escape oppositional violence but also as a way of reconceptualizing the African American who is imprisoned within normative society's restricted, dehumanizing, and otherizing category of race. But in his effort to redescribe the African American, Major embraces plural subjectivity and sexual difference and also minimizes/subordinates the feminine, creating a narratorial *I* that focuses its gaze almost exclusively on the body of Cora, the female character.

But how does *Reflex and Bone Structure* reconfigure race and redescribe the African American? In *Reflex and Bone Structure* and other novels published during the 1970s and 1980s, such as *Emergency Exit* and *All-Night Visitors,* Major subordinates race to what Bell calls "impressionistic and expressionistic explorations of sex, language, identity, and cultural hybridity as a liberating imaginative construction and affirmation of self" (2). Discussing one of life affirmations in his fiction, Major in "The Erotic Facts of Life" writes that "Eroticism or sensuality is one of the grandest expressions of the affirmation of life" (261). Because he wants to write "an interior novel" where there is not a great deal of landscape or context (Klinkowitz, "Clarence Major" 35), in *Reflex and Bone Structure* Major moves beyond traditional black sites of cultural production and consumption as well as beyond thematic and structural concerns with racial and political consciousness, thereby eschewing the problematic of race and racism as the central focus of the text. Major wants to affirm the African American self, to obviate the "tendency to stereotype the [black] Other," to humanize black people, and to "probe beyond its [the African American novel] merely political aspects to find the roots that link their [African American] experience to all human experience" (Major, *Calling the Wind* xvi, xxv).

Thus, in a fictive world where all normative unities or modern categories are defined as discursive and therefore are deconstructed/undermined, where the notion of language representing reality is rendered moot, Major in *Reflex and Bone Structure* also deconstructs the category of racial identity as a sole marker. As with most white American writers in their portrayal of white characters, Major presents (black) characters as being unmarked by race, tapping into "some elements of [the African American] human experience that transcend the merely cultural" (Scharper 65). Like Everett's characters in *Erasure,* Major's characters are black, but race is not the "totality of their identity" (Katz 53). Describing the kind of characters whose identities are not constructed totally by race, Major states that "They're very American in their obsessions: They want to make it. They want money. They have all these American values. Or they're very jaded and dejected and isolated. In other words, blackness isn't necessarily the most important thing about them" (Katz 53).

Because the characters in *Reflex and Bone Structure* are constructed as hybrid, plural, virtual, and complexly human, with free-flowing desires and intersubjectivity as part of their makeup, they cannot be pinned down by modern labeling and stereotyping of the logocentric engines because language cannot fulfill an obligation to fully represent subjectivity. The author/narrator, Cora, Dale, and Canada emerge from the narrator/author's consciousness as decentered, fragmented, and postmodern, with their plural subjectivities involved in and incorporating the Other—both human and inanimate, the actual and the virtual, the rational and the nonrational. From virtual tendencies or potentialities, these characters are actualized.

We know that the narrator/author/protagonist lives in Manhattan, but we know nothing about his past or his family. He has gray hair (18) and is concerned about getting older and coming to terms with dying. He becomes jealous when Cora, who is eight years his junior, is intimate with Dale and Canada. Keith Byerman argues that the fact that the author/narrator has sex with Cora is "an act of metafictional incest" (*Art and Life* 107). The author/narrator participates in much of the action of the novel, and throughout he remains aloof, detached, and fearful, having an eclectic work history. In addition to being a writer, he works construction with Canada in Maryland and runs an ice cream store in New York. For a time, the author/narrator is Cora's agent. When Cora dreams about him, he is "rich and militant" and has "a national name" (*Reflex and Bone Structure* 69).

In addition, the narrator/author/protagonist is a detective/writer who is searching for meaning. He is "a detective trying to solve a murder. No, not a murder. It's a life. Who hired me? I can't face the question" (32). Initially, this makes him something of a modern quester. But like Poe, Hammett, and Chandler who complicate the detective genre, the author/narrator hijacks the detective search and pursues an investigation into life, wanting the reader to think about meaning, subjectivity, and reality in new ways.

As a character, the narrator/author shows his limitations as author, not being all-knowing and not being omnipotent. He is tentative about his ability or power to author this book. In many instances, the narrator/author enters the story as though he were simply another character, with human limitations. But the reader witnesses him simultaneously narrating and building the reality in the text. He has coffee with Canada, talks to the police officers, and has sex with Cora (Byerman, *Fingering* 268). But he cannot master the creation/production of himself or his characters. He "realiz[es] that [he] not only cannot *own* her [Cora], but also [he] cannot even begin to own himself" (*Reflex and Bone Structure* 101). Two-thirds of the way through *Reflex and Bone Structure,* the narrator complains that "When I have to deal with Cora I'm forced to think too much. I'd rather drink beer with Cora and not try to untangle the mystery of her presence and her dreams of swollen food" (87). Near the end of *Reflex and Bone Structure,* Cora tells the narrator/author that "he still do[esn't] know [her]" (142), showing that she has an autonomous life. At times, he needs to ask characters about their motives: "When she [Cora] was like this, it often caused me to forget incidents or things I felt I should remember. Why, I don't know. But the inability to recall something would nag me until I'd have to ask Cora to help me" (29). Finally, at the end of *Reflex and Bone Structure,* the author/narrator states that "I study Cora, but not with the insult of anthropological thought. Nor the folly of some aspects of Freudian wisdom. I still don't know who Cora is or what Canada or Dale meant to her" (131). Here, simultaneously, the author/narrator/character's "conception and perception" of Cora transform the "witness function of the narrator into an active interpretative function" (Cagidemetrio 6). His existence both creates writing and is created by writing. The reader sees how the narrated world of *Reflex and Bone Structure* derives its reality and meaning from the process of narration. Finally, because the narrator/author cannot capture himself in language, certainly he cannot capture someone else.

Aware of his inadequacies, biases, and limitations in telling the story, the *I* narrator/author shatters the rational myths of origin, objectivity, and absolutes. "I want the mystery of this book to be an absolute mystery," says the narrator/author (*Reflex and Bone Structure* 61). As he attempts to tell the virtual stories of Dale, Canada, and Cora, the narrator's narrative continually falls back on itself as he deliberately chooses to tell his story in a shifting, unstable, and nonlinear manner. In addition to having difficulties constructing characters and events, the narrator/author is fully aware that his memory is faulty and selective. "I remember too much. I half remember things. I don't know the incidents which I should keep in mind" (91). When Cora is out of town, the narrator/author has "no memory of where she'd gone nor when it had taken place. Though she had told [him] everything. When where and what" (29). After describing Cora in a picture in great detail, the narrator/author concludes that "I may be dead wrong about all of this" (84). Memory is subjective and relative; it is unreliable in telling the truth.

There are also times when the narrator/author refuses to provide details (17) or to develop an idea, thereby showing the selective process and the fictiveness of the text. For example, after the deaths of Cora and Dale, the narrator/author visits the medical examiner's office but decides not to develop the examiner or describe the scene. "He is not a character but an idea. His office is an abstraction. Information on Cora and Dale is scribbled on sheets of paper, silently standing in files. It's a threat to the mystery" (9). Furthermore, his writing process is slowed because he lacks "examples. I still possess the spirit of Cora and I understand Canada, his moods and his deeds. I keep stopping to try to find out where I am" (52), the narrator/author says, maintaining incompleteness and mystery.

Showing his bias in character development, the narrator/author has difficulties characterizing Dale because he dislikes Dale immensely, particularly his relationship with Cora. The narrator/author does not know the role or the history of Dale, a minor character. "I have almost no sense of Dale except I know I don't like him" (11). The narrator/author does not know what it is that attracts Cora to Dale, with it remaining "a mystery" to him (42). Therefore, Dale never receives "justice" from his author (138). Later the narrator/author tells us that Dale "was never meant to make it. He was that side of myself that should be rewritten. Dale was an argument I had with the past" (144). Finally, there are times when the reader is not sure whether the narrator/author is telling the truth, using his imagination, or lying, especially as he admits that he himself is "only an act of [his] own imagination" (85). This knowledge forces the reader to view *Reflex and Bone Structure* as suspect, as contingent.

But in *Reflex and Bone Structure,* Major, through the power of the simulacra and/or virtuality, completely undermines the idea that the narrative *I* is unified and whole, in the modern Enlightenment sense. Major uses his personal life as a metaphor for difference subjectively in his fiction to show that individuals possess multiple selves. In the interview with McCaffery and Kutnik, Major states:

> Exploring different personae in my earlier novels was something that grew out of my sense of personal fragmentation. . . . Back when I was starting out to write, it felt perfectly natural to have my work reflect this sense that I was literally a different person every time I sat down to write. It was an interesting challenge to find narrative contexts for different parts of myself that needed voices to express themselves. So in something like *Reflex and Bone Structure* I consciously played with this whole concept of author/narrator identity, though in fact there were several personae there: the narrator, the protagonist, and the implied author. (73)

In a Lacanian sense, Major is defining subjectivity, including his own, as relative, multiple, and shifting.

In *Reflex and Bone Structure* the narrator/author/protagonist ultimately emerges as a decentered character, as a character with multiple selves, wandering around outside himself, exploding in different directions, and dwelling in many moments of time simultaneously. Wanting to see the world from another angle, he imagines seeing the world as if he were John Milton, Boris Karloff, and Zola. The narrator/author's *I* is in all of the text's dispersed geographical locations and events. In addition, he enters humanity via other people, taking risk with the Other, seeing the Other in himself. At one point later in the text, he reduces himself to Canada (100). In another part of the text, he spends "time in Canada" (138). Three pages later, Cora tells the narrator that he is "too much like Canada" (141). He even defines Dale as a "side of [him]self" (144). One could say that Dale and Canada are selves of the narrator/author. For the narrator/author, the boundaries of identity are exploded, exposed, transgressed, and expanded. Here, in expanding and reconfiguring the *I* narrator's character, Major is showing how instrumental reason (actuality) muzzles and imprisons life, how it mobilizes and stifles other possibilities, or how it shuts down the play of differences.

Besides the narrator/author, other characters in *Reflex and Bone Structure* appear open, mobile, virtual, curious, and multiple. Cora is also a character who is clearly complexly human and decentered, with desires flowing. She is described as being twenty-five years old; as being five feet, five inches tall; and weighing between 112 and 125 pounds (109). Although an erotic character, she was never a mother but "was pregnant several times" (55), losing the babies to miscarriage. Cora's bookshelf and coffee table are filled with criminal, sexual, psychological, anthropological, and historical books by Western scholars such as Wittgenstein, Tichner, Alverdes, S. Zuckerman, H. Soderman, and John J. O'Connell (26–27).

Before leaving Atlanta, Cora experienced racism. She is defined as "a Black woman from the South" (119), with grandparents living in a small town outside of Atlanta. We are told that at age twelve she witnessed her father being called a "nigger" by a white man. "The pain stays with her" (131). We are also told that Cora participates in "civil rights marches" (63) and experiences racism in New York. Crossing the street in New York City, she encounters a racist drunk white man who shouts to her, "*Hello pussy*!" (76)—a clear indication of how some white men have otherized/devalued black women. During a short time, a week, after she has her X-rays showing her bone structure framed, Cora is "concerned with racial differences and classification of human types. And searching her name, *Hull,* and ancestry" (104).

But we also know that Cora Hull, "a promising young Black Greenwich Village stage actress" (80), as the television anchorman describes her after her death, is more than a set of denigrated, racial experiences. At the age of fifteen when her father is telling her about the history of black people, she asks, "'Am I more than Black?'" (133). She is a complex individual who has human frailties and human virtues, who has a "pure spirit" (4), and who can also be silly. In addition to being American ambition, she goes against moral conventions. She is sexually free and adventurous and is attracted to young boys. Cora, writes Major, "is in touch with her own sexuality" ("Erotic Facts of Life" 261), which affirms her life. She has intimate relationships with the novel's three male characters. Cora gets out of the bed after having sex with the narrator/author and kisses Canada. With the narrator/protagonist looking on in the apartment, Dale "kisses Cora's neck. He strokes her thighs" (23). In Chicago, Cora is "casually and cynically involved with some very green young white man in the Black community working for his salvation and the crimes of the world" (113). Although she was born and raised in Atlanta where she experienced racial prejudice, in New York she is not concerned with race. Race is not the totality of her identity.

Thus, in New York after breaking with her family, Cora emerges as a virtual, plural, postmodern character who can live according to desire and curiosity and empathize with the Other. Her subjectivity is expanded by images from television, movies, the stage, and the author/narrator's imagination, allowing her to escape racial labeling by taking various subjective positions throughout the text. "She realizes she must not confine herself to the kitchen. It is too singular an image. Cora is aware that she has many other sides. . . . She has many dispositions, she has a round shape, her spirit is round her eyes, her arms and her legs. . . . Cora moves around and around. Cora moves up and down the spirit of her coiling self. She has an endless meaning" (41–42). Cora becomes many selves and plays several roles, including being an actress and a very serious secretary in an office on Madison Avenue. As a country preacher, the narrator comes to the city of Hull, where he meets "a gal named Cora" (108). While he is in a foreign country, he encounters Cora "in a coffin. I step closer to make sure it's Cora. It is. She sits up" (16). There is Cora being hijacked to Cuba, where she falls in love with Castro. "They have a big wedding and too many kids to count. Cora is both happy and sad" (25). There is Cora, rich and famous, "at a fancy party rubbing shoulders with Gina Lollobrigida, Alfred Hitchcock, Shirley MacLaine, Bing Crosby and Clark Gable" (40). There is Cora who is married to a policeman. "They have a house in Queens. . . . They have two children" (140). When the narrator/author is alone on an island, he heads for "an inlet called Cora" (103), and he also refers to Cora as Stella.

Thus, in a random, dispersed kind of way, we learn that in not being afraid of her unconscious life, Cora can believe in the free flow of desires. "She believed in the interplay between it [her unconscious life] and what she saw and felt everyday" (33). Through virtual power, she becomes animal/inanimal. Besides her role as the wife of a dirt farmer in the South in the movie made from the famous Negro writer's novel, Cora's movie roles are all mainstream leading lady roles, becoming a major movie star who is rich and famous, where in *The House of Strangers* she is paid to "become Susan Haywood" (56). In *The Cincinnati Kid,* Cora is "trying to pass herself off as Cab Calloway's daughter" (55). In the play *Voltage,* she is "playing the part of a cottonwood tree" (107). She is involved with a militant white group and is also part of a revolutionary black group. Furthermore, she is branching out into the women's liberation movement (31). Cora's subjectivity is constituted as hybrid, virtual, and multiple, with race being only one aspect. This characterization allows her to escape but not leave completely the stereotype of the black Other, or the symbolism of the burden of black inferiority.

Canada Jackson is also a virtual, plural, postmodern character. Like Cora, his subjectivity is expanded with images from television, movies, dreams, and the imagination. He plays several roles and takes various subject positions. From the various thoughts and images coming from the narrator/author's mind, we learn that because he is intimate with Cora, he is jealous of the relationship that Cora has with the young boy. At one point Canada becomes Cora, meaning that he can empathize with her. We also learn that Canada could have been a part of a revolutionary group, that he was once a policeman and a drama critic, and that he becomes a cop again. He wants to become God, he thinks of himself as a sledgehammer, and he, in watching television, turns into Edward G. Robinson (28). In a dream, Cora confuses Canada with the narrator (70). We also know that he is an actor who collects weapons and keeps a gun in a drawer in his kitchen. Along with the narrator/author, Canada operates "a crane on a construction site in Maryland" (35). He feels more at home in Harlem than in the Village, getting high on drugs and listening to jazz. Occasionally he "has terrible nights, sleepless nights, when he dreams of the godless world where he is an aimless victim" (51). Being deeply human, he seeks ways to improve the world. To keep his mind off Cora's death, he watches television because "it gives [him] a weird vegetable sort of copout security" (36). Other times, he pretends that "everything is all right and [that] she's very much alive. He invents and reinvents the world as he wishes it to be" (31).

Later Canada leaves town in a rented Mack truck, hauling "a trailer filled with traditional and realistic novels by Black and white authors" (128), which have obviously failed to represent him or to answer his questions. Driving north, he meets a blond female hitchhiker, and they settle down in a town where it takes their neighbors ten years to accept them. At this point they move to Quebec, where Canada learns French and politics and where his wife goes to college and learns how to teach college, calling "her Cora" (128). Jackson's subjectivity is also constructed as complex and multiple, making it difficult for normative society or the reader to successfully label him as the black Other or to define him as "the negative crap."

Finally, Dale is also a virtual, plural, decentered character. Dale, who is also intimate with Cora, is an off-Broadway actor who moves in and out of the text. The fact that the narrator/author cannot completely know or capture Dale reinforces this decenteredness, this multiplicity. "I have almost no sense of Dale except I know I don't like him. . . . I mean, I should be interested in him since he's one of my creations. He should have a character, a personality. And it is strange that I'm jealous of him since he's formless"

(11, 12). Unable to focus Dale, the narrator/author realizes that Dale is complexly human, that Dale "certainly is more than just Dale; Dale has to be a human being who is not simply Cora's lover. After all I'm Cora's lover too" (63). But Dale will not let the author "speak for him" (101), remaining a mystery.

Dale also moves in and out of movies and other characters, expanding his subjectivity. He dresses as Ava Gardner "to get a part in a melodrama on Broadway" (51). When he rests on the floor at the police station, he "turns into Cora" (20). In both instances, he challenges gender categories. In addition, the narrator/author "imagine[s] Dale [is] a fly" (11). Dale gives up acting and sells houseplants for a year and is sent by the narrator/author to South Dakota because he needs a break from him. Dale is also writing a novel that he plans to call "The Complete History of Cora Hull's Vagina" (21). Feeling isolated and jaded, he throws "himself on the mercy of the world, crawl[s] around begging people to believe him. . . . He [gets] shot in the ass with a bee bee gun" (12). Dale's multiple subjectivity, which mingles objects and gender, remains open. This makes it difficult for racial and sexual stereotyping to pin him down.

These characters are hybrid, having complex, multiple, virtual subjectivities, which risk the Other. As virtual characters, their subjectivities expand to include dreams, other subjectivities, created knowledge, and images/persons from televisions and movies but remain open. Like the author, they have several personae. The narrator/author cannot successfully capture his life in language. Certainly he cannot cross the boundaries into another. More important, the narrator does not construct himself and the other characters as victims of racism, as a set of denigrating experiences. "Blackness isn't necessarily the most important thing about them," states Major (Katz 53). As virtual subjects, he redefines and rethinks them outside the American norm and the Western consciousness, which have defined them as deviants. Here, Major in *Reflex and Bone Structure* gives us a virtual reality as an unalienated form of radical social action, which escapes the imprisoning force of the normal. But as a consequence of being socialized in a society that defines them as the negative Other, they can still have "reflex [racial] valuations that [they] continually carry" with them (Sylvia Wynter qtd. in Thomas, "ProudFlesh Inter/Views" 4).

In giving us limited personal histories, struggles, and desires of the narrator, Cora, Dale, and Canada and in constructing their subjectivities as complex and multiple, as virtual, with race being only one aspect, Major humanizes the African American, showing how his or her human experience and aspirations are the same as other human experiences. Major makes the African American as "good and bad" and as "complex" as any other human being (McCaffery and Kutnik 73). In constructing the African American as complex, Major, according to Stephen F. Soitos, contributes to "the emancipation of black American consciousness" (175), confronting the traditional methods of narrative discourse in which black people are reduced to the black Other. In this sense, in *Reflex and Bone Structure* there is a redescription of the African American.

In deconstructing the conventions of the novel/detective story, in undermining binary oppositions, in privileging differences, in eschewing closure and resolution, in constructing the characters as decentered and postmodern and virtual and not wholly rational, in using dreams, movies, the stage, and television, which allow the narrator to expand and to move "on to another place" (*Reflex and Bone Structure* 136) subjectively, and in using a digressive way of constructing the textual, Major uses virtuality and his imagination to create an artistic object in *Reflex and Bone Structure* that opens up the novel to other human potentialities, possibilities, impossibilities, and experiences, where life is deeper, richer, and fuller. He opens the novel to a different way of thinking about social reality, including constructing subjectivity, gender, and sexuality as being more fluid and open and constructing social reality as having mystery.

Fiction for Major in *Reflex and Bone Structure* becomes the way to burst asunder the traditional assumption that experience itself—in literature—is totalized and to transform reality, to rewrite reality/history, to imagine different spaces, and to tell different stories. Thus, as a jazz musician would treat a melody, Major uses and abuses language to renew it, to reform it, to make it work in a new and "more effective manner in order to unearth stronger, richer, deeper impressions of and extensions of life itself" (Bolling and Major 30), to exhume repressed ones and to open up new historical, psychological, social, sexual, racial, and human potentials and possibilities.

If *Reflex and Bone Structure* is a linguistic construct of the narrator's quest for authority and identity, it also serves as an ironic frame for Clarence Major's own logocentric quest for meaning, a quest that he continually defers. Major hopes that in attacking the universality of instrumental (Enlightenment) reason, humanizing the author, exposing narrative realism as a linguistic invention, and combining the actual and the virtual, he can produce nonreferential, indeterminate, fluid, and open postmodern fiction. He vaults borders, doing away with definitions that are closed and seeking permanent freedom—the poetry of life. He also challenges the white-black binary opposition and reframes the African American within a hegemonic, reasoned, Western truth that devalues the African American/otherness. Major is using and abusing language to scramble existing racial stereotypes and to redescribe the African American.

Although Major states that "a novel is anything" (*Reflex and Bone Structure* 61), there are blind spots in *Reflex and Bone Structure* where Major does not deconstruct, does not show differences, hybridity, and/or intermingling. These areas are protected by the privileged, masculine narratorial *I*, whose consciousness, desires, and interests ultimately shape the text. My purpose in discussing these blind spots is not to define the text as flawed. All texts have blind spots. I want to show further the text's inability to completely master its subject. Discussing this incompleteness of texts in *Of Grammatology*, Jacques Derrida writes that

> the writer writes *in* a language and *in* a logic whose proper systems, laws, and life his discourse by definition cannot dominate absolutely. He uses them only by letting himself . . . be governed by the system. And the reading must always aim at a certain relationship, unperceived by the writer, between

> what he commands and what he does not command of the patterns of the language that he uses. (158)

Texts simply cannot occupy all the space available to them. Their presence is constituted with certain absences. In discussing how *Reflex and Bone Structure* makes certain assumptions about universality, humanity, sex, and gender, I hope to make the text relevant and desirable to those readers and critics who share different assumptions about these issues.

First, unlike Wideman in *Philadelphia Fire* and Everett in *Erasure,* Major in *Reflex and Bone Structure* is aware of the violence of gender and sexual stereotyping. As someone who is in touch with her own fluid sexuality, Cora is fully aware of sexual difference, "that sexual difference develops out of bisexuality, which is the original condition of every individual and is subsequently displaced, transformed by culture" (Cixous, *White Ink* 60). She "senses [that] each man is partly female. And each woman is . . . partly male" (*Reflex and Bone Structure* 73). The narrator/author responds to Cora's manifesto, stating that he tries "to know these things. It is harder for [him] though. I'm arrogant. I'm male. I have certain weaknesses [that] spring from my [gender] orientation. I know them. I try to deal with them. I may not be very good at giving up what I imagine to be my status" (73). He is reluctant to give up his privileged, masculine position in the social. Yet, he admits that he possesses a femininity of the masculine. "I cook dinner. I wash dishes. I make the bed. I cook stuff like beets and carrots, bakes dishes with eggplant, mushrooms, veal, chicken, fish and onions. I have spent days in Cora's kitchen making fancy casseroles. . . . I bake fruit and make pies" (73). Also, the young boy in the "green cotton shirt" from downstairs displays sexual difference. In one instance, he sexually hungers for Cora, and, in another, he "licks Canada's earlobe" (7). Finally, despite the fact that both the narrator and Canada are sexually involved with Cora, while drunk Canada rams a Coke bottle up the narrator's rectum when "his thing [penis] had given out" and the narrator "still felt the itch" (30). Both are quite aware of sexual difference; it is simply repressed.

Later, the narrator further shows the arbitrariness and repression of gender labeling when "[a]n obvious homosexual person entered [the restaurant] and passed. Cora scribbled on a napkin: 'She/he is cute.' Which too was a way toward *naming.* Man *named* woman which condemned her to slavery" (*Reflex and Bone Structure* 120). Naming or labeling is a form of reduction, colonizing. Sexuality is desire, and once "desire is specified as sexuality, it enters into forms of [repressed] particularized power" (Guattari, *Soft Subversions* 35). In other words, once (sexual) desire takes a name or gender, a repressive system is established. The objective should be not the liberation of sex but instead the liberation of desire. Cora is aware of the violence of labeling. Also, equalizing the power relation in sex, "Canada fucks Cora and Cora fucks Canada" (*Reflex and Bone Structure* 11). There is also a moment when Canada becomes Cora, showing that sex is provisional, that it is performance, with the two attempting to shake their traditional heterosexual and masculine identities.

But despite his virtual reality of fluidity in gender and sex, the narrator/author's gaze remains somewhat entrapped in the actual masculine order/economy, never completely giving up what he imagines "to be his [masculine] status" (*Reflex and Bone Structure* 73). His gaze does not stare sexually at the male characters' bodies in the same way that it does Cora's. Throughout *Reflex and Bone Structure,* male characters are constantly writing their pornographic desires/fantasies on her body. There is the scene where the young boy "looks at [Cora] with hunger." In the same scene, Canada runs his hands under her skirt, and the narrator runs his "eyes over her [body]" (6). Later at the play, the narrator watches "Cora's breasts. They rise, they fall" (17–18). Even later, the narrator tickles "her clit as she wiggles her ass. Grinning and clicking her tongue against her teeth" (19). Going into a building, she sways "her wide hips, her high churning ass" (40). In one story about scientists who survived the Holocaust, Cora becomes the woman who "jumps out of the cake and shakes her naked ass and tits all over the place, in their faces" (57). While she is on the subway train, "men are grabbing [her] ass, squeezing it, pinching it" (139). Although she is branching out into the women's liberation movement, neither Cora nor Major ever critiques this objectification of her body.

In *Reflex and Bone Structure,* the reader gets a clear view/description of all of Cora's body parts but none of the men's body parts. When Cora appears at the Concept West Village Theatre, she is wearing a Fouke-dyed black fur seal coat, and "[e]very step she takes exposes her cunt. But she doesn't seem to care" (17). Yet in contrast, when Dale goes to the police station to have his fingerprints taken and the cop tells him to "strip," no one gazes at or objectifies his body. "Dale undresses and a dozen policemen lift him, holding him prone against the ceiling, rolling him along its surface" (20). When the narrator/author goes to the post office in only "an undershirt," he is not gazed at or sexually objectified by the white woman. Instead she offers him "a dollar to buy a pair of pants" (86). There is a clear discrepancy between how the text's authorial/narratorial *I* gazes/views Cora's body in contrast to how it views the males' bodies. Although he is aware and tries, the author/narrator never completely escapes the masculine economy.

Major in *Reflex and Bone Structure* uses other realities, represented and mediated by television, dreams, the movies, the stage, and the imagination, to deconstruct and to open up the modern novel form, to acknowledge excluded social, sexual, and psychological human dimensions—dimensions that have been repressed, subordinated, or excluded in Enlightenment reason. *Reflex and Bone Structure* establishes new ways of existing or inventing new possibilities of life. As with E. Franklin Frazier's African American subject in *The Negro Family,* Major's *Reflex and Bone Structure* is also reconfiguring African American subjectivity outside rigid rationalism, the linear model, racial essentialism, and normative society's negative racial labels and stereotypes. Like Frazier's African American subjectivity, *Reflex and Bone Structure*'s African American subjectivity is open, mobile, virtual, and fluid; it is a subjectivity that can empathize with the Other. But because it uncritically reproduces the masculine gaze of the feminine, *Reflex and Bone Structure* leaves but does not completely escape the American norm.

— 7 —

The Jungian/African Collective Unconscious, Jazz Aesthetics, and Xam Cartiér's *Muse-Echo Blues*

In the late 1980s and early 1990s, Xam Wilson Cartiér published two novels—*Muse-Echo Blues* and *Be-Bop, Re-Bop*—that deal with African American jazz music and how it informs African American life. I have chosen to focus on *Muse-Echo Blues* because its main character is a woman, and I am particularly interested in examining how gender plays a role in identity formation and postmodern subjectivity, especially as this subjectivity attempts to escape the conventions of the middle class and heteropatriarchy. Equally as important, *Muse-Echo Blues'* form is almost exclusively jazz-influenced. *Muse-Echo Blues* is, at its heart, a novel about the search for the flow of life and the inherent distortions and oppressions that necessarily accompany this epistemological quest. As in a jazz tune, the novel desperately wants to break free of the social and simply exists, becoming the pure essence of spirit and consciousness. In this chapter, first, I will demonstrate how *Muse-Echo Blues* uses the jazz idiom paradigm, discussed in the first chapter, and the Jungian/African American collective unconscious as counterspaces to discombobulate the ideology of rationality, middle-class respectability, heteropatriarchy, and the conventional boundaries of the novel, which colonize and weigh down the flow of life. Second, I will use Carl G. Jung's concept of the collective unconscious as a theoretical framework to show how *Muse-Echo Blues* redefines the African American with history, agency, and distinct subjectivity, outside heteropatriarchy, middle-class respectability, and Enlightenment reason, which has historically defined the African American as deviant or in devalued terms.

Muse-Echo Blues, which was published in 1992, uses the jazz paradigm and the collective unconscious to interrogate rigid identity politics and racial essentialism, which are modeled on the violent hierarchy of Western metaphysics, opening up African American consciousness to the flow of desire and advocating a different way to be human in the West. More important, *Muse-Echo Blues* uses jazz and the collective unconscious to give agency to the Other's alterity, with no aspect of human life being denied or objectified. Unlike Wideman's *Philadelphia Fire* and Everett's *Erasure* and like Greer's *Hanging by Her Teeth, Muse-Echo Blues* lets into its writing what has always been forbidden: the effects of femininity. This is a writing where the self has a relation to the Other. In divorcing the African American from signifiers of sex, gender, and power, *Muse-Echo Blues* offers an alternative to the entire masculine-rational worldview. Through the language and rhythm of jazz, the novel interprets the sweep and scope of modern American life.

First, *Muse-Echo Blues* challenges many of the suppositions of Enlightenment reason, choosing not to obey the limits. In presenting the troubled events/story of Kat, a 1990s San Francisco jazz pianist and composer who has a composer's blockage and men's complexes and who is in search of her inner clime, or spiritual core, in a nonchronological order, *Muse-Echo Blues* undermines reason's notion of linearity, which is a cornerstone of Western metaphysics. In using improvisation and play in constructing the narrative and Kat's consciousness, the text demonstrates its inability to master/pin down meaning, which contests the whole idea of absolute truth. In using italicized information to signify nonrational forms of speech such as fantasy, dreams, memories, and visions, the text opens up normative social reality and psychic consciousness and incorporates marginalized and nonrecognized cognitions or dimensions of human existence, plugging into other kinds of intelligence and/or forms of speech. *Muse-Echo Blues* also gives real and imaginary characters in the same textual space as a way of undermining that binary. Finally, in having Kat move through time and in and out of other characters, the text offers a different notion of consciousness/subjectivity. In short, in giving us a text that undermines the expected conventions of the modern novel and a human psyche that incorporates the conscious, the personal unconscious, and the collective unconscious, *Muse-Echo Blues* deconstructs the particular style of reason initiated by the Enlightenment that took a hegemonic hold and became the only valid form of rational thinking. The novel opens up the world to a planetary rather than a Eurocentric perspective on the human condition, making other forms of rational thinking valid.

Echoing the improvisatory spirit of jazz, *Muse-Echo Blues* values its own creativity, fusing the language of jazz music with its literary language and form and organizing not by chapters but instead by modes, which are based on the major musical scales instead of chords as the fodder for solos. The text is structured after the jazz model: music-like vamps, choruses, improvisation; syncopation of diverse material; the playing of blues, riffs, breaks, cycles, solos, repetitions, and new forms; instrumental and vocal conversations; and variations. The writing *swings*, coordinating its communication with the reader. Jazz musicians use modes to improvise over chord changes, to invent melodic patterns. Giving its structure and words a jazzlike quality, *Muse-Echo Blues* uses this jazz mode to play off and to improvise the blues tune/story of Kat, who is living her life in the "hard heart" of time, and it is squeezing the life out of her and her music (200). As a woman, how can she be a musician if she is "no one"? Everything in her and her environment forbids her to make music. In short, Kat has the blues: she is a "woman in search of [her] own need to *be*" (177). With Kat's blues, *Muse-Echo Blues* finds and celebrates meaning in the troubled part of her life. Through the music and history of jazz, Kat comes to recognize and to connect to her soul, the sacred Other, which will make her whole. During sleep and restless blues moments, her unconscious mind is released through dreams, memories, and visions and is returned to the "past for fulfillment"

(174), fantasizing and swinging in and out of her personal and the ancestral historical jazz musical past, the collective destiny of African Americans, like a jazz solo, and coming to wholeness.

It is obvious that Carl G. Jung's psychoanalysis, particularly his notion of the conscious/unconscious and the African collective unconscious, is a subtext to *Muse-Echo Blues.* The text refers to Jungian terms such as "shadow," "subconscious," "dream," "vision," "memory," and "fantasies." What functions in the unconscious of the text inscribes itself in the text on the signifier. I want to use Jung to establish a framework to elucidate Kat's unconscious psyche and her search for wholeness. Unlike Freud, who finds a rational cause for every problem and who defines the self as a reasonable commonsense ego in a struggle with an antagonistic id, Jung has a more expansive but less rational notion of the real and of the Self, which consists of the conscious ego and the unconscious, both the personal and the collective. In engaging mysteries, the nonrational, and the spirit and in adopting an attitude of reverence toward the whole of life or the daily need of the soul, Jung speaks to jazz, postmodernism, and post-Enlightenment.

In "The Concept of the Collective Unconscious," C. G. Jung divides the unconscious into two parts: the personal unconscious and the collective unconscious.[1] The personal unconscious is a storehouse of dreams, events, and desires that were once conscious but have been forgotten or suppressed. In additional to the repressed materials, the personal unconscious also contains "psychic components," "subliminal sense-perception," and "the seeds of future conscious contents" (Campbell 71). The collective unconscious "does not . . . owe its existence to personal experience. . . . [T]he contents of the collective unconscious have never been in consciousness, and therefore have never been individually acquired, but owe their existence exclusively to [evolution and racial] heredity" (Campbell 59–60).

This collective unconscious is peopled by interior selves and figures that correspond in part to the people of our everyday world but who are by no means reducible to exterior realities. It "consists . . . of the instinctual forces of the psyche and . . . of pre-existent forms, the archetypes . . . [that consist of] definite forms in the psyche which seem to be present always and everywhere . . . , which can only become conscious secondarily and which give definite forms to certain psyche contents" (Campbell 45, 60). Jung states that the archetypes or latent primordial images lie hidden in "the mythological and religious sphere in man" (Campbell 65), which could never be explained in rational terms. Man inherits these images from his racial inheritance or his ancestral past, a past that includes all of his human ancestors as well as his prehuman or animal ancestors. They are given with life, and they are accepted as the foundational structures of life. These mythical images are predispositions or potentialities for experiencing and responding to the world in the same ways that one's ancestors did. The collective unconscious is "an empirical matter" that is obviously shaped by history and culture (Campbell 62).

Since archetypes produce certain psychic forms/contents, Jung asks in what state psychic forms find themselves when not related to the conscious ego. How are they stimulated? Activated? For Jung, one answer is in "dreams," which are "spontaneous products of the unconscious psyche and are therefore pure products of nature not falsified by any conscious purpose" (Campbell 67). Another source of psychic forms/contents can be found in the "active imagination, . . . a sequence of fantasies produced by deliberate concentration" and unusual states of mind (Campbell 67). Jung finds that "the existence of unrealized, unconscious fantasies increases the frequency and intensity of dreams, and when these fantasies are made conscious the dreams change their character and become weaker and less frequent. . . . [D]reams often contain fantasies which 'want' to become conscious" (Campbell 67–68). These fantasies possess a power and energy of their own; they fascinate us and drive us to action that is entirely against our conscious intention (Fordham 27). Dreams are guides for men in darkness. "By extending a theory of the unconscious to embrace a vast historical and cultural range of human actuality and human potential," writes Christopher Hauke in *Jung and the Postmodern,* "Jung found that, in spite of several hundred years of 'liberal' Enlightenment, the citizen-subject of the industrialized West was only a human being as far as the dominant culture would allow. The cultural conditions of modernity had set a limit upon the permitted scope of the human psyche" (1). This means that the Enlightenment citizen-subject of the industrialized West is not natural but instead is constructed under historical conditions of exclusions and repressions. Of course, if the Enlightenment citizen-subject is constructed, he or she can change.

In *Muse-Echo Blues,* Kitty and Lena's improvised jazz stories as well as the actual swinging jazz musicians of the 1920s and 1930s and the beboppers of the 1940s belong to the African American collective unconscious. They serve as dreams, exemplars, inspirations, unrealized fantasies made conscious, fantasies produced by deliberate concentration, and energy for Kat to unleash her musical creativity and to resolve her complex about men. They teach Kat key lessons of jazz music and life, becoming her numinous source of wholeness and renewal. In an interview in *Essence,* Cartiér states that "I really like to show a dynamic of somebody in the present drawing strength from the past, from black heritage, and especially from black music" (Peterson). And just as Kitty, Charlie Parker, Lester "Prez" Young, Sarah Vaughan, Billy Eckstine, Duke Ellington, and Lena strove musically to cope with style and verse, Kat needs to find a way to compose her music, to find a style to solo with, to go it alone and thereby find inside herself and her traditions the strength to compose. Whereas Lena has the swinging jazz community of the 1920s and 1930s to give her sustenance and guidance and Kitty has the 1940s bebop era to nurture and ground her, Kat has the free jazz of the 1990s and Cecil Taylor to nurture her, needing the past, the ancestors, for guidance and instruction. But like Kitty and Lena and the jazz musicians, Kat also needs to find a way to use jazz to transcend her blues situation, to find harmony in the world. This becomes the problematic of the text.

Using jazz musical rhythm, scat syntax in the speech patterns, jazz language, the feel of improvisational impulse, deconstruction of chords, rhymes resonating off one another, a range of allusion, and off alliterative phrases, *Muse-Echo Blues,* like a jazz musician, invents new forms, new modes, and new idioms. *Muse-Echo Blues* instills jazz lingo and language in the syntax of its sentences to allude to the musical syntax that is evidenced in the music. Kitty scats, "I'm caught in a mid riff at a high note of hope when I hear 'Go's ride roll up to the curb down below" (35). In the sentence, Kitty's use of the terms "mid riff" and "high note" alludes to jazz lingo. Improvisation opens up and puts meaning and representation into play, creating a world and a self that are in flux and are perpetually becoming. It is both jazz and postmodern. *Muse-Echo Blues* gives us Kat's subjectivity, her consciousness/unconsciousness, the organizational mode of the text, in nonchronological and nonlinear, improvised order, with *Muse-Echo Blues* naming each chapter the way jazz musicians name their instrumental jazz tunes.

Cartiér's text plays with form and jazz history, putting the narratives of Kitty, 'Go, and Lena in unexpected order, as a jazz arranger/composer would do from concert to concert, hopping from one idea to another, playing variations of the same melody, moving in and out of other forms of jazz, actively conversing with the voices and tunes from the past, and seeking the sound of newness and surprise. As Sherrie Tucker states,"Cartiér invokes history in the same way that jazz does: by moving in and out of it spontaneously" (39). Moving chapter by chapter between the past and the present and putting the narratives in unexpected order to put meaning and representation into play permeate the text. A jazz musician approaches his or her music by having the melody appear and then reappear to be expanded and played upon. In each repetition the melody begins again, is renewed, or refuses to remain the same. Describing this jazz improvisational style in an interview with Rayfield Allen Waller, Cartiér states:

> You know . . . each time you get ready to walk away from [the music] . . . you come back and just happen to glance at something and you pick up something else out of it, so you have to . . . listen to it again,

> and the minute you listen to it again something else gets suggested, and you think, "Well, let me just hear that same thing again." But then something else suggests itself, and it has to be investigated. . . . [I]t was different each time, it wasn't sheer repetition. It was a variation. And that's what I hear each time is variations within those variations. (Waller 801)

Muse-Echo Blues reproduces this jazz improvisational style. First, with the tales of Kat, Lena, and Kitty, *Muse-Echo Blues,* like a bebop jazz tune, gives highly organized variations of the same tune. Kat, Kitty, and Lena's lives/narratives are variations of the same theme: their lives are about living free, taking risk, improvising, being spontaneous, and living the lives of independent women. In short, their narratives are variations on the theme of black women dealing with music and men in their contemporary moments.

Also, the historical but nonchronological arrangement of the various narratives seeks newness and surprise, allowing Kat to hear, in a jazz manner, the active conversations of the various voices and tunes that have preceded her. Although chronologically the 1930s swinging Lena comes before the 1940s bebop Kitty, the text tells us Kitty's tale first. And even within Lena's sections there is play, and with each play there is newness. The section on the mature, experienced Lena returning to Kansas City and reconnecting with her son 'Go/Chicago in 1938 comes before the section where she actually leaves him and follows her white lover Camvren to Montevideo, Uruguay, in 1933. Next, in 1936 *Muse-Echo Blues* has 'Go give a take on his encounter with Lena, his mother, at the malt joint in Kansas City, where she meets him for the first time since leaving the family. Unlike Lena, 'Go/Chicago knows that Lena is his mother. Finally, 'Go gives his riff on Lena to Kitty. But this happens before Lena's own version of herself in 1933. The nonchronological arrangement of the various narratives seeks unexpected newness and surprise. Like jazz music, with the surprise, *Muse-Echo Blues* is about the power of *now.*

Second, within the individual narratives, there is repetition and variations. On pages 106–09, Lena gives a version of leaving her son, leaving because her inside voice told her "Be you at all costs." Then Lena's husband Pop tells his version of Lena leaving their son (97–98), arguing that she was self-centered like a man who could not "stay put up for long" (97). Her dreams and ambitions made her continue to tour after she was married and had a son. Then, when Lena is conversing with 'Go about leaving her son, with Lady-day singing jazz in the background, Lena, as in a jam session with Pop, riffs an expanded version of leaving her son. Playing further upon this repeated theme, Lena accuses her husband of not understanding her; therefore, she "packed up and left for the green thought [she] had seen in [her] future" (108). In this variation or play, she expounds on her motive: "You've got to stride forward toward whatever it is that destiny's seen to fit to leave on your doorstep, be *you* at all costs, the best you" (108). Lena is trying to best Pop in representing what happened.

Even later, Lena returns to the theme/issue of leaving her husband and son but gives a different riff. This time, she focuses on her husband, whom she defines as a "dead-end" (114). Mixing her leaving Meech (Pop) and going with Camvren, along with her need to sing, Lena talks of the verbal abuse from Meech and the use of Camvren to escape America. This retold theme expands further where Lena through memory adds the issues of racism and limited opportunities (129–30). It is played upon again on page 137. This time she talks about her family, the Ames and Uncle Zeke. Here, there is repetition in a theme and/or variation. But it is in the variations that the new is conjured. In each of these retellings, beginnings, versions, and renewals, we get the notion that the representation of life or an event is always in flux and becoming.

Muse-Echo Blues also mixes verifiable historical jazz figures and events with fictional ones, further undermining the fact-fiction binary opposition. For example, *Muse-Echo Blues* creates jazz characters who are actual jazz players, such as Lester "Prez" Young, Duke Ellington, Sarah Vaughan, Count Basie, and Sonny Rollins, and others who are fictional jazz players, such as 'Go/Chicago. The text also creates vignettes in which jazz stories (Kitty and Lena) are improvised. These are creative tales in which the life/truth of the music is asserted and celebrated. *Muse-Echo Blues* creates an exilic consciousness that is opaque and uncompromising, wary of all group identity, cult, or mass. In capturing this flux, this consciousness/unconsciousness undermines the veracity of truth and falsity and demonstrates how the various characters are becoming.

Linguistically and rhythmically, the language of *Muse-Echo Blues* is jazz-influenced, replicating specific musical forms and structure through its prose, using Kat's blues story as a launching pad for spontaneous linguistic/thematic explorations, free-wheeling through long series of interconnected ideas, and following tangents but never getting lost. "Cartier is one of the very few writers," states Margaret Alic, "who has managed to successfully *replicate* in verbal form the experience of playing, listening to, and composing music." Throughout the text, the language has the feel of jazz improvisation, which is process, allowing *Muse-Echo Blues* to plug into other kinds of intelligences. Improvisation is a way, argues Scott DeVeaux, of "reasserting creative authority within the normally circumscribed role" (11). Whereas the jazz musician's performance departs radically from the legally recognized musical text or chord structure, *Muse-Echo Blues* departs radically from the conventions of the novel and normative, accepted language, creating something more than what it was.

Muse-Echo Blues uses the rhythmic freedom in jazz as a model to provide a literary/linguistic freedom, which allows for the continual renewal, variation, reinvention, and (multiple) repetition of a theme or event. Discussing her jazz-influenced style in an interview and echoing Morrison's comments on *Jazz,* Cartiér states that "I really wanted to consciously mirror the spontaneity of jazz, the improvisation from moment to moment. . . . Jazz seems to mirror key elements in black culture: spontaneity, improvisation . . . because your situation is always in flux" (qtd. in Alic). For example, at the buppy party after Nate and Chet cut off the discussion of black women dating white men with Sisternew, the narrator Kat describes the scene in a jazz rhythm and language style, capturing the electrifying note and line of bebop jazz and imitating in verbal form the experience of playing jazz: "Three quarternote beats then a series of rests worked their way through what had turned into blues in this measure during which Newsister seemed to be musing" (*Muse-Echo Blues* 16). Newsister's life is this blues life that is transcended by the improvisation of jazz.

In *Muse-Echo Blues,* there is the resonating off alliterative phrases where words are capturing the electrifying cadence of jazz music, creating multiplicity or what Jacques Derrida calls *differance.*[2] "But if you wanna play, you gotta pay" (*Muse-Echo Blues* 13) and "where co-guests are laid, sprayed, and ready to get laid" or "these coifs are all fried, dyed, and laid to the side" (5). After listening to the opera singer Leontyne Price, Kat says, "But don't let me elate when I ought to deflate" (11). When a buppy tells Nate that he knows how to simplify things, Nate retorts that "it's never to late to complicate" (18). Finally, when 'Go/Chicago meets Kitty for the first time and is trying to get her attention, he says, "I'm no flim-flam, and I don't scam" (28). Alliteratively, words are associated, which is mysterious. Throughout the text, language replicates the jazz rhythmic style and the improvisational feel of jazz, with the sound creating similar but different meanings. This is how jazz-influenced language plays: in several directions and at several levels.

In disrupting linearity and binarism and in giving us play and improvisation, *Muse-Echo Blues* undermines the Enlightenment notion that meaning and knowledge can be fully grasped through interpretation and language, becoming a space not of origin but instead of endless play of differences. Discussing playing his jazz, Lester Young makes his saxophone play multiple sounds. "I've developed my saxophone and I play it, make it sound like that alto, make it sound like a tenor, make it sound like a *bass* and everything, and I'm not through working at it *yet*" (42). He plays the tune within the melodic framework of jazz but with more play or improvisation, which keeps everything fresh. In his play, Young sounds like he is playing different musical instruments. Working not to repeat the same sound, Young's playing is fluid. He is "always loosening spaces, laying out, or something like that"; he is "always reaching" (42). His genius includes "[t]he warm, breathy, life-filled sound; the marvelously relaxed, flowing conception utilizing so subtly all the possibilities of time; the innate sense of form that shapes each interpretation or the message that is the sum of all the describable elements of what was truly a *style*" (Morgenstern 272). He is making the melody his own.

In improvising, Young alters the context of the sound so that no two performances are even similar, opening up the sound or melody to multiple meanings/versions and making the note not what you thought but something else. The creativity is right there, and what comes out is immediate. He is making it up as he goes along and depending on flexibility and resiliency, yet the playing has a sophisticated abstract reasoning. Young's playing is one of difference and becoming. It is open-ended. It is individual. With his playing, Young achieves a signature sound. Lester Young, according to Robert O'Meally, is telling the story, which is finding "an artistic voice and language" of his own and reciting his personal history with style (389). The playing is improvisational, spontaneous, ironic, and repetitious, aspects that question a certain style of rationality that is absolute and essential and present a pluralistic representation of a melody, a quality that is distinctly jazz and postmodern.

The varied shadings of the notes are also features of Sarah Vaughan's improvisation. Encountering Kitty in a bar in Kansas City, the emerging bebop singer Sarah, who is "close to [her] focus" (*Muse-Echo Blues* 44), tells Kitty that Mr. B, Billy Eckstine, unlike others who tend to see her just as she is, sees her "*will be,* so he tends to [her] druthers, he opens up wide, lets [her] play with a song" (44). Sarah asks Kitty about "her [Sarah's] chance for a gramophone date just for [her]" (45). As a woman, Sarah is aware of her own potentialities and abilities, but also the obstacles. As a bebop jazz singer, she scoops, bends, stretches, and slides around and into notes, instantly musically communicating exactly how she experiences life as it is felt. Sarah's swinging and playing continually make the song new and different, especially as she brings color to the melody and/or alters the melody's tone. Commenting on how the great Vaughan opens up a song and draws on the collective unconscious, sending it into all directions, Sonia Sanchez states that "*Sarah* left the universe sometimes. Sarah sang so that you would . . . move out of this world into another world. Sometimes she sounded ancient: She went back . . . to Africa, back to India, back to the Middle East, back to Spain" (365), exhuming her collective unconscious past that includes all of her human ancestors. These are both jazz and postmodern features.

Additionally, *Muse-Echo Blues* challenges the idea that meaning is total or absolute. In addition to the improvising and playing on meaning, the text shows those moments when the narrator imitates jazz by scatting words and using different words to defamiliarize and to open up concepts. Describing the rhythm of dancing to the be-bop beat of 'Go/ Chicago in Kansas City, Kitty describes one of her moves as "Wham! Whee-bop sha boop bam" (25), ending the description of the dance with "bloomp diddely boomp came the tail of the tune leadin into the head of the follow-up jam, a cool slowdrag bluesy wrap-em-up number" (26). This is spontaneous composition. Also, throughout, the text substitutes words that play on conventional words/concepts, opening them up to surprise and to fresh ideas. Describing the gathering of buppies at the downtown party, Kat says, "it's chock full of folks as far as the eye can see" (4). Thinking about the buppies at the party and their desire to enter the American melting pot, Kat says, "I'm chewing this through in my mind" (6). Acknowledging Nate returning to her at the party, Kat says, "I resee him making his way through pockets of people" (19). The words "chock full," "chewing," "pockets," and "resee" are fresh ways of signifying thinking, seeing, groups, and fullness. With depth and flexibility, *Muse-Echo Blues* exploits the surprise in words, the expected words or concepts, opening them up to multiple meanings. In signifying the referent, *Muse-Echo Blues* unleashes the play of difference.

Philosophically, jazz changes states of being, projecting subjectivity into a horizon beyond itself. Jazz enters the soul, opening it up to limitless possibilities, connecting it to other souls and entities, hoping for a different future, and liberating its consciousness from obstacles and barriers (the blues) that prevent the flow of desires. Jazz music, argues free-jazz bassist William Parker, uplifts "people and spiritually tap into things and help[s] people get into their optimium self—to better their personalities, better their spirit, better their understanding, better their idea of why we're here on earth and why we want to live" (French 40). Jazz accepts repetition, reinvention, or re-creation as an accepted fact of life, accepting difference and becoming. "It is an endless road of discovery leading to more maturity and acceptance of personal responsibility, a greater respect for cultures around the world, an invigorating playfulness, an excitement about change and an appetite for the unpredictable" (Marsalis, *Moving to Higher Ground* 10). Jazz is not judgmental; it is constantly in motion, avoiding being categorized. It teaches you to "[r]espect your own creativity," writes Wynton Marsalis, "*and* [to] respect the creativity and creative space of other people" (*Moving to Higher Ground* xiv), transcending self and accepting otherness.

Kitty demonstrates this philosophy of jazz, with jazz transforming her life, taking her from the mundane everydayness to the transcendence. Listening to 'Go play and feeling his music in her soul, Kitty narrates:

> Then, bloomp diddely *boomp* came the tail of the tune leadin into the head of the follow-up jam, a cool slowdrag bluesy wrap-em-up number which 'Go brought in with a wail. Whatever the riff 'Go rode it with a loping swing that arced out wide and then closed in, eyes closed—The *sound* of the man, it oozed right into your soul, made you rack back all the sad undertones of a life fulla doubledge color—I sank down into a breezy sea of endless possibility. (*Muse-Echo Blues* 26)

'Go's musical tale becomes "a stream of images that attach[] themselves to the notes" (Crouch 3). It reaches and fills some space inside Kitty, providing her brain with "an artificial environment, forcing it through that environment in controlled ways" (Jourdain 331). As a consequence, Kitty moves outside her conscious ego, which is grounded in rationality, and attains "a greater grasp of the world, as if rising from the ground to look down upon the confusing maze of ordinary existence" (Jourdain 331). She is connecting to something beyond her limited space and time, to the unknown Other/source, which is responsible for her existence. In this instance, Kitty experiences transcendence. Jazz allows Kitty to improve her life; to move beyond the blues, the "sad undertones" of life; to experience psychic wholeness; and to celebrate life's endless possibilities. When 'Go finishes, he asks Kitty how did she feels, and she says, "Almost cured" (*Muse-Echo Blues* 26). Jazz, argues Loren Schoenberg, has a "protean quality that drives some to distraction and others to ecstasy"; for Kitty, it is a music that drives her to ecstasy, a music that "inspires a great passion" (2).

In addition, jazz life is cool; it has a reflective attitude, dealing in the light and dark sides of life and playing off both sides. It is always open and mobile, encountering, questioning, and accepting of the spectrum of human life. Wynton Marsalis, in the "Foreword" to *The NPR Curious Listener's Guide to Jazz,* writes that

> Jazz music rewards a kind of restless, wide-ranging curiosity about life and the people and forces in it. . . . Comedy, tragedy, high-mindedness, downhomeness, sophistication, pathos, joy—Jazz contains and celebrates all of these things and more. . . . Jazz is an art form that depends on questioning, on challenging prevailing assumptions. (Schoenberg ix, x)

Through questioning, jazz deconstructs the status quo, the norm. Jazz life is living moment to moment and doing the best you can under any circumstances, including transcending the obstacles in life. Jazz expresses the life of the (African American) collective unconscious, which contains elements that point to new spiritual possibilities beyond the confusion of society.

The great jazz saxophonist Lester "Prez" Young, a character in *Muse-Echo Blues,* embodies jazz, taking life easy. In a blues kind of way, Young, to use the words of bell hooks in her discussion of black musicians, "confronts the hardships of life without allowing [his] spirit[] to be ravaged" (147). He had a hellish period in the military and is dishonorably discharged, returning with a broken spirit to the jazz world, where he becomes a drug user. Yet Young is self-assured, remaining calm under duress, taking his pain and disappointments and turning them into gold. He has "the ability to withstand the heat and remain centered" (hooks 147), playing at the peak of his power. He lives his life the way he plays. "[H]is movement is wrought in solid-caught rhythm, his every motion is taut as a drum" (*Muse-Echo Blues* 41). His cool sideways horn tells it like it is, whispering, chuckling, rhapsodizing the sweet thunder of rough-smooth melodies. He creates speech-like improvisations that are the epitome of cool. The playing sounds like it is motivated by feelings, like it is coming from the heart, where his spirit, energy, and power are unleashed. Prez is telling the listener who he is. "The message of Lester Young," writes Dan Morgenstern, "was intensely personal. Prez spoke into his horn, and what came out was always a story. As one listens to these creations torn from the womb of indifferent time, one marvels at the measure of this man, who in his own gentle way had the strength of a giant and the patience of an angel" (272). Even when Kitty tells him to his face that he should "cut that juice [heroin] loose," Prez keeps his cool, "Just like he jams on the stand, bendin round detours upcoming, flowin like sorghum round roadblocks right up to where sweet darkness ends" (43), viewing Billie Holiday as his jazz equal. Young's tone is light and floating, acknowledging but transcending the darkness. Later he keys in on Kitty's "waspish" (judgmental) way: "So why are you going to get into and say, 'He's an old junkie'. . . . Whatever we do, me *or* Lady, . . . whoever it is, let em do that and enjoy themselves and get your kicks yourself" (43). Young is telling Kitty that there are no ideals of purity and is asking her to accept the spectrum or the flow of life, to enjoy the music, and to be less judgmental of the musicians.

Muse-Echo Blues opens in San Francisco in 1990 with the "mace-colored" Kat, in a blues funk, attending a cocktail party, the guest of Nate, the new man in her life, to whom she is physically/sexually attracted. To Kat, Nate is "fine as wine, tall and divine, six feet four *flesh* . . . dressed in [a] charcoal three-piece" suit (14); she likes his élan, but his looks and vigorous enthusiasm are the only way she can relate to him. She cannot connect with him musically, culturally, or intellectually. Yet his debonair looks "exude capability/seem to demand, *Hey world, lean on me*" (19). Kat is defining Nate as a sexual object. At this moment in her life, Kat, like Violet in Morrison's *Jazz,* is at an impasse and is disoriented; she has not been getting "cues from the muse" (14). Therefore, she cannot compose her music, and she is unaware of what will inspire her to move past this blockage. Her present situation excludes anything to do with the imagination, causing her to become her own censor. As a creative person, Kat personifies the source of her inspiration as another person, a muse. She has sought out Nate, who is self-centered and egotistical, because she hopes to find herself in him or to find in Nate someone she can lean on. In *Black Feminist Thought,* Patricia Hill Collins discusses the historical reasoning for black women leaning on black men and for black men "protecting Black women from both economic and sexual exploitation" (156). Here, Kat's desire is expressed through an alienated form of submission, which represents a peculiar transposition of the desire for recognition. Kat's masochism, to use the words of the feminist psychoanalyst Jessica Benjamin in *The Bonds of Love,* "is to search for recognition [of the self] through an other who is powerful enough to bestow this recognition" (56). Kat hopes to get recognition of herself from Nate. At the party, she is doing her duty as "guest" in the atrium, while Urban Professnulls are comfortable upon the "peripheral floor," where people are more "laid back" (*Muse-Echo Blues* 4). There is a clean-cut woman who is shoeless, but below the uprising buppies are uptight. Kat is clearly alienated from both Nate and the buppy Valhalla, "this lash-n-dash showcase" in the "mobscene" below (5), who have become capitalism personified.

In contrast to jazz, this anticreative buppy group, which comes in all shades and colors, where the "half white blacks are darker skinned than full-black blacks who hail from fair-skinned kin" (13), represents the center, the rigid social norm, a "judging arena" (5), which is fatal to the care of the soul, the inner self. The buppy group lives an unbalanced and restrictive life, where the conscious ego rules its existence. Believing in the ideology of rationality but talking at times "overly blackly" (13), this bootstrapping group defines itself as hegemonic, as an ideal of middle-class racial purity, "judging" people such as Kat who dress differently, charging her with failure to "uplift the race by appearance," which she thinks is "a woeful waste of raw possibility" (5). As they are constructed in *Muse-Echo Blues,* the buppies belong to late-modern industrial capitalism, which emphasizes consumption, self-realization, and the release of the individual from traditional restraints and ascriptive ties. They also belong to the Enlightenment narrative of progress, individualism, and racial uplift, where their desires and beings are clearly traditionally American. In addition to being "meltingpot lickers" who stick to the "broth" where it is "spiceless" (6), they are also consumers, who are into appearances, clothes, and Beamers, inventing these obsessions to break out of their binality, which is created because of their refusal of transcendence.

In being rational rather than spiritual, the buppies are cut off from the universal symbols of the collective unconscious, which are necessary components of the psyche. They seek light but bring darkness upon themselves, substituting the material—jobs, hard work, industry—for the spiritual because, according to Jung, "they feel guilt[y] for [their] break with tradition," for being "disloyal to the past" (153). Never experiencing the soul, the sacred Other, they never know that they are more than their social mask or persona. The women look like they walked straight from the pages of *Onyx.* Their hair is perfectly styled, and they have "eyeshadowed eyes" (*Muse-Echo Blues* 5). They wear Gucci and gabardine suits. In addition to their preoccupation with their appearances, the female buppies are threatening to abandon the brothers and to deal with nonblack men, with "whoever can hang" (12).

On the other hand, the male buppies are mahogany men who are into three-pieced suits and horn-rimmed glasses. As heteropatriarchs, they are concerned with succeeding in corporate America, moving to the suburbs, and disassociating themselves from subaltern and working-class African Americans, "those rawrub ghetto niggers" (9), whom they think they must purify or erase. These buppies use Affirmative Action "as a stepping-stone" to become successful (7), then they abandon it. Those who defend it either live in the white suburbs or pimp the so-called community. They are inside the American Dream without being inside. Theoretically, economically, and socially, they are part of the American mainstream. But psychologically, they do not feel connected to a whole spectrum of normative American institutions and practices. In short, they do not enjoy the social power of being in the majority all the time. Thus, they live in the exclusion, without it becoming home, experiencing themselves in self-alienating terms. Without the experience of transcendence, argues Jung, the soul becomes sick of itself and tired of the world (Campbell 279). The buppies refuse transcendence.

At the party, Kat's presence threatens the buppies, exposing their limits and making them extremely uncomfortable. Her bohemian dress, her "sundress and opensling sandals" (*Muse-Echo Blues* 12), her love of jazz and her unmanicured hands betray their rigid, rational, middle-class world. They listen to "music of fusion, black muzak that girdles the scene with a no-challenge tease" (5), a bland elevator music that soothes and pacifies but does not force them to think or question. Muzak's subdued and steady rhythms exert a subtle control over the buppies. At the party when the band Frisco Finesse plays "no one gets off on or gives [himself] up to [the] musician or the music" (6), they have no response; they do not tap their toes to the music or say "Yeah!" or "Uh-huh!" (6). Deep into their conversation about black women and white men, the buppies ignore the bebop music being played by the saxophonist who screams from "spiritful throat, something to boost [them] away from homebase so [they can] gain new perspective, which is what good jazz does" (18). Good jazz "launches our visions by way of our ears" (18). The buppies ignore the "hope" in the form of the "saving-grace vocalist" whose "fullcurve lips kiss the lyrics" (5). They fail even to hear on the stereo the singing of the "soulful contralto" Leontyne Price's *Live from the Met,* where she comes to play on the other team's turf as "visiting star from racial afar" and knows how "to mow her way through those lone Euro welmisted modes of a few" (10). The buppies' insularity prevents them from hearing/appreciating good jazz or empathizing with otherness, which is necessary for transcendance.

In their ignorance of good jazz, the buppies, as they are constructed in *Muse-Echo Blues,* do not know its value, its spiritual and mentally liberating qualities, being totally oblivious to the force, or vision, of this bebop tradition. They are unaware of its ability to open up the world, to create multiple perspectives/possibilities, to provide the spiritual in music, and to transform life. In short, with their minds "untuned to improv and arch spontaneity" (6), they have no connection to a larger life, to the energy, spontaneity, and creativity of the African American jazz collective unconscious. They have murdered their capacity for critique, invention, and revolt. Less of a capacity for revolt also means the atrophying of the capacity to fantasize and to interpret the content of their actions. Because they emphasize the light, they end up as pallid, empty, bloodless, routine, and devoid of adventures, living a very surfaced, middle-class, consumer life, and their ignorance "disgusts [Kat] in [the] subconscious key" (6).

Among the buppies, with her natural hairdo style and her propensity for jazz, Kat is considered an outsider, especially being someone who, unlike the buppies, is spontaneous and open, who can plug into nonrational entities such as "coincidence" and "unprogrammed" joy (11). On their stage, Kat is "*stripless and plotless and wearing [a] fuckuped costume*" (12). But Kat cannot be her full self as a person and a musician/composer because part of herself, her soul, has been lost, neglected, or injured due to her current environment, or to what the Jungian analyst/scholar Christopher Hauke calls "the collective conditions of the era and culture" (109). Personally, Kat's consciousness is not broad enough to encompass the contents of the psyche that demand to be lived and that seek expression. Socially, she does not belong to a contemporary culture or community that will successfully nurture or regenerate her, that will give her a sense of identity, and that will unleash her musical creativity, her flow of desire. Instead she exists in a consumer culture that is squeezing the life out of her, and her hope lies in jazz and all that it represents.

Throughout *Muse-Echo Blues,* Kat, like Lorraine and the blues in *Hanging by Her Teeth,* listens for and hears good jazz, which gives her energy, vitality, and creativity. Good jazz allows her to create new music, new experiences, which can transform the self. She has an ear and an antenna for jazz music, music that speaks to the soul, which has a constant need to reach beyond itself to a larger life. At the newsmusic venue Koncepts, Kat hears the band Frisco Finesse "work up a lather on straight-to-it jazz," which has an "*avant garde* energy" (5). In the midst of the muzak at the party, she, unlike the buppies, immediately reacts to the bands' opening bars of Jackie Mac's *Jacknife,* to which "her mind turns on its axis like a green plant to [the] sun" (10). She hears the "soulful contralto" or the troubled blues sound in the voice of Leontyne Price, sowing her "ripe soul into furrows of . . . *Rigoletto*" (11). Smothered by the muzak, Kat pleads for Pope's *Saxophone Shop* to "feed [her] some muse-ic of nutrient energy, serve [her] some vibrant vitality, dish [her] up nourishing forwarding thrust" (18). Waiting for Chloe to arrive before they travel to Berkeley, Kat listens to Ladyday and Sun Ra on the radio, hoping the music will be a "cure-all muse-ic to loosen [her] blues" (56). Jazz allows Kat to think of things beyond the simple-minded concerns of consumerism and appearance, taking her out of the ordinary by aesthetically, spiritually, emotionally, and intellectually meeting "every anticipation with a graceful resolution" and raising "new anticipations at every turn" (Jourdain 303). Throwing her into overdrive, jazz expands her existence, and she realizes that she can be more than she normally is, that the world is more than it seems. Kat can listen to and appreciate good jazz music, but she fails to realize that in order to play music again, it is necessary for her to "hook to the past" (153).

At the party, Nate, her date, is preoccupied with his job at Townsend Behemoth and the black politic dominating the five African American professionals at his job. One brother thinks that Nate is an "oreo" because he does not "cover for him" (21), and other blacks look down on Nate. Ultimately Nate's dream is to become a lawyer, but he is having difficulties achieving this, which reminds Kat of her unfulfilled dream. Kat listens to Nate but does not occupy the same political or psychological space as he does. Because the two belong to two different worlds, they do not know each other, and Kat feels nervously uncomfortable when Nate shows public affection. "He's kissing my temple, letting lips linger a moment. I break out in laughs—now why'd I do that? I disavow me when I mince ultra-femininity or wince from sheer overstirred nerves" (18). Is Kat wincing because of her "overstirred nerves" or because she is resisting the heteropatriarchal Nate's need for her to carry a deprecated image of femininity to reinforce his masculinity? She is surprised that Nate is "unalarmed at [her] show of distress" (18), realizing and concluding that Nate is "used to juggling confusion" (18). More profoundly, she does not understand why Nate abruptly cuts the evening short and takes leave.

But after Nate takes leave, Kat dismisses him and decides to be true to her "shadow" (21), which is persistent and does not yield easily to suppression. For Jung, the shadow is an archetype of the psyche and is the source of all that is the best and the worst in a person, especially in one's relations with others. "The shadow is a moral problem that challenges the whole ego-personality," writes Jung, "for no one can become conscious of the shadow without considerable moral effort. To become conscious of it involves recognizing the dark aspects of the personality as present and real. This act is the essential condition for any kind of self knowledge, and it therefore, as a rule, meets with considerable resistance" (Campbell 145). The shadow exists in the unconscious; it is the gendered Other in ourselves that ego consciousness tends to reject. According to Christopher Hauke, the shadow represents "lost parts of the personality felt to be foreign and other to the ego but which is calling for inclusion and to be in dialogue with ego" (133). The shadow represents all those traits, desires, and contents that the conscious ego has found unacceptable and has been forced to repress.

The person who suppresses the animal side of her or his nature may become civilized and normative but does so at the expense of decreasing the motive power for spontaneity, creativity, strong emotions, and deep insights. To deny one's shadow is to cut one's self off from the wisdom of one's instinctual nature, a wisdom that may be more profound than any learning or culture can provide, and to disturb the flow of energy in the body-psyche. A shadowless life tends to become shallow and spiritless. In rejecting Nate, the black muzak, consumerism, and the middle-class buppy lifestyle, Kat is trying to avoid a shallow life. Feeling smothered at the party, she thinks that her "last hope of sanity [is] calling from outside in free pure night air of amazing escape" (20). It is very clear that Kat is not in harmony with her environment and that if she is going to be whole and alive, she needs to pursue her shadow.

After bidding Nate goodbye, Kat, who now wants a date with herself, finds herself out and alone, seated at the Waterloo West bistro near the scene of the party, which has put her in an unsettling, reflective, and blue mood, becoming aware of just how fundamentally alone and unhappy she is. She is aware of her need to master her inner vision, the inner urge that strives toward realization. But something is preventing this from happening. Jung attributes the reluctance, refusal, or resistance to engage unhappiness to "the inferiorities constituting the shadow" (Campbell 145). Although she knows, loves, and appreciates good jazz, Kat has also sought a conforming social identity that crushes the flow of the self, having always "lacked the heart to let go and let flow. *Just work out your wrackage of anguished fem-life stopped up for years under clamp-lids of* save-face *and other such self-crush suggestion, forlornities learned to conform with, or else*" (*Muse-Echo Blues* 166–67). She has denied her unrealized fantasies and dreams, her inner clime, her self, and has refused to move beyond her protected social identity. In this moment of aloneness and frustration, Kat regresses; as a woman, she does not know how to be in the world, to pursue her destiny alone, without a man.

For Jung, there are two important concepts of psychodynamics: the progressive and the regressive of psychic energy. Progressive is defined as one's daily experiences that advance the person's psychological adaptation. As the backward flow of libido, regressive psychic energy subtracts from psychic elements, while progressive psychic energy adds to them. Development may either follow a progressive, forward direction or a regressive, backward direction. When development is progressive, the self, which facilitates our journey toward wholeness, is harmonizing the reality of the environment with the needs of the whole psyche. When this harmony is broken by an environmental frustration or depravation, the libido is withdrawn from the extraverted values of the environment and invests itself in the introverted values of the unconscious. This withdrawing into one's collective unconscious is what Jung calls "regression." The regression, which refers to regeneration and psychological deepening, makes way for something new.

Kat's unconscious mind has the potential to open up and to make available her dreams, which are other dimensions to her being. *Muse-Echo Blues* assumes that the unconscious is the underlying levels of the mind below consciousness. Therefore, for Kat, at night "when consciousness sleeps . . . [the] unconscious can come out to play" (52). Retreating into sleep nightly is a time when the mind is cut off almost completely from the external world and turns upon itself and produces dreams. The passage from the unconscious to the conscious opens out. This nightly regression into the unconscious is capable of providing Kat with useful information about the nature of the obstacles that impede development and with suggestions as to how these obstacles may be overcome. Fortunately, although she resists, Kat increasingly pays attention to her dreams, which according to Jung are a rich source of psychic wisdom. Writing, composing, and creativity happen in the unconscious, where censorship is lighter.

Resisting her conscious ego, Kat's Self, the center of her entire psyche, retreats to the African American collective unconscious to revitalize itself, drawing on its wisdom and vast resources. In short, Kat seeks "the personal and psychological side-by-side with the collective and the socio-political" (Hauke 10). One of the ways that knowledge of the Self becomes accessible is through one's dreams. Kat's muse unearths the collective unconscious, particularly her jazz musical past, because jazz is the motif appearing in Kat's dream that is known to her. Unlike the buppies, Kat's individual jazz experiences make the expression of jazz predispositions or latent jazz images possible. What Lena and Kitty, the muse-ic selves of Kat, and the swing and bebop jazz musicians have to offer Kat is history, the wisdom of the ancestors. Lena and Kitty connect Kat to what Luce Irigaray calls the female "gender" or female "sexual culture" (*je, tu, nous* 12, 53), connecting her to earlier selves and to better selves to come. They provide her with past sustenance but with little authority, serving as successful alternative, female models of how to live an alive jazz life, striving to achieve and maintain harmony and balance.

As motifs from the collected unconscious, Kitty and Lena can "not possibly be known" to Kat (Campbell 67). Yet the two behave functionally in Kat's dream or vision in such a manner as to "coincide with the functioning of the archetype known from historical sources" (67). Kitty and Lena are "repressed instincts which have a natural tendency to influence the conscious mind" (67). As dream selves, repressed sacred Others, they are psychologically real; that is, they have emotional validity and have to be treated as if they were persons. But they are a disturbing presence. As Kat's shadows, her unconscious Others, they have been excluded from her conscious ego because they run contrary to her conforming social persona, her conscious ego. Kat is simply given the task of contemplating her fantasy to unblock her ability to compose "until its context becomes visible" (68).

Therefore, while sitting in the bistro in a concentrated or an unusual state of mind, Kat's muse attempts to take over her consciousness and her "insistent vision sudden-wafts in, seeming so far to be only a daydream, a harmless mere series of scenes of the sort that artists are all spacecase prey to" (*Muse-Echo Blues* 24). Dreams/daydreams contain fantasies, which want to become conscious, becoming symbolic expressions of the spiritual or universal aspect of reality and telling the dreamer what she does not want to know about herself. The "vision" suddenly bursts through against the intention of Kat's conscious ego. Without her psyche splitting the rational and the nonrational, splitting what Hauke calls the "social, collective norm and the individual" (2), Kat hears the voice of Kitty, the narrator, telling a "sequence of strange escapades" from the past (*Muse-Echo Blues* 24). Within Kitty's series of escapades, Kat receives the big band music of the 1940s, meets 'Go/Chicago, and gets a sense of the exilic lives of bebop musicians such as Lester Young, Billie Holiday, Count Basie, Sarah Vaughan, Dexter Gordon, Miles Davis, and Jacquet Illinois who are reclaiming or holding onto the wildness of the mind or wild imaginings. Kat sees how their marginal status makes them loyal and supportive of each other. They were self-possessed, sometimes inscrutable, and wrapped in a dialogue that excluded outsiders.

Within the music and the lives of the beboppers, Kat experiences a bebop jazz that is open, alive, different, and becoming, and as it redeems Kitty, it also transforms Kat. Listening to 'Go/Chicago, whose model is Lester "Prez" Young, take the stand, Kitty hears 'Go explode. It is a powerful on-the-spot creation. With his drug addiction, 'Go has come to embrace life under extreme circumstances, expressing his hard-earned optimism and his feelings on his saxophone. "Wham! Spliddledy jam, here it is yall, nothing but light-happy liquidy sound, 100-proof joy on the run, notes riffin for fun from down in a cave *a la* Dex Gordon, now up into hard droppin stop like the bopster called Yardbird, then easin on over an out in a long blowing gala of a wailll" (46). 'Go/Chicago is creating music in the moment, a music that thrusts forward, signaling openness, difference, and endless possibilities. 'Go's notes are full of "creative hope," and he is playing with personality. Realizing that the playing has redeemed 'Go, Kitty feels redeemed. "I've jumped from my seat to my feet from sheer bursten cheer, happy as a fat cheese-factory rat" (46). In 'Go's music, the satisfaction of anticipations accounts for the pleasure in Kitty's mind. Not only do we see 'Go telling his story, that is, reciting with style his own personal history, but we also see him telling others' stories. In this instance, we see jazz functioning in a spiritual way, touching people's souls affirmatively, opening them up to life possibilities, and connecting them to a larger spiritual life.

After experiencing Kitty's escapades, Kat's conscious mind is thrown by them. Her "mindplay [is] all weighted with strangers at odds in the forties" (50). But the "real-seaming fantasies," which inspire the creative process through remembered and improvised song and music, lures Kat to a challenge "that could serve as a gate to [her] own further fate" (50). Initially, these forces/visions that "burst out of the collective psyche have a confusing and blinding effects" (Campbell 109). Kat is not sure what to make of them. But it is in these stories/escapades of Kitty that Kat "first s[ees] the beckoning bet—*You a muse-ician, so musement your thang. Bet you can't hang an be cool 'nough to see what the muse of the soul's get to show you*" (*Muse-Echo Blues* 50). The fantasy/vision is asking Kat to engage her inner clime, the muse of her soul, for at the end of these "real-seeming fantasies" is "something to unstop her musical block" at a time when she could not compose. The fantasies are "some sort of herald . . . waiting to guide [her] through dreamscape to creative flow" (50). The visions had already caused her to face her worst fear: not being able to compose. These "strange chain of scenes from flybygone times . . . surfaced in [her] mind to fill in the creative blank where [her] real spark should be" (51). This experience for Kat is regressive, for the libido withdraws from the extraverted values of the environment and invests itself in the introverted values of the unconscious.

Yet, still unable to effectively play her piano, which means that aspects of the collective unconscious are having difficulty adapting to the conscious ego, and still in somewhat of a blues funk, Kat wants to escape her two-room apartment and "break free of [the] ingrown stultified life in San Fran" (51). Refusing to be land bound for long, Kat insists "on maintaining [her] own mental mecca of island design where [she tramps] in bare feelings, freeform type sand. Loose—call me loose, a loose woman of desperate intent bent on/determined to muster events of adventurous nature so's to waste not a drop of [her] own lopped-off life cleaned from the integral Whole" (51). When one is whole, the Self draws to itself and harmonizes all the archetypes and their manifestations in complexes and consciousness.

But before she can escape her apartment and "muster events of adventurous nature," Nate calls, and Kat has to listen again to him talk about his dream, a dream that she thinks is "deferred and rechanneled into plantation service at Townsend Behemoth" (54). Kat pledges not to let the negative thoughts and reckless opinions of Nate stop her. Still blocked, she decides again to leave her apartment. But this time, the "blond braids" and "hazel-eye blackfem" Chloe (13), her new best artist friend whom she met at the buppies party, calls and wants to visit. As usual, Kat has to listen to Chloe talk endlessly about her men troubles, her usual fights with her insecure artist boyfriend, Kamau. But in listening to Chloe, Kat, while smoking a joint and in an epiphany or revelation, recalls how being blocked and unable to "come from her music had caused her to seek out men" (58). Not able to settle on one man, she settles on two, Karl and Vibe, whom she pictures "as an object, a thing" (59). As with Nate, she needed the two to tell her who she is, but the relationships did not work. Karl leaves Kat because he thinks she does not support him (64), and Kat and Vibe break up because he smokes crack cocaine in her house and slaps her when she objects. Kat is not necessarily against drugs, but she believes in them "on special occasion" and "enough to stay sane" (80). Karl and Vibe, who are used by Kat as sexual objects, failed to show Kat her path of escape or help her find herself.

But as her collective unconscious mind breaks through and moves from the present to the bebop past, Kat's unconscious mind recognizes other subjects "as different and yet alike," as others who are "capable of sharing mental experience" (Benjamin 20). Kitty came of age during the bebop era, a period after World War II and the horrors of the Holocaust and the beginning of the nuclear age. It was a period when most, if not all, African Americans, including those who had gone to war to fight for democracy, lived racially segregated lives, when they were denied access to the basic public accommodations and the fruits of American democracy and capitalism. They were told daily that their lives had no value.

The underlying inequalities of race stiffened, especially in the music in the early 1940s when no music was produced. Entrenched patterns of segregation, both in the music industry and in society, automatically gave white musicians a nearly insuperable advantage in the mainstream market, blunting black ambitions and forcing jazz to reconfigure itself (DeVeaux 27). The Great Depression closed many of the jazz clubs that had thrived in the 1920s, and the repeal of Prohibition in 1933 sunk the speakeasies, which had provided many jazz musicians with a way to earn a living (Leland 121). In this atmosphere, white bandleaders such as Benny Goodman and the less talented Paul Whiteman overshadowed black acts.

But among African Americans, a new sense of militancy was one of the responses to the intransigent racism, and bebop, in its attempt to reconstitute jazz, comes out of this militancy, restoring the separateness that jazz had given up during the mainstreaming of the 1930s commercial swing. Rejecting assimilation but not integration because jazz was for everyone, bop demanded its own space. Boppers were outspoken on social issues. Beboppers, argues John Leland in *Hip*, "codified rebellion as personal style" (112). Rejecting the expected role of entertainer, they became artists. Ignoring commerce, they held themselves above the collective tastes of the public (Leland 118), forcing radical and disorienting innovations upon a reluctant and bewildered audience. "[A]udience expectations," writes Eddie S. Meadows in *Bebop to Cool*, "clashed with the reality of Beboppers' perceptions of who they were and what they were about; the result was audience confusion and rejection" (66).

Bebop emerged as a countercultural musical and social phenomenon, as "a movement and a spontaneous cultural crusade" (Baraka, *Digging* 225). The boppers presented themselves as the opposition, as nonconformists, especially in the way they dressed and presented themselves to the world, living in the present, always open and curious, doing what they wanted to do. They refused to let others define them, continuing to get through life's obstacles and find out who they are through their music. "[T]he life and the art," writes Dave Gelly in *Being Prez,* "enlighten one another" (x). Stepping outside the ideology of rationality and middle-class respectability and releasing their untapped power, spirit, and energy, they participate in life's flow, including the light and dark sides. This bebop music, argues Amiri Baraka in *Digging,* "took [you] somewhere [you] hadn't been before, made [you] think of things [you] hadn't thought of before" (224). It was transforming and liberating.

In their uncompromising complexity of the art, bebop musicians asserted their creative independence from the marketplace, seeking to create or, as a consequence, creating an idiom expressive of the black subculture, not the white mainstream. They jive and joke around with each other, "signifyin, cutting the dozens" (*Muse-Echo Blues* 37). There is laughter and camaraderie, and in life and on the bandstand there is a demonstrated mutual respect and trust, especially as they negotiate theirs and each other's musical freedom. They had their own language, calling one another "cats," calling their jobs "gigs" and their instruments "axes." They belonged to a shared sense of community and the accumulated wisdom of the musical ancestors. Drugs and alcohol were not only part of the social context in which the musicians performed but were also a part of the lives of artists, including Thelonious Monk, Fats Navarro, Bud Powell, Charles Mingus, and Miles Davis (Meadows 79), who were admonished by other musicians for their drug problems but were never alienated.

Through a subcultural wardrobe, berets, horn-rimmed glasses, and an impenetrable lingo, these African American bebop musicians musically revolted against big bands, arrangers, and vertical harmonies and asserted the individuality of jazz as creative artists, playing spontaneous and melodic music within the framework of jazz but with new tools, sounds, and concepts (DeVeaux 14). They took what they considered bland popular music and infused it with African American melodies, harmonies, rhythms, and artistic elevation through the art of improvisation. But they never abandoned the blues; they accepted and played out of the good and bad of their lives. "[T]heir own 'dirty' tones and 'unorthodox' fingerings, 'dark' timbres, 'Chinese' intervals, instruments, voices, etc.," argues Robert G. O'Meally in *The Jazz Cadence of American Culture,* allowed jazz musicians to thumb their noses at the conventional swing wisdom and create "something that was not only new and black but robustly, definitively *American*" (118). They were not bourgeois and middle class, and there is no evidence that they believed in Enlightenment ideas such as rationalism and the Protestant work ethic. Their art was not commodity; it was feeling and intelligence.

For example, Thelonious Monk was one of the founders of bebop of the 1940s. He did things his way: his way of addressing the fundamentals of the music, his way of playing the blues, or his way of negotiating melodies through harmonic progression. He forged a music that could make use of a variety of elements, taking you beyond the given and the ordinary. Showing attention to consistent thematic development in his improvisations, he accentuated the harmony; used short musical inserts, often in a call-and-response pattern; and played lines that swung within a moderate tempo (Meadows 222). He understood that the pianist should complement, not compete with, the horn players. He developed a style, writes Stanley Crouch, "that willfully shunned overt virtuosity in favor of a control of the elements in fresh ways" (87). Playing within the jazz tradition, Monk demanded that the listener appreciate "how he was playing around it [the tradition], off it, and through it" (Crouch 88). His genius was his ability to create variations based on the melody of the piece he was playing. Baraka in *Digging* writes that Monk was "uncovering old perceptions now being transformed into new rationales" (225). Through variations, Monk created the sound of newness and surprise.

But with all of his genius, Monk shunned traditional success and mainstream values. Although Robin D. G. Kelley in *Thelonious Monk* plays down Monk's bipolar/schizophrenia or his schizoaffective disorder, which is a mental condition that causes both a loss of contact with reality and depression or mood problems, as "the source of his [musical] genius" (215), psychoanalysts and philosophers such as Gilles Deleuze and Felix Guattari in *Anti-Oedipus* define the schizophrenic subject as the freest and most creative subject because he exists outside of the repressive Oedipus complex, transmitting "something that resists coding: flows, revolutionary active lines of flight, lines of absolutely decoding" (215). According to Deleuze and Guattari, "the schizophrenic is closest to the beating heart of reality, to an intense point identical with the production of the real," the flow of life (*Anti-Oedipus* 87). He is sick by "virtue of the oedipalization he is unable to bear" (91). Free of the oedipal socialization, the schizophrenic is able to be open and creative, to bask in the flow of life, violating all of the rules of the norm.

It is not difficult to interpret Monk's creative genius within Deleuze and Guattari's psychoanalytical paradigm. In many ways, Monk resists oedipalization and social coding, having what Deleuze and Guattari call a schizoid process of decoding and de-territorializing.[3] His behavior, states Marsalis, "was eccentric [and creative]—wearing strange hats, dancing 'round and 'round while others soloed, employing long periods of silence" (*Moving to Higher Ground* 143). Monk lived with his wife, Nellie, and his mother, and he was an individual in every way, simply not caring about social and economic conventions and norms. With the home situation financially secured, he did not have the need to hustle jobs. "He had his piano in his kitchen. And he didn't have to go out if he didn't want to. He didn't have to work. In his most creative period, he hardly worked" (Sinclair 389). And even when he worked, Monk was still creative and unconventional, being known for "enduring days without sleep followed by exhaustion, late-night forays in search of someone's piano to play" (Kelley 215). He could stay in his house or room for weeks at a time. He could be innocent and brilliant at the same time. He did not do much recording for the first twenty years of his musical career. Minton's was his second home, and he played there because he "wanted to play [his] own chords. [He] wanted to create and invent on little jobs" (DeVeaux 222). Monk's schizoaffective disorder was not the source of his musical genius, but it produced the alternative social and psychological space for it to flow, allowing him to move personally and musically to another level of consciousness.

Monk and bebop reflect this racially segregated era with a sound that was intense and unpredictable, dazzling and iconoclastic. The boppers' music was an autonomous art form. It captures the aspirations, frustrations, and subversive sensibilities, argues Scott DeVeaux in *The Birth of Bebop,* of an elite group of African American musicians. In addition to Monk, bebop musicians such as Charlie Parker, Coleman Hawkins, Dizzy Gillespie, Sarah Vaughan, and Ella Fitzgerald from the African American jazz collective unconscious come alive in the music. The life and the music are completely interwoven, and they do not separate one from the other. They use their imaginations to contest and transcend racial segregation, the daily devaluation of their humanity, economic oppression, and difficult life situations (the blues) that would keep them from celebrating life, from enjoying who they are. The spontaneity, improvisation, and flux of the music characterize or signify the consciousness of the musicians. In homage to the spirituals, bebop paves "the way from lush past to plush future of rounded, ripe, challenging notes full of creative hope" (DeVeaux 18). Their lives are their music, and their music is their lives.

Charlie Parker was another main innovator of bebop. Parker demonstrates, according to Marsalis, "the limitless potential of the mind to think fast and logically over long periods of time" (*Moving to Higher Ground* 147). This ability to invent compelling, meaningful melodies at breakneck speed is Parker's most astonishing musical achievement. He brought a deep feeling for blues and swing to everything he played. He was a "classicist whose improvisations were for the most part well ordered, played with immaculate precision, and largely within the boundaries of the established Jazz tradition" (Schoenberg 137). He created new harmonic structures, placing more emphasis on using seventh, ninth, and thirteenth intervals. According to the great Yusef Lateef, Parker "created different rhythmical aspects of developments that he played and he created a different sound on the alto saxophone that no one had produced before" (qtd. in Meadows 175).

At the personal level, Parker abandoned social conventions and allowed what Deleuze and Guattari in *Anti-Oedipus* would call his desiring machines to emerge, preferring "what is positive and multiple, different over uniformity, flows over unities" (xiii). For Parker, life is flow, and the forces of life exceed the physical body. Parker's flow contains not just the undesirable elements of life but also what Jung calls the "dark springs of instinct and intuition" (Campbell 140). The breaches of professional behavior, the multiple companion partners, his disheveled appearance, the four marriages, the taking off of his shoes while playing, the bohemian pleasures of New York's famous nightlife, and the liberating informality of playing in after-hours joints to steady (conventional) work on a bandstand are examples of Parker allowing and responding to his conflicting, contradictory flow of desires. This flow of desires, reinforced by the taste of heroin, which many critics judgmentally defined as self-destructive without acknowledging its value to his music, made him completely free, and the freedom shows in his music, where his rhythmic language is continually in flux. "His artistic power," writes Crouch, "was almost forever at war with the curse of his gift for self-destruction" (69). But Parker's drug use is not the source of his musical genius. Instead, the drugs produced the alternative state that creatively allowed his genius to flow. In this sense, the drugs are inseparable from the music. More importantly, he did not adhere to the notion of a pure, non–self-destructive body, since it does not exist.[4] He was always becoming, embracing the light and the dark. By the time audiences caught up to his early 1940s bebop music, Parker had changed/evolved, recording with strings and announcing his desire to study with Edgard Varese (Leland 126). "The anarchy onstage or in the musician's personal lives," writes Leland in *Hip,* "conspicuously signaled not sloppiness but intellectual curiosity, a rejection of limits" (124). Engaging the stuff of his shadow, Parker gives his life its highest values.

It is this bebop aura and sensibility that surround Kitty, who comes on the jazz scene in Kansas City in 1945. Kitty is a 1940s bebop singer in Kansas City, the heart of jazz, who lives a balanced, cool, successful bebop life with the jazz saxophonist 'Go/Chicago. It is winter in 1990, and Kat has a blues moment. One of Kitty's escapades reappears. In the escapade, Kat is called to Kitty's set because she (Kitty) thinks they have much in common. "*Between her and me there's more than ID; she's a woman like me, in search of her own need to be. Who are we to resist deep-rooted destiny*" (153). Kitty is one of Kat's unconscious female shadows, and she represents Kat's "deep-rooted destiny." Kitty can teach Kat lessons about life, about bebop music, about finding the Self. Echoing the jazz composition, Kitty's escapades are improvisations, eschewing categorization and absolute/total meaning. They are told from memory, and she doesn't "look for form among memories"; she is "not sure they add up or piece together" (24). Yet she still thinks that they should be "sifted through—accounted for" (24–25). With Kitty's fluid narrative, *Muse-Echo Blues* conveys meaning or experience without trying to codify a singular truth.

Kitty is an autonomous individual who has developed a culture of her own. Bebop allows her to transcend the mundane affairs of everyday life. She has a particular attitude about herself and her music that signifies independence. "No man snaps and I jump—I'm a woman full grown, not a new-dewed kid fulla trust and surprise" (36). But she is not a hard woman; she just plays "close to the chest, to *cover* as much as can be" (36). She is so light skinned that she could pass for white, and her crispness embodied her effort to straddle both fences at once—"the wood one to the race, the barbedwire to the other, an to maintain some semblance of savvy meanwhile, to maintain some . . . just to *maintain*" (93). Kitty is aware and is informed by her muse, her creative source, her inner clime that catapults her through time and away from the drift of day-to-day life with its creative-void type of strife. She is in tune with the rhythm, the cadence, and the language of jazz. Thinking in rhythm, she is "always workin the syncopate-theme of the sound into which or whatever surface [she] find[s]" (34).

Kitty, who is set in a time that Cartiér coins as "lindy hop & non-stop bop" (23), learns the lessons of life and jazz music from the beboppers who surround her daily. Listening to Mr. B at home on her RCA Victor while waiting for 'Go to arrive, Kitty observes how Mr. B is "blowin the brass outa 'I Love a Rhythm and a Riff,' workin the tune for all that it's worth, layin his horn down and loosnin his croon when it seems to be time to just bop past the stops" (34). Moving past the home base to gain a new perspective, Mr. B is making it recognizable and original at the same time. The experience of listening to Mr. B, to use the words of Robert Jourdain, "is so perfectly organized that every anticipation is roundly satisfied," filling Kitty "with intense pleasure" (318). Kitty is renewed spiritually by Mr. B's music. "I'm thinking of 'Go on his way all while I'm boppin, poppin my fingers" (*Muse-Echo Blues* 34).

In her encounter with other boppers, Kitty has similar moments of life and pleasure. Listening to Billie Holiday, Kitty knows that the art of Holiday did not come primarily from her words but instead came from the sound of her voice and her rhythmic phrasing. Kitty could hear the weight of humanity in Holiday's voice. Conversing and joking with Sonny Stitt at the club, Stitt tells her about growing and Count Basie's band—"sez he prefs it to Eckstine's cuz-a what Sonny calls Count B's 'stretch potential'" (39). Pioneering the use of space in both solo and accompaniment, Count Basie lets his players "roam far and wide, an that's how we *grow,* while him an the whole band just pockmark our melody" (40). The creative hope in Basie's music thrusts them forward. At the club when Jacquet soars "into a solo, trailin lanky long trills of high-register honks that loop through the air . . . like so many multi-toned steamers" (37), Kitty latches onto "one note and float[s] to remote uncharted stars til sixth sense" (37), experiencing ecstasy, transcending her conscious ego, and connecting with the otherness in the world. Jacquet's jazz boosts Kitty away from home base, opening her up to new possibilities. Finally, interacting with Prez, who is wise, level-headed, nonjudgmental, bluesy, and all grown up, Kitty is told about his and Ladyday's new Voodoo. After the talk, Kitty could "feel it already inside [her], that black-an-blue rhythm Prez won't let rest" (41). Here, in focusing on Mr. B, Basie, and

Prez, Kitty is amening those musicians who have achieved more than technical fluency and tricks of the trade; she is also "exhorting and high-praising those who have reached jazz's highest goal of attaining a personal artistic voice" (O'Meally 389). And as Kitty encounters and lives among these jazz giants, she wonders if she can be one of the singing "janes" who gets "a toehold on destiny" (45), wanting to continue to become.

Kitty lives and speaks in the lingo of bebop music, beginning a sentence with "while I was away in the music" (38). Kitty is renewed by 'Go's playing, becoming an integral part of his music. Hearing "All Too Soon" in boptime in her mind, Kitty says, "I know me and my own need that drives me: I want to be the life of this man, his indemnity plan for all the changes and bridges left in the tune. I want to be the heart of 'Go's solo, the tone note that glows with his brilliance that feeds me an already bleeds me" (90). She wants to live the moment to moment of 'Go's jazz life and music. In many ways, Kitty's consciousness/unconsciousness becomes mobile fragments that connect to the various aspects of 'Go's solo.

Furthermore, Kitty has a wonderful, healthy, spiritual, bluesy, nonhierarchical relationship with the drug-addicted 'Go/Chicago. They met first in Kansas City when she heard him play in one of the big bands. They met the second time on Christmas Eve in 1943 when he came to hear her perform. He was blue because the army had rejected him, having had "orange piss-test returns" (32). When she is down with the blues, she keeps to herself (32), knowing that love does not "lick the blues, that it [does not] pick[] people up in testy hard times" (33). Like the mature Joe and Violet in Morrison's *Jazz,* both Kitty and 'Go understand that it takes "two to tango in . . . love" (33). They are tender, gentle, and creative with each other. They have mutual respect for each other, moving in and out of each other's spaces, supporting and reinforcing each other, and knowing how to talk and listen to each other without denying each other's individual desires, difference, and distinct subjectivity. She likes his style; his "eyes size [her] up in [his] glory" (35). He gives her a song for Christmas.

The two live in the moment, which is "outside the quick loop of life" (90). Because 'Go, who plays in Mr. B's band, is a known jazz musician, other women in the club such as Mamie want to get close to him. In dealing with this, Kitty has to keep her balance, maintaining grace under pressure. When 'Go asks her if she is "roiled over Mamie," Kitty says, "No such luck," and thinks to herself: "I met him head-on with my lie. 'Think I'm screwy enough to think any sad skirt can work her way next to my man'" (88).

Kitty and 'Go are cool and calm, wearing a mask to cover not just sadness but exuberance as well. It is a mask that moves across the emotional spectrum, implying depths of feeling while showing none (Leland 132). It is defiant and protective. Entering the cab after playing his gig and detecting Kitty's blues attitude, 'Go asks, "Was I hard on you tonight" (*Muse-Echo Blues* 88). He is willing to confront reality, to face the truth and bear it. He is tender, gentle, and vulnerable. There is this smooth way that he carries himself. He can touch her in a way that makes fear vanish, and his lips caressing her body give her bliss. She challenges him, he tells her that he is grown, and she leaves him alone.

Kat's vision/dream of Kitty points to some "expected indications," or "at least hints, about certain basic trends" in her psyche process (Campbell 75). Kitty's situations/experiences are cycled and reverted back to Kat's experiences, allowing Kat to learn from the past. From Kitty, Kat learns not only about composing, how bebop jazz musicians lived and played, but also how a black woman in music is independent, lives an improvised life, is in constant contact with her muse, experiences ecstasy, transforms her ego, and is in charge of her destiny. Kitty's life shows Kat how jazz opens up life's possibilities and teaches one how to loosen and transcend the blues. Kat also sees a healthy bluesy man-woman relationship, particularly the image of a black man who does not believe in dominating masculinity and of a complete woman in a relationship. But Kat's anticreative social surroundings, particularly the buppies, are understood as being far more draining and listless when cycled between the descriptions of the vibrant club scenes in which Kitty thrives.

Like Kitty, Lena, another muse-ic self of Kat, also has this inner desire to seek freedom, to sing. Lena's dreams contain fantasies that want to become conscious. Music gets into her core, unleashes her power and spirit, and inspires her to be herself. Sitting in a malt joint in Kansas City in 1936, Lena, listening to Hampton work up a lather and to Ladyday singing on the jukebox and with deliberate concentration producing fantasies, tells her story. Young 'Go is her waiter, but she does not know that he is her son. She is a mature blues woman; therefore, she is prepared to confront and overcome her obstacles. "She seemed braced and angled to head full stream toward what she believed in, no matter how many hurdles stood tall in her way" (106). Her singing has a liberating and emancipatory dimension, which is about questioning and exploding the prevailing regime of power/knowledge. As an artist, she is in touch with her inner clime, and she is dying to get it out. It will be articulated in song, with a bluesy note of doubt and despair. "Singing . . . straight from soul's sad resources, was something that always had called her and lulled her; it had haunted her habits through home after home, from the homes of her growing-up motherless years to the three endless years spent with Meech and baby Chicago back in K C" (119). For Lena, life is full of the blues; her situation is always in flux. Jazz singing becomes the way she transcends her blues, the way to celebrate and define her existence joyously in spite of the hard times.

Lena's story, as had Kitty's, we are told afterward, had come to Kat through a dream/vision during the winter, at

> a turgid time when [Kat is] suffused with helplessicity, the cataplexed feeling of watching [her]self as dumbfounded caught-off-guard dreamer charmed into generative slumber. . . . Yet these visions from heretofore fascinate [her]! They could be mere offshoots of [her] stopped creativity. . . . [T]he images [she] see[s] in interior life could be only a scheme of [her] creative source enabling [her] to gather loose fruits of the muse and then say To hell with the tree, it's of no mind to [her]. (152)

Dreams, writes Jung, "contain images and thought-associations which we do not create with conscious intent" (Campbell 75). Without splitting the conscious and the unconscious, the rational and the nonrational, Kat's unconscious mind makes these transits to the past when she is feeling helpless. "[T]he past was the place to go when [she] was mad, sad, or too glad to stand it; past eras were full of more life than the *now* where [she] sustain[s her] self-inflicted identity" (*Muse-Echo Blues* 177). Looking to the past, or regression, has a creative, deconstructive function. It is making way for something new. Kat's unrealized unconscious fantasies increase the frequency and intensity of her dreams, which are offshoots of her "stopped creativity." Lena, along with Lionel Hampton and Billie Holiday, offers her inspiration, energy, and creative juice to drive her to action.

Initially, Kat wants to resist the dream/vision from the collective unconscious, embodied in Lena, to "shake" herself awake from it, "to swing suddenly to the right of [her] dream and plant [her] feet with resolution on sane-sapling floorboards of Now" (152). But the visions in the dream fascinate Kat, driving her to action against her conscious intention, against her "self inflicted identity" (177). Again, like Kitty, Lena is another of Kat's unconscious shadows, repressed sacred Others, who bursts through, catching Kat off guard. Because she is unadaptable, or cannot be influenced or modified, Lena represents the unconscious and all those tendencies and contents hitherto excluded from Kat's conscious life. Because Kat is fascinated with this vision, she lets Lena in. But it is still questionable if Kat is ready to give up her social mask, if she understands and knows how to assimilate Lena into her conscious ego.

Lena's story is one of struggle and triumph. She meets her husband Meech at the 1918 fair in Kansas City. They are married, and he laughs at her desire to sing, to "let something outa [her] that [she] got all stopped up inside" (119). Frustrated by the gender restriction in the marriage, Lena "packed up and left for the green [she] thought [she] had seen in her future" (108), leaving her husband and son in Kansas City. She believes in listening to and doing what her inside voice (muse) tells her. "You've got to do what your own inside voice tells you . . . and nevermind folks' bitterness, calculated or not, nevermind how they missed your dreams—You can't expect them to get ready for what you're hardly ready for yourself. . . . You've got to stride forward toward whatever it is that destiny's seen fit to leave on your doorstep, be *you* at all costs, the best you" (108). Before she meets Cam, Lena is singing in Kansas City. She thinks of going to Chicago and joining a jazz-oriented white dance band as a vocalist, "*where women like her were making their mark on the Jim Crow–controlled industry*" (130), but she never gets around to going.

Seeing the limited options available to her by segregated America, Lena, remaining cool in the face of racial oppression, passes for white so that she can become a secretary, affording her the financial opportunity to go to Montevideo, Uruguay, with Cam, a white man who has a fetish for dark-skinned women. She sings a blues-flavored jazz at Cam's hotel, El Hotel Bjorn. Singing in Montevideo, Lena could easily "lose what was left of herself in songs that pushed themselves through mellow minor keys"; her songs "melted like raw sugar, sharp and strong flavored, flowed from the heart as plain harshsweet cane" (119). Singing jazz allows Lena to transcend her "soul's sad resources," to turn pain into an aspect of art and beauty. Lena's sad resources in art are experienced as pleasurable because the aesthetic illusion acts as a protective device (Garon 16–17). Lena has followed Cam to Montevideo because he wants her to be happy, but she finds herself again in a restricted, subordinated position in a relationship.

In Uruguay, Cam becomes combative, demanding his freedom to have other women, and Lena is tested. Despite the marriage, he is a "grown man who must have his sport" (*Muse-Echo Blues* 122), other women. They fight over these situations, and afterward Lena listens to jazz, to Ladyday and Duke Ellington and the Cotton Club band, who provide her with sustenance and guidance. Initially, Lena works hard to maintain her balance, her pride and integrity. She is calm under duress, for she is determined not to let Cam be in control of her. "I've been doing for myself since Day One and I'll be damned if I need you to navigate me"

(117), she says to him. Declaring her independence, Lena later tells Cam, "I don't need no man to complete me or be my advisor" (121). This means enduring not only Cam's infidelity but also the indignities of Harry, who defines her as an exotic sex object. She comes to feel diminished in "a world . . . tailored to fit [Cam and Harry] and [their] kind" (123). She becomes their object.

But because of her ambition, she is forced into compromising situations. At one point, to survive, she decides to play Cam's game, to "play as Cam wanted and refuse to be bruised by her role in his rich-tempered skits; she would adapt to his heat-seeking ways" (133). But she is bruised by her role, whereby she is forced to set "aside her sense of herself to get her work done" (143), abandoning "top-heavy rules" and joining the 1930s "flux and ripe flexibility" (144). Finally, she "loose[ns] the bindings she'd used to gird herself" and becomes a prostitute, fighting "with her self after each of her roles in Cam's playscenes" (144). This period becomes a low point in Lena's life. She has a bad case of the blues.

But Lena regains her bearings, using jazz to transcend her troubled blues life and continuing to become, to be in flux. In 1938, after Jesse Owens strode blackly through the Olympics in 1936, Lena promises herself to leave Cam and his schemes and to return to Kansas City and her son, who, upon her return, claims "her as mother with no reservation" (138). In Kansas City, she returns to her independence and balance, without a man. She doesn't "look up to anybody . . . and no one can look down on [her]" (93). In 1938, musically, Kansas City is in the grip of the swing big band era.

Developed in the 1930s, swing bands use a strong anchoring rhythm section, which supports a brass section including saxophones, trumpets, and trombones; medium to fast tempos; and a changing swing-time rhythm. Swing bands usually feature soloists who improvise a new melody over the arrangement. In the 1930s, these swing bands became jazz-oriented swing bands. "There are few sharp dividing lines," argues Scott DeVeaux, "between preceding styles ('early jazz' or 'New Orleans jazz') and the common practice of the 1930s. The obvious distinction is in instrumentation and sheer size of the ensemble" (116–17). Some of the prominent 1930s leaders of big bands are Goodman, Henderson, Ellington, Calloway, and Basie.

In Kansas City in 1938, Lena encounters her son 'Go/Chicago outside a club where Count Basie and Lester "Prez" Young are playing. She later escorts him into the club, with Basie's "huge sound swell[ing] up in a roar" (94). In the club, people are alive. Everyone is dressed to the nines, "cats on the move to a groove of their own, independent and dapper, on the upswing of crash times" (94). Inside 'Go witnesses Prez approach the mike with his saxophone, "easing into liquid lilts that bobbed like buoys on a bountiful bay . . . the Buck Clayton blew in K.C. Style/riff to solo/trailing a sassy bright kitetail of brass, and 'Go could hear Helen Humes's lighthearted lyrics bounce in the breeze of the Count's punch-up background licks. . . . *Life can be so sweet . . . on the sun-nay side-a the street"* (95)! These swinging musicians and the listeners use jazz to keep pain at bay, refusing to let bad times prevent them from living and celebrating life.

Later Lena takes 'Go to the library, smiling and staying friendly when he loses his cool and talks strong to her. At the library she introduces him to black history, to Marcus Garvey, W. E. B. Du Bois, and Booker T. Washington, for she wants to teach him about differences. When 'Go asks her why Garvery, Du Bois, and Washington do not "come to grips with one grove," Lena responds, "As long as we have more than one head among us . . . we'll have more than one way of life" (100). And when 'Go decides to flow only into Garvey because "he knows what he wants" (101), Lena admonishes him that blacks "can afford not to be aware of our choices" (101). She ends with "As far as I'm concerned, we could use some of each" (102), seeing value not in a hegemonic form of rational thinking but instead in multiplicity, in many truths. This mode of thinking is very jazz and quite postmodern. Both advocate difference and equal. But Lena later commits suicide in hope of "redemption for what she had done because life is a song that scourges your sins from around you and clears passage to heaven or down toward the hell of our birth on this earth" (210).

Again, Kat's dream/vision of Lena, as with Kitty, points to certain psychic trends: the idea of dealing with and overcoming obstacles and of being an independent woman who comes to take care of and teach her child. Hearing Lena blow her tune, Kat understands that she can also blow hers. This idea of reverting back to the same theme within a coherent whole defines what Thomas Brothers calls "cycle" within a jazz composition (489). From Lena, Kat learns the experience and the history of 1930s swing music. Additionally, from Lena, Kat observes a fiercely ambitious and independent black (blues) woman who listens to her inner voice, makes mistakes, but eventually grows to overcome her barriers/obstacles. She comes to be in the world, to live a complete life, without a man. Like Kitty, Lena lives an improvised life, one that is constantly changing and in motion, one whose dreams contained fantasies that became conscious and were eventually actualized. There is nothing middle class and bourgeois about her existence. Certainly, Lena does not live according to the dictates of Enlightenment reason. But it is important for Kat to know that even if Lena looks on things as they are, she still might not survive them.

As her female muse-ic selves in Lena and Kitty give Kat her history, as they teach her how to get back in touch with her inner clime, how to have a transcendent or harmonious experience with music, how life is risky and also dark, and as they teach her how to deal with men, she begins to take control of her life, to assert her own authority. Giving up her need for the male gaze, which is the attempt to constitute herself by having her feminine colonized into the masculine selfsame, in her rerememberings, she fires Vide, who gives her great oral sex, and Karl, whom she uses "as a thing to stave off the worst thug of all, the feminized mugger called destiny" (*Muse-Echo Blues* 190), from her life. Realizing that she cannot find her identity/subjectivity in a man and "resisting Brothers insisting on locking [her] up in their own male delusion" (Baraka, "Toni" 109), Kat moves to resolve her complex for men and accepts life as a "solo of crink-tinkling keys on their own with a prehensile hook to the past that nobody can see" (*Muse-Echo Blues* 153). Finally, heading to Berkeley "where life and times are free as a bee"

(153), she listens to bebop and the free jazz of Cecil Taylor, who functions, according to V. R. Peterson, as a "guardian spirit" (54). Berkeley, which is "brimming with creative *stim*" (*Muse-Echo Blues* 153), possesses people—"ofays"—who compliment "free open spirits like [hers]" (154). Hopefully, in Berkeley she will get in touch with her muse.

And although she still cannot play her Plexus, Kat has an audiotape of the free jazz, hyperkinetic pianist Cecil Taylor—"jumping for joy on his keys, working the juice from each piano note with a stac-ca-to tease and then *longato squeeze*" (78). Free jazz was a movement in jazz music that developed in the 1960s by artists such as Ornette Coleman, Albert Ayler, Don Cherry, and Cecil Taylor. Most of the free jazzers were outsiders and African Americans. For many years they lacked access to the concert halls, grants, prestigious commissions, and other symbolic measures of artistic achievement. Advocating radical flux and becoming, free jazz reacts against bebop, breaking down/deconstructing or extending the conventions of jazz by subverting the various bebop jazz conventions—discarding fixed chord changes and tempos, song forms, and structured solos.

Free jazz works from "the idea that an improvisation need not be based on any chord structure, or governed by any preordained rhythm or meter, or bar length" (Schoenberg 39). Instead, it relies on a "far ranging, stream-of-conscious approach to melodic variation" (Schoenberg 56). What emerged in free jazz are "[l]onger, uninhibited, loosely structured, often disturbing performances, explosions of sound" (Gioia 344). Although freedom/atonality had appeared before in jazz music, Coleman and Taylor "raised it into a decisive issue" (Gioia 339). And although the sound was spontaneous and explosive, it was also the product of a highly sophisticated abstract reasoning. For Taylor, free jazz does not mean that anything can happen. It requires a lot of control over the instrument ("working the juice from each piano note with a stac-ca-to tease") and over the telling of the story (*Muse-Echo Blues* 78). Coleman, Taylor, and Ayler forced more established bebop jazz musicians such as Coltrane, Dolphy, Rollins, and Davis who were still playing tonal music to dance to *their* time (Gioia 340).

As she works through her musical blockage and struggles to get in touch with her soul and find her destiny, Kat increasingly listens to the classical and modern Western compositional–influenced but still blues-based jazz pianist Cecil Taylor, whose music is free but has a sense of direction. But the free is redefined every second. When she listens to Cecil Taylor, because of his "musical stimulation and creativity" (Spellman 4), she comes alive and is able to make decision, making "off just as mean Cecil T had stopped milking each key of its hidden-stash rash harmony" (*Muse-Echo Blues* 82). Again, listening to the atonal stylist Cecil T work his way through labyrinth keys, Kat is able to move forward. En route to Berkeley and listening to Cecil on her walkman, Kat states, "I'd just flipped the switch so that Cecil'd begun to wend in from the bend of where music imps meet, flash Cecil T captured on wax in Dark Forest of Germany, nevermind Aryan superiority dream, C T'd brought his own scheme of brash get-to-this! brilliance, a tune he must've first heard in hermetic elliptical craters of moon" (158). Taylor and his group, whose music remains truly beyond category, whirl Kat up. Kat's refusal to be bound for long, her desire to mentally escape earthly spaces, makes her attraction to Taylor logical. For Kat, Taylor's music brings a "flood of anticipations" (Jourdain 319); particular chords lead to particular harmonic directions. As long as Taylor's music travels in this external, away-from-the-earth ("crates of moon") direction, it registers immediate pleasure for Kat (*Muse-Echo Blues* 158).

But Kat is in Berkeley to meet Chloe, and the meeting turns into another moment of feminist soul-searching and truth-telling. As Kat listens to Taylor's "Dark to Themselves," which whirls her up in "formative tornado funnel when earthly impulse takes leave" (158), she finds Chloe standing beside her. Taylor's music is providing Kat with extreme pleasure, or ecstasy, momentarily taking her outside of her conscious ego, which is caught in time, space, and rationality, and transforming and connecting her to the Other, the external world. "Ecstasy melts the boundaries of our being," writes Robert Jourdain, "reveals our bonds to the external world, engulfs us in feelings that are 'oceanic'"

(327). In projecting herself into a horizon beyond herself, in establishing a relation with something that is Other/different, Kat experiences transcendence.

But Chloe's presence brings Kat back to earth. Chloe is constantly fighting with her domineering, heteropatriarchal boyfriends, who have a designated submissive gender role for her. "[T]he usual notions of sexual differentiation in roles," writes Toni Cade Bambara in "On the Issue of Roles," "is an obstacle to political consciousness, . . . is a hindrance to full development" (101). After listening to Chloe's men troubles again, Kat held her center and "lent her a lyric of uplift, mind to muse-echo mind" (*Muse-Echo Blues* 167). Again, ruminating on her own complex relationships with men, Kat gives another take on dealing with men. In the retelling, she expands her version, acknowledging that neither Vide, Karl, nor Nate "had mustered the dearness to stab [her] heart's core from close range," that she had "made sure of that and [she] knew it but didn't know *Why* yet and still; surrounding [her] heart was a moat of No Admittance" (167). She counsels Chloe, informing her to keep her art, because "Art's one arena where a woman's equal to a man, and black and white merge on the dance floor" (167). The two visit Telegraph Street, Moe's, and Cody's bookstore before settling on Counter Culture for food. While walking down Telegraph Street, Kat, thinking of her visits to malls, comments to Chloe about the "rabid consumption of lookalike wares" (172) and the mindless shopping. En route to Shattuck from Berkeley, Kat recognizes her natural surroundings, the "incomparable scene of bayside green dotted by wildcolor, wildflower growth, all of its potted by reckless-joy nature" (170). She is in tuned with nature, with the otherness in the world.

In this pensive moment, Kat thinks about telling Chloe about "the real story of [her] men and [her]self, how [she] hid in their fleshly connection in order to *ground*," to find herself, but decides against it. She knows she is "caught in a dream" but does not know why she is "haunted" (175). But Kat is aware that "some sort of detox solution seemed at the verge of [her] dam, trying like hell to work its way through" (175). Obviously, a breakthrough is inevitable. Then, ignoring Chloe, Kat mentally floats out into space, remembering and hearing in her head the music of Hamiett Bluiett, a member of the postmodern World Saxophone Quartet, which works without a rhythm section and makes music that cuts across boundaries, moving from swing to atonality to African music, soul, and rhythm and blues, and Willie Colon, the jazz trombonist of Puerto Rican descent who combines elements of jazz, rock, and salsa, along with the rhythms of traditional music from Cuba, Puerto Rico, Brazil, and Africa, and it is ecstacy.

Finally, needing "to talk to herself," to regress, Kat abandons Chloe and withdraws (176). As Kat becomes inundated with more dreams, visions, and memories of her past, she becomes open and fascinated, hurrying up Dwight Way to Shattuck with Ladyday's voice "jagged in a jig through [her] heart with Benny Carter honkytonk tumbling on clarinet" (177). Kat wonders if "these *riddling dreams* fuse a bridge to her muse" (177), allowing her to understand her visions and fantasies of Kitty, Lena, and Chicago. Rummaging through the personal and the collective unconscious past, Kat again revisits and reremembers the men in her life, along with visions from the past. Ultimately, what Kat wants is to resolve her complexes and to try to be the pure essence of consciousness, which is energy.

In the last section of *Muse-Echo Blues,* both Lena and Kitty return. Kat is seated at her Plexus, and Lena comes to talk to her, telling Kat, "You need a lead and I'm here to provide it" (198). Lena sits "not beside me but in me and of me; her form seemed to mesh with my own. Her warmth merged with mine and the shine of her presence shimmered within me so that I felt more than heard each of her words" (198). Lena will help Kat "let loose that hide-and-seek sound that [she was] struggling to find" (199). She is there to help Kat "find [her] lost you." Actually, Lena is Kat's "lost you," her muse, her inner clime, being a self-representation of Kat's interior reality. Lena also tells Kat that in order to grow, she must let herself go, "to move backward through time as [she knows] it. Feel what I tell you. What you need is a sense of yourself with the firm understanding that talent's the spring bud of ancestral roots. Think on it. You know it already as I do" (199). Earlier, Kat "could feel Kitty . . . welled up inside [her]" (183); Kitty is a spiritual symbol of an unknown aspect of Kat. Kat ends her conversation with Lena about 'Go, saying "I couldn't help but light into Lena, the Kitty in me, she had to come through" (203). For Kat, life becomes an open and creative whole of proliferating connections. She is successfully getting cues from her muse. To create her own female musical voice, Kat had to cycle back and enter into conversations with other female musical voices from the past, just as bebop was in conversation with swing and just as free jazz is continually in conversation with bebop. The conversations allow Kat to change her perception of the present.

Finally, in altering her perception, Kat allows Kitty and Lena, Kat's otherness, her power and her spirit, to enter her consciousness. Kat's confrontation with the unconscious precedes the birth of a new Self, which costs her an investment in a conforming social persona. As a new Self, her conscious ego is now "capable of assimilating the contents produced by the unconscious, i.e., of understanding and digesting" (Campbell 111). Kat can now make the first step toward integration, which is the individuation—the spiritual art of becoming a whole person—of all aspects of her personality. Differentiation and unification are coexisting processes in the development of personality. Together they produce the ultimate achievement of a completely realized selfhood, which can renounce dependence and real autonomy and which always partly amounts to a solitary destiny. According to Jung, this is progressive. Kat is moving toward wholeness and has discovered what Irigaray calls a "natural belonging" to herself (*Conversations* 158).

After accessing the ancestral past, readjusting her conscious ego, and finally allowing herself to interpret her dreams and visions, which connect her to swing and bebop, which provide her with blueprints for healing and surviving, and which are the source of her talent, Kat is ready to use jazz to move beyond her blues life. "In Jazz . . . the blues is used as a medium of transcendence—one plays or sings the blues to vanquish them" (Schoenberg xv). With her nature no longer "at the service of the other's [male's] desire" (3), to use Irigaray's terms in *Conversations*, Kat, alone, is now ready for "new times of Welcome! To Plexus, digging what [she] had to do. The moment [she] posed fingers on keys of proud Plexus, [she] started to real-eyes that rhythm's the glimmer that sparkles the motion of [her] in ecstasy, free. . . . [T]he stirrings within [her] demanded fidelity" (210–11). With her shadow, Lena, dead from a suicide, Kat recognizes the dark aspects of her personality as present and real, which is the essential condition for any kind of self-knowledge, and lets her "foresister Kit, alternative [her] in [her] own fantasy," come through (211). Here, the world that annulled Kat as a woman now recovers her as a neutral being. Who and what Kat has become has a lot to do with her militantly getting in touch with her spiritual core, which allows life to flow.

Like Taylor, Kat is prepared to transcend her conscious ego, to become someone who is connected to and inspired by but is not restricted by the ancestral swing and bebop past. Her creative work originates in her visions and dreams. Now Kat does something that all of her previous ancestors have done: "she come[s] from within" (211), coming to a realization/understanding of her personal and collective unconscious. She has been able to constitute her concrete life by getting in touch with the fateful, spiritual inner side of her life, the inner process of maturation and growth. Spiritual meaning nourishes the soul by offering it connectedness to a larger life. Now Kat, unlike the uncreative buppies, realizes that she is not alone, that intelligent forces, both light and dark, interact with her life and provide meaning and direction if she is receptive to them. In this transcendence Kat has autonomy but, unlike Kitty, does not have a new way of relating to and with men.

As a creative person whose ego has learned to understand the interior process, Kat is not confined to a single self located in the conscious ego; she is able to harness a sense of plurality, to work with it and become conscious of it. Therefore, her subjectivity extends across a spectrum of possibilities, a subjectivity defined always in terms of its relations to the Other. Kat's engagement with otherness leads to a rich flow of images, inspirations, and ideas. She is "aware that joy in life is achieved by and through a just, vigilant, and fecund relationship with a different other" (Cherif 24). Now, Kat can play her Plexus because she has found inside herself and her traditions the strength to compose.

In allowing the muse to take over her consciousness, thereby opening it up to the African American collective/jazz musical unconscious, Kat embodies a different kind of consciousness. Like Joe and Violet in Morrison's *Jazz* and Lorraine in Greer's *Hanging by Her Teeth,* Kat undergoes an epistemic change in subjectivity. In *The Order of Things,* Michel Foucault discusses the unfolding of a post-/non-Cartesian subjectivity/consciousness (a unified social body) in which it is "once more possible to think" (342). It looks very much like jazz. According to Deleuze and Guattari in *Anti-Oedipus,* within the construction of the Cartesian subject is the breakup of old, corroded oedipal structures. This consciousness, according to Foucault, "explode[s] in different directions" (346), involving a constantly shifting identity. It has the capacity to flow readily between different aspects of itself, traversed by alterity. Therefore, it can move from the past to the present, from the self to the Other, and from the light to the dark. It "can dwell in many moments of time simultaneously," argues Jane Flax in *Thinking Fragments,* "or move relatively free through past, present, and . . . future experiences" (94).

Kat embodies this non-Cartesian psyche, this plural, fluid conscious and unconscious mind. Through the African American collective/jazz musical unconscious, *Muse-Echo Blues* breaks up old, corroded oedipal structures. Dreams, fantasies, and visions from her unconscious psyche allow Kat to unstop her musical blockage and release culturally unregulated and unmediated flows of pure desire and energy. Kat's "*own inner clime . . . catapults [her] through time:* away from the drift of day-to-day life with its creative-void type of strife, toward bygone times of grace and face-saving, of okay delay" (*Muse-Echo Blues* 153). The African American collective/jazz musical unconscious saves her and makes her whole.

With jazz aesthetics and the Jungian/African American collective unconscious, Cartiér in *Muse-Echo Blues* shows the limits of the ideology of rationality, of middle-class respectability, of the Freudian psyche, and of the traditional modern novel, undermining its notion of linearity, putting its stable language back into play, and deconstructing its ability to fully grasp meaning and representation. She opens up the novel and incorporates otherness, nonrational components of life. In addition, Cartiér, through Jung, in *Muse-Echo Blues* redescribes human consciousness, which becomes one that incorporates the nonrational and the instinctual—dreams, fantasies, visions, memories, etc.—the collective unconscious. Jung calls the whole of the conscious-unconscious psyche the Self. This sense of Self is a total challenge to the West's concept of human consciousness as belonging to a rational being and political subject, with the non-West, nonwhite being defined as the human Other—the animal, the instinctual, the nonrational, etc. In fact, Cartiér uses Jung to redescribe human consciousness, which consists of the rational and the nonrational (spiritual), the personal and the collective unconscious, to deconstruct the rational/irrational violent hierarchy in the West. It is a human psyche in which "the ego, and hence consciousness and subjectivity, is utterly relativised against an unconscious which is experienced by the subject as profoundly *other*" (Hauke 150). Because of the fluidity of this human psyche, it, like the psyche in Cooper's reconfigured African American subject in *A Voice From the South* and Charles Johnson's complex human portrait of the psyche of African American youth in *Growing Up in the Black Belt*, eschews rigid racial identity and racial essentialism, which, because of their rationalism, cannot engage the nonrational, the darkness, and the mysteries of life. Because of its flow, this human psyche opposes masculine narratives that demand traditional morality and subordination to preexisting ethical codes. This is a conception of human consciousness that is different from that of the Enlightenment. It is also a conception that is not recognized by the public norm. Unlike the modern Freudian psyche, Kat's ego never takes charge; it is subordinate to the Self and is related to it like a part of the whole. As a consequence, Cartiér creates counterspaces that represent the modern conventional novel as a limited Eurocentric construct and that define the African American with history and agency, outside Enlightenment reason, which, like Cooper in *A Voice From the South*, opposes and pushes beyond America's representation of the African American as devalued Other.

— 8 —

Conclusion

I began *Postmodernism, Traditional Cultural Forms, and African American Narratives* with a historical survey of African American scholars, social and political movements, and cultural forms such as the civil rights movement, the Black Power movement, the blues, and jazz, examining how they have historically resisted or countered the dominant American society's historical representation of the African American as "deviant" or as devalued Other. My intention was not to get involved in a long and drawn-out discussion about blacks being victims of racial oppression, the white norm, or the Eurocentric gaze, although all of these issues are valid and necessary areas of research endeavors. Instead, I wanted to examine African American theorists, educators, historians, sociologists, and writers who not only resisted the West's negative definition of the African American but also dealt with the African American in terms of his or her own agency, logic, complex history, and distinct subjectivity. I wanted to ferret out an African American subjectivity that knows the law of the Other, of difference, that can coexist with subjects of different but equal worth, thereby challenging and marginalizing the dominant Eurocentric gaze and striving for an American/African American elsewhere.

First, to get to this other place, this elsewhere, I used current postmodern, poststructural, postcolonial, African American cultural as well as current psychoanalytical theories and feminist theories to reread and rethink certain African American scholars, educators, sociologists, and historians such as Anna Julia Cooper, W. E. B. Du Bois, Charles Johnson, Carter G. Woodson, and E. Franklin Frazier, liberating their potentialities from restrictive and erroneous interpretations, dramatizing latencies in their works, and allowing them to speak to the contemporary, cosmopolitan, multicultural American moment. To my surprise, these African American scholars, as theorists and visionaries, reconfigure and remap the American symbolic order, making the African American an integral part of that order. In addition, in constructing African American subjectivities, these scholars offer plural subjectivities that are not deviant or devalued but instead are comfortable in their existential, hybrid existences and can empathize with and know the Other. This is a place where African American subjectivities are most alive, providing models of subjectivities for a multicultural, cosmopolitan American society.

Second and more important, I explored how certain canonical and noncanonical African American texts reposition/plug into African and African American cultural and religious forms such as the blues, jazz, spirituals, the African American trickster figure, Yoruba gods, and African belief systems—which are spaces that still retain a wildness, that have not been completely colonized by normative American society—to speak to contemporary issues in American/African American life. As with the scholars, historians, and sociologists mentioned above, these texts, in drawing on American, African, and African American cultural forms and belief systems, construct the African American as a complex entity with his or her own potency, agency, history, wildness, and distinct subjectivity, leaving but not completely escaping the Eurocentric gaze.

Wanting three male and three female writers to be the focus of my study and to explore how each deals with the Other, I settled on Wideman's *Philadelphia Fire,* Everett's *Erasure,* Morrison's *Jazz,* Greer's *Hanging by Her Teeth,* Major's *Reflex and Bone Structure,* and Cartiér's *Muse-Echo Blues,* reading them along an axis, which moves away from Enlightenment reason, heteropatriarchy, the Eurocentric gaze, and Freudian subjectivity and toward less hierarchical forms of reason, to plural subjectivities that can "take the risk of *other,* of difference, without feeling threatened by the existence of an otherness" (Cixous and Clément, *Newly Born Woman* 78). In focusing on Wideman's Cudjoe in *Philadelphia Fire* and Everett's Monk in *Erasure,* who bring difference to African American male subjectivity, I was able to capture African American males escaping but not completely leaving Western heteropatriarchy. Certainly, they challenge the West's construction of the African American male as primitive or devalued Other. With Joe and Violet in Morrison's *Jazz,* I illustrated how Morrison's text demonstrates how common urban African American subjects reconnect to their rural past and the improvisational aspects of jazz music/aesthetic and transform their lives, opening themselves to nature and Others. In this instance, Morrison redefines the African American outside the Eurocentric gaze. And with Lorraine in Greer's *Hanging by Her Teeth* and Kat in Cartiér's *Muse-Echo Blues,* I was able to show how these texts capture images/representations of black women that defy all of their social, sexual, and subjective stereotypes, rerepresenting black women as complex, plural human beings who engage otherness and who exist outside of Western reason, white supremacy, black essentialism, identity politics, and heteropatriarchy.

I read Wideman's *Philadelphia Fire,* Everett's *Erasure,* Morrison's *Jazz,* Greer's *Hanging by Her Teeth,* Major's *Reflex and Bone Structure,* and Xam Cartiér's *Muse-Echo Blues* as counterhegemonic texts that write back to or contest the regimes of power/knowledge in the West/the United States and that construct the African American as victim, as devalue Other, as deviant, or as the same. These texts reconfigure the African American in a new constellation, outside the white middle-class puritan norm/gaze. Rather than view African American life as a stamp of oppression, these texts affirm African American life, opening doors to different and alternative forms of consciousness, to new ways of thinking of the world, to new and different ways of defining subjectivity, to new ways of being in the world: of our entrances into it, our encounters with it, and, ultimately, our voyages out of it and into something else. They give us some idea of how to be human in the West/the

United States in the twenty-first century without dominating, subordinating, or being violent toward the Other.

But for this different subjectivity to become hegemonic or for this different way to be human in the West/the United States in the twenty-first century to be normalized, American politics (including African American social and political movements) has to embrace differences, plurality, and hybridity. America has to practice an alliance and coalition politics that defines subjectivity as diverse and that engages multiple identities and social movements. American politics has to accept diversity as the norm, accept differences without hierarchy, which leads to a multiplicity of justice. Finally, American politics has to equally engage a diverse and conflicting set of social, economic, religious, sexual, gender, and racial/ethnic positions.

Notes

CHAPTER 1

1. There are many blacks who know white or mainstream culture and some whites who know black culture. Therefore, there is division in the halves. There are many whites, and there are many blacks. The notion of these terms must be divided.

2. I use the term "subjectivity" because I am concern with individuals who are produced through language and systems of meaning. I am concerned with how individuals are constituted as subjects and given unified identities or subject positions.

3. Here I am thinking of cosmopolitan in terms of viewing all people around the world as equal, as equally respected and valued. For further explanation, see Anthony Appiah's *Cosmopolitanism* and Seyla Benhabib's *Another Cosmopolitanism.*

4. Here, I use the term "bicultural" to indicate that Cooper belonged culturally to both American and African American societies.

5. See Francois Guizot's *The History of Civilization in Europe* (1828), translated by William Hazbitt and edited by Larry Seidentop (New York: Penguin, 1997).

6. There is a history of African American scholars and intellectuals misreading Du Bois's concept of double consciousness. In most instances, it is defined as a conflict that is to be resolved. Therefore, it is ultimately read

negatively, as the pathological curse that condemns the African American to victimhood. In the "Introduction" to the 2003 Barnes and Noble edition of *The Souls of Black Folk,* Farah Jasmine Griffin writes that "Double consciousness defines a psychological sense experienced by African Americans whereby they possess a national identity, 'an American,' within a nation that despises their racial identity, 'a Negro'" (xvi). In *A Home Elsewhere,* Robert B. Stepto, discussing Du Bois and double consciousness, writes that "What happened to Du Bois that day was he was initiated into double-consciousness, which is precisely the 'peculiar sensation' of 'looking at one's self through the eyes of others'" (29). Here Stepto avoids the conflict by only citing one half of the binary. Even Cornel West in *Brother West* reduces Du Bois's double consciousness to "an idea that says, in essence, we're looking at ourselves through the eyes of others who devalue us" (172).

7. Frazier came to Du Bois through the *Crisis,* which Du Bois edited. Between 1912 and 1916, Frazier's resume, writes Mio Matsumoto, "reads as if he were already a seasoned activist in Du Bois's mold" (56). Du Bois was given significance in Frazier's master's thesis at Clark University. But Frazier gradually became discontented with Du Bois, culminating in his attack on Du Bois's Depression-era program in 1935. Frazier represented Du Bois as elitist and semiaristocratic and as having very little sympathy for common people. However, Frazier comes to Du Bois's defense in the 1950s when Du Bois is publicly arrested and persecuted by the U.S. government. Frazier refused to cancel an honorary dinner for Du Bois after he had been indicted by a federal jury for his refusal to register as a "foreign agent" (Matsumoto 67).

8. According to Abdul Alkalimat, who directs the Africana Studies Program at the University of Toledo and who keeps track of figures nationwide, there are still about 450 colleges and universities that offer undergraduate or graduate programs in some form of black studies (Wilson A10).

9. This is particularly true with the programs and departments at Temple University, Florida State University, Northwestern University, Cornell University, the

University of California–Berkeley, Georgia State University, Ohio State University, Syracuse University, Indiana University, and others.

10. Many of these programs and departments belong to the National Council of Black Studies, which came into existence seven years after the first program at San Francisco State University. On its website, the council lists as one of its goals "promoting scholarly Afrocentric research on all aspects of the African world experience. . . . Our members include top scholars, community leaders and students focused on a variety of issues related to the African world experience."

11. See UC Berkeley's Department of Ethnic Studies' website at ethnicstudies.berkeley.edu.

12. See the website for the Department of African American Studies at Northwestern University at www.afam.northwestern.edu/graduate/graduate.html.

13. Although there are contemporary African American poets and playwrights such as Suzan Lori-Park and Harryette Mullen who are taking similar cultural-specific approaches, I am limiting my study and focus to fiction, mostly in the 1990s.

CHAPTER 2

1. Wideman's first phase includes his semiexistential novels *A Glance Away, Hurry Home,* and the *Lynchers.* His second phase includes his Homewood trilogy: *Hiding Place, Damballah,* and *Sent for You Yesterday.*

2. I take the term "selfsame" from Hélène Cixious in *The Newly Born Woman,* where the term is used in the context of Western phallocentrism, which only sees and reproduces itself in the Other.

3. Here, reason of the Other refers to a different organization of meaning within and outside of Western phallocentric metaphysics. The reason of the Other has its own logic.

4. My strategic composite of MOVE is drawn from several sources, which are quoted in the text and are in the bibliography. My objective is not to be definitive but instead to draw a sufficiently large portrait to expose the gaps and

silences and omissions in *Philadelphia Fire*'s representation, to show that it does not occupy all of the spaces concerning the bombing, and to show that *Philadelphia Fire* is the product of signifying practice.

5. It is Margaret who makes Cudjoe aware of his almost exotic desire for white women. In his first conversation with Margaret, Cudjoe questions, "How did she know so much about him, not only her but all her sisters, how, after the briefest of conversations, did they know his history, that he'd married a white woman and fathered half-white kids?" (9). Since the reader never hears any corroboration from Margaret or any other character in the novel concerning this matter, the assumptionn is that it exists only in Cudjoe's head.

CHAPTER 3

1. Percival Everett is a prolific American writer, having written more than twelve books of fiction. Many of his novels do not have black characters and do not deal with the problematic of race. Interestingly, despite his protestation, he is known for the one novel that is actively about race.

2. Although Monk tells us that he reads the fiction of Jean Toomer and Zora Neale Hurston, it is interesting that Percival Everett assumes that there is *only* one kind of African American novel. He is refusing to see the black novel of victimized black life as a space of repressed difference, where different kinds of black novels are simply excluded. He is forgetting that there are existential, postmodern, modern, jazz, and blues novels that do not construct the African American as a victim, as being black in a racist society. He has forgotten the fiction of William Demby, John Edgar Wideman, Charles Wright, James Baldwin, Toni Morrison, and others who do not make race and racism the problematic of the text.

3. In "Race under Erasure," Margaret Russett points out that the paper on *S/Z* that Monk delivers at the conference in Washington, D.C., was actually published by Everett "as a piece of fiction" in *Making Callaloo.* Also, Russett learns from Everett that *My Pafology* was "originally written as a

freestanding novella [by Everett] and only later fathered my Monk" (359).

4. Despite the fact that they critiqued reason, expressed skepticism, and pointed out the limitations of the Enlightenment in their numerous writings, Hume, Kant, and Hegel played a strong role in articulating Europe's sense of not only its cultural but also its racial superiority (Eze 5). In their writings, "reason" and "civilization" became almost synonymous with "white" people and northern Europe, while unreason and savagery were conveniently located among the nonwhites, the "black," the "red," and the "yellow" outside Europe. What follows are some excerpts of the writing of Hume, Kant, and Hegel. In "Of the Populousness of Ancient Nations" (1748), Hume, writing about Africans and Mexicans, states:

> And indeed there is some reason to think, that all the nations, which live beyond the polar circles or between the tropics, are inferior to the rest of the species, and are incapable of all the higher attainments of the human race. . . . I am apt to suspect the negroes and in general all other species of men . . . to be naturally inferior to the whites. There never was a civilized nation of any other complexion than white, nor even any individual eminent either in action or speculation. No ingenious manufactures among them, no arts, no science. On the other hand, the most rude and barbarous of the whites . . . have still something eminent about them, in their valour, form of government, or some other particular. (qtd. in Eze 32–33)

Reinforcing Hume's racist position, Kant, in "On National characteristics . . . Distinct Feeling of the Beautiful and Sublime," states:

> The Negro of Africa has no nature no feeling that rises above the trifling. Mr. Hume challenges anyone to cite a single example in which a negro has shown talents, and asserts that among the hundreds

> of thousands of blacks who are transported elsewhere from their countries, although many of them have even been set free still not a single one was ever found who presented anything great in art or science or any other praiseworthy quality. (qtd. in Eze 55)

In "What Is Enlightenment" (1784), Kant writes:

> Enlightenment is the exit of humanity by itself from a state of culpable immaturity. . . . Laziness and cowardliness are the causes which bind the great part of humanity in this frivolous sate of immaturity. (qtd. in Dussel, *The Invention of the Americas* 19).

In his "Observations on the Feeling of the Beautiful and the Sublime," Kant notes that American Indians and Blacks "are lower in their mental capacities than all other races" (qtd. in Shohat and Stam 88). Hegel, very representative of the Western white male philosophical tradition, is equally as racist as Kant. In "Lectures on the Philosophy of World History" (1822–28), Hegel argues that from a philosophical point of view, "non-European peoples—American Indians, Africans, and Asians—are less human than Europeans because, to varying degrees, they are not fully aware of themselves as conscious, historical beings" (qtd. in Eze 127). On Africa, Hegel writes:

> The characteristic feature of the Negroes is that their consciousness has not yet reached an awareness of any substantial objectivity—for example, of God or the law—in which the will of man could participate and in which he could become aware of his own being. The African . . . has not yet succeeded in making this distinction between himself as an individual and his essential universality, so that he knows nothing of an absolute being which is other and higher than his own self. . . . The Negro is an example of animal man in all his savagery and lawlessness. (qtd. in Eze 127)

Because they defined the African as immature, Kant and Hegel excluded them from world history.

5. In terms of popular songs, Stagolee becomes the subject of the song "Frankie and Johnnie." He is also reproduced in Ellison's *Invisible Man* as Rhinehart and is the subject of Cecil Brown's *I, Stagolee.*

6. Monk's attempt to erase the African American subaltern is shown again when he visits Lisa's clinic and talks to the young black mother, Tamika Jones, asking her if she had "gone to college" after she talks intelligently about Toomer's *Cane* and Hurston's *Their Eyes Were Watching God.* Monk "had expected this young woman with blue fingernails to be a certain way, to be low and stupid, but she was neither" (21). Like Van Go, Tamika Jones threatens to erase Monk's presence of the selfsame.

CHAPTER 4

1. Since jazz begins with the blues, I use the term "jazz/blues" to connote this black musical lifestyle.

CHAPTER 7

1. In the 1920s after his big break with Freud, Jung began to travel extensively. In addition to places in Europe, he went to Tunis and the Sahara. He developed a fascination with what he called the mentality of "primitive people." On one trip to Africa, he journeyed to the heart of the continent on a safari, returning by way of Egypt. This journey provided a profound learning experience for Jung because it brought him in contact with indigenous Africans and the collective unconscious. Documenting this further, in "The Collective Unconscious: An Opportunity for New Thought on the Existence of Independent Black Institutions and Black Achievement Theories," Bush, Bush, and Causey-Bush argue that although Jung is the most celebrated pioneer and authority concerning the theory of the collective unconscious, "the theory of the collective unconscious was a basic concept that was developed in the

African universities and secret societies of ancient Egypt" (57). Also, in *The African Unconscious,* Edward Bynum discusses how Jung intended to establish "a more universal perspective on this collective unconscious by studying the dreams of Blacks in Africa and in the United States" (79). Finally, in *African Origin of Biological Psychiatry,* Richard D. King traces the archetype of humanity, the hidden doorway to the collective unconscious to Africa.

2. "Differance" comes from both "defer" and "differ." For Derrida, there is no absolute identity or essential meaning for a person or an object. Nothing stands outside the system of differences. Meaning exists in language in a relational system where signs themselves do not have essential meanings. They are continually defined in terms of difference and play. See Derrida's interviews in *Positions* for his discussion of differance.

3. Deleuze and Guattari make a distinction between schizophrenia as a process and the way schizophrenics are produced as clinical cases that need hospitalizing. "The schizophrenics in hospitals are people who've tried to do something and failed, cracked up. We're not saying revolutionaries are schizophrenics. We're saying there's a schizoid process of decoding and de-territorializing, which only revolutionary activity can stop turning into the production of schizophrenia" (Deleuze, *Negotiations* 23–24).

4. The question is not whether jazz musicians possessed contaminated bodies but rather which contaminants. Alcohol is a contaminant. Do you resist it?

Works Cited

Alic, Margaret. "Gale Contemporary Black Biography: Xam Wilson Cartiér." www.answers.com/topic/xam-wilson-cartier.

Anderson, John, and Hilary Hevenor. *Burning Down the House: MOVE and the Tragedy of Philadelphia.* New York: Norton, 1987.

Appiah, Kwame Anthony. *Cosmopolitanism: Ethics in a World of Strangers.* New York: Norton, 2007.

Asante, Molefi Kete. *Afrocentricity.* Trenton, NJ: Africa World, 1988.

———. "Black Studies and Henry Louis Gates." *Chronicle of Higher Education* 39 (September 2, 1992): B-6.

Assefa, Hizkias, and Paul Wahrhaftig. *Extremist Groups and Conflict Resolution: The MOVE Crisis in Philadelphia.* New York: Praeger, 1988.

Baker, Lisa. "Storytelling and Democracy (in the Radical Sense): A Conversation with John Edgar Wideman." *African American Review* 34 (Summer 2000): 263–72.

Bakhtin, M. M. *The Dialogic Imagination: Four Essays.* Ed. Michael Holquist. Trans. Caryl Emerson and Michael Holquist. Austin: U of Texas P, 1981.

Baraka, Amiri. *Digging: The Afro-American Soul of American Classical Music.* Berkeley and Los Angeles: U of California P, 2009.

———. "Toni." *Savoring the Salt: The Legacy of Toni Cade Bambara.* Ed. Linda Janet Holmes and Cheryl A. Wall. Philadelphia: Temple UP, 2008. 108–12.

Barry, Stacey L. "The Individual and the Collective: Threatening Blackness in Wideman's *Philadelphia Fire.*" *Critical Essays on John Wideman.* Ed. Bonnie TuSmith and Keith Byerman. Knoxville: U of Tennessee P, 2006. 161–173.

Barthes, Roland. *S/Z: An Essay.* Trans. Richard Miller. New York: Hill and Wang, 1974.

Beeber, Steven. "The Art of Fiction: John Edgar Wideman." *Paris Review* 161 (Spring 2002): 137–60.

Bell, Bernard W., ed. *Clarence Major and His Art: Portraits of an African American Postmodernist.* Chapel Hill: U of North Carolina P, 2001.

Benhabib, Seyla. *Another Cosmopolitanism (Berkeley Tanner Lectures).* New York: Oxford UP, 2008.

Benjamin, Jessica. *The Bonds of Love: Psychoanalysis, Feminism, and the Problem of Domination.* New York: Pantheon Books, 1988.

Berliner, Paul F. *Thinking of Jazz: The Infinite Art of Improvisation.* Chicago: U of Chicago P, 1994.

Bobo, Jacqueline, Cynthia Hudley, and Claudine Michel, ed. *The Black Studies Reader.* New York: Routledge, 2004.

Bolling, Doug, and Clarence Major. "Reality, Fiction, and Criticism: An Interview/Essay." *Conversations with Clarence Major.* Ed. Nancy Bunge. Jackson: UP of Mississippi, 2002. 28–34.

Bourdieu, Pierre. *Masculine Domination.* Trans. Richard Nice. Stanford, CA: Stanford UP, 2001.

Bowser, Charles W. *Let the Bunker Burn: the Final Battle with MOVE.* Philadelphia: Camino, 1989.

Boynton, Robert S. "The Professor of Connection." *New Yorker* 71.35 (November 6, 1995): 114.

Bracey, John H., August Meier, and Elliott Rudwick, eds. *Black Nationalism in America.* New York: Bobbs-Merrill, 1970.

Bradfield, Larry D. "Beyond Mimetic Exhaustion: The *Reflex and Bone Structure* Experiment." *Black American Literature Forum* 17.3 (1983): 119–23.

Bremen, Brian A. "Du Bois, Emerson, and the 'Fate' of Black Folk." *American Literary Realism* 24 (Spring 1992): 80–88.

Brothers, Thomas. "Solo and Cycle in African-American Jazz." *Musical Quarterly* 78.3 (Autumn 1999): 479–509.

Brown, Cecil. *I, Stagolee: A Novel.* Berkeley, CA: North Atlantic Books, 2006.

Bunge, Nancy. "Clarence Major." *Conversations with Clarence Major.* Ed. Nancy Bunge. Jackson: UP of Mississippi, 2002. 35–47.

Bush, Lawson, Edward Bush, and Tonia Causey-Bush. "The Collective Unconscious: An Opportunity for New Thought on the Existence of Independent Black Institutions and Black Achievement Theories." *Journal of Pan African Studies* 1.6 (December 2006): 48–66.

Butler, Judith. *Precarious Life: The Powers of Mourning and Violence.* London and New York: Verso, 2004.

Byerman, Keith E. *The Art and Life of Clarence Major.* Athens: U of Georgia P, 2012.

———. *Fingering the Jagged Grain.* Athens: U of Georgia P, 1985.

Bynum, Edward Bruce. *The African Unconscious: Roots of Ancient Mysticism and Modern Psychology.* New York: Teachers College Press, 1999.

Cade [Bambara], Toni. "On the Issue of Roles." *The Black Woman: An Anthology.* Ed. Toni Cade. New York: New American Library, 1970. 101–10.

Cagidemetrio, Alide. "The 'Real Thing': Notes on an American Strategy." *Critical Angles: European Views of Contemporary American Literature.* Ed. Marc Chenetier. Carbondale: Southern Illinois UP, 1989. 3–14.

Campbell, Joseph, ed. *The Portable Jung.* Trans. F. F. C. Hull. New York: Viking Penguin, 1971.

Carabi, Angels. "Interview with Toni Morrison." *Belles letters.* 10.2 (1995): 40–43.

Carby, Hazel V. *Reconstructing Womanhood: The Emergence of the Afro-American Woman Novelist.* New York: Oxford UP, 1987.

Carden, Mary Paniccia. "'If the City Is a Man': Founders and Fathers, Cities and Sons in John Edgar Wideman's *Philadelphia Fire.*" *Contemporary Literature* 44.3 (Fall 2003): 472–500.

Cartiér, Xam. *Muse-Echo Blues.* New York: Ballantine Books, 1991.

Chakravorty, Swapan, et al., ed. *Conversations with Gayatri Chakravorty Spivak.* London and Calcutta: Seagull Books, 2006.

Cherif, Mustapha. *Islam and the West: A Conversation with Jacques Derrida.* Trans. Teresa Lavender Fagan. Chicago and London: U of Chicago P, 2008.

Cixous, Hélène. *Coming to Writing and Other Essays.* Ed. Deborah Jenson. Trans. Sarah Cornell, Deborah Jenson, Ann Liddle, and Susan Sellers. Cambridge: Harvard UP, 1991.

———. "Rethinking Differences: An Interview." *Homosexualities and French Literature.* Ed. George Stambolean and Elaine Marks. Ithaca, NY, and London: Cornell UP, 1979. 70–86.

———. *White Ink: Interviews on Sex, Text and Politics.* Ed. Susan Sellers. New York: Columbia UP, 2008.

Cixous, Hélène, and Mireille Calle-Gruber. *Hélène Cixous rootprints: Memory and Life Writing.* Trans. Eric Prenowitz. London and New York: Routledge, 1997.

Cixous, Hélène, and Catherine Clément. *The Newly Born Woman.* Trans. Betsy Wing. Minneapolis: U of Minnesota P, 1986.

Code, Lorraine. *What Can She Know? Feminist Theory and the Construction of Knowledge.* Ithaca, NY, and London: Cornell UP, 1991.

Coleman, James W. *Blackness & Modernism: The Literary Career of John Edgar Wideman.* Jackson: UP of Mississippi, 1989.

Collins, Patricia Hill. *Black Feminist Thought: Knowledge, Consciousness, and the Politics of Empowerment.* 2nd ed. New York: Routledge, 2000.

Cooper, Anna Julia. *A Voice From the South.* 1892. New York: Oxford UP, 1998.

Cox, Edward L. "Carter G. Woodson." *Writers of American History in the 20th Century.* Ed. Clyde Wilson. Columbia, SC: Bruccoli Clark, 1983. 458–65.

Crouch, Stanley. *Considering Genius: Writings on Jazz.* New York: Basic Civitas Books, 2006.

Cruse, Harold. "The Integrationist Ethic as a Basis for Scholarly Endeavors." *Black Studies in the University: A Symposium.* Ed. Armstead L. Robinson, Craig C. Foster, and Donald H. Ogilvie. New Haven, CT: Yale UP, 1969. 4–12, 17–36.

Davis, Angela Y. *Blues Legacies and Black Feminism: Gertrude "Ma" Rainey, Bessie Smith, and Billie Holiday.* New York: Pantheon Books, 1998.

Davis, Francis. *The History of the Blues.* New York: Hyperion, 1995.

Davis, Kimberly Chabot. "'Postmodern Blackness': Toni Morrison's *Beloved* and the End of History." *Productive Postmodernism Consuming Histories and Cultural Studies.* Ed. John N. Duvall. Albany: SUNY Press, 2002. 75–92.

Deleuze, Gilles. *Difference and Repetition.* Trans. Paul Patton. New York: Columbia UP, 1994.

———. *Negotiations: 1972–1990.* Trans. Martin Joughin. New York: Columbia UP, 1995.

Deleuze, Gilles, and Felix Guattari. *Anti-Oedipus: Capitalism and Schizophrenia.* Minneapolis: U of Minnesota P, 1983.

———. *A Thousand Plateaus: Capitalism and Schizophrenia.* Trans. Brian Massumi. Minneapolis and London: U of Minnesota P, 1987.

DelRosso, Jeana. "Catholicism's Other(ed) Holy Trinity: Race, Class, and Gender in Black Catholic Girl School Narratives." *NWSA Journal* 12.1 (Spring 2000): 24–43.

Derrida, Jacques. *Dissemination.* Trans. Barbara Johnson. Chicago: U of Chicago P, 1981.

———. *Of Grammatology.* Trans. Gayatri Chakravorty Spivak. Baltimore and London: Johns Hopkins UP, 1976.

———. *Positions.* Chicago: U of Chicago P, 1981.

Derrida, Jacques, and Christie V. McDonald. "Choreographies: Interview." Trans. Christie V. McDonald. *Feminist Interpretations of Jacques Derrida.* Ed. Nancy J. Holland. University Park: Penn State UP, 1997. 23–42.

DeVeaux, Scott. *The Birth of Bebop: A Social and Musical History.* Berkeley: U of California P, 1997.

Dickson-Carr, Darryl. "The Project of the Beast: Subverting Mythologies in Toni Morrison's *Jazz.*" *CLA Journal* 49.2 (2005): 168–83.

Dubey, Madhu. "Contemporary African American Fiction and the Politics of Postmodernism: Introduction." *Novel: A Forum on Fiction* 35.2–3 (Spring/Summer 2002): 151–68.

———. *Signs and Cities: Black Literary Postmodernism.* Chicago: U of Chicago P, 2003.

Du Bois, W. E. B. *The Souls of Black Folk.* 1903. New York: Barnes and Noble Classics, 2003.

Dussel, Enrique. "Beyond Eurocentrism: The World-System and the Limits of Modernity." *The Cultures of Globalization.* Ed. Fredric Jameson and Masao Miyoshi. Durham: Duke UP, 1998. 3–31.

———. *The Inventions of the Americas: Eclipse of "the Other" and the Myth of Modernity.* Trans. Michael D. Barber. New York: Continuum, 1995.

Eaton, Kimberly. "Deconstructing the Narrative, Language, Genre, and Experience in *Erasure.*" *Nebula* 3 (2006): 220–32.

Ellison, Ralph. "Remembering Jimmy." *Living with Music: Ralph Ellison's Jazz Writings.* Ed. Robert G. O'Meally. New York: Modern Library, 2002. 43–49.

Evans, Stephanie Y. "The State and Future of the Ph.D. in Black Studies: Assessing the Role of the Comprehensive Examinations." *The Griot: The Journal of African American Studies* 25.1 (Spring 2006): 1–16.

Everett, Percival. *Erasure.* New York: Hyperion, 2001.

———. "Foreword." *Making Callaloo: 25 Years of Black Literature.* Ed. Charles Henry Rowell. New York: St. Martin's Griffin, 2002. xv–xvii.

———. "F/V: Placing the Experimental Novel." *Callaloo* 22.1 (1999): 18–23.

Eze, Emmanuel Chukwudi, ed. *Race and the Enlightenment: A Reader.* Cambridge, MA.: Blackwell, 1997.

Fernheimer, Janice W. "Arguing from Difference: Cooper, Emerson, Guizot, and a More Harmonious America." *Black Women's Intellectual Traditions: Speaking Their Minds.* Ed. Kristin Waters and Carol B. Conaway. Burlington: U of Vermont P, 2007. 287–305.

Finley, Toiya Kristen. "Archtypical Metafiction: Scrutinizing Fallen Archetypes." *Farragot's Wainscot.* http://www.farragoswainscot.com/2008/6/archetypical.html.

Flax, Jane. *Thinking Fragments: Psychoanalysis, Feminism, and Postmodernism in the Contemporary West.* Berkeley: U of California P, 1990.

Fordham, Frieda. *An Introduction to Jung's Psychology.* Baltimore: Penguin Books, 1966.

Foucault, Michel. *The Archaeology of Knowledge & the Discourse on Language.* Trans. A. M. Sheridan Smith. New York: Harper, 1976.

———. *The Order of Things: An Archaeology of Human Sciences.* New York: Vintage Books, 1973.

———. "Truth and Power." *Power/Knowledge: Selected Interviews and Other Writings, 1972–1977.* Ed. Colin Gordon. Trans. Colin Gordon et al. New York: Pantheon, 1980. 109–33.

Fraser, Nancy. *Justice Interruptus: Critical Reflections on the "Post-Socialist" Condition.* New York and London: Routledge, 1997.

Fraser, Nancy, and Alex Honneth. *Redistribution or Recognition? A Political-Philosophical Exchange.* Trans. Joel Golb, James Ingram, and Christiane Wilke. New York and London: Verso, 2003.

Frazier, E. Franklin. "The Failure of the Negro Intellectual." *The Death of White Sociology: Essays on Race and Culture.* Ed. Joyce A. Ladner. Baltimore: Black Classic Press, 1973. 52–66.

———. *The Negro Family in the United States.* Chicago: U of Chicago P, 1966.

French, David. "His Own 'New Thing.'" *Downbeat* 75.10 (October 2008): 40–46.

Gabel, Leona C. *From Slavery to the Sorbonne and Beyond: The Life & Writings of Anna J. Cooper.* Studies in History Vol. 49. Northampton, MA: Smith College, 1982.

Gaines, Kevin. "E. Franklin Frazier's Revenge: Anticolonialism, Nonalignment, and Black Intellectuals' Critique of Western Culture." *American Literary History* 17.2 (2005): 506–29.

Gallop, Jane. *Reading Lacan.* Ithaca, NY: Cornell UP, 1985.

Garon, Paul. *Blues and the Poetic Spirit.* San Francisco: City Lights, 1996.

Gates, Henry Louis, Jr. "Review of Morrison's *Jazz.*" *Toni Morrison: Critical Perspectives Past and Present.* Ed. Henry Louis Gates Jr. and K. A. Appiah. New York: Amistad, 1993. 53–55.

Gelly, Dave. *Being Prez: The Life and Music of Lester Young.* New York: Oxford UP, 2007.

Gilpin, Patrick J. "Charles S. Johnson: Entrepreneur of the Harlem Renaissance." *The Harlem Renaissance Remembered: Essays Edited with a Memoir* by Arna Bontemps. New York: Dodd, Mead, 1972. 215–146.

Gilroy, Paul. *Black Atlantic: Modernity and Double Consciousness.* Cambridge: Harvard UP, 1993.

———. *Small Acts: Thoughts on the Politics of Black Cultures.* New York: Serpent Tail, 1993.

Gioia, Ted. *The History of Jazz.* New York: Oxford UP, 1997.

Goffman, Erving. *Stigma: Notes on the Management of Spoiled Identity.* New York: Simon & Schuster, 1963.

Grandt, Jungen E. "Kinds of Blue: Toni Morrison, Hans Janowitz, and the Jazz Aesthetic." *African American Review* 38.2 (2004): 303–22.

Greer, Bonnie. *Hanging by Her Teeth.* London: Serpent's Tale, 1994.

Griffin, Farah Jasmine. "Introduction." *The Souls of Black Folk* by W. E. B. Du Bois. New York: Barnes and Noble Classics, 2003. xv–xxviii.

Guattari, Felix. *Soft Subversions.* Ed. Sylvere Lotringer. Trans. David L. Sweet and Chet Wiener. New York: Semiotext(e), 1996.

Guizot, Francois. *The History of Civilization in Europe.* 1828. Trans. William Hazbitt. Ed. Larry Seidentop. New York: Penguin, 1997.

Guzzio, Tracie Church. "'All My Father's Texts': John Edgar Wideman's Historical Vision in *Philadelphia Fire, The Cattle Killing,* and *Fatheralong.*" *Critical Essays on John Edgar Wideman.* Ed. Bonnie TuSmith and Keith E. Byerman. Knoxville: U of Tennessee P, 2006. 175–89.

Gysin, Fritz. "The Pitfalls of Parody: Melancholic Satire in Percival Everett's *Erasure.*" *Reading Percival Everett: European Perspective.* Tours, France: U Francois Rebalais, 2007. 63–80.

Hauke, Christopher. *Jung and the Postmodern: The Interpretation of Realities.* London and Philadelphia: Routledge, 2000.

Healy, Paul. "Between Habermas and Foucault: On the Limits and Possibilities of Critical and Emancipatory Reason." *South Africa Journal of Philosophy* 16 (November 1997): 1–13.

Hentoff, Nat. "Duke Ellington's Posthumous Revenge." *Jazztimes* (November 2004): 146.

Holloway, Joseph E., ed. *Africanisms in American Culture.* Bloomington: Indiana UP, 1990.

hooks, bell. *We Real Cool: Black Men and Masculinity.* New York: Routledge, 2004.

Howard, Richard. "Preface." *S/Z: An Essay.* Trans. Richard Miller. New York: Hill and Wang, 1974. ix–xii.

Huggins, Nathan. *Afro-American Studies: A Report to the Ford Foundation.* New York: Ford Foundation, 1985.

Hutcheon, Linda. *A Poetics of Postmodernism: History, Theory, Fiction.* New York: Routledge, 1988.

Irigaray, Luce. *Conversations.* New York: Continuum, 2008.

———. *je, tu, nous: Toward a Culture of Difference.* Trans. Alison Martin. New York: Routledge, 1993.

———. *Speculum of the Other Woman.* Trans. Gillian C. Gill. Ithaca, NY: Cornell UP, 1985.

———. *This Sex Which Is Not One.* Trans. Catherine Porter. Ithaca, NY: Cornell University Press, 1985.

———. *to be two.* Trans. Monique M. Rhodes. New York: Routledge, 2001.

James, Frank. "Enchanted Forrest Pens Works of Epic Proportion." *Emerge: Black America's Newsmagazine* 5 (July/August 1994): 58.

Johnson, Charles S. *Growing Up in the Black Belt: Negro Youth in the Rural South.* New York: Schocken Books, 1941.

Jones, LeRoi [Amiri Baraka]. *Blues People: Negro Music in White America.* New York: William Morrow, 1963.

Jourdain, Robert. *Music, the Brain, and Ecstasy: How Music Captures Our Imagination.* New York: HarperCollins, 2002.

Jung, C. G. *The Collected Works of C. G. Jung.* Vol. 10. Trans. RFC Hull. Princeton: Princeton UP, 1978.

Karenga, Maulana. "Black Cultural Nationalism." *The Black Aesthetic.* Ed. Addison Gayle Jr. New York: Anchor Press/Doubleday, 1972. 31–37.

———. *Introduction to Black Studies.* 3rd ed. Los Angeles: U of Sankore P, 2002.

Katz, Alan. "Transition Is Tugging at a Local Avant-Garde Author." *Conversations with Clarence Major.* Ed. Nancy Bunge. Jackson: UP of Mississippi, 2002. 51–54.

Kelley, Robin D. G. *Thelonious Monk: The Life and Times of an American Original.* New York: Free Press, 2009.

Kilson, Martin. "The Intellectual Validity of Studying the Black Experience." *Black Studies in the University: A Symposium.* Ed. Armstead L. Robinson, Craig C. Foster, and Donald H. Ogilvie. New Haven, CT: Yale UP, 1969. 13–16.

King, Richard D. *African Origin of Biological Psychiatry.* Bensenville, IL: Lushena Books, 2001.

Klinkowitz, Jerome. "Clarence Major: An Interview with a Post-Contemporary Author." *Black American Literature Forum* 12 (Spring 1978): 32–37.

———. "The Self-Apparent Word: Clarence Major's Innovative Fiction." In *Studies in Black American Literature.* Vol. 1. *Black American Prose Theory.* Ed. Joe Weixlmann and Chester Fontenot. Greenwood, FL: Penkevill, 1984. 199–214.

Kristeva, Julia. *Revolt, She Said: An Interview by Philippe Petit.* Trans. Brian O'Keefe. Los Angeles and New York: Semiotext(e), 2002.

———. *The Sense and Non-Sense of Revolt: The Powers and Limits of Psychoanalysis.* Trans. Jeanine Herman. New York: Columbia UP, 1993.

———. *Strangers to Ourselves.* Trans. Leon S. Roudiez. New York: Columbia UP, 1991.

Lacan, Jacques. *Ecrits: A Selection.* Trans. Alan Sheridan. New York: Norton, 1977.

———. *The Seminars of Jacques Lacan, Book II: The Ego in Freud's Theory and in the Technique of Psychoanalysis 1954–1955.* Ed. J. A. Miller. Trans. S. Tomaselli: New York: Norton, 1991.

Laclau, Ernesto, and Chantel Mouffe. *Hegemony and Socialist Strategy: Towards a Radical Democratic Politics.* Trans. Winston Moore and Paul Cammack. London: Verso, 1985.

Lai, Wei-ching. "Re-Membering the Song of My Self—African American Self-Formation in Toni Morrison's *Jazz.*" *EurAmerica* 36.4 (2006): 591–612.

Landrum, Larry. *American Mystery and Detective Novels: A Reference Guide.* Westport, CT, and London: Greenwood, 1999.

Landrum, Larry N., Pat Browne, and Ray B. Browne. *Dimensions of Detective Fiction.* New York: Popular Press, 1976.

Lee, James Kyung-Jin. "Where the Talented Tenth Meets the Model Minority: The Price of Privilege in Wideman's *Philadelphia Fire* and Lee's *Native Speaker.*" *Novel: A Forum on Fiction* 35 (Spring/Summer 2002): 231–57.

Leland, John. *Hip: The History.* New York: HarperCollins, 2004.

Lemke, Sieglinde. *Primitivist Modernism: Black Culture and the Origins of Transatlantic Modernism.* New York: Oxford UP, 1998.

Leonard, Neil. *Jazz and the White Americans: The Acceptance of A New Art Form.* Chicago: U of Chicago P, 1962.

LeSeur, Geta. "'Sweet Desolation' and Seduction in Toni Morrison's *Jazz.*" *Popular Culture Review* 16.1 (2005): 21–30.

Levinas, Emmanuel. *Totality and Infinity.* Trans. Alphonso Lingis. The Hague: Martinus Nijhoff, 1964.

Lewis, Barbara Williams. "The Function of Jazz in Toni Morrison's *Jazz.*" *Toni Morrison's Fiction: Contemporary Criticism.* Ed. David L. Meddleton. New York: Garland, 1997. 271–81.

Lewis, David Levering. *W. E. B. Du Bois: Biography of a Race, 1868–1919.* New York: Henry Holt, 1993.

Lewis, Leslie W. "*Philadelphia Fire* and *The Fire Next Time:* Wideman Responds to Baldwin." *Critical Essays on John Edgar Wideman.* Ed. Bonnie TuSmith and Keith E. Byerman. Knoxville: U of Tennessee P, 2006. 145–59.

Lilienfeld, Jane. "'To Have the Reader Work with the Author: The Circulations of Knowledge in Virginia Woolf's *To the Lighthouse* and Toni Morrison's *Jazz.*" *Modern Fiction Studies* 52.1 (Spring 2006): 43–65.

Magner, Denise K. "Afrocentrism at Temple U: Ph.D. Program Stirs a Debate on the Future of Black Studies." *Chronicle of Higher Education* 47.40 (June 19, 1991): A1, A113.

Major, Clarence, ed. *Calling the Wind: Twentieth-Century African American Short Stories.* New York: HarperCollins, 1993.

———. "The Erotic Facts of Life: A Personal View." *Revue Francaise d'Etudes Americaines* 9 (May 1984): 261–64.

———. *Reflex and Bone Structure: A Novel.* New York: Fiction Collective, 1975.

Marsalis, Wynton, with Geoffrey C. Ward. *Moving to Higher Ground: How Jazz Can Change Your Life.* New York: Random House, 2008.

Matsumoto, Mio. "E. Franklin Frazier on W. E. B. Du Bois: Sociologist, Critic, and Friend." *Souls: A Critical Journal of Black Politics, Culture, and Society* 7.3–4 (2005): 55–71.

McCaffery, Larry, and Jerzy Kutnik. "Beneath a Precipice: An Interview with Clarence Major." *Conversations with Clarence Major.* Ed. Nancy Bunge. Jackson: UP of Mississippi, 2002. 70–92.

McDaniel, Vanessa. "Author Percival Everett." http://fiction addicton.net/author-percival-everett-interview.html.

McEvilley, Thomas. *Art & Otherness: Crisis in Cultural Identity.* Kingston, NY: McPherson, 1992.

McKay, Nellie. "Black Studies in the Midwest." *Three Essays: Black Studies in the United States.* New York: Ford Foundation, 1990. 23–29.

———. "An Interview with Toni Morrison." *Conversations with Toni Morrison.* Ed. Danille Taylor-Guthie. Jackson: UP of Mississippi, 1994. 138–55.

McLuhan, Marshall. *Understanding Media: The Extension of Man.* New York: McGraw-Hill, 1964.

McWhorter, Gerald A. "Deck the Ivy Racist Halls: The Case of Black Studies." *Black Studies in the University: A Symposium.* Ed. Armstead L. Robinson, Craig C. Foster, and Donald H. Ogilvie. New Haven, CT: Yale UP, 1969. 55–74.

Meadows, Eddie S. *Bebop to Cool: Context, Ideology, and Musical Identity.* Westport, CT: Praeger, 2003.

Memmi, Albert. *The Colonizer and the Colonized.* Boston: Beacon, 1991.

Micucci, Dana. "An Inspired Life: Toni Morrison Writes and a Generation Listens." *Conversations with Toni Morrison.* Ed. Danille Taylor-Guthie. Jackson: UP of Mississippi, 1994. 275–79.

Morace, Robert A. "The Facts in Black and White: Cheever's *Falconer,* Wideman's *Philadelphia Fire.*" *Powerless Fictions? Ethics, Cultural Critique, and American Fiction in the Age of Postmodernism.* Ed. Ricardo Miguel Alfonso. Amsterdam and Atlanta, GA: Rodopi, 1996. 85–112.

Morgenstern, Dan. "Consideration." *Ask Me Now: Conversations on Jazz & Literature.* Ed. Sascha Feinstein. Bloomington: Indiana UP, 2007. 269–92.

Morrison, Toni. *Jazz.* New York: Plume, 1992.

Morrison, Toni, and Cornel West. "Blues, Love and Politics: A Conversation between Toni Morrison and Cornel West." *Nation* 278 (May 24, 2004): 18–28.

Moynihan, Sinead. "Living Parchments, Human Documents: Racial Identity and Authorship in Percival Everett's *Erasure* and Hannah Crafts' *The Bondwoman.*" *Engaging Tradition, Making It New: Essays on Teaching Recent African American Literature.* Ed. Stephanie Brown and Eva Tettenborn. Newcastle upon Tyne: Cambridge Scholars, 2008. 103–21.

Norment, Nathaniel. *The African American Studies Reader.* 2nd ed. Durham, NC: Carolina Academic, 2007.

O'Brien, John. "Clarence Major." *Interviews with Black Writers.* New York: Liveright, 1973. 125–39.

O'Hagan, Sean. "Colour Bind." *The Guardian/The Observer,* March 15, 2003. http://books.guardian.co.uk/departments/generalfiction/story/0,6000,914871,00.html.

Oliver, Paul. *The Meaning of the Blues.* New York: Collier, 1960.

O'Meally, Robert G., ed. *The Jazz Cadence of American Culture.* New York: Columbia UP, 1998.

O'Meally, Robert G., and Valeria Smith. "Evaluation of Ford-Funded African American Studies Departments, Centers, and Institutes (1994)." *Inclusive Scholarship: Developing Black Studies in the United States; A 25th Anniversary Retrospective of Ford Foundation Grant Making, 1982–2007.* New York: Ford Foundation, 2007. 123–58.

O'Reilly, Andrea. "In Search of My Mother's Garden, I Found My Own: Mother-Love, Healing, and Identity in Toni Morrison's *Jazz.*" *African American Review* 30 (Spring 1996): 367–79.

Page, Philip. "Traces of Derrida in Toni Morrison's *Jazz.*" *African American Review* 29 (Spring 1995): 55–66.

Patton, Stacey. "Black Studies: 'Swaggering into the Future.'" *Chronicle of Higher Education,* April 12, 2012. http://chronicle.com/article/Black-Studies-Swaggering/131533/. . .

Pearsall, Susan M. "'Narratives of Self' and the Abduction of Authority in Wideman's *Philadelphia Fire.*" *MELUS* 26 (Summer 2001): 15–46.

Pearson, Ralph L. "Combatting Racism with Art: Charles S. Johnson and the Harlem Renaissance." *American Studies* 18.1 (1977): 123–34.

Peperzak, Adriaan. *To the Other: An Introduction to the Philosophy of Emmanuel Levinas.* New Haven, CT, and London: Yale UP, 1992.

Perry, Carolyn, and Tonya Maddox. "Repetition and Revision in Toni Morrison's *Jazz.*" *Publication of the Missouri Philological Association* 21 (1996): 62–68.

Peterson, V. R. "Xam Cartiér." *Essence* 23.2 (June 1992): 54.

Pici, Nick. "Trading Meanings: The Breath of Music in Toni Morrison's *Jazz.*" *CEA Critic: An Official Journal of the College English Association* 62.3 (Summer 2000): 18–38.

Powell, Tara. "Percival Everett: *Erasure.*" *Still in Print: The Southern Novel Today.* Ed. Jan Wordby Gretlund. Columbia: U of South Carolina P, 2010. 73–87.

Prager, Jeffery. "Self Reflection(s): Subjectivity and Racial Subordination in Contemporary African American Writers." *Social Identities* 1 (August 1995): 1–13.

Pratt, Anthony M. *E. Franklin Frazier Reconsidered.* New Brunswick, NJ: Rutgers UP, 1991.

Presson, Rebekah. "John Edgar Wideman." *Conversations with John Edgar Wideman.* Ed. Bonnie TuSmith. Jackson: UP of Mississippi, 1998. 105–12.

Richard, Jean-Pierre. "*Philadelphia Fire,* or the Shape of a City." *Calalloo* 22.3 (1999): 603–13.

Rodrigues, Eusebio L. "Experiencing Jazz." *Toni Morrison: Critical and Theoretical Approaches.* Ed. Nancy Peterson. Baltimore: John Hopkins UP, 1997. 245–66.

Rody, Caroline. "Impossible Voices: Ethnic Postmodern Narrative in Toni Morrison's *Jazz* and Karen Tei Yamashito's *Through the Arc of the Rain Forest.*" *Contemporary Literature* 41 (Winter 2000): 619–41.

Rogers, J. A. "Jazz at Home." *The Black Aesthetic.* Ed. Addison Gayle Jr. Garden City, NY: Doubleday/Anchor, 1972. 104–111.

Rowell, Charles H. "An Interview with John Edgar Wideman." *Conversations with John Edgar Wideman.* Ed. Bonnie TuSmith. Jackson: UP of Mississippi, 1998. 86–104.

Russett, Margaret. "Race under Erasure: For Percival Everett, 'A Piece of Fiction.'" *Callaloo* 28 (2005): 358–68.

Rutherford, Jonathan. "Who's That Man?" *Male Order: Unwrapping Masculinity.* Ed. Rowena Chapman and Jonathan Rutherford. London: Lawrence & Wishart, 1988. 21–67.

Said, Edward W. *Culture and Imperialism.* New York: Vintage Books, 1994.

———. *Freud and the Non-European.* New York: Verso, 2003.

Salaam, Kalamu. "Searching for the Mother Tongue: An Interview with Toni Cade Bambara." *Savoring the Salt: The Legacy of Toni Cade Bambara.* Ed. Linda Janet Holmes and Cheryl A. Wall. Philadelphia: Temple UP, 2008. 58–69.

Sanchez, Sonia. "Cante Jondo." *Ask Me Now: Conversations on Jazz & Literature.* Ed. Sascha Feinstein. Bloomington: Indiana UP, 2007. 339–69.

Sanchez-Arce, Ana Maria. "'Authenticism,' or the Authority of Authenticity." *Mosaic: A Journal for the Comparative Study of Literature* 40.3 (September 2007): 139–55.

Scanlon, Thomas M. *What We Owe to Each Other.* Cambridge and London: Belknap Press of Harvard University, 1998.

Scharper, Alice. "Clarence Major." *Conversations with Clarence Major.* Ed. Nancy Bunge. Jackson: UP of Mississippi, 2002. 63–69.

Scheiber, Andrew. "Jazz and the Future Blues: Toni Morrison's Urban Folk Zone." *Modern Fiction Studies* 52.2 (Summer 2006): 470–94.

Schoenberg, Loren. *The NPR Curious Listener's Guide to Jazz.* New York: Perigee, 2002.

Scott, David. "The Re-Enchantment of Humanism: An Interview with Sylvia Wynter." *Small Axe* 8 (September 2000): 119–207.

Shohat, Ella, and Robert Stam. *Unthinking Eurocentrism: Multiculturalism and the Media.* London and New York: Routledge, 1994.

Sinclair, John. "Ask Me Now." *Ask Me Now: Conversations on Jazz and Literature.* Ed. Sascha Feinstein. Bloomington: Indiana UP, 2007. 371–98.

Soitos, Stephen F. "*Reflex and Bone Structure:* The Black Anti-Detective Novel." *Clarence Major and His Art.* Ed. Bernard W. Bell. Chapel Hill: U of North Carolina P, 2001. 175–87.

Spellman, A. B. *Four Lives in the Bebop Business.* New York: Limelight Editions, 1988.

Spivak, Gayatri. "Subaltern Talk: Interview with the Editor." *The Spivak Reader: Selected Works of Gayatri Chakravorty Spivak.* Ed. Donna Landry and Gerald Maclean. New York: Routledge, 1996. 287–308.

Spohrer, Erika. "Colonizing Consciousness: 'Race,' Pictorial Epistemology, and Toni Morrison's *Jazz.*" *Amerikastudien/American Studies* 54.1 (2009): 79–98.

Stepto, Robert B. *A Home Elsewhere: Reading African American Classics in the Age of Obama.* Cambridge, MA: Harvard UP, 2010.

Stewart, Anthony. "Uncategorizable Is Still a Category: An Interview with Percival Everett." *Canadian Review of American Studies* 37.2 (2007): 293–324.

Stillman-Webb, Natalie. "'Be What You Want': Clothing and Subjectivity in Toni Morrison's *Jazz.*" *Styling Texts: Dress and Fashion in Literature.* Ed. Cynthia Kuhn and Cindy Karlson. Youngtown, NY: Cambria, 2007. 333–50.

Stroman, Carolyn A. "Charles S. Johnson." *American Magazine Journalists, 1900–1960* 1st ser. (1990): 157–64.

Tate, Claudia. "Toni Morrison." *Black Women Writers at Work.* Ed. Claudia Tate. New York: Continuum, 1983. 117–31.

Thomas, Greg. "ProudFlesh Inter/Views: Sylvia Wynter." *ProudFlesh: A New African Journal of Culture, Politics, and Consciousness.* www.africanknowledgeproject.org.

Torgovnick, Marianna. *Gone Primitive: Savage Intellects, Modern Lives.* Chicago and London: U of Chicago P, 1990.

Tucker, Sherrie. "When the Blues and the Truth Lay Hiding: Rememory of Jazz in Black Women's Fiction." *Frontiers: A Journal of Women's Studies* 13.2 (1993): 26–44.

Turner, James. "The Sociology of Black Nationalism." *The Death of White Sociology: Essays on Race and Culture.* Ed. Joyce A. Ladner. Baltimore: Black Classic Press, 1973. 234–52.

TuSmith, Bonnie. "Benefit of the Doubt: A Conversation with John Edgar Wideman." *Conversations with John Edgar Wideman.* Ed. Bonnie TuSmith. Jackson: UP of Mississippi, 1998. 195–219.

Varsava, Jerry. "'Woven of Many Strands': Multiple Subjectivity in John Edgar Wideman's *Philadelphia Fire.*" *Critique* 41 (Summer 2000): 425–44.

Wagner-Pacifici, Robin. *Discourse and Destruction: The City of Philadelphia versus MOVE.* Chicago and London: U of Chicago P, 1994.

Waller, Rayfield Allen. "'Sheets of Sound': A Woman's Bop Prosody." *Black American Literature Forum* 24.4 (Winter 1990): 791–802.

Weeks, Jeffrey. "Preface to the 1978 Edition." *Homosexual Desire* by Guy Hocquenghem. Durham, NC: Duke UP, 1993. 23–47.

Weiss, Phillip. "How He Bombed in Philadelphia: Goode, Bad, and Ugly." *New Republic,* June 10, 1985: 12–13.

Weixlmann. Joseph. "African American Deconstruction of the Novel in the Work of Ishmael Reed and Clarence Major." *MELUS* 17 (Winter 1991–92): 57–79.

———. "Clarence Major's Singing Voice(s)." *Clarence Major and His Art.* Ed. Bernard Bell. Chapel Hill: U of North Carolina P, 2001. 243–63.

West, Cornel. *Beyond Eurocentrism and Multiculturalism: Prophetic Thought in Postmodern Times.* Vol. 1. Monroe, ME: Common Courage, 1993.

West, Cornel, with David Ritz. *Brother West: Living and Loving Out Loud.* New York: Smiley Books, 2009.

White, Curtis. *The Middle Mind: Why Americans Don't Think for Themselves.* New York: Harper San Francisco, 2004.

Wideman, John Edgar. "The Architectonics of Fiction." *Callaloo* 13.1 (1990): 42–46.

———. *Philadelphia Fire.* New York: Random House, 1991.

Wilson, Robin. "Past Their Prime? After 35 Years on Campus, Black-Studies Programs Struggle to Survive." *Chronicle of Higher Education* 51.33 (April 22, 2005): A9–A11.

Woodson, Carter G. *The Mis-Education of the Negro.* New York: Classic House Books, 2008.

Wright, Michelle M. *Becoming Black: Creating Identity in the African Diaspora.* Durham, NC: Duke UP, 2004.

Wright, Richard. "Blueprint for Negro Writing." *The Black Aesthetic.* Ed. Addison Gayle Jr. Garden City, NY: Doubleday/Anchor, 1972. 315–32.

Young, Iris Marion. *Justice and the Politics of Difference.* Princeton, NJ: Princeton UP, 1990.

Zizek, Slavoj. *Violence: Six Sideways Reflections.* New York: Picador, 2008.

Index